Mastering Christianity

Figure 1. Detail from "St. Philip's Church and Moncreiffe in Barbados," from Robert H. Schomburgk, *The History of Barbados* ... (London, 1848). (Courtesy of the Rare Book and Manuscript Library, University of Pennsylvania.)

Mastering Christianity

*Missionary Anglicanism and
Slavery in the Atlantic World*

TRAVIS GLASSON

OXFORD
UNIVERSITY PRESS

OXFORD
UNIVERSITY PRESS

Oxford University Press is a department of the University of Oxford. It furthers
the University's objective of excellence in research, scholarship, and education
by publishing worldwide. Oxford is a registered trade mark of Oxford University
Press in the UK and certain other countries.

Published in the United States of America by Oxford University Press
198 Madison Avenue, New York, NY 10016, United States of America.

© Oxford University Press 2012

First issued as an Oxford University Press paperback, 2017

Library of Congress Cataloging-in-Publication Data
Glasson, Travis.
Mastering Christianity : missionary Anglicanism and slavery in the
Atlantic world / Travis Glasson.
p.   cm.
Includes bibliographical references and index.
ISBN 978-0-19-977396-1 (hardcover : alk. paper); 978-0-19-068301-6 (paperback : alk. paper)
1. Slavery and the church—Church of England—History. 2. Society for the Propagation of
the Gospel in Foreign Parts (Great Britain)—History. 3. Racism—Great Britain—History. I. Title.
HT917.C3G55   2011
283.086'25—dc22   2011008489

For Lucy

CONTENTS

ACKNOWLEDGMENTS

I would like to thank a number of people and institutions for their support. Grants from the American Historical Association, the Huntington Library, the John Carter Brown Library, the Harvard University International Seminar on the History of the Atlantic World, Columbia University, and the Whiting Foundation supported the research and writing of the dissertation that led to this book. My thanks to Richard Bushman, Evan Haefeli, Marcia Wright, and Christopher Brown for their guidance at that stage. Alexandra Gillespie, Joanna Innes, Perry Gauci, and the postgraduate students of Balliol College welcomed me during research in Oxford and the staffs of the Rhodes House, Vere Harmsworth, and Bodleian Libraries were generous with their assistance. The opportunity to teach Contemporary Civilization at Columbia University, then under the chairmanship of Philip Kitcher, provided welcome financial support and a mind-expanding experience. A sabbatical from Temple University helped me complete this project.

I presented portions of this book before a number of groups, and I thank the organizers and participants for their encouragement and many incisive comments. In particular I would like to thank Bernard Bailyn and my fellow members of the 2003 Harvard University Atlantic History Seminar; Joyce Chaplin, Laurel Thatcher Ulrich, Jill Lepore, Vincent Brown, and history graduate students at Harvard for opening their colonial American history seminar to me; Richard Bushman and the Columbia University Seminar on Early American History; Daniel Richter and the McNeil Center for Early American History; Peter Mancall, Carole Shammas, and the American Origins Seminar of the USC/ Huntington Library Early Modern Studies Institute; and Peter Logan, Elizabeth Varon, and the Nineteenth Century Forum at the Center for the Humanities at Temple University. Vincent Brown, Christopher Hodson, Jon Sensbach, and Rowan Strong kindly read and thoughtfully commented on conference papers and other work. I am particularly grateful to Katherine Carté Engel for reading the entire manuscript and providing many valuable suggestions. Susan Ferber, my editor at Oxford University Press, helped improve the book in many ways big and small.

Portions of Chapter 3 first appeared in the *William and Mary Quarterly*. My thanks to Christopher Grasso and those anonymous readers for their assistance and to the *William and Mary Quarterly* for permission to reprint that material here. Segments of Chapter 6 first appeared in *the Journal of British Studies*. Thank you to Anna Clark and those readers, and to *the Journal of British Studies* for allowing me to include that material. My readers for Oxford University Press provided much appreciated advice on many general and particular points. My thanks to the United Society for the Propagation of the Gospel and the Bodleian Library of Commonwealth and African Studies at Rhodes House for permission to quote from the SPG archive.

Rebecca Goetz has generously shared her own research, discussed religion in the Atlantic world with me, and been a constant source of encouragement. Philip Stern commented on portions of this manuscript, housed me in London, and advised me on the publication process with good humor. My colleagues at Temple University have been stimulating and generous and made our department a wonderful place to be a historian, particularly one early in his career. I would especially like to thank my chairs Andrew Isenberg, William Hitchcock, Beth Bailey, and Jonathan Wells for their support. Elizabeth Varon served as my wise faculty mentor and read a draft of this book in its entirety. I am grateful for her good sense, advocacy, and encouragement.

David Armitage served as my graduate adviser and read and commented on several versions of this work. Besides inspiring my interest in the Atlantic world and fostering my development as a historian, David has been an unfailingly generous source of intellectual and professional guidance over many years. Members of my family have provided enthusiastic backing. My thanks to all of them, especially my mother Mary Susan Mulligan, William Eccleston, Donald and Nancy Fowler, James and Claire Glasson, and my grandparents, Phyllis and the late Edward Glasson. Hilary Glasson provided a late shot of adrenalin. Lucy Glasson did more to help this book appear than any other person. She has encouraged, edited, listened, advised, and inspired. This book is for Lucy, with love.

Mastering Christianity

Introduction

The Society for the Propagation of the Gospel in Foreign Parts (SPG) was the largest and most influential missionary organization in the eighteenth-century British Atlantic world. It sent hundreds of Anglican clergymen to widely dispersed posts, circulated large amounts of religious literature, lobbied politicians and the public, and helped found many churches and schools. Its work among European settlers helped transplant the Church of England to Britain's far-flung empire and laid the foundation for American Episcopalianism. The SPG's ministers endeavored to Christianize Native Americans and bring them into Britain's cultural and political orbit. The Society also launched the first concerted Protestant effort to convert enslaved black people to Christianity. In colonial parishes and at a number of specially dedicated missionary stations, the SPG worked for many decades to Christianize enslaved people as part of an ambitious program for making colonial societies more godly, orderly, and English.

This book examines the missionary encounters that occurred between the Anglican missionaries of the Society and black people in early America, the Caribbean, and west Africa in the eighteenth and early nineteenth centuries. It aims to uncover the ideas and practices promulgated by the SPG's clergymen and British supporters, and how and why those principles were accepted, rejected, or modified by the people the Society hoped to convert. This book also examines these missionary encounters as sites where changing ideas about human difference and slavery played out. Across the eighteenth century, the Society functioned as a circum-Atlantic network, one that widely circulated people, texts, and ideas. This period saw new developments in natural philosophy and religion, the growth of slavery's economic importance, and increasing contact among the different regions of the world. Eighteenth-century social, cultural, and economic changes provided the context for the hardening of European and Euro-American understandings of human difference, a process usefully conceived of as the "creation of race." Against this backdrop, new justifications for slavery developed. Missionary texts and experiences were fected by and contributed to these wider processes, which shaped cultural life in Britain, early America, and the wider Atlantic world.

The first generation of SPG supporters envisioned the Church of England as a global institution, a supranational church with a reach commensurate with England's expanding power. From the start, the Society's supporters regarded the Roman Catholic Church and other Protestant groups as their rivals. Convinced that episcopal Protestantism was the best form of Christianity and that a close alliance between the church and the state was essential to the health of both, the Society's backers saw the Atlantic world as a field of intense religious competition. In their expansionist vision, the conversion of non-Christian populations was a good to be worked for in its own right and part of a worldwide struggle against national and religious foes.

The Society's initial approach to converting non-Europeans was informed by a reformist zeal and a religiously grounded belief in the essential unity of humankind. As George Stanhope, Dean of Canterbury, put it in an SPG sermon in 1714, "Birth and Fortune, Climate and Complexion, Barbarism and Servitude, are only Circumstantial Differences."[1] The Society began its missionary program before race as a biological "fact" was a major way of understanding human difference. While the Society's supporters had multiple views on the origins of human diversity and were certainly attuned to variations among people, it was religion and culture, not the body, that were the essential markers of such difference when the Society began its missionary work. In consequence, the Society's members and colonial representatives tended to view Native Americans and black populations as "heathens" first and foremost. As imperial expansion drew the Anglican establishment's attention to the religious needs of Britons abroad, so too it brought reports of populations that were being incorporated into transatlantic political, military, and economic systems but who remained outside the bonds of Christian fellowship. It was in this environment, in which national and religious interests were seen as closely aligned, that the SPG began its operations.

The possibility of converting Native Americans had long fascinated and inspired Europeans, including those seventeenth-century Protestants who supported the New England Company's program in Massachusetts.[2] The Society's engagement in this branch of its missionary project continued a drive that had been established by others in British North America. The SPG's interest in the Christianization of the black population of the British colonies, on the other hand, broke newer ground. Particular attention to the religious condition of black people was the product of population transfers that remade the Atlantic world in the late seventeenth and eighteenth centuries. As was the case for Native Americans, the belief in essential human unity prevalent among SPG supporters led to attempts to convert enslaved Africans and their African American and Afro-Caribbean descendants. American experiences, in turn, led the Society to undertake a missionary program in Africa in the latter half of the century.

While this inclusive conception of humanity was critical to how the Society's history unfolded, so too was missionary Anglicanism's attitude toward slavery. The SPG, like other eighteenth-century religious organizations, accepted slavery as sanctioned by both the Bible and human law. Bishop John Williams, whose 1706 Annual Sermon was an early call for the Society to focus on converting enslaved people, noted that slavery had existed "throughout all Ages in the most Parts of the World," cited passages in Genesis, Leviticus, 2 Timothy, and 1 Corinthians that sanctioned slavery, and noted that "Christianity did not intermeddle with" the legal position of the enslaved.[3] For Anglicans, who often identified themselves as defenders of Protestant theological orthodoxy and as allies of properly constituted civil authority, such justifications were potent as the Society began its work. However, over the course of the eighteenth century the SPG did not just passively reflect a circum-Atlantic consensus on slavery. Its growing material and intellectual entanglement with slavery had serious implications for its religious program. The Society's members and ministers also contributed to changes in the cultural and political history of Atlantic slavery.

The SPG's foundation and early activity abroad occurred during a period of explosive growth in black chattel slavery.[4] In the late seventeenth century, slavery was economically critical in relatively few English colonies and centered on the production of a small number of commodities. In the eighteenth century, it became the predominant system of production in a crescent of colonies stretching from the Chesapeake to the eastern Caribbean. It is a striking aspect of this story that slavery and Anglicanism grew together in several colonies and that Anglicanism was often most influential where slavery was most important. Colonies including Virginia, South Carolina, and Barbados had strong Anglican establishments and societies ultimately organized around slavery. The SPG was not a direct presence in the predominantly Anglican Chesapeake colonies, but it was active in the mainland colonies south of Virginia. It likewise operated in many port towns including Newport, Philadelphia, and New York, where slavery became an important aspect of urban life. In the early eighteenth century the Society also became the owner of Codrington, a large sugar plantation in Barbados. This estate gave the SPG a significant presence in the Caribbean and became central to its missionary program among the black population of the Atlantic world.

The beliefs that all people were capable of Christianization and that slavery was biblically permitted continued to predominate within the Society well into the nineteenth century. That, however, does not mean that the views of SPG affiliates on these points were monolithic or static, or that its missionary approaches were unchanging. In the first three decades of the Society's history, many of its founding generation exhibited a particularly strong commitment to converting Native American and black people. Early SPG supporters envisioned the conversion of Indians would be a speedy and glorious work that would lead many souls to Christ while providing Britain with reliable allies in America, but converting Native Americans proved difficult. Many SPG supporters were ultimately convinced that true conversion would come about only after a long period of "civilizing" Native American people.

Similarly, initial zeal for converting enslaved people gradually waned. There were some important figures among the Society's early affiliates who, in pursuit of their religious goals, were willing to challenge the way that slaveholding was being practiced around the British Empire. Their successors, however, became increasingly sympathetic toward the Atlantic world's planters. The deepening participation of the Society and its clergymen in slaveholding was an integral part of this development. Over the course of the eighteenth century, the SPG owned more people as slaves than it employed as missionaries.[5] From the mid-1730s, the Great Awakening in colonial America also had an effect as it offered enslaved people new religious alternatives and exacerbated missionary Anglicanism's tendency to fear disruptions of the social order. Reforming slavery never disappeared from the SPG's agenda, but the Society became increasingly loath to undertake any religious program that threatened the position or prerogatives of colonial elites. The ideological and practical alliances that the Society forged with fellow slaveholders in these decades remained powerful as antislavery activism grew from the 1760s. Paradoxically, while part of its missionary program was inspired by a commitment to the unity of humankind and by a desire to reform enslaved people, masters, and slavery itself, the SPG's ideological and material investment in slaveholding deepened across the eighteenth century.

The Society's interactions with black and Native American populations have featured in many studies of the religious history of colonial America, the emergence of black and Native American Christianity, the histories of individual colonies, and the intellectual and cultural history of slavery and antislavery. While the bulk of the existing scholarship on the SPG focuses on territories that would become part of the United States, this book adopts a deliberately broader Atlantic framework by connecting events in places including South Carolina, New York, and Rhode Island to developments in Britain and to missionary sites in the Caribbean and West Africa.[6]

The life histories of key figures connected with the Society provide striking evidence of the Atlantic nature of its eighteenth-century project. Francis Le Jau (1665–1717), an important early figure in the SPG's history, was born in Angers, France, educated at Trinity College, Dublin, was a canon of St. Paul's Cathedral in London for several years, and served as a West Indian clergyman before set-tling as SPG missionary at Goose Creek in South Carolina.[7] Thomas Thompson (1709–73) was born in Yorkshire, educated at Cambridge, lived in New Jersey for several years as an SPG missionary, traveled to Africa and began the Society's efforts there, and finished his life as a beneficed clergyman in Kent.[8] Even when serving at remote stations, the Society's missionaries remained connected to London, and via the metropolis to the rest of the Atlantic world, through regular correspondence and the circulation of SPG instructions, sermons, and books. While recent work has examined how white and black people encountered Anglican ritual life in the key plantation societies of Barbados, Jamaica, and South Carolina between 1650 and 1780, there remains no broad history of the SPG other than those produced under the aegis of the Society, and no study has attempted to comprehensively consider the Society's efforts among black people and its relationship with slavery around the Atlantic world.[9]

This book relies on an analysis of the SPG's extensive archive and eighteenth- and nineteenth-century printed material—including sermons—to reconsider several themes in the existing literature on the Society. Many works have focused on the SPG's work among the European settler population or on the Church of England in a particular colony, and a number of historians have examined the SPG's role in the build up to the American Revolution.[10] Much other work on the Society has been produced within a denominational milieu, which has typi-cally celebrated its missionaries for their role in building the foundations of American Episcopalianism. Some of the most important studies of the SPG have been produced by the organization itself as official histories, the most recent of which breaks new ground in addressing contentious aspects of the organization's past.[11] Yet, at their core such official histories are intended to highlight achieve-ments rather than explore the significance of SPG activities for wider historical developments. The eighteenth century also has come to occupy a smaller space in such accounts. The SPG, operating since 1965 as the United Society for the Propagation of the Gospel (USPG), continues to function as an Anglican mis-sionary organization, and as it expanded into new regions and different types of work, official histories responded by giving more attention to nineteenth- and twentieth-century developments.

The most important scholarly studies of the SPG were produced by Frank Klingberg, who delved deep into the Society's archive and, more than any other scholar, integrated the Society's activities into wider narratives of British and American history. Klingberg's scholarship on the SPG, which grew out of his interest in abolitionism, stressed a consistent theme: the Society was a major source for what he conceived of as "humanitarianism" in the colonies.[12] Such a reading now appears overly optimistic and celebratory. The SPG's missionary work and the interactions between its missionaries and the diverse populations of the Atlantic world were complex and often contested.[13] As a whole, existing accounts also tell us too little about the varied ways in which Native American and black people responded to the organization's missionary program. This book seeks to redress these imbalances by recognizing the agency of non-European peoples in missionary encounters and offering new assessments of the impact of the Society's eighteenth-century efforts.

More generally, a generation of influential studies has stressed the centrality of Protestantism in general and Anglican values in particular to eighteenth-century British culture, while scholars of colonial American religion have uncovered the commitment and effectiveness of colonial Anglican clergymen and asserted the importance of Anglicanism to the wider development of American Christianity. British missionary groups, including the eighteenth-century SPG, have also been considered as a largely autonomous force within Britain's long-term imperial history. Together, these studies highlight the importance of the Society not just as a critical institution within transatlantic Protestantism but also as an agent for the dissemination of a robust, influential, and religiously influenced British culture.[14]

The experiences of black members of the Church of England have been studied less extensively than those of black Baptists, Methodists, and Moravians. While often acknowledging Anglican activity as an early phase in Protestant missionary work among enslaved people, most historians have emphasized the ways that the Great Awakening, which unsettled hierarchies of race, class, and gender, gave rise to black Christianity. As a result, finding a place for Anglicanism, which was often closely identified with planter elites, can be difficult. For example, the key history of the development of black Protestantism concluded that "Anglican doctrines and rituals held little intrinsic appeal for the enslaved populations of the Southern mainland and British Caribbean."[15] In many locations, especially where Anglicanism was most entangled with slavery, this appears to have been the case. Yet, one paradoxical consequence of the close correlation between the developments of slavery and Anglicanism was that, especially before the 1740s, the Church of England was the institution through which many enslaved people first experienced Christianity in the colonies. We know relatively little about the motivations or numbers of early black Anglicans, but they certainly numbered in the thousands around the British Atlantic by the mid-eighteenth century.[16] It is worth considering why some black people adopted Anglicanism even as most did not.

I use the term "missionary Anglicanism," and both parts of the phrase merit explanation. While the pre-Reformation English Church was referred to as the

Ecclesia Anglicana, and the Church of England was being described as the "Angli-can Church" by the late sixteenth century, the term "Anglicanism" is a nine-teenth-century one that originally had affiliations with the Oxford Movement.[17] I use it, as other writers on eighteenth-century English and colonial history have done, only to represent the beliefs and practices associated with the Church of England. Through the use of the term "missionary Anglicanism" I aim to capture the ethos of those who supported the SPG, allied organizations including the SPCK and the Associates of Dr. Bray, and like-minded churchmen. I want to distinguish their beliefs and practices from those of English Anglicans who were not interested in promoting the Church of England abroad. The term also helps distinguish the circum-Atlantic, at times even global, orientation of SPG sup-porters from the localism of some colonial Anglicans, particularly some cler-gymen in colonies where the Church of England was legally established, who were hostile to interference from London. Proponents of missionary Anglican-ism, as I use the term, were typically united in their beliefs in the necessity of episcopacy and close church-state cooperation. These ideas, and others, differ-entiated them from many supporters of the new evangelical forms of Protestant-ism that emerged in the mid-eighteenth century.

Those connected with the SPG, reflecting their own concerns and then pre-dominant understandings of human difference, grouped a wide array of people they encountered in the Atlantic world under such terms as "heathens." The per-ceived connections between Native American and black populations that such terminology implies are important to understanding the history of SPG mis-sionary work in this period. I have attempted sometimes to maintain a sense of these animating connections while employing less pejorative language by refer-ring to Native American and black people collectively as "non-Europeans."

The Society's affiliates, like many Britons, typically used the terms "Negroes" or "slaves" when referring to Africans and their descendants in the colonies. I have used the collective term "black people." "African," "African American," and "Afro-Caribbean" denote subdivisions within this population. "Africans" were born in Africa; "African American" and "Afro-Caribbean" people were born in the colonies. I have tried to use the term "enslaved people" frequently to miti-gate the dehumanizing effects of repeatedly calling people "slaves." Slavery was something imposed on some people in the Atlantic world, not something intrin-sic to who they were. The names of individual black people are rarely given in SPG materials, but where individual names are recoverable, I have tried to include them.

The Society also encountered people who were descended from different combinations of African, European, and Native American ancestors. In a testa-ment to the indeterminateness of categories of human difference operative in the period, these people were labeled variously in different communities. The words "mulatto," "coloured," "tawny," "near-kind," and "mustee" all appear in SPG records as references to people of joint European and African descent. While historians have employed a variety of terms to designate these popula- tions—including "Eurafrican," "Creole," and "Mestizo"—I have employed the term "mixed-race" people, which can be used for various people around the Atlantic world. It has the disadvantage of perhaps suggesting that race was an operative concept in the eighteenth century. Its use should not be taken as im- plying that categories of "race" were either fixed or defined in the eighteenth century in the same ways they would be defined in the nineteenth, twentieth, or twenty-first centuries. I have used "Creole" in places to denote people born in the colonies. I have used "people of color" as an umbrella term to refer to groups containing both black and mixed-race people.

The SPG supported some lay schoolmasters and catechists, but most of its colonial employees were clergymen who had been episcopally ordained as priests in the Church of England. Reflecting the self-conscious and assertive Protestantism of the pre-Oxford Movement Church of England, those affiliated with the Society in the eighteenth century frequently referred to these ordained missionaries as "ministers" and tended to use the term "priest" only in pejorative reference to Catholic clerics. I have used "missionary," "minister," and "cler- gyman" interchangeably when discussing the Society's ordained missionaries. All quotations from the Bible are drawn from the King James Version (KJV).

Part 1 of this book treats the way the Society operated as an influential circum- Atlantic institution and how the SPG's founders drew on and contributed to wider philosophical and theological debates about the origins and meaning of human difference and slavery as they began their missionary program. In an era when many of the most significant markers of difference were cultural, not bio- logical, religion played a critical role in defining where individuals fit into the divisions of humankind.[18] The creation of concepts of race was a multistrand process that unfolded over the course of the eighteenth century. This study sug- gests that around the Atlantic world, the process was shaped both by some of the intellectual and cultural trends captured in metropolitan-produced texts and by more diffuse responses to the cross-cultural encounters that occurred in the col- onies. The Society's program facilitated the circum-imperial flow of both learned texts on philosophical and theological themes relevant to understandings of human difference and a stream of reports and reflections on interactions between Europeans and non-Europeans at many locations. In this sense the SPG can be seen as an institutional link between the front lines of colonization and debates that unfolded in intellectual circles in metropolitan Europe.

Part 2 charts the SPG's efforts to convert enslaved people and the organization's growing entanglement with slavery in the colonies. Through the 1730s, missionary Anglicanism was at the forefront of efforts to convert enslaved people in the British Empire. The Society's clergymen led this push in many places, but over time they increasingly came to sympathize with the concerns of slaveholders and participate in slaveholding themselves. By around 1740, the SPG's tightening relationship with slavery had begun to have serious effects on its missionary program. The Society's members came to embrace slavery as a missionary tool and to shape their religious message to appeal more to masters than to enslaved people themselves. While the Society aligned itself with economic and political colonial elites, the Great Awakening was enabling enslaved people to access and appropriate Christianity in new ways. Part 3 explores two particularly important sites of long-lasting SPG missionary activity—Codrington Plantation on Barbados and Cape Coast Castle in West Africa—to understand how such encounters were shaped by the differing concerns and cultures of Anglican clergymen and the black people they hoped to Christianize, by the pressures of slavery and the slave trade, and by the chronological changes charted in Part 2.

Part 4 returns to England to consider how, after sixty years of working to convert enslaved people, the SPG's supporters became engaged in debates over the abolition of the slave trade and the emancipation of enslaved people. Considerable attention has been paid to the intellectual origins of antislavery thought and the antislavery movement in Britain and its empire, and SPG interest in the condition of enslaved people is sometimes seen as part of this history. Many eighteenth-century SPG annual sermons did make calls for reforming slavery and, indeed, some criticized the slave trade. Yet, such reformism did not lead to widespread advocacy for abolitionism or emancipationism within the Society. In fact, from the 1760s through the 1830s, a number of SPG figures emerged as proslavery spokespeople and the Society's history was used to defend slaveholding. This book traces the SPG's transformation from an organization characterized by a reform-minded acceptance of slavery as a permitted but troubling institution to one that embraced slavery as an instrument of financial support and missionary manpower. In doing so it suggests one way in which slavery became an entrenched feature of cultural and social life in many British Atlantic colonies.

PART ONE

INSTITUTIONAL AND INTELLECTUAL FOUNDATIONS

"My Constitution is Constellated for Any Meridian"

Creating Transatlantic Missionary Anglicanism

In 1711 Edward Bishop applied to serve as an SPG missionary. In making his case, he avowed that "I was not born for myself only, nor made a Minister to live always at home; my Constitution is Constellated for any Meridian, and I shall be in England in any part of the World."[1] Bishop failed to convince the Society to send him to America, but his claim to a calling and his belief in his robustness echoed how the Society's founding generation viewed the Church of England in the early eighteenth century. Like Bishop, they believed that the Church of England too had a constitution "constellated for any Meridian" and could be successfully planted abroad. In their view their church was no longer strictly a national one but an institution with a wider responsibility in the world. In the coming decades, the SPG would attempt to spread Anglicanism throughout Britain's Atlantic empire. In doing so it affected the spiritual and material lives of European settlers, Native Americans, Africans, and African Americans.

The founding and development of the Society reflected several developments in early eighteenth-century British Atlantic culture. The creation of an overseas Anglican missionary society was the product of the growth of religious voluntarism in post-1688 Britain, the Church of England's rivalry with other churches, and the English experience of attempting to support episcopal Protestantism in Ireland and Scotland. The SPG drew interest from across eighteenth-century Anglicanism, and it was a shared commitment to common religious principles, more than any other factor, which united the Society's politically, theologically, and nationally diverse membership and missionaries. From the start, the SPG operated within an Atlantic framework. The institutional structure of the Society meant that individual missionaries maintained ties both to their local stations and to the SPG leadership in London. That leadership's prominence and the Society's commitment to the publication and dissemination of texts also ensured that the group had connections to a wider public in the eighteenth century. These arrangements meant the SPG did more than just facilitate the one-way transference of the Church of England to the colonies; it also spread missionary-minded Anglicans' ideas about human difference and the social order among a circum-Atlantic audience.

In the years following the Glorious Revolution (1688/89), the Church of England was growing in power and confidence, and the SPG's founders envisioned the overseas extension of developments at home. In the half century prior to 1688 the Church of England had been battered by the successive storms of the growth of Dissent, the Civil Wars, and Stuart support for Catholicism. The Glorious Revolution replaced the religiously suspect James II with the firmly Protestant monarchs William and Mary and the accompanying Revolution Settlement, while providing for the legal toleration of Protestant Dissent also secured the established church's privileged political position. In this new environment, in the 1690s and 1700s committed churchmen began drives to make England godlier and the Church of England a more prominent part of the national life. By 1701, the Church of England had been an established presence in America for nearly a century. Yet, it was only after the Glorious Revolution that it was sufficiently internally cohesive and doctrinally united to systematically evaluate its position abroad.

The SPG's founders were often active in other dimensions of this post-1688 resurgence within the Church of England, and their missionary aims were shaped by their connections to the period's other religious reform movements. One important feature of this revival was the establishment of a number of voluntary societies aimed at improving public morality, promoting regular worship, and spreading religious education.[2] They included multidenominational Societies for the Reformation of Manners, which aimed to suppress public immorality through cooperation between religiously minded activist informants and civil authority. A 1699 report counted ninety-three such organizations and by the late 1730s, when they largely ceased to function, their activities had resulted in some 100,000 convictions for various forms of immoral behavior.[3] There was also a more particularly Anglican movement to found parish-based organizations intended to promote more active and ardent Christian living. Forty-two of these so-called Religious Societies were established in London and Westminster alone in the last few years of the seventeenth century, where they were seen as "very instrumental in promoting, in some churches, Daily Prayers, Preparatory Sermons to the Holy Communion, the administration of the Sacrament every Lord's Day and Holy Day, and many other excellent designs conformable to the Doctrine and Constitution of the Church of England."[4] These organizations, which were based on cooperation between clerics and laypeople, created a foundation of Anglican activism, and several people involved in them helped establish the SPG.

Alongside these developments, a drive developed to improve the general population's knowledge of essential Christian doctrine. This strain of the post-1688 revival was closely associated with the clergyman Thomas Bray (1656–1730). Bray, who had published lectures on the catechism and been a supporter of the Religious Societies in the mid-1690s, initially hoped to form an organization for promoting religious education, which would be chartered and backed by

Figure 2. Thomas Bray (ca. 1658–1730). Founder of the SPG, SPCK, and the Associates of Dr. Bray (Courtesy of the Society for Promoting Christian Knowledge.)

the Crown.[5] These hopes remained unfulfilled, but he and a group of four lay associates formed the voluntary Society for Promoting Christian Knowledge (SPCK) for that purpose in 1699.[6] The SPG would subsequently develop out of the SPCK, and concern for the condition of the Church of England abroad was always intertwined with the domestic interests of Bray and his collaborators. The SPCK's and other voluntary societies' various hopes for moral reform, regularizing religious practice, and improving the laity's knowledge of Christianity would all resurface in the Society's dealings with enslaved people.

By the frequent admission of many Society backers, the Church of England had long been remiss in its duties to ensure the proper religious development of the colonies. Before the creation of the SPG, Anglican missionary efforts in England's overseas territories were uncoordinated and sporadic. While Anglican establishments had been created in the Chesapeake and a few Caribbean colonies in the seventeenth century, even there churchmen believed their church was in a precarious and underdeveloped position with little regularity in worship, poor internal discipline, and many empty pulpits. The situation was worse elsewhere. In contrast, by the beginning of the eighteenth century some of the religious movements that Anglicans regarded as most threatening to political and ecclesiastical order had been working overseas for decades. New England's Independent churches were deeply entrenched, supported by a comprehensive legal establishment, and staffed by a professional, homegrown clergy. Not only were Dissenters numerous and powerful in many colonies, they were also reaching out to "heathen" populations. By 1700 the Puritan-oriented New England Company, which undertook missionary work among the Native Americans of New England, had been operating for more than fifty years.[7] Even more concerning to some churchmen, Quakers and Baptists too had become widespread in the colonies, corrupting the religious life of settler communities and spreading their errors to non-European populations.

In particular, Bray's concerns about the weakness of colonial Anglicanism were deepened by his own experiences in ecclesiastical administration. In the absence of a colonial episcopate, the bishop of London, Henry Compton, began in the late 1680s to assert his diocese's authority over the Church of England overseas by appointing commissaries to act as his representatives abroad. With Bray's English reputation growing, in 1695 Compton appointed him Commissary for Maryland. Bray spent several years lobbying for Maryland's Anglican interest in London and a short period actually resident in the Chesapeake, work central to the ultimately successful push to secure the colony's fragile Anglican legal establishment.[8] Some of the strongest opposition Bray's efforts faced in Maryland came from Quakers, and he and many other Anglicans of his generation were particularly worried by their presence and political power in England's colonies.[9]

Bray saw Maryland as one theater in an epic struggle between the Church of England and its diverse opponents. In 1698, he provided a world-spanning survey that unfavorably contrasted Anglican overseas missionary efforts to those of Muslims, Roman Catholics, and the Protestant Dutch, and lamented "that so little should yet be done" to even "preserve in Being that Pure and Undefil'd Religion, which we profess" among "Colonies of English Men, from when the whole Kingdom has been so much Enrich'd."[10] Quakerism and other forms of Dissent unsettled life in England's colonies, but for Bray and other Society founders Roman Catholicism was an even more dangerous threat. England's imperial rivals, France and Spain, had long been sending Catholic missionaries to their North and South American colonies and elsewhere to serve their own emigrants and to work among indigenous peoples. As Bray put it, "Papists, we do well know, spare no Cost in sending their *Missions* into all the parts of the known World."[11] In the 1690s, Bray envisioned establishing "a Protestant Congregation, pro Fide propaganda, by Charter from the King" in the hope it would act as a counterweight to Rome's *Congregatio de Propaganda Fide*, which had provided a centralized administrative apparatus to coordinate Catholic missions worldwide since 1622.[12] Throughout the century the Society's backers regularly expressed a mixture of admiration and anxiety about Catholic missionary activity and warnings about Roman Catholicism featured regularly in SPG sermons.[13] With the Glorious Revolution a recent memory, and the Jacobite threat still seen as very real, many early Society members saw their work as a counter to Catholicism's universalistic ambitions. In light of coordinated Dissenting and Catholic missionary activity around the Atlantic world, Bray and other SPG backers believed their group was a late starter in a crucial race.

It was against this backdrop of Anglican religious revival and multisided confessional rivalry that the SPCK and then the SPG were formed. The intersections between the domestic and imperial concerns of Bray and other active members of the Williamite Church of England were captured in the minutes of the first meeting of the SPCK in March 1699, which laid out three initial tasks for the organization. First, Bray and another founder were to "go and discourse George Keith" on "what progress he has hitherto made towards the instruction and conversion of Quakers" and to offer him assistance. Keith, himself a convert from Quakerism, subsequently became the SPG's first missionary. Second, the SPCK was to "further and promote that good design of erecting Catechetical Schools in each parish in and about London" and promote the catechetical instruction of poor children. The erection and promotion of such schools was to be a cornerstone of the SPCK's work for the rest of the century, while supporting religious education abroad would also become part of the SPG's mission. Third, the SPCK desired that Bray would present "his scheme of promoting Religion in the Plantations."[14]

It was this third plank in the SPCK's initial agenda that would lead directly to the foundation of the SPG. Bray and others soon concluded that making Anglicanism a stronger presence overseas required the status and financial backing of an independent organization that had the support of government and Crown. Consequently, as the SPCK added members and expanded its activities, years in which Bray was also working as Maryland's commissary, the momentum for the creation of a body specifically aimed at supporting the colonial Church of England continued to build. In March 1701, the Lower House of Convocation, the assembly of Anglican clergymen, appointed a committee to cooperate with the bishop of London in considering "Ways and Means for promoting Christian Religion in our Foreign Plantations." In 1701, with the support of the SPCK and influential ecclesiastical leaders including Thomas Tenison, archbishop of Canterbury, and Henry Compton, bishop of London, Bray succeeded in obtaining the royal charter that established the SPG.[15]

The decision of Bray and others to found a distinct missionary organization was largely due to the scale of the task that confronted them. By 1700, the combined nonnative population of British North America and the British West Indies was already approximately 412,000, and it was to grow rapidly to more than 2.7 million people by 1770. Changing colonial demographics played a major part in how the Society's missionary strategy would evolve. Continuing emigration from England, including the movement of members of the established church, was part of this population growth, but it was also fueled by migrants from elsewhere in the British isles and Europe. The Society's backers hoped that French Huguenots, Germans, Scots, Welsh, Irish, and others who were moving into the empire would all conform to the Church of England. The colonies' burgeoning, overwhelmingly enslaved, black population was another important component of this demographic growth. The combined black population of British colonies on the Continent and in the Caribbean grew from approximately 86,000 in 1680 to perhaps 555,000 in 1750. This population increase made the religious condition of enslaved people impossible for the SPG's supporters to ignore.[16]

The founding members of the Society included fifty-two clergymen and forty-two laymen.[17] They included many from the rolls of the SPCK, and over the next decades the two organizations would remain tightly allied.[18] The SPCK focused its efforts on charity schools for religious instruction in Britain, and on the publication and distribution of sound religious literature at home and worldwide; the SPG assumed responsibility for dispatching missionaries to the colonies.[19] However, while the SPCK was a strictly voluntary and independent organization, the SPG's charter made it something of a hybrid: a relatively open body but one that remained closely identified with the leadership of the Church of England. Membership in the SPG was voluntary, and it relied on the energy and donations of its lay and clerical supporters, but the granting of a royal charter also made the organization an organ of the establishment. Most significantly, it placed stewardship of the Society clearly in the hands of the Anglican hierarchy. The charter named the archbishops of Canterbury and York and nine other

Figure 3. The Seal of the Society for the Propagation of the Gospel in Foreign Parts. From a bookplate in *A collection of papers, printed by order of the Society for the Propagation of the Gospel in Foreign Parts*... (London, 1741). (Courtesy of the Rare Book and Manuscript Library, University of Pennsylvania.)

English and Welsh bishops among the organization's founding members.[20] The charter also named Archbishop Tenison as the first president of the Society, and his involvement—he was constantly involved in SPG business and personally presided over 20 percent of the meetings held during his lifetime—is a good indication of the close interest the Anglican leadership took in the organization.[21] It became routine to elect each new archbishop of Canterbury as president of the SPG. The upper clergy and influential London clerics were also prominent within the membership. This tight connection with the church's leadership insulated the SPG from some of the criticisms leveled against other voluntary societies by High Churchmen who resented the loss of clerical power to the laity, and well into the nineteenth century the Society remained closely identified with the bench of bishops.[22]

Before the American Revolution, the Society was most active in mainland North American colonies in New England, the mid-Atlantic, and the South, while also sending smaller numbers of missionaries elsewhere, including Nova Scotia, the Caribbean, and West Africa. The Society's particularly Atlantic footprint in the eighteenth century was largely the product of its charter, which limited its activities to those "Plantations, Colonies and Factories beyond the Seas, belonging to our Kingdom of England." This clause was long interpreted as limiting the Society's operations to Britain's formal colonies and as prohibiting the SPG from operating in East India Company–controlled territories. It was not until the middle decades of the nineteenth century that the Society became a truly global organization with a substantial presence across Africa, Asia, and the Pacific. Its sphere of action was also constrained by the decision taken early in the SPG's history to concentrate resources in those colonies without legal Anglican establishments. Consequently, neither the Chesapeake colonies nor most of those in the Caribbean were major fields of SPG activity. The exception was Barbados, where the SPG operated Codrington Plantation, constructed Codrington College, and sent a sizeable number of clergymen to act as schoolmasters and as catechists to the Society's slaves. Ministers to the island's parishes were supported by an establishment and not dispatched or salaried by the SPG, although a succession of them did serve as local attorneys who helped the Society manage its estate from afar.

To administer its far-flung enterprise, the Society rapidly developed a durable set of institutional practices. For most of the eighteenth century the Society held full meetings once a month. These meetings were typically chaired by a bishop or other high-ranking clergyman; more rarely a long-serving lay member might preside. Members were entitled to participate in and vote at meetings and required to pay annual dues, which provided the organization with the largest portion of its certain annual income. New members were added on the basis of nomination by an existing member and a vote. By 1705, clergymen and laity from every diocese in England and Wales had joined.[23]

Across the century most new members were English clerics or Anglican laymen with reputations for piety and philanthropy. Prominent early lay members included the devout Welsh MP Sir John Philipps and Robert Nelson, a nonjuror who had refused to take the oath of allegiance to King William after 1688. The early membership also included a few noblemen like Francis North, second Baron Guilford, and Thomas Thynne, first Viscount Weymouth, lawyers including the serjeant-at-law John Hooke, Sir Humphrey Mackworth, and William Melmoth, and medical doctors such as Gideon Harvey. The Society also made periodic efforts to recruit particular categories of new supporters. In the first two decades of the eighteenth century especially, many SPG supporters saw themselves as members of an international Protestant movement, and the Society voted more than forty European Protestant ministers as members.[24] As Charles Trimnell, bishop of Norwich, noted in 1710, Society supporters also believed "Christian Governours" had a special responsibility to promote Christianity because their "Authority and Power cannot but spread the Truth they profess."[25] To foster alliances between church and state, over thirty colonial governors were recruited into the membership before the American Revolution.[26] Some of these types of members were more honorary then active, but commitments varied. There were also periodic efforts to bring in supporters from merchant circles; annual sermons often called for donations from those who had become rich through colonial trade. Over time, the membership was augmented by small numbers of prominent colonial Anglicans and highly regarded former missionaries. By the early 1720s, the Society had more than 250 members. Deaths among the first wave of supporters saw membership fall to just over 180 by the early 1730s, but there were again more than 250 members by the early 1760s. The number of members never exceeded three hundred in the eighteenth century.[27]

The SPG's tight continuing connection to the Anglican hierarchy does not mean that all the attitudes of its members were uniform. The SPCK had a "bipartisan nature" in the early eighteenth century, incorporating members who could be characterized as High and Low Church, Tory and Whig.[28] Similarly, among the charter members of the SPG were both White Kennett, a notable Whig polemicist detested by Tories for having switched his loyalties from James II to Parliament at the time of the Glorious Revolution, and Offspring Blackhall, a suspected Jacobite and avowed High Churchman.[29] William Fleetwood, one of the most celebrated preachers of his generation, was an SPG founder and an ardent Whig.[30] George Smalridge, later bishop of Bristol, was a very active SPG member but also a friend of Francis Atterbury, whose politicized

High Churchmanship made him one of the most polarizing figures within the post-1688 church. Like Atterbury, Smalridge refused to disavow loyalty to the "Old Pretender" James Francis Edward Stuart following the Jacobite Rebellion of 1715. Participation in the Society did require enough moderation to cooperate with Anglicans of various stripes, and tellingly Smalridge has been characterized as a man whose churchmanship, despite his reputation, "included a willingness to conciliate, compromise, and incorporate heterodox latitudinarianism."[31] Edmund Gibson, who as bishop of London was a predominant figure in the Society in the 1720s and 1730s, rose to prominence as a young clergyman as an opponent of Atterbury during the Convocation controversy, a dispute that roiled church politics between 1690 and 1701 over the privileges, ordering, and powers of the corporate assembly of Anglican clergymen. He subsequently became the nation's leading Whig cleric and a chief ecclesiastical powerbroker during the regime of Robert Walpole.[32] A similar political and theological diversity existed among the bishops and other high clergy who gave the Society's annual sermons in its early years.[33] As a whole, the membership of the Society across the eighteenth century was one that, within the boundaries of political and theological Anglican orthodoxy, reflected the range of opinions on many issues confronting the period's churchmen.

These members were all men, but beginning in the 1750s a relatively small number of women were regularly listed in the Society's reports as "Ladies Annual Subscribers," a designation signaling that they provided regular financial support but did not have the right to participate in meetings. The essential aid these women gave to the Society points out an important dynamic at play in its domestic administration. The Society's members determined its program and provided it with its most secure funding. However, this reliable income never enabled the Society to meet its annual expenses, which were made up primarily of the salaries paid to colonial clergymen. By 1707, for example, the Society was already aware that its certain annual expenses totaled £1,065 while the amount pledged in member subscriptions only amounted to approximately £750. The SPG's connections to the Anglican hierarchy and Queen Anne's early interest in it did inaugurate the periodic granting of royal permission to hold special collections in English churches for the Society. These collections, first taken up in the parishes of greater London and other port towns and then across the country in later decades, provided valuable financial windfalls, but they occurred only six times in the eighteenth century.[34] The problem of financial uncertainty grew as the number of missions supported by the Society increased. In 1716, for example, the Society's auditors reported that certain annual expenses exceeded certain annual income by more than £1,400, and the Society was forced to discharge several schoolmasters in its pay.[35]

This financial situation meant that the Society was continually soliciting donations from beyond the membership and that one-time gifts or legacies from
laypeople around Britain were essential to its ability to continue its operations.[36]
Contributing to religious charities became an important expression of Anglican
piety in the early eighteenth century, and donations made by laymen and lay-
women feature continuously in the Society's records.[37] The £1,000 given to the
Society by Dame Jane Holman of Northamptonshire in 1702 was the first very
large gift received by the organization; it enabled the Society to undertake its
missionary work in earnest.[38] As early as 1711, the active SPG member Philip
Stubbs noted the importance of the donations of "Honourable and Devout
Women" and both men and women contributed to the Society across the century.[39] In consequence, members had to be sensitive to wider public attitudes.
This need to continually raise funds was part of the reason why the Society
adopted the practice of printing the charter-mandated annual sermon delivered
each February. Those sermons, which often included pleas for financial support,
were published along with summaries of the Society's activities and lists of
recent donors and then sent around Britain and abroad.

While the organization's financial viability depended on a wide network of
donors, the bulk of its regular business was conducted by a body significantly
smaller than even the membership. From the start, the Society had one paid secretary, usually a clergyman who was sometimes aided by a clerk and a messenger.
He was responsible for maintaining the transatlantic and domestic correspondences essential to its activities. These typically long-serving secretaries—there
were only nine between 1701 and 1843—were the individuals best placed to
understand the totality of the Society's business at any given moment. They
wielded a considerable amount of authority as sources of institutional memory
and as the principal intermediaries between the missionaries and the membership. The charter also called for the Society to have one or more vice presidents,
who were usually member bishops, one or more treasurers, who were usually
member laymen with business experience, and two or more auditors to review
its accounts.

Within a mere six months of the Society's founding, the volume of correspondence generated by its operations and the array of issues that had to be considered at each full meeting of the membership led to the formation of a Standing
Committee to "receive all Proposals" and "to prepare matters for the Consideration of the Society." The committee was to be made up of at least five members
drawn from among "all the Dignitaries of St. Pauls & all the London Clergy" and
any other members who wanted to attend.[40] As the Society's practices became
entrenched, these arrangements meant that a very large portion of the membership's work was conducted by a relatively small group of London clergymen and

a few active laymen, often in consultation with a bishop or bishops who were particularly committed to the Society. It became, for example, standard practice for the Standing Committee, meeting in the chapterhouse of St. Paul's Cathedral, to screen prospective missionaries and to be tasked with preparing recommendations or reports on particular issues, which would then be voted on by the whole Society. Typically, though not invariably, the Society adopted the recommendations made by the Standing Committee. These arrangements are significant for understanding how the Society operated as an Atlantic institution because the most active London-based members who steered SPG policies were often also figures of note within other philanthropic organizations, the domestic ecclesiastical establishment, political and court circles, and other networks that converged on the empire's capital city.

One expression of the Society's capacity for using these contacts to exert wider influence was its political lobbying.[41] SPG backers from Bray onward embraced cooperation between the church and state as a fundamental principle, gave scrupulous attention to the legal framework under which the colonial church operated, and therefore saw politicking as part of their mission.[42] The Society exploited various types of political connections. Most directly, supportive bishops sat in the House of Lords. Some of these men, like Edmund Gibson, wielded great power and deployed it on behalf of the Society. The Society's membership also regularly included a handful of office holders, Members of Parliament, colonial governors, merchants, lawyers, and other players in national and imperial political life. For example, John Pownall, who became secretary of the Board of Trade, and his brother Thomas Pownall, colonial governor and then Member of Parliament, became members of the SPG in the 1750s. In 1760, when the Society decided to review the financial position of its Codrington plantation, the special committee formed included John Pownall, Bishop Robert Hay Drummond, and the former customs official and lieutenant governor of Virginia Robert Dinwiddie. In turn, when the Board of Trade was founding the new colonies of East and West Florida in 1764, John Pownall wrote to the Society asking that it recommend men to serve as ministers and schoolmasters in the Anglican parishes being established there.[43] The Society drew on such men for their expertise in colonial matters and worked to capitalize on their influence.

Given the varied agendas of the membership, the size of Britain's overseas empire, and the financial constraints the SPG operated under, there were sometimes different views on what policies the Society should pursue. Most importantly, there were recurring debates about whether it had a primary responsibility to work toward the salvation of the nominal, lapsed, and uncared for Christians who made up the settler population of the Atlantic colonies, or if its main duty lay in spreading the gospel to those "heathens" who had never heard it. Most SPG members hoped to do as much as possible to minister to both groups, but there was a continuing gap between the organization's ambitions and its funds. This affected the Society's push to convert non-Christian populations because it meant that those efforts were always competing for attention with plans to send missionaries to work among European colonists.

The SPG charter provided little definitive guidance on the issue. Several early members believed that the colonies' European population should be the focus. At the first Annual Meeting in 1702, Richard Willis noted, "The design is in the first place to settle the State of Religion as well as may be among our *own People* there, which by all accounts we have, very much wants their Pious care; and then to proceed in the best Methods they can toward the *Conversion* of the *Natives*."[44] Promoters of work among European emigrants often extended this argument, claiming that the transformation of settler religious life was a necessary precondition for the conversion of non-Christian populations. As Gilbert Burnet, bishop of Salisbury, noted in 1704, "Our Designs upon Aliens and Infidels must begin in the Instructing and Reforming our own People, in opening Schools every where, in sending over Books of good Instruction, and above all things, in encouraging and preparing many Labourers to go into that Harvest."[45] Even among some strong supporters of missionary outreach to non-Europeans, this notion of "settlers first" persisted after decades of SPG work.[46]

However, bringing the gospel to the "heathen" continued to seem to many to be the main reason for the organization's existence. In one of the earliest accounts of the proceedings of the new Society, published in 1704, it was noted that missionaries had been dispatched to serve among the Iroquois in order that the Society "might answer the main end of their incorporation."[47] If there was to be missionary work among settlers, this should be properly understood as preparatory. As Bishop Trimnell put it in 1710, converting non-Christians was "that for which this Corporation was primarily erected" and "the Christianity taught and inculcated to our own People, should be calculated for the better bringing of others to the Belief of it."[48] In 1710, this view was strong enough to see a meeting of members formally adopt the policy that the Society's primary mission was the "conversion of the heathens and infidels; and therefore that branch of it ought to be prosecuted preferably to all others."[49] The new regulation, however, did not signal a permanent, clear new direction and its practical ramifications seem slight. By 1714 George Stanhope, dean of Canterbury, again noted in the Society's annual sermon that "Nature, as well as Religion, obliged us to begin" with "our Own People," of whom "vast Numbers long had lived, as Sheep without a Shepherd."[50]

In the hopes of doing more work in more places, the Society attempted, often ineffectually, to get mission stations to supplement the salaries of their SPG ministers. In 1707, it was resolved that the "Society will supply those Places before others which are most willing to contribute to such Maintenance."[51] Of course, those areas most likely to contribute to the financial maintenance of a minister were the wealthiest settler communities—already the most Anglicized and Anglican areas of the British Atlantic. Missions among Native Americans and black slaves were unlikely to receive much local financial assistance. This dynamic meant that those who favored a focus on the religious needs of European settlers had a powerful argument: missionary work among the heathen was not only difficult but costly, and the Society might expect better results with less expense among the needy colonial Christian population. To counter this tendency, a fund dedicated to supporting catechists employed solely in slave conversion was established in 1729, but it never grew large enough to enable major new initiatives, and it was quietly folded back into the Society's general operating fund in 1752.[52] The bulk of the money the Society spent over the course of the eighteenth century supported parish clergymen stationed among settlers. Tensions over the essence of the Society's purpose remained unresolved throughout the eighteenth century and simmered behind many debates over missionary strategy and support.

The Society worked to make the church abroad as much like the church at home as possible, but major institutional differences distinguished the two settings and affected the SPG's program. Most obviously, the absence of a colonial episcopate affected the relations between the church and state. Without bishops exercising the authority they wielded domestically, the governance of the church in the empire varied considerably from colony to colony. Commissaries, royal governors, colonial assemblies, and parish vestries all claimed and wielded powers over ecclesiastical matters.[53] These ill-defined and conflicting lines of authority made it difficult to superintend the appointment and conduct of Anglican clergymen abroad. Church leaders adopted a number of measures including the bishop of London's appointing commissaries and issuing licenses for colonial clergymen, and practices like clerical conventions in response to these difficulties. There remained little, though, that the Anglican hierarchy could do to make sure that colonial ministers were properly qualified for their offices, to prevent and punish clerical misconduct, or to adjudicate disputes between clergymen or between ministers and their congregations. The lack of bishops also impacted religious practice. It made the rite of confirmation, which had to be conducted by a bishop, an effective impossibility for colonial Anglicans. Because preparation for confirmation provided a focus for the catechizing of young people, its absence also probably undermined religious education.[54] Finally, it made it difficult for colonials to become Anglican ministers, requiring candidates to undertake a round-trip journey to London for episcopal ordination.[55]

Aware of these multiple effects, most of the Society's supporters saw the absence of bishops as a crippling weakness for the colonial church, and the SPG repeatedly attempted to persuade British politicians to sanction an American episcopate. However, the only partial transference of the structure of domestic Anglicanism to the colonies magnified the importance of the SPG as an imperial institution and kept the transatlantic bonds between the overseas church and the Society's London-based membership strong over a long period of time. As the Fulham Papers (the records of the bishops of London) and the SPG's archive chronicle, the absence of colonial bishops meant that appeals, complaints, and questions of all sorts relating to the church abroad continued to flow through London. This meant that colonial ministers had to be attuned to the English political and ecclesiastical situation, and that the Anglican hierarchy and the membership of the SPG retained substantial decision-making power over the colonial church even as Caribbean and North American settler societies matured.

The Society's provision of ministerial salaries illustrates how this institutional situation affected missionary work among non-European peoples. The membership initially envisioned that it would provide financial support to colonial parish clergymen for a limited period of time, until the gathering of viable Anglican congregations and the securing of legal establishments would allow the church in a given colony to rely fully on local resources. However, this process only really played out in South Carolina, where the provincial government assumed responsibility for clerical salaries in 1759.[56] Elsewhere the Society continued to provide salaries for the missionaries it dispatched throughout the eighteenth century. While this limited Anglicanism's growth, it also kept Society-supported clergymen more directly tied to London and, in distinction to establishment colonies like Virginia and Maryland, probably mitigated the power of local vestries. Though still strongly influenced by the views of their congregations, and often dependent on them for supplements to their salaries, London-paid missionaries were probably more able to risk local anger at their efforts to convert enslaved people than their ministerial counterparts in the Chesapeake or Caribbean. The South Carolina missionary Francis Le Jau was a proponent of slave conversion who had previously served as a parish clergyman on the island of St. Christopher. In one of his earliest reports to the SPG, in which he advocated establishing new missions in the Caribbean, he recommended to the Society that any new ministers' salaries "may not be precarious & at the Mercy of the People, for then they may do their Duty without fear of disobliging 'em."[57] More than fifty years later, the New York minister Samuel Auchmuty encouraged the SPG to continue its salary to the town's catechist because he was "very confident that the Masters of the poor Slaves will not pay for their Instruction" and preferred that they remained unconverted.[58] If these conditions limited the number of missionaries the SPG could deploy, they also allowed some SPG ministers to work among enslaved people despite local opposition. Even for missionaries who shared colonial planters' skepticism about the work, their financial dependence on the Society meant that they could never entirely ignore it.

The SPG supported more than four hundred missionaries around the Atlantic in the eighteenth century. Compared with other British transatlantic institutions, the size and scope of the Society's operations were impressive. At the end of Queen Anne's reign in 1714, there were only approximately 240 English officials of all types serving in all the American colonies.[59] In 1715 the Society already had thirty-three missionaries, schoolmasters, and catechists on its annual payroll. By 1750 the SPG had eighty-three men working simultaneously in the colonies.[60] Cumulatively, between 1701 and 1785, the SPG financially supported 309 clergymen, schoolmasters, and catechists to the colonies that became the United States. Before 1800, an additional forty-three worked in the Caribbean, slightly under half of whom served on Codrington Plantation, and at least seventy-three missionaries worked in territories that became part of Canada. The Society also sent three missionaries to West Africa before 1800, marking the beginning of Anglican missionary work on that continent.[61]

Like the Society's membership, its missionaries embodied a range of Anglican religious opinion. As a whole, the missionaries of the SPG favored a strong colonial church, believed in a close relationship between church and state, and had a high regard for their own status as episcopally ordained clergymen. Collectively, like rank and file Anglican clerics in England, they were probably more High Church than the congregations they served, but their views and backgrounds varied considerably. George Keith, the Society's first missionary, ended his life as a vociferous advocate for an overtly sacramental and priest-led Anglicanism, but he was a convert from Quakerism.[62] Another early SPG missionary, John Talbot, was dismissed from SPG service in 1724 for his Jacobite sympathies. After years of pressing for colonial bishops, Talbot was allegedly secretly consecrated as one himself by a nonjuring prelate in England in the early 1720s. Elias Neau, who began SPG work among African Americans, was by contrast a lay catechist who served as an elder of the non-Anglican French Protestant congregation in New York prior to being appointed by the SPG.[63] Later, SPG missionaries had different responses to the rise of evangelical religion during the Great Awakening. While most SPG clergymen, for example, vehemently opposed George Whitefield's itinerant preaching and his criticism of their work, a few shared his evangelical orientation.[64]

The Society's missionaries were also drawn from across the map of Atlantic Protestantism.[65] Only about one-third of those employed by the Society in the eighteenth century were English. The dangers, difficulties, and low pay of overseas work meant that the Society could rarely find enough university-educated English ministers to meet the needs of the colonial church. Ireland, Scotland, and Wales were important sources of manpower. George Keith and several other early SPG clergymen were Scottish, and the Williamite re-establishment of Presbyterianism in Scotland created a large group of displaced Scottish episcopally ordained ministers on which the Society could draw.[66] The presence of many Scottish episcopal clergymen in the colonies was underlined in 1717 by the churchwardens and vestry of St. James Parish in South Carolina, who requested that the Society send them a new clergyman but "humbly desire that he may not be a North Brittain."[67] A contingent of Welsh-born missionaries served Welsh communities in Pennsylvania.[68] In the case of Ireland, the lack of good livings for Protestant ministers seems to have led some to consider SPG service. At least seventy-eight Irishmen served in the colonies that became part of the United States. The Society also supported a number of continental European-born missionaries to German, Swedish, and French-speaking congregations that it had encouraged to conform to the Church of England. While the number of colonial-born Anglican clergymen increased as the eighteenth century progressed, only 28 percent of the Church of England ministers with known origins who served in the thirteen colonies between 1607 and 1783 were born in America.[69] These dynamics meant that, in the overwhelming majority of cases, SPG clergymen were not natives of the places where they ministered. Unordained schoolmasters and catechists, including a very small contingent of Native American and black teachers who worked within their own communities, were more likely to have been born in the colonies. The Society also arranged for the education and ordination of one African-born man in the eighteenth century, Philip Quaque. These patterns suggest that it was ministers' affiliation with the Church of England, rather than any single common national cultural perspective, that is most important to understanding how they collectively approached converting non-European people.

When seen in their totality, the efforts the Society and its missionaries undertook to convert "heathens" were substantial, diverse, and persistent. In most locations, this work was dependent on the varying commitment and initiative of local ministers, but in many cases SPG missionaries attempted to convert nearby black and Native American peoples. The Society's missionaries were active in a number of colonies with large black populations, including Rhode Island, New York, North Carolina, South Carolina, Georgia, and Bermuda.[70] SPG missionaries were stationed at Cape Coast in modern Ghana from 1750 to 1754 and from 1766 to 1816. Clergyman supported by the Society ministered to black "Loyalists" when they resettled in Canada following the American

Revolution, and one accompanied a group that subsequently migrated to Sierra Leone.[71] Non-SPG colonial Anglican clergymen were also encouraged by the Society's members and the English ecclesiastical leadership to work for the conversion of slaves.

In locations where the SPG supported parish schools, people of color were sometimes in attendance. The Society also supported a number of schools aimed specifically at the education and conversion of free and enslaved black people. The first of these, founded in 1703 by Elias Neau in New York, represented the beginning of concerted Society efforts to convert the Atlantic world's black population. Enslaved people on Codrington were also the subjects of a long-running missionary program. In Charleston, South Carolina, a school for the instruction of enslaved people was supported between 1743 and 1768, and an SPG catechist worked among Philadelphia's black population between 1747 and 1762.[72] These schools existed in addition to schools in Philadelphia, New York, Newport, Williamsburg, and Fredericksburg, Virginia, founded by the Associates of Dr. Bray between 1758 and 1765. This was a small organization allied to but distinct from the SPG—it was independent and less closely identified with the Anglican hierarchy—that dedicated itself to the creation of parochial libraries in the colonies and to the education and conversion of enslaved people. Local SPG ministers were often heavily involved in the administration of the Associates' schools.[73]

The Society's efforts to convert African and African American people were interconnected with those made among the Atlantic world's other "heathen" population, Native Americans. One recent account calculates that the Society undertook some form of work among forty-six Indian peoples in the eighteenth century.[74] The heart of this endeavor was the Society's mission to the Iroquois, which began in 1710 and continued into the nineteenth century. SPG ministers primarily served a community of pro-English Mohawks during the eighteenth century and accompanied pro-English Iroquois who relocated to Canada in the aftermath of the American Revolution. Early in its history, the Society dispatched a missionary to the Yamasee people of the southeast, but this effort collapsed with the outbreak of war between South Carolina and the Yamasee in 1715. In New England, the Society ministered among the Narragansetts frequently throughout the eighteenth century. The SPG's interest in the conversion of Native Americans extended into the Caribbean, where it supported ministers to the Native American and mixed-race people of coastal modern Nicaragua and Honduras.[75] These missionary efforts produced uneven results, but their variety and persistence indicate how seriously the Society took the conversion of non-European peoples and how integral this work was to initial plans for remaking religious life in the colonies.

As examples like the mission to the Iroquois suggest, the connections that existed between Anglican missionary activity and the aims of the British government in America were often strong and important.[76] The political roles of bishops and other members, and Anglican conceptions of the nature of the relationship between church and state, promoted such cooperation. Likewise, the Society's supporters typically believed that proper, hierarchical forms of order in religious and political life went hand in hand. It would be a mistake, though, to think that in most matters, government ministers set the course, and the Society simply complied or that the SPG's agenda was essentially political. In some cases, notably the Society's continuing, divisive advocacy for the creation of an American episcopate, the interests of missionary Anglicanism and effective imperial governance might be seen as at odds. For all the heat they generated, Anglican efforts to establish American bishoprics failed, and rather than helping to strengthen metropolitan control over the colonies these attempts seem to have made imperial governance more complicated. Here, to be sure, many in the Society had a vision of church and government cooperation, but it was not one in which officials in London were ultimately willing to participate. It was only in the dramatically changed, post-1783 political landscape that colonial and American bishops would be created.[77] In most areas, the SPG's goals cannot be subsumed easily within secular politics, even if its activities sometimes had political repercussions. The most important case in point is the Society's extended drive to convert black people, which was primarily the product of religious motivations rather than any other aims.[78]

As is widely recognized, the effects of that missionary program among black people are harder to gauge than its scale. While it is clear that the SPG failed to convert the large majority of the British Atlantic world's black populations to Anglicanism in the eighteenth century, it is equally clear that the Society's missionaries brought thousands of free and enslaved black people into the Church of England to some degree. Part of the difficulty in assessing this branch of the SPG's missionary work lies in the nature of eighteenth-century Anglicanism itself. Church of England services were in many ways more community events than opportunities for personal religious expression. The centrality of the clergy to Anglican worship meant practicing involved more listening than speaking for all lay members of gathered congregations. Since Anglican clerics were typically careful to foster seemliness and due respect for social hierarchy in the services they conducted, black attendance was also probably less likely to attract anxious elite commentary than black participation in the more open and egalitarian worship conducted by Baptists, Methodists, or Quakers. Moreover, black people's participation in church rituals like adult baptism could signal a tremendous personal commitment to the church, or it could mean something significantly different. Unlike Methodists or other evangelicals, few eighteenth-century Anglicans left behind the sorts of personal religious testimonies that have helped historians to reconstruct the experiences of black and Native American Christians of other denominations around the Atlantic world. We know, for example, that the former slave and author Olaudah Equiano was a baptized member and regular attendant of the Church of England primarily because he subsequently embraced Methodism, which led him to produce his spiritually oriented autobiography.[79] Black people who stayed within the Church of England and who remained enslaved had less motivation and even fewer opportunities for leaving behind evidence of their personal beliefs.

Although the SPG records are full of references to the baptism of black and Native American people, they often report the baptism or religious instruction of one or two individuals at a time, making an overall picture difficult to assemble. These numbers are probably larger than has traditionally been recognized. It has been observed that the colonial Church of England in Virginia "was by no means a 'for whites only' institution" and "African Americans were present at Sunday services and thereby must be counted among the Anglican adherents."[80] People of color also participated in regular Anglican worship in places like Jamaica and Barbados.[81] A similar situation prevailed in many of the places where the SPG operated. It has been estimated that the Associates of Dr. Bray, a much smaller organization than the SPG, which operated only from the 1730s, reached some two thousand to three thousand slaves through its catechists, schools, and book distributions. One recent estimate has put the number of baptized black Anglicans in colonial South Carolina at between 3 and 5 percent of its total slave population, a percentage that, while small, would have meant there were about 2,500 baptized enslaved people there alone in 1750.[82] In light of these considerations, Thomas Newton's 1769 statement that the Society had by then converted "many thousands" of a total colonial black population "computed to be considerably above half a million" seems credible if imprecise.[83] In any case, numbers alone tell us little about how black people baptized by Anglican clergymen may have understood their relationship to the Church of England, what "conversion" was understood to entail, or how black people practiced or did not practice Anglican Christianity in their own lives. Diversity in all these areas was probably more characteristic than uniformity. What can be said is that while the great majority of colonial black people remained outside of the Church of England in the eighteenth century, there were small but sustained numbers of black Anglicans in parishes around the Atlantic world.

The scope of the Society's efforts and the way it functioned as an Atlantic institution make it a valuable lens through which to observe the changing relationship between religious ideas and attitudes toward human difference and slavery.[84] An important by-product of its religious agenda was the way the SPG facilitated the movement of people. Its missionaries fanned out across the Atlantic world and frequently moved from place to place over the course of their careers. Throughout the century, the Society also helped move small numbers of indigenous peoples from America and Africa to Britain and back, aiding such voyagers as the "Four Indian Kings" of the Iroquois and the Yamasee "Prince George" in the 1710s, the African-born Philip Quaque in the 1750s, and the Mohawk leader Thayendanegea, known to the English as Joseph Brant, in the 1770s. More grimly, the ownership of enslaved people by SPG missionaries and the Society's corporate ownership of Codrington Plantation involved it in the transatlantic and intercolonial slave trades, connecting the organization to one of the period's principal forms of population transference.

This society of people in motion was also a society of letters. In the absence of colonial bishops and faced with the daunting task of coordinating a far-flung program, the Society depended on correspondence to make plans drawn up in London a reality, instruct and superintend its employees, and solicit support. The letters missionaries sent home were at the heart of this system. The Society required each of them to write to the secretary every six months and include answers to a set of standard questions designed to summarize their efforts and progress among both the Christians and heathens they found in their districts. These *Notitia Parochialis* and the letters that accompanied them provide the most detailed and revealing information available about what occurred at individual missionary stations. These reporting requirements made reflecting on and writing about the condition of local non-European people part of missionaries' routine responsibilities; they also framed and limited those reflections in certain ways. For their part, often feeling isolated in their postings, many clergymen wrote more expansively to the Society than the terms of their appointments required. In their letters they sought financial aid and practical advice, defended their reputations, lamented their troubles, and offered suggestions based on their experiences. Many simply looked to retain connections to the lives they had left behind.

For similar reasons, SPG clergymen wrote to each other, often across thousands of miles. The Rhode Island missionary James MacSparran corresponded with fellow ministers Alexander Garden in South Carolina and Samuel Auchmuty in New York; Philip Quaque in West Africa exchanged letters with missionary Samuel Johnson in Connecticut.[85] These webs of correspondence carried missionary strategies, attitudes toward slavery, views on the origins of Native Americans, and a host of other ideas around the Atlantic world. Collectively, the letters written by the organization's missionaries, secretaries,

N°. II.	
Notitia Parochialis ; Or an Account to be fent Home every Six Months to the *Society* by each Minifter, concerning the Spiritual State of their refpective Parifhes.	
I. *Number of Inhabitants.*	
II. *No. of the Baptized.*	
III. *No. of Adult Perfons Baptized this half Year.*	
IV. *No. of actual Communicants of the Church of* England.	
V. *No. of thofe who profefs themfelves of the Church of* England.	
VI. *No. of Diffenters of all Sorts, particularly Papifts.*	
VII. *No. of Heathens and Infidels.*	
VIII. *No. of Converts from a prophane, diforderly and unchriftian Courfe, to a Life of Chriftian Purity, Meeknefs, and Charity.*	

Figure 4. Form for SPG Missionaries' *Notitia Parochialis.* From *A collection of papers, printed by order of the Society for the Propagation of the Gospel in Foreign Parts* . . . (London, 1741). (Courtesy of the Rare Book and Manuscript Library, University of Pennsylvania.)

members, and other affiliates provide insights into what the organization was doing in the eighteenth century and how the people it missionized responded. These epistolary linkages and the organizational structure of the SPG meant that decisions about whom to convert and how to go about doing it were never made in isolation or just in the colonies but were rather the product of transatlantic discussion and debate.

Besides these letters, published materials produced by the Society's members and supporters also moved around the Atlantic world. The most significant example of this was the Society's wide distribution of its annual sermons in both Britain and the colonies. These sermons were mandated by the SPG's charter and their delivery in a London church each February became the organization's central yearly ritual. They afforded the invited preachers, drawn from the ranks of the Anglican upper clergy and often Society members, the opportunity to address the assembled membership. Sometimes, speakers urged the Society to adopt a particular policy or direction, but in published form these annual sermons became the SPG's key means of appealing to a wider public, and most preachers aimed their message at that broader expected readership. For example, many sermons called for the creation of a colonial episcopate or for moral reform at home or abroad. Many of these sermons also reflected and commented on the effort to convert Native American and black populations, and in doing so they provided a mechanism for the circum-Atlantic circulation of SPG supporters' thoughts about human difference and slavery.

The Society's supporters believed its communications network gave them special insight into American conditions and invoked it to give authority to their reports and recommendations. In 1706, the early promotional *Account of the Society for Propagating the Gospel in Foreign Parts* boasted that "the Society have obtained many large and good Accounts of the State of Religion in all our several Colonies and Plantations abroad, which they carefully preserve among their other Books and Papers." These collected letters gave the Society the ability, "by having recourse to them," to "understand the present Condition and Circumstances of every Place; and know how most effectually to answer the Wants and Occasions of them."[86] The Society's correspondence was cited in various annual sermons and came to feature prominently in internally produced accounts of its work. Secretary David Humphreys noted that his 1730 history of the Society was "compiled from Papers, transmitted to the Society, by Governors of Colonies, or Persons of Note Abroad; or from Congregations of People, and the Missionaries in the Plantations." Capitalizing on his own privileged position at the center of this web of correspondence, Humphreys claimed the "original Papers may still be seen" and that there did not "appear any Reason to question their Veracity, and sufficient Exactness in all material Points."[87] Afforded the honor of being invited to deliver the 1745 annual sermon, the SPG secretary Philip Bearcroft took the opportunity to "lay before you from authentick Papers" an account of the Society's activities up to that point "as the great Motive for Perseverance in this well doing."[88] Reports on the previous year's work, which were usually published with each annual sermon, were typically synopses of recent correspondence from clergymen. The migration of missionaries' letters and *Notitia Parochialis* into these printed, public reports ensured that what happened at sites of missionary encounter crisscrossed the Atlantic and resonated in much wider circles.

Beyond enabling the Society to coordinate, finance, and publicize its work, the circulation of texts was also integral to its religious aims. "Knowledge," Thomas Bray wrote, "is the fairest Ornament of the Soul of Man," and he believed in the power of books to promote piety.[89] After the provision of salaries for missionaries, distributing texts was the main way the Society spent its funds. Each clergyman appointed as an SPG missionary was granted an allowance of £10 to purchase books for his own use and an additional £5 for short tracts to be dispersed among his new congregation. From an early date, the Society drew up and revised lists of approved works on which these allowances could be spent. Often cooperating with the SPCK, the SPG also shipped large numbers of books to missionaries and correspondents already in the colonies for them to distribute: the Bibles and Books of Common Prayer believed necessary for orthodox Anglican practice, schoolbooks and catechisms for children and "heathens," small tracts designed to encourage lay piety, polemical pamphlets aiming to counter the arguments of the Church of England's diverse opponents, works of theology and ecclesiastical history intended for parish libraries and ministerial use, and the Society's own sermons and reports. George Keith carried hundreds of copies of a number of anti-Quaker tracts, two thousand catechisms, two thousand copies of *A Pastoral Letter from a Minister to his Parishioners*, and hundreds of other books with him on his inaugural missionary tour.[90] In ensuing decades the Society likewise donated thousands of books to create or augment larger libraries at institutions including Codrington College, Yale, Harvard, and New York's King's College. By mid-century, the Society was already estimating that it had sent some 130,000 Bibles and Prayer Books to the colonies, along with many other educational and devotional books and an "innumerable quantity" of small tracts.[91] This carefully managed flow of printed works provided another means for the Society to affect cultural and intellectual developments.

The way that the Society operated on both sides of the Atlantic had important long-term implications for its missionary program among slaves. As a product of the religious revival that grew up in the wake of the turmoil surrounding 1688, the formation of the SPG was one expression among several of resurgence and confidence within the Church of England. The Church of England in this period had global ambitions, out of which early SPG members' interest in the conversion of non-European peoples often grew. This vision was common among a politically, theologically, and nationally diverse membership and a missionary staff, that engaged in a serious and sustained effort to convert Native American and black populations around the British Atlantic world. More than any other factor, what united these people was a shared belief that episcopal Protestantism should have a larger presence in Britain's colonies. Rivalries with other Protestant denominations and with the Roman Catholic Church helped spur the SPG's foundation, and its supporters continued to see the power of Dissenters and Catholics as posing a multipronged political, social, and spiritual threat to the good order of Britain's colonies. These attitudes helped inspire Anglican interest in the diverse populations of the British Empire, but as the eighteenth century unfolded and new religious movements such as the Great Awakening and Methodism along with new social and political ideas like antislavery developed, this propensity to conceptualize the colonies as sites of religious competition and potential disorder would make the Society suspicious of other groups' efforts to Christianize slaves or ameliorate their conditions.

The particular institutional structure of colonial Anglicanism, characterized by an absence of local bishops and a continuing dependence on financial support from Britain, and the enduring patterns of internal and external communication that the Society's practices created, meant that the SPG functioned as a notably "Atlantic" organization. Decisions about its priorities and strategies were made neither exclusively in the colonies nor in London, but rather emerged out of an interplay between the experiences of missionaries in the field and the efforts of well-connected metropolitan members to coordinate and steer an extensive enterprise. The organization's reliance on letters and texts to administer its program, the membership's belief in the power of print to foster Christianity, and the financial need to encourage public interest in its efforts also combined to make the Society function as a system for the internal and external circulation of ideas about a range of subjects relevant to its aims. As a result, the Society's efforts to convert enslaved people were the subject of continuing transatlantic significance and debate across the eighteenth century.

2

Natural Religion and the Sons of Noah

The Society, Human Difference, and Slavery

As the enslaved population of the colonies continued to grow in the years surrounding the chartering of the SPG, defining the place of black people in colonial societies began to seem increasingly pressing to missionary-minded Anglicans. In the late seventeenth and early eighteenth centuries, debates developed in English intellectual circles about the nature and implications of global humanity's increasingly observable physical, cultural, and religious diversity. In this context, the Society's developing interest in the position of black people in Britain's expanding empire was shaped, in part, by discussions about how the people of the world, including those of African birth or descent, were related to each other. Making decisions about if and how to attempt to convert enslaved people also involved making judgments about the fitness of enslaved people to receive the Society's clergymen and how to respond to slavery within colonial societies, and these issues too were affected by developments in metropolitan learned culture. This chapter explores the intellectual history of SPG supporters' views on these subjects to illuminate the ways they framed the organization's plans and contributed to wider discourses about the nature of human difference and the place of slavery within the British empire.

The involvement of SPG affiliates in discussions of human difference and slavery took place against a backdrop in which Protestantism, Anglican clergymen, and religious thought more generally played central parts in eighteenth-century English intellectual life.[1] While classic narratives of the Enlightenment portrayed it as a struggle between traditional Christianity and modern skepticism, in England some clergymen with apologist intentions were among the most prominent supporters of Enlightenment ideas and "the new intellectual fashions which developed during the eighteenth century did so, to an overwhelming extent, within a Christian context, and moreover, were frequently justified on religious grounds."[2] For example, a pro-Anglican belief that mankind's

religious knowledge had gradually improved over the course of history contributed to the quintessential Enlightenment doctrine of progress.[3] One particularly
important dimension of these broader intellectual developments was the way
that Newtonianism interacted with religious belief, but emerging understandings of ethnicity and race were also affected by religious thought.[4]

Many such discussions engaged in by those affiliated with the Society
emerged out of wider early modern debates about whether reason or scripture
was the better tool for understanding the natural world and people's place in it.
Reflecting its broad-based Anglican origins, the SPG's founding generation included those who enthusiastically embraced reason and new forms of learning
and those who advocated a stricter, more traditional reliance on the Bible as a
guide to nature. While such differences meant that the Society's backers had
various understandings of the origins and implications of human difference,
thinkers from across the spectrum of Anglicanism supported missionary work
among the non-European peoples of the British Atlantic world. However, both
the embrace of reason and an emphasis on the ongoing utility of the Bible for
comprehending the natural world had double-edged implications for the SPG's
activities. Reliance on the Bible, particularly understandings of human difference rooted in interpretations of Genesis, emphasized the shared descent of all
the earth's people but opened the door to arguments that black slavery was divinely sanctioned. In some permutations, such arguments depicted black chattel
slavery as the fulfillment of scriptural prophecies, thereby freighting the particular features of slavery as it existed in the Atlantic world with an apologetic purpose. For their part, explanations for human difference that were not anchored
in scripture could lead to claims that human populations did not have a common
ancestor. In the eighteenth century, such positions remained marginal and heterodox, and they found no support among the committed Christians who constituted the SPG. There were, however, many within the Society who sought to
use rationalist ideas and approaches including natural religion as tools in the
service of their apologetic and missionary goals. Some early SPG supporters
thought that natural religion, especially the notion that all humanity could arrive
at a basic belief in God through the exercise of reason, would serve as an entry-
way for "heathens" into the church. It was also thought that their conversion
would bolster arguments that portrayed Christianity as the truest, ultimate
expression of a universal human religiosity. However, as evidence appeared to
mount that the colonial "heathens" who should have been primed by the existence of natural religion to accept Anglican Christianity were proving resistant
to it, SPG supporters were loathe to accept that their message or methodologies
were at fault. Over the course of the eighteenth century, Anglicans concerned in
the Society's project looked for explanations as to why they did not achieve mass

conversions of non-European peoples. In part, these ideas led them to increasingly find answers in the faults of the populations they sought to convert.

Anglican thought on human difference was rich in the first decades of the eighteenth century. Through Society members' engagement in debates about the origins and significance of human diversity, metropolitan intellectual currents mingled with a stream of information about life in the ethnically diverse colonies. In a reciprocal process, SPG supporters' ideas about the nature of human difference first formed the backdrop for Anglican religious outreach and then, in turn, were reformulated in light of accounts of colonial missionary encounters. The Society's institutional arrangements meant that supporters of missionary Anglicanism simultaneously participated in scholarly and religious speculation *and* determined policies that impacted colonial communities. SPG supporters never considered their work among "heathens" in isolation from their other interests and commitments. Debates about the origins and implications of human variation were not mechanically political ones, nor did the range of views on related theological and philosophical issues of importance for the Society's missionary work correspond automatically to the positioning of participants on the continuum that existed between "High" and "Low" churchmanship. Such differences sometimes emerged, but too much stress on such categorizations can suggest artificial distinctions between figures who had much in common and does little justice to the nuances of Anglican thought.[5] Much of the SPG's program relied on finding common ground between Anglicans of differing persuasions and, more often than not, the compatibility of reason and revelation was stressed when its members considered whom they should convert and how to go about it.

The Society's foundation occurred amid important developments in the ways Europeans understood human difference. François Bernier's 1684 *Nouvelle division de la terre par les differents espèces ou races qui l'habitent*, which divided humanity into groups on the basis of geography, skin color, and physical characteristics—as opposed to older divisions between Christians and heathens or men and brutes—can be seen as marking the start of the first stage in the development of an idea of race, a stage that spanned the "long eighteenth century." What made this period particularly important was the adoption of a new methodology, "the setting aside of the metaphysical and theological scheme of things for a more logical description and classification that ordered humankind in terms of physiological and mental criteria based on observable 'facts' and tested evidence."[6] The late seventeenth and early eighteenth centuries were a transitional period in which questions about differences between human populations were being formulated and explored against the backdrop of European imperial expansion.

As this chronology implies, the replacement of older, religiously inspired ways of understanding humanity occurred gradually. Even as new ideas emerged, those who retained a belief in the literal historical truth of the Bible had ways to understand human diversity. In the late seventeenth and eighteenth centuries, there was a sustained rear-guard defense of scripturally based approaches across fields of knowledge. One manifestation of this was what Colin Kidd has termed "ethnic theology": the effort to reconcile scripture with observations of global human difference reported by European travelers, traders, and settlers. While other approaches were emerging, in the eighteenth century "matters of race, ethnicity, and the genealogies and relationships of peoples and nations were, in the first instance, part of the province of theology."[7] Based on scriptural exegesis, ethnic theology attempted to organize all humanity according to genealogies derived from the Bible. At its most basic level, ethnic theology stressed that every person was descended from a pair of biblical parents—Adam and Eve. In sharp contrast to the ideas of human polygenesis advanced first by Isaac de La Peyrère (1596–1676) in his *Prae-Adamitae* (1655), orthodox ethnic theology emphasized a shared Edenic origin for all.[8] Ethnic theology was important both as a discipline in its own right, and because human taxonomy—like geology would become in relation to scriptural chronology—was believed by skeptics to be good ground from which to launch assaults on the Bible as literal truth. The defense of biblically inspired explanations of human difference, therefore, helped uphold the Bible as an accurate guide to history and nature.[9] Universal descent from Adam and Eve also meant that all the world's population groups, at least theoretically, could include people entitled to and capable of salvation. In this most important way, global humanity was more united than divided.

The book of Genesis was ethnic theology's central text. Genesis 9 chronicles the story of Noah and his family after the great flood. Because the flood had destroyed all people except those preserved on the ark, Noah's three sons—Shem, Ham, and Japheth—and their wives were held to be the progenitors of all humanity's successive generations. Crucially, Genesis 9 also contains a perplexing story of sin and punishment. Genesis 9:20–27 recounts that, after the flood, Noah began to farm and planted a vineyard. Noah became drunk on wine and lay naked in his tent. Ham saw his father in that state and told his brothers, but Shem and Japheth took a robe, and entering the tent backward so as not to look at Noah, used it to cover their father's nakedness. When Noah awoke from his drunken sleep, he learned what Ham had done and issued a curse against Canaan, the son of Ham, saying:

> Cursed be Canaan; a servant of servants shall he be unto his brethren.
> And he said, Blessed be the Lord God of Shem; and Canaan shall be his

servant. God shall enlarge Japheth, and he shall dwell in the tents of
Shem; and Canaan shall be his servant. (Gen 9:22–27)

Ham's sin, the meaning of which has puzzled many scriptural commentators,
was punished by a curse not on him, but on his son.[10]

Genesis 10 provides genealogies of the descendants of Noah, listing the offspring of Shem, Ham, and Japheth. Japheth's descendants included the groups of
peoples collectively called "Gentiles." Ham's descendants included Nimrod, the
mighty hunter and empire builder, and, through Ham's cursed son, the Canaanites,
whose cities included Sodom and Gomorrah. Shem's descendants included Abra-
ham, who entered into a covenant and became patriarch of God's chosen people.
Genesis 11 begins with the story of the Tower of Babel, when "the whole earth was
of one language, and of one speech" (Gen. 11:1). As mankind moved east, they
settled in the "land of Shinar," where they decided to build a city and a tower (Gen.
11:4). The story recounts that the Lord saw this effort, and said, "Behold, the people
is one, and they have all one language; and this they begin to do: and now nothing
will be restrained from them, which they have imagined to do" (Gen. 11:6). To
prevent their completing the tower, God confused the people's language and scat-
tered them all over the earth from that place, which was thereafter called Babel.

Although a total of only ninety-three verses, these three chapters of Genesis
gave many early modern scriptural commentators means to understand the dis-
persion and division of humankind, and ways to explain why God appeared to
favor some peoples over others as history unfolded. The international interpretation of these confusing and even contradictory passages in Genesis has a history of its own, one which was dependent on changes in printing and the
standardization of the Bible, on changes in cartography and conceptions of
geography, and on changes in the interpretive needs of successive generations of
commentators. Because Genesis 9 made clear that all people were descended
from Noah's sons, efforts were long made to link the people and places in the
book's ensuing genealogies with current populations and geographic designa-
tions. Increasingly Ham and his descendants were associated with black skin
and the continent of Africa, and the curse laid upon Canaan was often linked to
slavery. Such interpretations were never uncontested, but they grew in strength
and prevalence across the early modern period.[11] While Ham's identification
with Africa and slavery was well underway when the SPG was founded, it was
not completed before the arrival of "the full-blown racism of the nineteenth and
twentieth centuries."[12] Ethnic theology in the late seventeenth and early eighteenth centuries, therefore, was neither merely received wisdom nor rigid in its
interpretive possibilities, but rather an approach that enabled an author to carve
out his own position within limits imposed by scripture.

Several early SPG members authored commentaries on the Bible, including the stories in Genesis 9–11 that were central to ethnic theology. Richard Kidder, bishop of Bath and Wells and a founding member of the SPG, wrote *A Commentary on the Five Books of Moses* (1694), in which he attempted to support the reasonableness of Scriptural chronology by arguing that the biblical patriarchs lived longer lives than modern people.[13] Kidder noted the "servile and base condition of *Canaan's* Race" and identified the descendents of Ham with Africa.[14] Simon Patrick, the bishop of Ely, and another SPG charter member, authored *A Commentary upon the first book of Moses, called Genesis* (1695).[15] Despite his prominent role among the latitudinarians—he had been the first to defend the "Latitude men" in print—Patrick was committed to upholding the historical accuracy of the Bible.[16] Patrick argued there was "very good reason to believe every thing that Moses hath related; without forsaking the literal Sence" and resorting to "Allegorical Interpretations."

Patrick saw Genesis as particularly powerful in its account of the "Original of Nations," rapturously claiming that Moses's "account of the Families by whom the Earth was Peopled after the Flood, is so surprisingly agreeable to all the Records that remain in any Language, of the several Nations of the Earth; that it carries with it an uncontroulable Evidence of his Sincerity and Truth, as well as of his admirable Universal Knowledge." Patrick believed that Moses's Genesis provided the best guide to understanding human diversity, since "no Writer that hath given us an Account of so many Nations, and so remote as he hath done." Moses had "acquainted us with their original; and told us at what time, and from what place, and on what occasion they were dispersed into far distant countries." Through Genesis, Patrick argued, Moses had "informed us of more in one Chapter, than we can find in the great Volumes of all other Authors" and demonstrated "from whom all [t]hose People descended, who are spread over the Face of the Earth."[17] Like Kidder, Patrick identified the children of Ham with Africa. However, he saw Noah's curse as falling not on all Africans but as being fulfilled when the Israelites used "the Gibeonites . . . as mere Drudges for the service of the Tabernacle."[18] As Kidder and Patrick show, a range of interpretive possibilities was open to students of ethnic theology.

Like many Society supporters, Kidder and Patrick saw the defense of scripture's historical accuracy and the promotion of heathen conversion as linked parts of the fight against Deism and skepticism.[19] Another early Society member, the latitudinarian bishop of Peterborough Richard Cumberland (1632–1718), wrote several tracts considering points of ethnic theology that were published after his death as *Origines gentium antiquissimæ; or, attempts for discovering the times of the first planting of nations* (1724). Cumberland too was interested in reconciling scriptural and secular history to combat skepticism and, like Kidder, argued that the long lives of the biblical patriarchs explained how it was possible for Noah's sons and their wives to produce enough children to populate the earth.[20] Another case in point was the moderate churchman Humphrey Prideaux (1648–1724), dean of Norwich, who defended orthodoxy by publishing, among other works, *A Letter to the Deists* (1696).[21] As a scholar, Prideaux was an orientalist primarily known for his *The Old and New Testament connected in the history of the Jews and neighboring nations* (1716–18), which aimed to demonstrate the compatibility of sacred and secular history by bridging the chronological gap between the Hebrew and Christian scriptures.[22] Prideaux's interests in defending and applying revelation and combating Deism blended with his sustained support for overseas missionary work. He supported "a designe de propaganda in fide in the East Indys" in 1681, he advocated for the expansion of Anglican missionary activity in the 1690s, and he became a member of the SPG in 1702.[23] As figures like Kidder, Patrick, Cumberland, and Prideaux suggest, ethnic theology gave many SPG supporters a way to understand human history and difference and, because its ideas were often wielded in the struggle against freethinking, further motivated them to promote missionary work among "heathens" whose successful conversion would not only be an intrinsic good but also help demonstrate the unique truthfulness of Christian revelation.

While ethnic theology was one part of the intellectual background to the Society's interest in black people, its early supporters could also draw on the writings of Morgan Godwyn, George Keith, and Anthony Hill, Anglican ministers who were among the tiny group of English people who critically examined slavery and its relationship to developing colonial Christianity in the late seventeenth century. The publication of *The Negro's & Indians Advocate* by Morgan Godwyn (1641–90?) in 1680 first brought many churchmen's attention to the rising numbers of slaves held by Anglo-American colonists and decried the lack of attention paid to their religious salvation.[24] Godwyn's writings were later well known by SPG members, cited by Thomas Bray, and both noted by White Kennett in his 1712 annual sermon and appearing on a short list of works he particularly recommended for study by missionaries.[25] Godwyn was the son of an Anglican clergyman who was a royalist during the Civil Wars of the mid-seventeenth century and the grandson and great-grandson of Anglican bishops. After receiving his BA in 1664 from Oxford, where he was tutored by a young John Locke, Godwyn traveled to Virginia and ministered for several years before moving to Barbados. By 1680 Godwyn had returned to England, where he occupied a string of benefices.[26] Most of the other Anglican clergymen of Godwyn's day who saw slavery close up remained in their colonial parishes and probably felt compelled to maintain good relations with the local slave owners who often formed the backbones of their congregations. Godwyn's return to England enabled him to publish his unexpurgated thoughts on slavery from outside of plantation society.

Godwyn's central message was that colonists and the Church of England should do more to convert enslaved people. His book combined moral outrage with an admixture of arguments based on scripture, classical authors, travelers' accounts, his own observations of colonial life, and appeals to the reason and self-interest of slaveholders. Throughout, he insisted on the paternal responsibilities of Christian masters. Enslaved people, he argued, were planters' "*Servants*, and even branches of *each Family*, by whom they in a manner wholly subsist" and "*for whose Souls they are as certainly accountable to God,* as for *their own.*"[27] In Godwyn's view, enslaved people could not be blamed for rejecting Christianity—a claim that some used as a justification for their bondage—because "our *Negro's* are not guilty" of the charge, Christianity "having never been *tendered* to them" (ibid., 54). Portraying masters as the spiritual heads of extended families, Godwyn cited their reluctance to do their duty as the major obstacle to the conversion of enslaved people. The SPG would subsequently share Godwyn's assessment and focus on slave owners' support as the key to Christianization.

As Godwyn recognized, calls for the conversion of enslaved people were also implicitly arguments for their full humanity. Godwyn thought the "monstrous opinion" that Africans were less than fully human was ridiculous but so dangerous that it required a thorough answer. He provided a host of empirical objections to any such claims: "the consideration of the shape and figure of our *Negro's* Bodies," their "Voice and Countenance," which were like other peoples', "their *Risibility* and *Discourse* (Man's *peculiar* Faculties)," their ability to master "*Trades*, and no other less Manly imployments," and the ability to read, write, and show "Discretion in management of Business." These characteristics were "the most clear *emanations* and results of *Reason*, and therefore the most genuine and perfect characters of *Homoniety*" (ibid., 12–13). Yet, according to Godwyn, despite the patent falsehood of such notions, white residents of Barbados still claimed that Africans were less than fully human. One woman told him "that I might as well Baptize a Puppy" as a young enslaved person (ibid., 38).[28]

Godwyn also attempted to refute slaveholders' arguments that stood on the more slippery terrain of scriptural exegesis. Like many SPG founders, Godwyn was well versed in late-seventeenth-century controversies over human origins and the relationship between biblical genealogies, contemporary populations, and slavery. Not surprisingly, the first, and to Godwyn's mind, most dangerous arguments were those grounded in "Pre-Adamatism," which "strain hard to derive our Negro's from a stock *different* from *Adam's.*" These were particularly troublesome because, as subsequent SPG supporters also saw, their proponents saw them as "so exceeding useful to undermine the *Bible* and *Religion*, unto both which they have vowed never to be *reconciled*." However, unlike some influential Society members, Godwyn was skeptical of even more orthodox ethnic theology's application to the populations of Britain's Atlantic colonies and attuned to the inconsistencies of such claims regardless of who deployed them. While critiques of polygenetic concepts entailed attacking heterodoxy, Godwyn was also willing to challenge more mainstream defenses of slavery. He criticized the contention made by some that contemporary black populations were "descendants from *Cain*" who "carry his *Mark*," an argument rooted in Genesis 4 that typically sought to justify black slavery by identifying the "mark of Cain" with black skin and portraying black enslavement as the transgenerational fulfillment of the curse that God leveled against Cain for the murder of his brother, Abel. Finally, Godwyn addressed the more common scriptural justification for slavery that emphasized black descent not from Cain but from Ham (also known as Cham) "that unhappy Son of *Noah*, who, they say, was, together with his whole *Family* and *Race, cursed* by his *Father*."[29] These final two interpretations were more orthodox, but Godwyn rejected them too as "impertinent and blasphemous *distortions of Scripture*" and, more directly, as mutually contradictory (ibid., 14).

Godwyn's criticisms of these biblically inspired arguments led him well down the road of questioning the legitimacy of slavery itself. Godwyn questioned the whole mechanism of the transmission of Noah's curse by arguing that any curse on "Cham's *African* Race" cannot visit any punishment on *American* (nor yet *Asian*) *Slaves*." Proslavery arguments resting on Noah's curse, he argued, were:

> [F]ounded on a Supposition, including in it these five *Falsehoods*, or (at best) *Uncertainties*. 1. That the *Negro's* are of *Cham's* Race. 2. That both *Cham* and his *whole Posterity* were under the *Curse*. 3. That this *Curse* was in its effects to be *perpetual*, even to the last Generation. 4. That it extended to their *very Souls*, and was a kind of *Reprobation*. 5. That this is a sufficient Ground not only for *enslaving* them, but for keeping them from the exercise of *Religion*.

Even if all this was proved, none of it could demonstrate that "we are the *Brethren*, whom they were to serve; and that the *Curse* did confer on us a full and perfect *Right of Dominion* [over] them" (ibid., 19, 43). Godwyn's arguments amounted to a far-reaching attack on ethnic theological justifications for the particular form of slavery developing in Britain's empire. Given his interest in defending orthodoxy against skepticism, though, Godwyn's approach was risky. While his work illustrates the array of ideas circulating within Anglican circles and several of his arguments would recur in SPG-associated texts, none went so far in challenging the comfortable cover for Atlantic slavery that Genesis seemed to many to provide.

Also unlike many subsequent Anglican authors, Godwyn allowed his readers no illusions about the brutality of plantation slavery. He reported masters "Emasculating and Beheading" enslaved people, and "cropping off their Ears (which they usually cause the Wretches to broyl, and then compel to eat them themselves)" as well as the more mundane tortures of overwork and insufficient diet (ibid., 41). This awareness again led him to the brink of questioning the legitimacy of such slaveholding. If Christianizing plantation slavery truly was impossible, Godwyn argued, "it might be considered, how monstrous and inhumanly cruel they are, who do both buy and retain in this *Soul-murthering and Brutifying state of Bondage*, those whom they might so easily restore to their pristine *Homoneity*." Slave owners risked damnation, he argued, if mistreated slaves died through their greed. Godwyn likewise implied that voluntarily emancipating enslaved people would be moral and humane, observing that masters might "with one little blast of their Mouths, even but a word or two" convert brutalized enslaved people "into Men; and be at the same time the happy *Authors* of life to Souls, as well as freedom to Bodies" (ibid., 29–30).

Seen from the perspective of how Anglican thought on slavery subsequently developed, Godwyn's writings read as jeremiads pervaded by a reformist passion. Yet he stopped short of advocating an immediate end to slavery. He thought, counter to masters' self-interested arguments, that Christianity and slavery *could* be reconciled. While willing to challenge any easy identification of enslaved black people with Noah's curse, Godwyn still believed slaveholding was sanctioned by scripture. He thought "it clear enough that *Christianity* doth not lessen any obligations of Servants to their lawful *Masters*." In this way, while Godwyn's critique was broad and explosive, his text also articulated the idea that a reformed slavery was theoretically compatible with Christianity. The key for Godwyn was that colonial societies had to be properly ordered so that any potential conflicts between slavery and Christianity were eliminated.

Consequently, in a line of advocacy that *would* be echoed by the Society, Godwyn supported using the law to alleviate masters' concerns and facilitate slave Christianization. If there were any *"positive Laws"* that stipulated that baptized people could not be kept as slaves, Godwyn recommended "the *Bermudian caution* of Indentures for 99 years Service, to our Peoples *imitation*" until any such laws linking baptism with temporal freedom "might by *Authority* be fairly removed" (ibid., 143). Virginia passed such a law clarifying that baptism did not entail emancipation in 1667, during Godwyn's time in the colony.[30] The 1669 *Fundamental Constitutions of Carolina*, which were at least partially authored by

Godwyn's former tutor John Locke, contained a similar provision. Such laws were also mooted, though not passed, in England in ensuing years.[31]

Godwyn's strident critique of slaveholders' behavior and his acceptance of slavery's theoretical acceptability and legality marked the two points between which missionary Anglican thinking on slavery would oscillate across the late seventeenth and early eighteenth centuries. Given Godwyn's awareness of slavery's brutality, his willingness to accept its legitimacy might be seen as surprising. But Godwyn's text further suggests that Anglican concerns with order and stability, which would continue to affect thinking about slavery in the eighteenth century, were affected by memories of Britain's Civil Wars. Godwyn's clerical family had been traumatized by those conflicts—his father had been ejected from his parish—and in his text royalist positions regarding attitudes toward authority were applied directly to the emerging institution of slavery. As much as he detested the savagery he witnessed and how masters sinned in pursuit of profit, Godwyn noted, the Bible "presseth *absolute* and entire *Obedience* to *Rulers* and *Superiours,* as may be collected from almost innumerable places of Scripture" and "establisheth the *Authority of Masters,* over their Servants and Slaves." The experience of the Civil Wars figured directly, as Godwyn dismissed "any *Levelling Tenets*" and "the Delusions of those *Atheists,* and *Impostors* in 1642 and afterwards, [. . .] to whom *Christ* will one day return but small thanks for *occasioning his Doctrine thus to be blasphemed*."[32] Slavery was accepted both because of biblical sanction and because upsetting the established social order was anathema to many defenders of the Church of England. Like Godwyn, subsequent supporters of missionary Anglicanism used their respect for authority to differentiate themselves from nonconformists whose origins lay in the ferment of the mid-seventeenth century.

This posture was important partly because Quakers became important critics of slavery.[33] Despite the Church of England's antipathy to the Friends, Godwyn's passionate reformism was quite similar to early Quaker impulses. It was only subsequently that missionary Anglican and Quaker approaches to slavery would dramatically diverge. The founder of Quakerism, George Fox, severely criticized Barbados masters for their cruelty and Anglican ministers for failing in their pastoral duties when he visited the island in 1671, but he did not call for an end to the ownership of slaves.[34] William Edmunson, who was "probably the first Quaker to denounce slave-holding outright," did so in 1676, but emancipationists remained a very small minority among the Friends deep into the eighteenth century.[35] For his part, Godwyn had been motivated to write *The Negro's & Indians Advocate* at least in part by a public letter from Fox to the Anglican clergymen of Barbados, which Godwyn described as a "petty *Reformado* Pamphlet" given to him by "an *officious FRIEND*, or Quaker of this Island." It asked

Anglican clergymen "Who made you Ministers of the Gospel to the White People only, and not to the Tawneys and Blacks also?"[36] Godwyn's recognition of the truthfulness of Fox's criticism and concerns over allowing Quaker attacks on colonial Anglicanism to go unanswered seem to have furthered his interest in the conversion of slaves.

The biography of the SPG's first missionary, George Keith, also illustrates the intersections between early Anglican interests in the conversion of enslaved people and concern with Quakerism. In 1702 the Society dispatched Keith to travel widely in the colonies, proselytize, and report back on what he observed. In choosing Keith, a prominent convert from Quakerism, the SPG signaled its intention to challenge the Friends' position in America. Keith had become a convinced Quaker in about 1662, and some thirty subsequent years of travel, preaching, and writing on behalf of the movement made him a prominent figure and gave him ties to various early Quaker leaders including George Whitehead, William Penn, Robert Barclay, and George Fox himself.[37] Keith lived in North America from the mid-1680s, and by 1691 his atypically doctrinaire approach to theology and strident personality brought him into serious conflict with Quaker leaders in Pennsylvania. Keith came to believe that American Quakers were losing touch with the fundamentally Christian nature of their faith, and he objected particularly to "their Notion of the Sufficiency of the Light within every man to Salvation without anything else."[38] Keith's calls for a more scripturally based and theologically systematic Quakerism resulted in a long dispute that saw Keith become the head of a separatist group of "Christian Quakers."[39] Keith was disowned first by Pennsylvania Quakers and then, when he took his cause back to Britain, by the London Yearly Meeting. By 1699 Keith's polemics came to the attention of Thomas Bray and the newly formed SPCK, which sponsored his writings and English preaching tours in which he "detected" the Friends' errors. Keith came into communion with the Church of England in 1700, and in 1702 he was ordained as an Anglican priest.

In 1693, as Keith was engaged in his increasingly bitter feud with Pennsylvania's Quaker leadership, his Christian Quaker group began discussing what their attitude should be toward slaveholding. The result was a precocious antislavery tract, Keith's *An Exhortation & Caution to Friends Concerning Buying or Keeping of Negroes*, which urged Quakers to buy no slaves unless to free them and to manumit any enslaved people already owned "after some reasonable time of moderate Service . . . that may reasonably answer to the charge of what they have laid out." He did not focus primarily on the theoretical morality of the institution but rather on the incompatibility of the Golden Rule with the reality of black chattel slavery. Like other early Quaker critics, he also claimed that the slave trade and slave ownership should be avoided because they led Christians to sin in the pursuit of profit. Enslaved people were "some of the Merchandize of Babylon, by which the Merchants of the Earth are made Rich" but since that wealth was accumulated "through the cruel Oppression of these miserable Creatures" it would "be a Means to draw God's Judgments upon them." While many affiliated with the SPG subsequently used the Bible to sanction slavery, Keith quoted it to warn that Christians were prohibited from buying "Prize or Stollen Goods," which, he said, many of the slaves for sale in Pennsylvania were.[40] Like Godwyn, Keith was keenly aware of the practical difficulties inherent in reconciling actual mastership with a genuinely lived Christianity.

The tract's publication dovetailed with the final collapse of Keith's connections to Philadelphia's Quaker establishment. After 1693, Keith did not discuss slavery in his many publications nor did he make particular efforts to work among enslaved people as an SPG missionary. This may be because Keith seized on slavery primarily to embarrass the wealthy Philadelphia merchants who were among his religious opponents.[41] Keith was too disputatious and too given to changing his mind to be sure of his long-term opinion. But it might also be the case that Keith's statements on slavery were politically motivated *and* sincere, especially because they seem compatible with both the sentiments of Friends like Fox and Anglicans like Godwyn. There is no record that Keith found the Church of England's position on slavery objectionable when he conformed in 1700 nor, evidently and more tellingly, did his printed views on slavery disqualify him as a missionary in the eyes of the SPG's founders. It may be that Keith abandoned his antislavery sentiments, although there seems to be no positive evidence for this, or that once an Anglican clergyman he became more sensitive to the radical implications his views had for the wider colonial economic and social order. After his missionary tour, Keith returned to England and an Anglican benefice, and was rewarded with membership in the SPG, which looked to him for advice on Quakerism and other matters.

Anthony Hill's 1702 sermon *Afer Baptizatus: Or, the Negro turn'd Christian* provides a final example of some of the discussions of slavery on which the Society could draw as it began operating.[42] Like Godwyn, Hill was the Oxford-educated scion of a clerical family.[43] His sermon, however, was less concerned than Godwyn's text with the details of plantation life and more restricted to purely theoretical considerations. In consequence, while he shared Godwyn's desire to encourage the conversion of enslaved people, Hill was far less critical of planters and emphasized the duties required of any Christian. Milder in its language than Godwyn's earlier blistering critique, his text concentrated on winning masters' support, arguing that "*Christianity* is a Law of Obedience, as well as a System of Belief."[44] Hill devoted much of his sermon to disproving that slavery was threatened by Christianity, presenting biblical evidence and arguing it was allowed by international historical practice and the canons and councils of the early church. Hill even claimed, despite the considerable difference of opinion that would exist on this issue for decades, that slavery was sanctioned by English laws.[45]

Christianizing slavery as Godwyn envisioned would have entailed massive changes in how it functioned. Yet, Godwyn's work also shows how Anglican belief in the necessity of hierarchy as a guarantor of social stability, fueled by memories of the Civil Wars and applied to the novel situation emerging in the Atlantic world, could act as a counterweight to desires for moral reform. Few subsequent Anglican supporters of slave conversion matched Godwyn's crusading passion, and they were at greater pains to foreground the compatibility of Christianity with existing slaveholding practices. The difference between Godwyn and Hill was largely one of emphasis, but that difference suggests how thin the line could be between reformism and the legitimation of the status quo regarding slavery. As Hill saw it, "Our holy Religion is the best Security against Dishonesty and Unfaithfulness; it teaches Men to do as they wou'd be done by, to acquiesce in their Condition, and to be contented with the Appointments of Providence; to acknowledge their Benefactors, and to pay a Deference to those above them."[46] While some SPG supporters, especially early ones, would share Godwyn's zeal for reform, most across the eighteenth century were more like Hill and intent on co-opting masters rather than risking alienating them. Though Godwyn, Keith, and Hill all shared the view that the Bible provided the best way to understand how Christians should conceptualize and practice slaveholding, they disagreed on many specific points of interpretation and emphasis. These early texts reveal that Anglican responses to slavery were not predetermined or unanimous when the Society began its work in 1701. Its members and missionaries would make many choices about how to approach Atlantic slavery, masters, and the enslaved people whom they hoped to convert.

As Godwyn's skepticism about many arguments grounded in ethnic theology suggests, those who emphasized it were not the only Anglicans who believed in the conversion of non-Christian peoples. A number of influential figures within the SPG were interested in supporting religion through the claims of reason and new developments in natural philosophy. One way this can be seen is through the connections between the early SPG membership and one of the period's most prominent venues for Anglican theology, the Boyle Lectures. Robert Boyle, who had promoted missionary work in the colonies, endowed the lectures at his death in 1691 for "proving the Christian Religion, against notorious Infidels, viz Atheists, Theists, Pagans, Jews and Mahometans, not descending lower to any Controversies, that are among Christians themselves."[47] The men who gave the lectures largely shared Boyle's twin commitments to battling the forces of skepticism at home and paganism abroad.[48] Fifteen of the twenty-one Boyle lecturers between 1692 and 1731 were members of the SPG, including all of the initial ten.

Whiggish latitudinarian clergymen interested in promoting Newtonianism and natural religion were particularly prominent among the Boyle lecturers.[49] This connection should not be overstated since the early lecturers also included men like the subsequent Jacobite Offspring Blackhall and the Tory Francis Gastrell, as well as several SPG members who used their Boyle Lectures primarily to defend revelation rather than mount rationalist defenses of Christian truth. It is clear, however, that important rationalistic churchmen were prominent among the Boyle Lecturers, and these sorts of Anglicans too supported the Society's work.[50] Richard Bentley and Samuel Clarke, the two most important Newtonians among the early lecturers, were SPG members. The long career of the classicist and controversialist Bentley, who gave the first Boyle Lecture in 1692, included being a Society member for over thirty years.[51] Clarke, who gave the 1704 and 1705 Boyle Lectures, became an SPG member in 1710.[52] Clarke's views on the Trinity were of questioned orthodoxy after the publication of his *Scripture Doctrine of the Trinity* (1712), but he remained an Anglican clergyman and a Society member until his death in 1729.[53]

More generally, the rationalist project was well represented in the actions of those SPG affiliates who attempted to assemble and harness secular knowledge in the service of religious outreach. As Thomas Bray noted in his plan for creating parochial libraries, "The Knowledge of *Nature* affords the best, the plainest, and the most demonstrative Proofs of the Existence, and Providence of God, to the Establishing of our Faith, and the Raising the Admiration and Devotion towards the Divine Majesty, both of the most Intelligent and of the Meanest of the People."[54] This ethos was embodied in Patrick Gordon, a member of the Royal Society whose 1693 textbook *Geography Anatomized* aimed to provide young men with a grounding in global geography, in the explicit hope that the diffusion of such knowledge would help spread Christianity worldwide. For each region of the earth, Gordon provided information on its cities and soil, and assessments of the manners, language, government, and religion of the area's inhabitants. As an appendix to his geography, Gordon included "A Proposal for the Propagation of the Blessed Gospel in all Pagan Countries," where he called for an expanded missionary program on the grounds that "Christianity taken in its largest Latitude, bears no greater proportion to the other grossly false Religions, than 5 to 25" and suggested that "Rational Methods might be taken to have several Pagan Tongues taught in this our own Island."[55] The work was steadily updated, running to a twentieth edition by 1749. Gordon's desire to use his knowledge to expand Christianity was more than a literary conceit. In 1702, Gordon volunteered as the SPG's second missionary and was dispatched to New York. Gordon died only a few months after his arrival in America, but subsequent editions of *Geography Anatomized* included a dedication to Archbishop Thomas Tenison that observed with satisfaction that "our implacable Adversaries can no longer upbraid us with a *supine Neglect* of our *Heathen American Neighbours* in their *Spiritual Concerns*."[56]

Reason-oriented Anglicans contributed significantly to the Society's program by emphasizing natural religion within its missionary methodology. This was a delicate issue. The concept of natural religion had multiple interconnected and contested meanings in the decades surrounding the SPG's founding. Natural religion's proponents differed on many points of emphasis and interpretation, but central to it was the notion that God's existence could be discovered and demonstrated through the proper exercise of human reason, independent of any divine revelation. Many advocates of these ideas argued that one way this could be done was by carefully observing the design and purpose evident in the workings of the natural world. This natural theology, as it was also known, had deep roots within the history of Christian apologetics, but it was particularly powerful in late seventeenth- and early eighteenth-century British intellectual life because it seemed to offer a way to harmonize new "scientific" discoveries with a continuing belief in God.[57] These ideas intersected with missionary outreach because many proponents of natural religion also argued that all people, because they could exercise reason, shared an awareness of God's existence regardless of their particular historical and cultural circumstances. This was seen as a valuable tool for connecting with an array of potential "heathen" converts, whose supposedly common, basic beliefs could serve as a foundation for the inculcation of the fuller truth of Christianity.

The dilemma for self-consciously orthodox Christians lay in the relationship between natural religion and the unique aspects of Christian revelation. While many firmly Christian thinkers were attracted to natural religion in this period, English Deists also utilized it in an effort to critique orthodoxy and offer alternatives to it. Deists argued that the proper use of reason and the observation of nature not only enabled knowledge of God but also showed that many specific features of historical revealed religions, including Christianity, were superfluous or even false. In turn, Society members were also aware that some Deists claimed that the cross-cultural existence of a pure, superior, and sufficient natural religion obviated the need for a specifically Christian missionary effort among "heathens." John Williams, who used his Boyle Lectures to defend revelation, made that point in his 1706 SPG annual sermon, imagining a conversation between a "native" and a missionary who preached natural religion but did not do enough to stress the necessity of a belief in Christ. "Then, saith the Native, let the Fault lie upon me, and if I may be saved in the Religion of my own Country, I shall need no farther Instructor, nor shall I desire any Change."[58] Williams's point was clear: natural religion alone could not ensure salvation.

As Williams's sermon also suggests, there was not an unbridgeable gulf between the acolytes of reason and revelation within the Society's ranks. Many Anglicans believed that arguments in defense of Christianity could be made— indeed could best be made—on the grounds of *both* revealed and natural religion, and that reason and authority could be mutually supporting in many other areas. Similarly, an array of missionary-minded churchmen thought that properly framed appeals to natural religion could help promote Christianity at home and abroad. In 1712, for example, the Society's printed instructions to its missionaries ordered that in teaching "*Heathens* and *Infidels*, they begin with the Principles of Natural Religion, appealing to their Reason and Conscience; and thence proceed to shew them the Necessity of Revelation, and the Certainty of that contained in the Holy Scriptures, by the plain and most obvious Arguments."[59] In 1719 the SPG directed its Codrington catechist to begin his work among its slaves with natural religion:

> *First,* Put them upon considering what sort of Creatures they are; and how they came into Being. *Secondly,* From whom they received their Being. *Thirdly,* What sort of Apprehensions they ought to have of the Author of their Beings. *Fourthly,* Shew them, from that invisible Spirit which moves and acts their Bodies, and by which they are enabled to think, to reason, and to remember, that there may be other Beings which they do not see with their Eyes; and particularly that Being which we call GOD. *Fifthly,* Shew them, that there is such a Being as we call GOD, from his Works of Creation and Providence; and particularly from the Frame of their own Beings.

Only after completing this initial phase should the catechist "shew them farther, How [God] has made Himself and his Will known to Men, by a certain Book, called the *Bible*."[60] Such instructions were reissued to missionaries subsequently in the century.[61]

Likewise, some SPG supporters claimed religion and natural philosophy could be combined to explain human difference. Society member John Harris's 1698 Boyle Lecture *Atheistical Objections against the Being and Attributes of a God fairly considered and fairly refuted* was part of a lifetime of work devoted to furthering religion through reason. Harris was a committed Whig, a Fellow and later Secretary of the Royal Society, a lecturer on Newtonianism, and an active clergyman. The year before his Boyle Lecture, Harris published his own work on Genesis, *Remarks on some late papers, relating to the Universal Deluge* (1697), which neatly merged his joint dedication to religious and scientific truth by claiming that it could be proven that black African people were descended from Ham *and* that blackness was determined by environment.[62] In 1705 Harris produced a collection of global travel accounts that sought to update the compendia of Hakluyt and Purchas.[63] He prefaced this collection with an introduction that made his apologetic aims clear. It treated "the Origination of Mankind, the Peopling of the World, and the Migration of Nations" and argued that "the History which *Moses* gives us of the Original of Mankind and the Peopling of the World ought to claim the greatest state of our Veneration and Regard."[64]

Harris's effort to reconcile the human diversity cataloged in his collection of voyages with Genesis and global Noachian descent led him to argue expansively for the mutability of human beings. It was, he claimed, "not difficult to conceive how very different Colours and Shapes of Men may easily arise from the difference of Climates, Humours and Fashions of Mankind, and from the Power of the Mother's Imagination operating on the *Foetus*." His example was "the Case of the *Cafres* or *Negroes* of *Africa, New Guinea, Madagascar*, &c," the bodies of the first of whom might have "become very swarthy, burnt and black" by "the vast Heat and Drought of the Climate." Those who were most active in such an environment were likely to have the darkest skin and, stressing the relativity of assessments of human beauty, Harris asked if they would "not despise the effeminate Whiteness and Softness of those that staid at home?" A desire to achieve black skin, he suggested, might even lead such people to "use *Artes* and *Pigments* to procure it." In such an environment, women would desire to see such traits in their children, and as a result "the *Foetus* in the Womb of the Mother (which is but like a Graft on a Tree) would be tinged with the same Colour, Form and Complexion."[65] History and observation, Harris thought, provided ample evidence of the power of mothers to effect such changes in their offspring. In Harris's argument, efforts to support scripture and a focus on climate as a determining factor in human appearance combined to produce patterns of thought that minimized the distance between human populations. For Harris, as for other SPG supporters, reason and scripture combined to encourage and shape missionary work among non-European peoples.

Another concrete expression of SPG members' desire to deploy reason and secular learning was the London library that the organization assembled. In 1714 White Kennett, then dean, and later bishop, of Peterborough, gave the Society his large collection of books, pamphlets, and maps on America.[66] Kennett's library, which the SPG maintained in London for nearly two centuries, was a landmark—the first English attempt to assemble all of the works that had been published on America. Kennett gathered these materials, which ran to over 1,200 separately cataloged titles, over many years as part of an unrealized plan to write a history of the spread of Christianity in the Americas. His collection aimed to establish "a religious genealogy for the British Empire," marking a new effort to link the nation's burgeoning colonial project with the spread of Protestantism.[67] He saw the English church and English commerce as mutually supporting and wanted the library stocked with texts that "may best serve for the Conduct of our Missionaries, the Help of Mariners and Merchants, the

Figure 5. White Kennett (1660–1728). Bishop of Peterborough (© Trustees of the British Museum.)

Information of Strangers, and the Entertainment of all Persons, who wish well to the Propagation of our Faith, and to the Trade and Commerce of our Country, among ALL NATIONS."[68]

Kennett's donation coincided with the Anglican consensus that clergymen should be well educated and with Bray's hopes for creating a better-read ministry in England and the colonies. Kennett suggested that prospective missionaries might be required to spend several weeks in the library before leaving England. There "a Man of Conscience with his Thoughts upon the *Indies*" could "prosecute his preparatory Studies with so much advantage and delight." No records of the library's use appear to exist and the SPG sold the collection in 1913. It may have taken some years to find a proper location to house the donation and make it available for use, but the leading expert on the library has observed that there can be no doubt its books were consulted extensively.[69] Clergymen who entered the Society's service typically spent considerable time in London before they sailed for the colonies. The Society instructed them to engage in prayer, preaching, "or in such Studies as may tend to fit them for their Employment."[70]

The library included a wide range of materials. The accounts of travelers and voyages were prominent, with the stories collected by Hakluyt and Purchas cataloged individually by Kennett. As he noted in his catalog, the library's five-volume set of the 1626 edition of *Purchas his Pilgrimage* was donated by an influential member, Francis Nicholson. As a central text for surveying human difference into the early eighteenth century, *Purchas his Pilgrimage* provided powerful support for the idea that all peoples of the Atlantic world were worthy of conversion. Its section on Africa concluded with a prayer that, "The tawnie Moore, blacke Negro, duskie Libyan, Ash-coloured Indian, olive-coloured American, should, with the whiter European become one sheep-fold, under one Great Sheepheard, till this mortalite being swallowed up of life, wee may all bee one, as Hee and the Father are one."[71] Works by New Englanders, including Cotton Mather, Matthew Mayhew, Daniel Leeds, and John Eliot provided missionary exemplars and reminders of the comparative inadequacy of Anglican efforts. A hallmark of the library was its mixture of works from across approximately two centuries of European knowledge of the Americas. Hakluyt's and Purchas's collected stories stood alongside such state-of-the-art works as Hans Sloane's 1707 traveler's account and natural history of the Caribbean.

The library's subject was America, but in Kennett's broad vision missionaries could understand it and its peoples only if they grasped their connections to the wider world. He saw "a sort of necessary Dependence of Things and Places upon one another" so he gathered works on "Voyages and Travels to all Parts of the World, especially to AFRICA and the EAST-INDIES, that chiefly supply our Traffick to AMERICA."[72] Accordingly, the library included texts like *A Reporte of* the Kingdom of Congo, a Region of Africa, and of the Countries that border round about the same, &c (1597) and *A Geographical Historie of Africa* (1600), both English translations of Italian accounts, and more recent political and economic treatises on the African and Asian trades.[73]

Kennett believed that the library's works on Africans and Native Americans would be particularly useful for future missionaries, who "might here examine the various Accounts that have been given by Eye witnesses of their Genius and Capacity, their Notions and Manners, their Prejudices and their Obstinacy in them." Those who hoped to "converse a little with those ignorant Natives" could "dip into the Indian languages, or the Chief Dialects of the Borderers on us."[74] The library also included numerous works of ethnic theology. Explaining the relationship of Native Americans to scripture genealogies and the rest of humankind was a particularly important subfield of ethnic theology, and a "wide variety of imaginative solutions emerged in answer to the riddle of American origins."[75] Among the works Kennett collected were Thomas Thorowgood's *Jewes in America, or probabilities that the Americans are of that race* (1650), which argued that Native Americans were descended from the lost tribes of Israel and ripe for conversion, and Giles Fletcher's *Israel Redux* (1677), which used ethnic theology to argue that the lost tribes were located in Tartary, not America.[76] Though the collected books were primarily in English, the library included many Latin works including those of the Spanish Jesuit José de Acosta (1540–1600) and the German Georg Horn (1620–70), which offered competing biblically based explanations for the peopling of the Americas.[77] A belief in the relationship between Native Americans and the Israelites was not necessary to embrace missionary work, but the issue was seen as one worthy of consideration.[78]

Kennett seems to have been open-minded on such questions. He included the competing works by Thorowgood, Fletcher, Acosta, and Horn, and Morgan Godwyn's *The Negro's and Indians Advocate* (1680), which was skeptical of ethnic theological claims, in a subset of "such Tracts and Dissertations as recommend and explain the Great Duty of Planting the Gospel in All Nations, and direct the most effectual ways and means of bringing over the poor Pagan Souls to Christian Knowledge and Salvation." He thought these books ought to be included in the personal library of every SPG missionary.[79] Kennett's effort to assemble the sum total of English knowledge of America in one place for the use of the Society is a striking example of a belief that reason and secular knowledge could help spread Anglicanism. The inclusion of so many works of ethnic theology in that library is also an indication of the way that religiously based understandings of history and nature continued to be seen as having practical applications.

The books that the Society sent to the colonies illustrate a similar dynamic. On the whole, books approved for purchase for missionaries' personal use or in parochial libraries reflect the desire to harmonize human and natural history with revelation. Edward Stillingfleet's 1662 work *Origines Sacrae: Or a Rational Account of the Grounds of Christian Faith, As to the Truth and Divine Authority of the Scriptures, And the matters therein contained,* a learned attempt to show that biblical stories could be factually correct, is representative of the Anglican classics often bought for missionaries by the Society. *Origines Sacrae* went through at least nine editions by 1708 and was included, for example, in both Thomas Bray's 1697 plan of books to be included in parochial libraries—under the heading "Upon the Mosaick History of the Creation and the Deluge"—and in a 1705 list of books approved for inclusion in missionaries' libraries.[80] Stillingfleet was committed to reconciling religion with new learning and as originally written *Origines Sacrae* had relied on Robert Boyle's natural philosophy in its examination of religious questions. By 1697 Stillingfleet updated the work to reflect the growing influence of Newtonianism.[81] Other notable works on these lists of approved books included Hugo Grotius's widely influential apologetic *De Veritate Religionis Christianae* and a number of Boyle Lectures.[82]

Works considering human difference from a primarily religious perspective were also on these lists, with those emphasizing the utility of natural religion and those presenting ethnic theology appearing side by side. John Wilkins's *Of the Principles and Duties of Natural Religion* (1675) was included in lists approved in 1705 and 1741. Simon Patrick's ethnic theology-informed commentary on the Old Testament was present on lists approved in 1705, 1741, and 1788. Similarly, Humphrey Prideaux's *The Old and New Testament connected in the history of the Jews and neighboring nations* appeared on such lists. These lists served practical purposes. Stillingfleet's *Origines Sacrae* and Grotius's *De Veritate* were among the eleven works James Gigullat purchased with Society funds in 1710 before he sailed for his mission in Santee, South Carolina. Thomas Poyer, who was stationed to Jamaica, Long Island, in the same year spent £3 12s. of his book allowance on nine volumes of Simon Patrick's *Commentaries*.[83]

The Society's records also demonstrate attempts by some early missionaries to deploy concepts of ethnic theology in the field, particularly as they tried to understand the Native Americans they encountered. Francis Le Jau was deeply committed to the conversion of "heathen" people, and ethnic theology was central to his understanding of the situation he confronted on the ground.[84] Le Jau believed that rituals he witnessed among South Carolina Indians suggested that "they had some Tradition ab[ou]t Noahs Ark and his 3 Sons."[85] Le Jau also saw connections between local Native American peoples and the Israelites. For example, in 1708 he wrote to the Society to inform them, "I hear of several

Nations that are Circumcised; I take notice of several Old Legal Ceremonies still
kept among our Neighbours chiefly their feast, and a kind of Offering of first
fruits when their Corn is ripe."[86] This proved an enduring fascination, with
Le Jau writing again in 1716 about circumcision among some Carolina tribes.[87]
Le Jau systematically approached his study of links between secular knowledge,
the Bible, and the multiethnic landscape of his mission. In 1710 he made detailed
references to the 1625 edition of *Purchas his Pilgrimage* he owned when inform-
ing the Society about the Savannah Indians.[88] Other missionaries, including
Carolina-based Francis Varnod, also thought they detected linguistic and cultural connections between Native Americans and the Lost Tribes. Varnod, like
Le Jau, would be one of the SPG clergymen most committed to the conversion
of enslaved people.[89]

As these missionaries' experiences suggest, an interest in ethnic theology could
spur an interest in converting, and often considerable sympathy for, some "heathen" peoples. However, ethnic theology also had more dismal implications. It
has been argued that in nineteenth-century America, "from the perspective of
moral science no argument was more important for the proslavery case than
proving the biblical authorization for American slavery."[90] Eighteenth-century
texts produced by those affiliated with the Society helped to develop and circulate such ideas around the Atlantic world. In an age when overtly antireligious
explanations for human difference remained beyond the pale of acceptability for
most people, the strain of ethnic theology advanced most often by SPG supporters yoked missionary outreach to the acceptance of slavery.

A theme with particularly far-reaching implications was the portrayal of
black Atlantic slavery as a fulfillment of scriptural prophecy. Philip Bisse
(1661–1721), the moderate Tory bishop of Hereford, concluded his 1718
annual sermon by assuring his audience that the Americas would "be brought
under the banner of CHRIST's Kingdom." He also wanted to "intimate" something of "a higher nature:" what was happening in the colonies was the coming
to pass of a specific biblical prophecy, that "ancient Prophecy of our Father
Noah; that first of all Prophecies on record in Scripture," that "*GOD shall enlarge
Japhet, and Canaan shall be his servant.*" Bisse thought it remarkable that Noah's
words seemed "so literally to foretel, what hath befallen these *Western* Nations
(the Sons of *Japhet*) in these latter days." In Bisse's view, European colonialism
and African enslavement in the Americas were divinely ordained.

In interpreting Noah's blessing upon Japhet and curse upon Canaan as
prophecy, Bisse cast Atlantic chattel slavery as compelling real-world evidence of
the unfolding of God's plan. "Was there," Bisse asked, "ever an Enlargement of a
People, equal to that of taking a Possession of a New World! Or was there ever so

remarkable a Generation of servants, or such a kind of slavery, as is that of the miserable *Negroes*, the Sons of *Ham!*" These parallels, Bisse concluded, "cannot but affect us with some Wonder: the discovery of these Regions is scarcely more remarkable in itself, than the Words of this Prophecy, so plainly foretelling it."[91] Elsewhere in his sermon Bisse criticized British planters and how little they had done to promote their slaves' conversion. Nevertheless, his text points to the way ethnic theology led some Society supporters to not only accept generic slavery as divinely permitted but also to impute apologetic and philosophical importance to the particular harsh and racialized form that it took in Britain's Atlantic colonies. In Bisse's hands, the literal and prophetical meanings of Genesis provided frameworks for understanding who the peoples of the Atlantic world were, for understanding the SPG's obligation to convert non-European peoples, and for understanding how and why slavery existed in Britain's empire. Such prophetical interpretations of Genesis 9 went beyond more common claims that slavery was sanctioned by various biblical passages, taking Atlantic slavery's starkest characteristics as welcome evidence of God's hand in human affairs.

Philip Bearcroft, who served as the Society's secretary from 1739 to 1761, gave the 1745 annual sermon, which he used to provide an overview of SPG accomplishments in its first four decades. When he discussed the Society's work among enslaved people, Bearcroft too argued that Atlantic slavery demonstrated the truthfulness of scripture prophecy. "Most remarkable is the Prophecy of the great Ancestor of this post-diluvian World, concerning the Fate of his Posterity; Cursed be Canaan, a Servant of Servants shall he be to his Brethren. This the poor African Negroes of his Race prove in their hard Slavery to their great Sorrow fulfilled." Bearcroft extended his use of ethnic theology by identifying Europeans with the descendants of Japhet. He observed that "The European Posterity of Japhet have greatly enlarged themselves in America, and the unhappy Children of Canaan are most certainly their Servants there."[92] Bearcroft's position gave him an important place in steering the Society's circum-Atlantic operations. As it had earlier for Philip Bisse, his seeing black slavery as the fulfillment of a prophecy entailed that there was not only a divine sanction for slavery, there was also a divine purpose behind its growth and spread in Britain's colonies.

This way of thinking about slavery was not esoteric. The various threads of opposition to Deism, the Anglican effort to reconcile reason with scripture, interest in explaining human difference, the desire to support missionary work, and assessing the place of slavery in the Atlantic world were also woven together in the work of Thomas Newton (1704–82). Newton was a member of the Society by the early 1750s and remained one over the course of a career that culminated in his serving for twenty years as bishop of Bristol. In 1754 he published *Dissertations on the Prophecies*, a work that sought to counter Deism by demonstrating the many ways that scriptural prophecies had been fulfilled in biblical times and subsequent human history.[93] Newton's work was widely distributed in Britain and the colonies. By 1794 the book had been produced in eleven British editions, and it was published by several American printers in the late 1780s and 1790s. A study of the distribution of millennial literature—a category in which Newton's work is included because of its focus on prophecy—has found that *Dissertations on the Prophecies* was listed on 42 percent of a representative sample of booksellers' catalogs in late eighteenth-century America. This suggests that besides being by far the most available book on prophecy to North American readers of the period, Newton's work was more widely offered by booksellers than many other now well-known

Figure 6. Thomas Newton (1704–1782). Bishop of Bristol (© Trustees of the British Museum.)

titles including Locke's *Two Treatises of Government* and Samuel Richardson's popular novel *Pamela*.[94]

In this work, Newton's very first example of the historical fulfillment of prophecy was provided by the story of Noah, whose prophetic curse was realized not only by the subjugation of the Canaanites by the Israelites but also by the enslavement of the later descendants of Ham. As Newton observed:

> The whole continent of Africa was peopled principally by the children of Ham: and for how many ages have the better parts of that country lain under the dominion of the Romans, and then of the Saracens, and now of the Turks? in what wickedness, ignorance, barbarity, slavery, misery live most of the inhabitants? and of the poor negroes how many hundreds every year are sold and bought like beasts in the market, and are conveyed from one quarter of the world to do the work of beasts in another?[95]

In Newton's conception the story of the sons of Noah did more than explain the origins of human diversity. As it had for earlier Society supporters, the existence of African slavery served an explicitly apologetic purpose. Defenders of orthodoxy believed that pointing to examples of the fulfillment of scriptural prophecies helped make the case that the Bible was divinely inspired, that God's hand could be seen in natural and human history, and that, at the most fundamental level, God existed. Newton appeared to sympathize with the plight of slaves, but his characterization of Atlantic chattel slavery as the continuing fulfillment of prophecy not only justified slavery but also invested the continuing enslavement of African people with theological and philosophical meaning. As Newton proclaimed, "And is not this a most extraordinary prophecy; a prophecy that was delivered near four thousand years ago, and yet hath been fulfilling thro' the several periods of time to this day! It is both wonderful and instructive. It is the history of the world as it were in epitome."[96] Through Newton, such ideas became included in a circum-Atlantic best seller. Newton's apologetic intentions aside, *Dissertations on the Prophecies* became an important text in the equation of Ham with Africa. These ideas had an enduring effect on thinking about slavery in the Atlantic world. In the nineteenth century, proslavery writers in America made use of Newton's work to support their position.[97]

The attention devoted to natural religion by those Anglicans sympathetic to rationalist theology likewise had long-term implications for how SPG members thought about missionary work and human difference. Early in the Society's history, belief in the ubiquity of natural religion generated hopefulness that the conversion of non-Europeans would be a relatively straightforward matter. In 1704, for example, the first SPG missionary to North Carolina, James Blair, reported to the Society in glowing terms that minimized the distance between Native Americans and other inhabitants of the colonies.

> I think it likewise reasonable to give you an Account of a Great Nation of Indians, that live in that Government computed to be no less than 100000 many of which live amongst the English, and all as I can under-stand a very Civilz'd People.
> I have often convers'd with 'em, and have been frequently in their Towns, Those that can speak English among them seem to be very willing & fond of being Christians & in my Opinion there might be Methods taken, to bring over a great many of them.[98]

Once it undertook missionary work in earnest, the SPG found the going rougher than expected. Its efforts produced some conversions, but after several decades of work there still had not been the wholesale conversion of black and Native American populations that early members of the Society anticipated.

Part of the picture was simply the fading away of early naiveté. However, there was more to this process than the replacement of unrealistic hopes with more realistic expectations and better-informed understandings of "heathen" peoples and their cultures. Increasingly, members of the Society thought that the conversion of non-European peoples would not happen through building on natural religion, but could only occur after a long process of civilization. In his 1730 history of the Society's first decades, the SPG secretary David Humphreys recited a litany of missionaries' complaints about the manners and morals of the Mohawks and said the membership had concluded "that it was not possible to teach them the Christian Religion, before they were in some Degree civilized."[99] Humphreys wrote at a momentary low point for the Society's mission among the Iroquois, but the sentiments he expressed were on the rise. Because calls for the conversion of black people were frequently made in paternalistic language that framed enslaved people as part of the colonial "family" (and thereby often effectually denied that they had a distinct culture that affected missionary encounters), this hardening of attitudes about human difference was clearest in the way that Society members spoke about the conversion of Native Americans. Henry Stebbing captured the growing mood in 1742, telling the Society that "of a *general* Conversion of the native *Indians* I see no great likelihood at present." Native Americans first "must be polished into good Manners; there must be some common intercourse between us; we must bring them to some good liking of our Laws, and Customs." On the other hand, Stebbing observed that "our *Negroe* Slaves are within our Authority; Branches, as it were, of our Families; many of them born, and bred up among us; and these may be taught our Religion, as easily as they may be taught any Thing else, if proper Care be taken to instruct them.[100] Henry Stebbing and other post-1740 deliverers of SPG annual sermons may have been willing to question the Society's missionary work among Native Americans in part because the Deist threat had largely subsided by that period.[101] It was also the case that the Society's inability to effect mass conversions of "heathen" peoples provided another context for SPG supporters' changing conceptualizations of their missionary project and for related developments in their ideas about the nature and depth of human difference.

Doubts about the Society's work among "heathens" and arguments that accentuated the disparities, rather than the commonalities, between European and non-European populations became increasingly important by mid-century. Samuel Lisle, the bishop of St. Asaph, used his 1748 annual sermon to consider the unequal distribution of God's favors on humanity. Lisle, like some other SPG preachers, wanted to stress the centrality of a uniquely Christian revelation to salvation, but his development of the point indicates a growing uneasiness about how the SPG had been approaching non-European peoples. Revelation, Lisle observed, is not a right but a gift from God, and in both individual cases and in "his dealing with whole Nations" his "Bounties are bestowed with a very unequal Hand." While some thinkers saw climate as an explanation for observable difference that underlined humankind's essential unity, Lisle thought that "even originally from the Nature of their State and Situation, some Nations seem to be condemned to perpetual Distress and Misery. Inclemency of Climates, unfruitful Soils, unwholesome Airs, are the natural Lot of many of them. And all this is frequently attended with such Dulness of Apprehension, such Darkness of Understanding, and such Barbarity of Life and Manners, as sets them but a small Degree above the Brute Creation." By contrast, people from other "Parts of the Earth," a category clearly including Britain, were "by Nature blessed with all possible Means of Happiness; with mild and fruitful Seasons; with clearer Faculties and riper Judgment; with social Graces, and all the Refinements of civil Life." One product of this divinely ordained difference was the Society's responsibility to send catechists to "civilize and instruct in the Knowledge of Christianity the rude Minds of the Negroes, who are so usefully employed in our several Colonies."[102]

Lisle's sermon made potent connections between nationality, climate, civilization, and God's distribution of blessings, all in favor of his own countrymen and at the expense of non-European peoples. John Thomas, bishop of Peterborough, struck a similar note when he told the SPG's membership in 1751 that

"Diversity in the Understandings, as well as Situation and Circumstances of Mankind," was a beneficial thing for society.[103] The 1757 SPG annual report contained the observation that while the Society had been "very careful to endeavour to convert to Christianity both Indians and Negroes on every proper Opportunity," results had not been what the Society had hoped. "It is to be found to be to no Purpose, to talk to them about our Holy Religion in their wild native State." Instead, "they must be reduced from their Barbarity, I had almost said Brutality, and be made Men, that is rational considerate Creatures, before they will become good Christians."[104] Whereas, missionary strategies rooted in natural religion had been premised on the common human rationality shared by Europeans and non-Europeans, Lisle argued that black and Native American people needed to "be made Men." Experience had shown that despite optimistic hopes about the conversions of non-European peoples, there were major, God-sanctioned differences that separated human populations.

Such growing pessimism had wider cultural resonances. The late eighteenth century saw important changes in the way that cultural difference was understood by British people. Whereas in earlier periods culture was seen as a "driving force of human mutability," it came to have "an aspect of racialized permanence."[105] The thought of the supporters of the SPG provides early examples of such a movement and reveals an element that may have contributed broader shifts. William Warburton's 1766 annual sermon expanded such lines of argument. A representative of England's largely clerical experience of the Enlightenment and the quintessential polemical divine of the period, Warburton was both a Whig bishop and an active participant in wide-ranging philosophical and theological debates for decades.[106] Warburton was a combative author, and the often unorthodox way he defended orthodoxy made some fellow clerics, including figures associated with the SPG, doubtful about his true philosophical and theological loyalties. However, he wielded considerable influence in European literary and philosophic circles. Warburton's SPG sermon has received attention from historians for its passionate attack on colonial slaveholders.[107] While Warburton's views on slavery were largely rejected by the Society's membership, his arguments about converting Native Americans appear to have been more influential and reveal how views on the nature and significance of human difference were shifting.

His sermon's treatment of the subject was based on an argument that Warburton had made in his most influential work, *The Divine Legation of Moses Demonstrated*, which addressed missionary work in the context of defending Christianity from the attacks made on it by Deists.[108] *The Divine Legation* employed a counterintuitive and ambitious strategy in which Warburton attempted to transform many of the arguments of Deists themselves into defenses of orthodoxy. Warburton claimed in the *Divine Legation* that British missionary history had been marked by "continued ill Success." While missionary failures seemed on their face to undermine the case for the truth of Christianity, Warburton argued they really showed that "Religion cannot long subsist without the Aid of Civil Government."[109] While some believed that Warburton envisioned a church that was overly subservient to the state, he intended to defend the Anglican establishment and hoped that government and the church would cooperate in a needed reformation of the nation's manners.[110] Based on his insistence on the need for state strong support for religion, Warburton argued that missionaries' repeated failures showed that most of them "have begun at the wrong End." While Christianity "requires an Intellect above that of a Savage to comprehend," Indians lived "without Civil Government" and consequently had "very uncultivated Minds." These arguments led Warburton to argue for a civilization-first missionary strategy. Many SPG preachers had stressed the civil benefits such as increased security and commerce that would flow from Indian conversion. Warburton inverted this traditional argument and argued that "the spiritual benefits arising from the labour of civilizing are many and substantial," because civilization would make Native Americans grateful to Europeans and more amenable to religious instruction.[111]

The notion that civilization might have to precede Christianity was not a new one, but Warburton's sermon marks the growth of pessimism within the Society's ranks about its efforts among "heathens." In 1767 John Ewer argued that both black slaves and "that other race of savages, our neighbours in America" demonstrated that "morality and religion" could not be understood "by the mere strength of nature." Whereas the idea of natural religion had once seemed powerful to many Society supporters, Ewer drew on SPG history to claim "these untutored people we experimentally know to be ignorant of arts and sciences, of morality, of God."[112] Ewer also noted critically that enslaved people were purchased and treated "as cattle," but such arguments led other SPG supporters to argue that slavery was a positive good because it would foster the necessary civilization of black peoples.

Because Native Americans were, unlike enslaved black people, seen as largely outside of colonial control, there were in this period growing calls for the radical transformations of their societies through the introduction of settled agriculture.[113] In 1773, for example, Jonathan Shipley noted that Indians had an "untameable savage spirit" and observed "we have little reason to hope for their conversion, till some great change in their manners has made them abandon their savage vagrant life, and prepared them for the discipline of law and religion." Implicitly disparaging seventy years of missionary endeavor, Edmund Law argued in 1774 that any attempts to bring Indians into the church without "admitting them to the privileges of a more advanced humanity" would "prove as vain and fruitless, as they have evidently been preposterous." Such arguments did not become universal among the Society's preachers, nor did these still-committed Christians abandon the principle of essential human unity to deploy the fully developed vocabulary of "scientific" racism that would emerge in the nineteenth century. Writing about enslaved people, Law reminded his circum-Atlantic readers that "we well know (whatsoever our pride and arrogance may suggest to the contrary) that these are of the very same nature and origin with ourselves" and that God "has communicated to them all an equal capacity of knowledge, virtue, and religion."[114] The Society, in continuing its missionary work among non-European peoples, largely retained the belief in the theoretical possibility of "improvement" in the manners, morals, and religious beliefs of these people. At the same time, many of the Society's supporters presented increasingly critical and essentializing characterizations of non-European peoples, and these assessments circulated widely in the Atlantic world. The writings of figures associated with the Society can, in this way, be seen as reflecting and contributing to developing ideas about race.

Motivated by natural religion and ethnic theology, in the years after 1700 SPG members inaugurated a circum-Atlantic missionary program that sought to convert Native American and black populations. The intellectual circumstances out of which the Society's program emerged gave its supporters powerful motivations to Christianize non-European peoples and a widespread and deeply held belief in the essential unity of humankind. Christian compassion, as the SPG's supporters understood it, merged with perceptions of national and denominational interest to put the conversion of "heathens" permanently on the Society's agenda. These motivations were remarkably enduring—they sustained SPG activity across the eighteenth century. However, the particular intellectual milieu that furthered many churchmen's interest in missionary activism in the first place also had implications for the way the SPG's program would develop over time. Fears of Deism, a belief in the literal truth of scripture, and the ideas of ethnic theology led Society members to accept black chattel slavery even as these same motivations spurred an interest in converting enslaved people. In a particularly revealing form of such arguments, some prominent Society supporters came to hold up black chattel slavery as evidence of God's existence and power.

As the Society's missionary program matured, doubts about its efficacy grew. What initially appeared to be a glorious opportunity to convert the "heathen" was increasingly seen as a pious but difficult obligation. While not yet recognizable as the more fully developed racism that developed later, by mid-century many metropolitan backers of the Society frequently saw Europeans as separated from other people by a deep, almost unbridgeable, gulf. The SPG's transatlantic structure, the intellectual prominence of many of its members, and its ability to circulate texts and ideas gave such developments wider importance. Over the course of the century, missionary Anglican ideas about the essential unity of humankind and calls for the better treatment and Christianization of "heathens" circulated widely, but so too did religious justifications for slavery and growing doubts about the cultures and capacities of non-Europeans. This intellectual history helps explain why the Society's activities often had double-edged implications for the position of enslaved people within colonial societies.

PART TWO

THE SOCIETY AND COLONIAL SLAVERY

3

"The Two Great Articles of Faith and Obedience"

Anglican Missionaries and Slavery, 1701–40

In the early eighteenth century, the SPG was at the forefront of Protestant Christianity's outreach to enslaved people; supporters of missionary Anglicanism were early and continuing advocates for what they understood to be the religious and material interests of enslaved people. This chapter explores how the Society's missionaries tried to convert enslaved people, the ways that enslaved people responded to missionary Anglicanism, and how the Society's program was affected by contact with slavery in its first four decades. For Anglicans, as for members of most Christian communities in the Atlantic world when the Society began its work, scriptural references attesting to the presence of slaves among the Israelites and early Christians opened the door to the acceptance of slaveholding as a divinely permitted practice. However, Anglican attitudes toward slavery were not static in the first half of the eighteenth century. Despite the reformist activism of figures like Morgan Godwyn and some early SPG affiliates, many Anglicans moved from seeing slavery as a troubling, alien practice to holding that slavery and conversion to Christianity were not only compatible but could indeed be mutually beneficial.

Transatlantic Anglicanism's goal of making colonial societies more orderly played an important part in this development. The desire to support proper patterns of subordination and hierarchy in the colonies, and to align the church as closely as possible with civil authority, led the Society's supporters to seek alliances with slaveholding elites who wielded growing economic and political power. As slavery became more entrenched, more direct ties to the institution also came to shape the SPG's activities. The Society went beyond accepting slave ownership by others as individual SPG affiliates and the Society as a body became increasingly enmeshed in slavery themselves. Many SPG clergymen became slaveholders, and the Society became the long-term corporate owners of enslaved people after it received Codrington Plantation in 1710. Expanding connections to mastership affected the way many of the Society's members thought about the place of slavery in Atlantic societies. Understanding the SPG's efforts in its first four decades to incorporate black populations into the Church of England involves simultaneously examining the sometimes under-appreciated, long-term commitment of the Society to this project, the diverse responses of enslaved people to its program, and the ways that slavery shaped the spaces in which missionary encounters occurred.

While pro-conversion texts like those by Morgan Godwyn and Anthony Hill were known in London and Bray and other early Society supporters were interested in the religious condition of slaves, the SPG's direct efforts among enslaved people originated in the colonies. In 1703, as part of the Society's attempt to start work among the Iroquois, its secretary wrote to Elias Neau, a New York merchant, to ask if he would serve as a catechist to them. Neau suggested that instead of traveling to the Indians at the colonial frontier, he should begin a mission in the town of New York, where there were "a great Number of Slaves . . . who are without God in the World and of whom there is no manner of Care taken."[1] Though lacking the potential strategic benefits of a mission among the Iroquois, Neau's proposal was taken up.[2] In the ensuing years Neau's commitment to slave conversion and the regular, positive reports that he relayed to London seemed to demonstrate how success might be achieved. The Society's leadership was soon holding up Neau to its other missionaries as a man to emulate and trumpeting his work in its promotional literature.[3]

Like other early SPG figures, international Protestantism was a cause for Neau even before he became involved with the Society. A Huguenot, Neau emigrated to America as a young man. In 1692, while on a trading voyage to Jamaica, his ship was captured by a French privateer. He was carried to France and prosecuted for having illegally emigrated, but Neau refused to abjure Protestantism. His constancy led to several years of captivity aboard French galleys, nearly two years of solitary confinement in Marseille's infamous Chateau d'If, and finally, because he persistently sang psalms aloud, several months of being held in a "subterraneous Hole." After being released in 1697, on the grounds that he had been previously naturalized as an English subject, Neau traveled across Europe before returning to New York, seeking aid for still imprisoned Huguenots and publishing an account of his tribulations.[4] It was this story of steadfast, exhortative Protestant faith that brought Neau to the SPG's attention. As the Society's secretary put it, "his former Sufferings on the Account of his Religion, did with great Advantage, recommend him to be a Teacher of the Christian Faith; and his

Humility enabled him to bear with the many Inconveniences in teaching those poor People."[5]

Neau's students were primarily adult black slaves, but they also included enslaved children, several enslaved Indians, a few free black people, and black sailors, who attended when their vessels were in port.[6] In the mission's early years, Neau experimented with various educational techniques, including basic attempts to utilize his students' native languages. He sent the Society copies of the Lord's Prayer in "Indian," "Curmantin," and "Cymodingo."[7] Neau initially visited students in their homes. By 1707 he had outfitted a large room in his own house as a classroom. The meetings he conducted were largely devoid of ceremony, in part because Neau remained a lay catechist, which he claimed would "seem less affected."[8] Because his catechumens were "not Masters of their own time," Neau held classes in the late afternoons or evenings after they had completed their daily work. Students prayed aloud, and Neau used a catechism to quiz them. Singing became a particularly important part of the gatherings. Neau observed that it "encourages both them and me" and that although many participants remained unbaptized, "they strive who shall sing best."[9] Neau himself composed a "great Number of Hymns and spiritual songs" for use in the school.[10]

Some aspects of Neau's approach had potentially unsettling implications for New York society. Once Neau's school was well established, white apprentices began attending alongside slaves, raising the possibility of closer relations among different peoples of the town's underclasses.[11] Neau also believed, like other Society supporters, in the transformative power of good religious literature. Neau employed primarily oral instruction, but he also furnished his enslaved students with religious books to read or, since many were illiterate, to find others to read to them.[12] In 1705, for example, he gave catechisms and "other good Books" to some enslaved students and distributed a parcel of texts "equally to the Whites & Blacks."[13] In Neau's view circulating religious books promoted communal piety, but many of New York's masters believed Neau's activities placed the dangerous tool of literacy within enslaved peoples' reach. He decided not to give books to some of his catechumens "because there was no body in their Masters houses that either cou'd or would teach them the [Creed], the Lord's Prayer, and the Ten Comandments."[14]

Through Neau, the SPG first directly encountered masters' objections to the conversion of their slaves. Foremost among these was the oft-stated concern that baptism would lead to their temporal freedom. Neau complained of the "vulgar Prejudice in those Parts, that if the *Negroes* were baptized, they would cease to be Slaves; tho' neither the Law nor the Gospel does authorize any such Opinion."[15] Neau doubted whether masters' fears were genuine, deriding such claims as "a Pretence which Covetousness furnishes them with."[16] Neau's assessment of

slaveholders' motives is plausible, and his assertion that there was no legal relationship between slaves' religious and legal status harmonized with the views of
Anglican authors like Morgan Godwyn and Anthony Hill. However, Neau's as-
surance papered over an area of continuing uncertainty and change in colonial
and British society.

Between 1664 and 1706 at least six mainland colonies passed laws stating that
baptism would not result in an enslaved person's manumission.[17] This process
was underway but not completed as Neau considered how to achieve conversions. While Virginia law stipulated that baptism did not result in freedom in
1667, a 1670 statute declaring that "all servants not being christians imported
into this country by shipping shalbe slaves for life" suggested that religious status
remained an important conceptual justification for slavery. Laws passed in 1682
and 1705 restated that baptism was not grounds for manumission.[18] In South
Carolina any link between baptism and emancipation was denied in the 1669
Fundamental Constitutions and reiterated in 1691 and 1713.[19] The frequency
and repetition of such legislation probably reflects the desires of politically active elites to make slavery more legally secure and to counteract persistent popular beliefs that holding Christian slaves was problematic.

While this issue was being repeatedly treated in several colonies, wider questions remained. In England an array of conflicting and ambiguous rulings meant
that the relationship between religious status and slavery, the legality of chattel
slavery under the common law, and the relationship between colonial laws on
slavery and English law would long remain uncertain. Missionary Anglicanism's
transatlantic supporters, who were attuned to the legal and political framework
under which the church operated in both metropole and colonies, were among
those sensitive to this situation. Slavery arose most often in English courts in the
context of commercial disputes, and cases there often revolved around which
causes of action plaintiffs could deploy to recover claimed property in slaves.
The form of these cases gave judges opportunities to consider the origins and
extent of slaveholders' property rights, and the religious status of people being
held as slaves was frequently noted in this context. Circum-imperial doubts
about the relationship between slavery and religious status may have been stoked
by the 1677 English case *Butts v. Penny*. The case seemed to bolster slaveholders'
property rights by allowing a litigant to use trover—a common law form of action used to recover the value of personal property—in his attempt to obtain
compensation for the loss of slaves he had owned, but it also called for the
"negroes" being disputed over in the case to "go to administrator until they
become Christians; and thereby they are infranchised."[20] Other cases probably
further muddied the waters. "Sir Thomas Grantham's Case" (1686/87) saw a
possibly enslaved man brought to England from "the Indies" and then baptized

and "detained from his Master," but its outcome is unclear. In *Gelly v. Cleve* (1694) the Court of Common Pleas "adjudged that trover will lie for a negro boy; for they are heathens, and therefore a man may have property in them." The implications this reasoning might have had for a slave who was baptized are uncertain. John Holt, chief justice of King's Bench, issued rulings between 1696 and 1706 that undermined the notion that enslaved people in England could be held as chattel property. The 1697 case *Chamberlain v. Harvey* was a factually complex one in which an heir unsuccessfully tried to use trespass as a cause of action to recover ownership of an enslaved man who had been brought to England from Barbados and "baptized without the knowledge of [his mistress] while there." The question of whether the baptism of a slave resulted in manumission was raised in *Chamberlain*, but Holt's court left the issue without opinion in its decision.[21] These cases collectively meant that despite several colonial legislatures' enactments, the question of how a person's religious condition affected her or his status as free or unfree, like much related to slavery, was considerably less certain in English law. Similarly, those with a circum-Atlantic perspective on slavery were probably aware that English statutory law remained silent on the issue. While some efforts had been made in the late seventeenth century to have the Westminster Parliament pass declarative laws like those passed in Virginia, these efforts had not borne any fruit by 1703.[22]

Most importantly, the legal relationship between slavery and Christianity was sufficiently cloudy in New York to concern Neau. The 1665 "Duke's Laws" for the newly English colony said that no Christians could be held as slaves, but at least one extant copy of the manuscript laws contains the proviso that no "Negroe or Indian Servant who shall turne Christian after he shall have been bought" would thereby be freed.[23] A 1702 law imposed a duty on "every Negro or Indian Slave Imported in this Province from their own Countries."[24] Even as this act pointed to a future of entrenched racial slavery, another 1702 law, "An Act for Regulateing of Slaves," continued to use religion to distinguish between freedom and bondage. It stipulated punishment for "any slave [who] presumed to assault or strike any Freeman or Woman professing Christianity" and observed that "slaves are the property of Christians."[25] While New York law, like that of other colonies, was moving toward fully racialized slavery and away from distinctions based on religion, this process was not complete as Neau contemplated how to achieve conversions.

Applying a widely shared SPG ethos, Neau believed that government should support his religious efforts. In 1703 he told the Society, "If the Parliament or our General Assembly would concern themselves therein, I mean if there were a law which permitted the Inhabitants to cause their Negroes to be Instructed and Baptized, I believe that would be of great Advantage provided nevertheless that the Slaves might have no Right to pretend to a Temporal Liberty," which "would be a great Injury to the Plantations which are only Supported by the Labour of those People." Otherwise, Neau thought "all the Inhabitants would oppose it, for there are very few who have not Slaves."[26] In 1704 Neau again advocated legislative intervention, suggesting that the SPG lobby New York's governor for a law "that all the Inhabitants should be obliged to permit all their Slaves to be instructed & that their Religion should make no Alteration in their Condition."[27]

In a prime example of how the SPG's communications network and transatlantic structure could produce wider cultural and political ramifications, Neau's requests initiated a metropolitan drive to secure changes in English and "imperial" law. In October 1703, at the same meeting in which Neau's letter advocating the involvement of "Parliament or our General Assembly" was read, the SPG took collective action. It delegated one of its members, John Hooke, a senior figure in the English Bar, to prepare "a Draught of a Bill to be offer'd to Parliament for the conversion of the Negroes in the Plantations to the Christian Faith."[28] Though this bill made no recorded progress, the Society would revisit the issue repeatedly in the coming years.

Since Neau was not ordained, he depended on New York's Anglican minister William Vesey to baptize his pupils. Vesey vacillated over the wisdom of baptizing slaves and was skeptical of Neau's fitness, as a layman and a Huguenot, to serve as an Anglican catechist. In September 1705, to Neau's pleasure, Vesey used his pulpit to deliver an "Exhortation to the Masters and Mistresses to take Care to send me their Slaves" three evenings a week.[29] Enslaved people themselves might have appreciated Neau's classes, since by March 1706 he was optimistically reporting that he saw "almost every time new Faces, [which] makes me believe they tell one another that we intend to Instruct them."[30] In April 1706, however, Neau's mission suffered a severe setback. Vesey had baptized some enslaved people without the knowledge of their masters, who had claimed they feared baptism would mean the loss of their human property. Angry masters began refusing to allow slaves to attend religious instruction lest they be baptized surreptitiously. To counter this, Neau returned to the idea of legislation: "We are resolved Sir to do all we can, for to obtain an Act of Assembly, to confirm the right of the Inhabitants over their Slaves after Baptism, in the same manner that they had it before."[31]

Neau's recent experiences had also put the issue back on the SPG membership's agenda. In his 1706 annual sermon, which was the first to treat the conversion of black people extensively, John Williams averred that "I know nothing as to Christianity that alters Mens['] Rights for the sake of it; but such as they were, so they remain till alter'd by a humane Law" and that among the first Christians "their being Christians did not discharge the Servant, and give him Authority to claim his Liberty from the believing Master."[32] Williams's language suggests some early Society members might have preferred that a "humane law" be passed to explicitly free Christian slaves, but this possibility was not pursued by the Society. Instead it mobilized its political resources to support laws that were designed to secure masters' cooperation by clarifying, and thereby strengthening, their power over enslaved people.

At an April 1706 meeting chaired by Henry Compton, the bishop of London, and attended by numerous members including two other bishops, the Society considered a report from its standing committee on letters from Vesey and Neau advocating laws designed to facilitate conversions. The committee had also heard from Francis Nicholson, the widely experienced colonial administrator whose career had already included service as lieutenant-governor of the Dominion of New England and governor of Virginia and Maryland.[33] Nicholson was one of the Society's most active and generous lay members, and he wielded considerable influence within the organization in its first decades. Nicholson told his fellow Society members that it had "formerly been a vulgar Error in Virginia" that slave baptism led to freedom and that a similar "Common Error" prevailed in other colonies. Nicholson provided samples of Virginia, Maryland, and Jamaica laws that severed the link between baptism and freedom. After considering the issue, the assembled membership decided "that it is the Opinion of the Society that it may be proper to make some Application to her Majesty for making such Declarative Laws concerning Slaves in other of her Majesty's Plantation as in Virginia."[34] In doing so the members looked to use their influence to solve a problem that, from their perspective in London, was comprehensible not just as a local but an imperial one.

Despite the SPG's political connections, these efforts produced no comprehensive Westminster legislation that would create "imperial" law regulating slavery.[35] Neau, however, had more success with his parallel effort in New York. In November 1706, he informed the Society that he had secured the passage of an act to encourage the baptism of slaves: "I have made a great stir here to procure an Act of Assembly in Favor of Propagation of the Faith, His Excellency My Lord Cornbury approved of my Sollicitations so that God has blessed my smal Cares, the Act is publickly pass't, whereof I send you enclosed a Copy, which makes me hope for better success than I have had hitherto."[36] The new law had the desired effect. In the summer of 1707, Neau reported he now had over one hundred students and requested an additional two hundred catechisms for his expanding school.[37]

Notwithstanding the act's benefits for his mission, Neau accomplished a tightening of New York's slave code. The act replaced the ambiguity of previous legislation with rigorous racial categorizations, noting that conversion efforts had been hindered by "a Groundless opinion that hath spread itself in this Colony, that by the Baptizing of such Negro, Indian or Mulatto slave they would become free and ought to be sett at Liberty." It was "to put an end to all such Doubts and Scruples" that it was enacted "that the Baptizing of any Negro, Indian or Mulatto Slave shall not be any Cause or reason for the setting them or any of them at Liberty."[38] Like the SPG's membership, Neau viewed such laws as expanding missionaries' access to enslaved people. Yet a principal product of this new act was an increase in the severity and restrictiveness of the colony's law on slavery. This is especially apparent in light of the act's subsequent paragraphs, which added two new provisions to New York law. The first stated that any child "born of any Negro, Indian, Mulatto or Mestee shall follow the State and Condi- tion of the Mother," placing a new group of mixed-race people definitively in bondage. The second further degraded enslaved people's civic position by pro- hibiting them from being "admitted as a Witness for, or against, any Freeman" in any court case.[39] Although Neau did not report this, the inclusion of these provi- sions could have been the product of cooperation or compromise with slave owning interests. Neau expressed no concern about these dimensions of the act when he sent copies of it to the SPG.[40]

It was characteristic of Neau's approach that he welcomed other assistance from figures of authority. In January 1712, Governor Robert Hunter issued a proclamation enjoining New York's legal officers to vigilantly execute various laws against "Immoral and Disorderly Practices" and encouraging parents and masters to send their children, servants, and slaves to Neau's school.[41] Neau saw the proclamation as important and urged its regular reading in New York's churches. He hoped that governmental power could be wielded to bind both slaves and masters to the project of religious reform.

Neau's hopes were dashed by an explosion of violence in New York. On April 7, 1712, a group of approximately twenty-five enslaved people set fire to several houses and then, using clubs, knives, and a few guns, ambushed men that responded to the fire. Nine white New Yorkers were killed and several others seriously wounded. In the fighting and pursuit that followed, a number of the rebels com- mitted suicide, with some killing their wives first, rather than be taken prisoner. Authorities responded to the incident with a deluge of gruesome reprisals. Some seventy slaves were alleged to be conspirators, and twenty-one people were exe- cuted. The goal was to see "the most exemplary punishment inflicted that could be possibly thought of."[42] Many of the executed were hanged. Others were burned to death, another hung up alive in chains, and one man was broken on the wheel.[43]

In the aftermath of the revolt, enraged white townspeople believed that Neau's classes had facilitated a conspiracy. Neau could "hardly appear abroad for some days" as his "School was blamed as the main occasion of this barbarous Plot."[44] Two of Neau's students were among those executed. One of them, Robin, had belonged to Adrian Hoghlandt, a townsman killed by the rebels. Robin was convicted of murdering Hoghlandt and sentenced to be hung up in chains until dead.[45] While the Society acknowledged that Robin was implicated in the plot, it denied he had killed his master and later tried to limit his connection to Neau's school by noting that he was not baptized. The missionary John Sharpe, however, reported that Robin's lack of baptism was not because he was not a true convert but "had for two years solicited his master for leave to be baptized but could not obtain it."[46] The second of Neau's executed students was an unnamed enslaved man who had been baptized, but according to a subsequent SPG account he was "in the Peoples Heat, upon slender evidence, perhaps too hastily condemned; for soon after he was acknowledged to be innocent by the common voice."[47]

Panicked New Yorkers were particularly concerned that Neau's school had allowed enslaved people to meet at night with minimal supervision. Soon after the revolt, the town's Common Council barred slaves from the streets after dark without a lantern or candle, a measure that limited their access to Neau's classes. The Provincial Council and Assembly also passed a draconian "Act for Preventing, Suppressing, and Punishing the Conspiracy and Insurrection of Negroes, and other Slaves" in December 1712. It criminalized unauthorized meetings of more than three slaves, gave justices of the peace powers to inflict corporal punishment on any enslaved person who should "assault or strike any Freeman or Woman, professing Christianity," and severely limited the possibility of manumission.[48] Whether Neau's school actually facilitated the rebellion seems impossible to discern from this distance. Governor Hunter personally cleared Neau of any responsibility for the uprising and urged masters to again send people to him.[49] It is clear, however, that the Society made strenuous attempts to distance itself from the conspiracy. As the Society's secretary put it when recounting the events in his 1730 history, "Upon full Tryal, the guilty Negroes, were found to be such as never came to Mr. Neau's School; and what is very observable, the Persons, whose Negroes were found to be most guilty, were such as were the declared Opposers of making them Christians."[50]

Despite Governor Hunter's efforts, slave owners only gradually allowed their people to resume participating in Neau's classes as their fears subsided. Many, including William Vesey, who was always attuned to the views of his parishioners, remained deeply suspicious of Neau's school. In the immediate aftermath of the rebellion Vesey "refused to baptize a Mulatress aged 18 years & named Jane, tho she had before hand obtained a letter from her mistress directed to Mr. Vesey." For several years after the rebellion, Vesey would not use his pulpit to read Hunter's proclamation instructing masters to send their slaves to Neau's classes, and his own three slaves stopped attending Neau's meetings.[51]

Threatened and isolated, Neau nevertheless remained committed to catechizing enslaved people. He gradually rebuilt his school, but these traumatic events affected the way he approached his religious work. After the rebellion he was at greater pains to emphasize the earthly utility of slave conversion. In December 1712 Neau complained that masters were suspicious of sending him their slaves, "as if the Christian Religion should not Command Obedience to all Inferiors." In 1713 Neau complained that New Yorkers were "strangely prejudiced with a horrid Notion Thinking that the Christian Knowledge will be a Mean[s] to make their Slaves more cunning and apt to wickedness th[a]n they are."[52] To continue his mission, he emphasized the ways that Christianity could improve the behavior of slaves. As Neau noted in October 1719, in his catechizing "I enlarge upon the two great Articles, of Faith and Obedience, besides I teach them to pray and to Sing, as the publick may well know."[53] His postrebellion coupling of those "two great Articles" as the heart of his missionary message was an early example of how slavery would increasingly shape the SPG's religious program.

Neau served the SPG until his death in 1722. The Society continued to support a catechist to New York's black population until the American Revolution, but few of Neau's successors equaled his achievements. James Wetmore, who took up the post, reported in 1726 that his "Catechumens are now very few" and that New York's slave owners "choose to instruct them at home, rather th[a]n venture them into Companies together." Ordered to explain further why Neau's years of effort appeared to be melting away, Wetmore insisted that he had worked hard to fulfill his duty. While masters were largely at fault for not sending their slaves to his school, he added that black people "are so vicious that People don't care to trust 'em in Companies together and some have under pretence of going to Catechizing taken opportunity to absent from the Masters Service many days."[54] Further altering the dynamic after Neau's death was the fact that while he had been a layman, his successors were ordained clergymen. At Vesey's prompting and beginning with Wetmore, Neau's former post became a joint appointment in which the holder served simultaneously as instructor to the town's black community and as assistant to the rector of New York's growing Trinity Church.[55] While some subsequent catechist/assistants were committed to working among the town's slaves, the change blunted the mission's focus. The post came to be occupied by a succession of young clergymen often more interested in moving up the ecclesiastical career ladder than in pursuing the controversial work Neau had pioneered.

Neau's mission left a complicated legacy for later SPG efforts. Society members were proud of his dedication and accomplishments, but his experiences and the traumatic 1712 rebellion affected the Society's strategic vision of how to convert the Atlantic world's black population. Neau, whose teaching style may have been shaped by his own long captivity, seems to have been particularly skilled in reaching enslaved people, but in the ensuing decades the Society did little to help its many other less charismatic missionaries develop effective strategies for making Anglicanism specifically appealing to enslaved people. Moreover, most enslaved people in the Atlantic world lived in rural, plantation-dominated communities rather than in urban environments, so many missionaries faced different sets of challenges. Neau's mission also raised troubling questions for the Society about the potential connections between slave education and slave rebellion. Whether the New Yorkers who accused Neau's mission of contributing to the 1712 revolt had any grounds for doing so, their charges put the Society and its missionaries on the defensive. The fear that there might be a real or believed link between its catechetical efforts and slave rebellion shaped how the SPG's members and missionaries approached advocating for the conversion of enslaved people in the coming decades. The specter of rebellion made the Society even more anxious to stress its adherence to the emerging colonial social order and at pains to emphasize how conversion would transform enslaved people into better servants.

Neau's mission also seemed to demonstrate that legal measures could help produce conversions. Despite its early failures to achieve changes in English law on slavery, the Society continued to look to wield its political connections and clout in this area in ensuing years. Between 1710 and 1714, the Society made a number of efforts to attach amendments to Parliamentary bills that underpinned and regulated British involvement in the transatlantic slave trade. These amendments sought to add clauses stipulating that all "Negro children" should be baptized, that there should be proper sureties for their being brought up as Christians, that missionaries should have access to enslaved people, and that enslaved people should be allowed to attend church on Sundays. These attempts to Christianize slavery, however, simultaneously looked to make masters more secure in their property in the hopes of winning their cooperation. All these legislative initiatives included the attaching of "a reassuring postscript about the civil position of the baptized."[56]

As Neau's letters demonstrated, the Society's transatlantic communications network regularly put the concerns of colonial masters and missionaries into the ears of influential churchmen in London. In 1719, for example, Ebenezer Taylor wrote from his new posting in North Carolina to tell the Society that his hopes for converting the people owned by one of his parishioners were being undermined by the "silly Buckbear" that "all slaves that were Baptiz'd were to be set free." His parishioner told Taylor "plainly I should Baptize no more of his Slaves till the Society had got a Law made in England that no Baptiz'd Slave should be set free because he is Baptiz'd and send it here."[57] In the face of such reports and with a penchant for seeking church-state cooperation, the Society and other Anglican networks promoted measures intended to make slavery more uniform and regulated, and at the same time, more secure.

The most important example of such politicking, which had long-term implications for the legal history of slavery in the British empire, was the part that the clergyman and philosopher George Berkeley and a circle of his supporters played in securing and promoting the subsequently infamous Yorke-Talbot opinion in 1729. Unlike earlier lobbying, this was not a corporate project of the SPG, but it was pursued by several people closely connected to the Society and committed to the expansion of the Church of England in the colonies. In the Yorke-Talbot opinion, the Crown's attorney general and solicitor general interpreted existing English law to mean that "a Slave, by coming from the West-Indies to Great Britain or Ireland . . . doth not become free," "that Baptism doth not bestow Freedom on him, nor make any alteration in his temporal Condition in these Kingdoms," and that "his Master may legally compel him to return again to the Plantations." Berkeley's interest in the conversion of enslaved people developed alongside his plans for establishing an Anglican college in Bermuda. Motivated as Neau had been by a desire to overcome masters' objections to converting slaves, a network of Berkeley's backers—including his fellow prominent SPG members Edmund Gibson, Martin Benson, and Thomas Secker and others—appears to have lobbied Yorke and Talbot to issue their opinion and then publicized it in the colonies and Britain. The Yorke-Talbot opinion, a close metropolitan analogue to the change in New York law that Neau had secured, operated as a key proslavery authority. Within a continuously contested and evolving English legal landscape, it remained an important defense of slaveholders' interests until the antislavery movement and Lord Mansfield's 1772 ruling in the Somerset case opened up a new era in the history of British Atlantic slavery.[58] As in Neau's case, through the Yorke-Talbot opinion supporters of missionary Anglicanism strengthened slavery and the power of masters in the interest of overcoming their resistance to the Christianization of enslaved people.

Neau's mission was dedicated to converting slaves, but contact between enslaved people, masters, and many other SPG representatives also quickly became common. As a matter of policy, the Society urged all missionaries to report on and attempt to convert any "heathens" in their parishes. By 1706 similar responsibility was formally extended to all its schoolmasters, when it was mandated that "they be ready as they have opportunity, to teach and instruct the Indians and Negroes, and their Children."[59] The religious condition of enslaved people was seen as most pressing in those colonies where their numbers were growing most rapidly. In South Carolina, where the SPG mounted a major push to staff the colony's newly established churches just as the province was turning to the large-scale production of rice and other staples through slave labor, the continuing "heathenism" of enslaved people was particularly apparent. The SPG's first generation of missionaries in the colony saw its primary duty as nurturing infant Anglican congregations; some also worked to catechize and baptize enslaved people.

By the 1720s, it was clear that while the Society's support had played a major part in helping make South Carolina one of the most strongly Anglican colonies on the continent, its efforts to Christianize black people had not kept up with the growth of slavery. Thomas Hasell reported in March 1723 that in St. Thomas parish approximately one hundred families of white settlers owned between nine hundred and one thousand enslaved black people and around ninety enslaved Native Americans. There were also ten or twelve free blacks in the

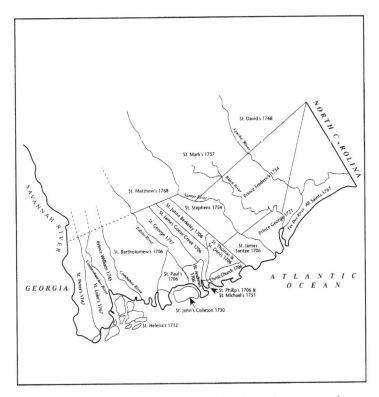

Figure 7. Church of England Parishes in Colonial South Carolina. Dates refer to a parish's founding or splitting off from another parish. (Image courtesy of the South Carolina Department of Archives and History.)

parish. In total less than a dozen black people—free or slave—were baptized.[60] Another missionary reported in 1728 that St. Andrew parish contained approximately eighteen hundred enslaved people, three of whom were baptized.[61]

In 1721 Richard Ludlam estimated that only about forty of the fifteen hundred enslaved people in his Goose Creek parish were baptized. Ludlam feared such large, unconverted populations of black slaves and Indians in South Carolina meant that "by their Vastly Superior numbers we should be crushed by one or the other." Ludlam thought the precariousness of their position made planters unwilling "that their sensible slaves should be converted" because they might "make an ill use" of religious classes or Church services "to take the opportunity of such times of seizing & destroying their owners." He urged the creation of suffragan colonial bishops, whose powers of ordination might create enough clerics so that thousands of slaves could be safely converted in smaller groups and "enjoy the Benefits (in their Masters Plantations) of Christianity without endangering their own or their owners happiness."[62] In the same period, the missionary Brian Hunt argued for the necessity of an act of the Carolina assembly requiring planters to have one in every ten enslaved people they owned "taught to read the Bible and learn the Catechism." Otherwise, Hunt said, "all we clergy" believe the mass conversion of slaves "impracticable in the present posture of affairs."[63] While this sense of the scale of the challenge came to be widely shared, neither the Society, South Carolina's Anglican establishment, nor the colonial government ever launched genuinely commensurate Christianization initiatives. As Richard Clarke, the rector of St. Phillip's, Charleston, complained in 1757, there was still not "one Civil Establishment in the Colony for the Christian Instruction of fifty Thousand Negroe Slaves." The clergy did their best, he thought, but "it by no Means is in their Power to perform the more immediate Duties of their proper Stations, and at the same Time instruct so very large a Number of Negroes."[64] Similar challenges existed even in those colonies where the numbers of the enslaved were smaller.

As Neau had, SPG ministers everywhere reported numerous objections to their working among enslaved people. John Adams, an itinerant missionary in North Carolina, wrote in 1709 that masters had "a false Notion that a Christen'd Slave is by Law free." Robert Maule noted "a mistaken Notion that they are free after they are baptized" in South Carolina. If missionaries convinced masters that baptism did not threaten their property rights, they still faced obstacles. James Gigullat claimed in 1710 that masters in Santee, South Carolina, were opposed to Christianization because "they observ'd that those that had been made Christians were the worst of their Slaves, and that all other Slaves do laugh at 'em and render 'em worse and worse." John Bartow in Westchester, New York, wrote in 1710 that while "Negroes and Indians come to our Assembly and behave themselves orderly," the "Slight and Contempt of Baptism by Quakers and many Others" dissuaded them from receiving it.[65]

Francis Le Jau recorded a lengthy catalog of planters' claims. In 1711 he reported that while some recent slave baptisms he performed were to the "satisfaction of some pious Masters," others complained, and "their Chief Argum[en]t was from the Impossiblity of bringing the Slaves into a right order." Other parishioners rejected the spiritual leveling and social mixing that would have been entailed by enslaved people's incorporation into the community's religious life. A woman asked "Is it possible that any of my slaves could go to heaven, & must I see them there?" A young man "resolv'd never to come to the holy Table while slaves are Rec[eive]d." In 1712 Le Jau reported "New Opposition" on "the Old pretext that Baptism makes the Slaves proud and undutifull." In 1713 the "main argument" he now confronted was that "knowledge makes them worse."[66] Like Neau, Le Jau and some other missionaries believed that such objections were often insincere. William Treadwell Bull observed in 1715 that "the Truth out, let them pretend what they will," was that planters feared that their "Worldly Business" might be "a little impaired thro the Loss of Time & taking their Slaves from their work."[67]

Reports of such obstructionism persisted for decades. Francis Varnod told the Society in 1724 that his parishioners opposed slaves' instruction because it gave them "an opportunity of gathering together on the Lord's day to make Insurrections." Varnod thought owners' objections could only be overcome if "the Civil Power permitted the Ministers and other approved persons to resort to the Negroes houses when they think proper," as it "was practiced at Martinico." Richard Ludlam claimed "the Masters Fear of having Slaves train'd up for Baptism arises from the ingratitude of some bloody villains who have returned 'em the greatest of evils for the greatest of good." In 1727 the Rhode Island missionary John Usher repeated the claim that masters feared baptism would result in emancipation. After fifty years of SPG work in the colonies, James Harrison still reported in 1752 that masters had an "obstinate aversion" to baptizing slaves because it led to their becoming less governable. In 1765 Samuel Auchmuty told the SPG that New York masters simply preferred that enslaved people "were kept in intire Ignorance."[68]

The Society also encountered occasional English hostility to its work among slaves. In 1719 the Bristol minister William Cary noted that while local clergymen had promoted a recent SPG fundraising effort, the Society could expect a "Cold Answer" to their appeals from that port city. Noting that both "planters and Traders agree" on the issue, Cary was told "it was an Impracticable thing which the Society pretended to" and that it was "well known" there that "those few among the slaves who had been converted and baptiz'd learn'd only to be more cunningly villainous." Cary himself had received "letters from a Gentleman in Antigua" that were filled with what he thought to be "unanswerable arguments against the conversion of the Negroes" and claimed that "the real ground of their Aversion to baptize them is a Notion that their Slaves as soon as Baptized or in Seven Years after become free."[69]

In a number of instances where masters were supportive and enslaved people were amenable, missionaries made converts. Baptisms never kept pace with Goose Creek's rapidly growing slave population, but with some white parishioners' aid Le Jau was able to instruct and baptize small numbers of enslaved people continuously during his eleven-year mission. Moreover, this support facilitated some enslaved people being even more fully incorporated into Goose Creek's Anglican community. The new schoolmaster Benjamin Dennis reported that four black men, which "really surpriz'd me," were among the parish's communicants in 1711. "Several Gent[lemen] & Gentlewomen" communicated too, but "the blacks were as Constant as any."[70] Likewise, Le Jau performed marriage and burial services for black members of his congregation.[71]

An even more striking case occurred in the South Carolina parish of St. George, which was split off from St. Andrew parish in 1717. Despite most local masters' indifference or hostility, Ebenezer Taylor reported in 1713 that two women in his parish, Lilia Haigue and her companion, Mrs. Edwards, had begun instructing enslaved people. Lilia Haigue was the widowed sister of the secretary of Barbados, Alexander Skene, and Haigue and Edwards had recently resettled on Skene's Carolina plantation. Having found there "a very considerable Number of Negroes that were very loose and wicked and little inclined to Christianity," the women began a program to "Instruct those Negroes in the principles of Christian Religion" and "reclaime and reform them." Within a year, Taylor had baptized twenty-seven people owned by the Skene family. The Society celebrated this example of pious mastership in its publications.[72]

This initial spate of baptisms was the foundation for a long-enduring community of black Anglicans. Francis Varnod, who arrived as SPG missionary in 1723, reported that seventeen black people were among the forty communicants he had at the first Christmas service he performed. About fifty white people and "29 or 30" black people attended church most Sundays. Like Le Jau and Neau, Varnod was a French-speaking "foreigner," seemingly from a Huguenot background. With the support of the extended Skene family, Varnod continued to baptize those enslaved persons belonging to them. They regularly formed between 40 and 50 percent of St. George's communicants for well over a decade, a situation seemingly without parallel in any other colonial Anglican parish. Yet, even with Varnod's commitment to the cause and the support of a powerful planter family, the number of baptized or practicing black Anglicans in

St. George remained proportionally small. Varnod reported in 1728 that there were some 1,300 slaves in his parish, of whom 108 were baptized. All of these people were owned by the Skene/Haigue family except for one, who was the property of the Carolina merchant, slave trader, colonial agent, and SPG member Samuel Wragg.[73]

The long-term fate of St. George's black Anglican community is also instructive. While it survived for perhaps twenty-five years, this group declined after Lilia Haigue, Alexander Skene, and Varnod passed from the scene. Varnod had twenty-three black communicants at Easter in 1734. In 1740, four years after Varnod's death, his successor George Rowe had only eleven black communicants at his Easter service. By 1748 Rowe's successor, William Cotes, told the Society that there were "but few" enslaved people baptized in his parish and "the few Negroe Communicants that if I heard off [*sic*] in my Predecessors time" had been "sold and dispersed into various Parishes." Even deep incorporation into parish life evidently could not protect St. George's enslaved Anglicans from the traumatic dislocations of the internal slave trade.[74]

Other missionaries sometimes also managed to baptize or otherwise incorporate enslaved people into the Church of England in larger numbers. William Tredwell Bull convinced some of his white parishioners to teach the Lord's Prayer to black and Indian slaves in St. Paul's, South Carolina, and this led to a spate of twenty-six baptisms in 1714.[75] In 1751 Hugh Neill, having "prevailed on their Masters and Mistresses to permit them to come to Church for Instruction," baptized one hundred and nine black adults and seventeen black children during the first year of his mission in Dover, Delaware.[76] In other places, steady effort combined with local support led to the more gradual building up of sizeable and lasting groups of non-European Anglicans. In 1727 James Honyman regularly had between sixty and seventy black and Indian slaves at weekly worship in Newport, Rhode Island; by the mid-1740s he was claiming one hundred black people "constantly attend." In nearby Narragansett, "70 Negroes and Indians" joined "a large Congregation of our own People" in the same period.[77] James Greaton, the SPG missionary to Huntington, Long Island, reported in 1771 that between thirty and forty black people came to his services, "the Masters of most of which come to Church; the rest belong to Dissenters."[78]

However, mass conversions and such conspicuous groups of black people within Anglican congregations were atypical. Because successful catechizing depended on a combination of the commitment of local ministers, the attitudes of masters, and the interest of enslaved people, results varied considerably. Most SPG clergymen typically baptized just a few enslaved people each year within their parishes. To take one long-serving example, William Guy, who ministered to several different parishes in South Carolina between 1712 and 1751, averaged

Figure 8. James Honyman (1675–1750). SPG Missionary to Newport, Rhode Island
(© Trustees of the British Museum.)

about one baptism of an enslaved person per year over his career.[79] Household
servants, rather than field laborers, were likely overrepresented among the
enslaved people who were baptized and participated in church life. Richard Ludlam told the Society in 1724 that "the diffidence of Owners" and the "treach-
eries" of some black converts made it "at present almost impracticable to convert
any but here & there a favorite house Slave."[80] Missionaries also often found it
easier to convert American-born enslaved people. Thomas Hasell thought that
teaching children was most efficacious because "those that are born & brought
up among us are both civilized and Speak English," while those "brought hither
from their own Country . . . seldom or never Speak good English, but mix with

their own barbarous Dialect which make it so difficult to teach them any thing."[81] The Society heard similar reports from Codrington plantation.

While most SPG ministers instructed and baptized enslaved people in small numbers, sometimes in the face of local opposition, other missionaries and Anglican clergymen were more openly skeptical or hostile. John Thomas told the Society, which had encouraged him to emulate Elias Neau, that he had "many Negroes who are constant hearers" at his parish in Hempstead, Long Island. Thomas was not entirely averse to this, but he did not think ministering to them was his primary responsibility. He told the Society that "I conceive my self sent here as Minister of this parish" and that while "to Convert a heathen to Christianity is a very good & pious work" he thought that to "reconcile the English" to Christianity was "a far worthier employement" because it was "feasible & practicable."[82] In 1707, two non-SPG Jamaican Anglican clergymen wrote to the Society and observed that though they were "not unsenseable of the blame that is laid upon us by many zealous & good men at home for suffering our Negroes to continue Infidels," there were a host of problems with converting them. "These miserable wretches," they wrote, "are naturally of a False, base, & Slavish temper" and in them "Barbarism is so radicated, that tho' born here, they will still retain their Heathenish Customs, among which polygamy is one, that they will never be perswaded against." Added to this was the fact that "they will retain their own several languages" and that "they seem to have no notion of Spiritual things."[83] SPG clergyman Thomas Standard reported in 1729 that he had tried to teach enslaved people but that he had little success because, he claimed, they could not even count to ten.[84]

John Bartow, missionary to Westchester, New York, pleaded his conscience. He replied to the Society's instructions by "begging leave to answer that I can[n]ot be very Zealous to baptise Slaves" because "they will not or can[n]ot live up to the Christian Covenant" with regard to marriage. Bartow claimed that enslaved people were reluctant to remain monogamous and that masters would never permit their slaves to be properly married because it would limit their freedom to separate couples through the sale of one partner.[85] On another occasion, Bartow claimed that it was "very rare that those people can be brought to have any true sense of the Christian Religion."[86] Similarly, Robert Jenney was troubled by what he saw as enslaved people's sexual immorality, arguing that baptizing slaves was problematic because they "change their wives upon every Disgust" and were often guilty of "fornication" and because honoring enslaved people's marriage commitments would limit masters' ability to sell them.[87]

While such protestations were often disingenuous, they may have sometimes reflected missionaries' sincere concerns and an awareness of the social implications of conversion. Francis Le Jau's clear commitment to Christianizing enslaved people makes him an interesting example. Like others, he was particularly troubled by what he perceived as the sexual immorality of enslaved people. He asked the Society for advice on how to "prevent the promiscuous Cohabitation of Slaves which is horrid." On another occasion he complained that one of the "most scandalous and common Crimes of our slaves is their perpetual changing of wives and husbands." He required enslaved adult converts to publicly aver that "The Christian Religion does not allow plurality of Wives, nor any changing of them" before he would agree to baptize them.[88] Le Jau worried over baptizing children with unbaptized parents and also about who would serve as godparents for enslaved converts.[89] For all the Society's promotion of slave conversion, it never really grappled with Le Jau's concerns or articulated a clear vision of how it would address the practical implications of the inclusion of large numbers of enslaved people into the church.

For clergymen less committed than Le Jau, raising such scruples justified their lack of success to the Society. Likewise, repeatedly emphasizing the intransigence of slave owners insulated individual clergymen, and indeed the Society as a whole, from the suggestion that not enough time, effort, and money were being spent on the work. Masters' hostility appears to have been real, but invoking it also became a matter of routine in many missionaries' correspondence and in the Society's annual sermons and reports. An example of this dynamic at work is provided by a collective letter of the clergymen of South Carolina to the Society, which was delivered personally by Commissary Gideon Johnston in 1713. No doubt mindful of repeated SPG prodding, Carolina's ministers informed the Society that slave conversion was, "considering the present circumstances of things scarcely possible." While they noted that "an odd slave here and there may be converted when a minister has leisure and opportunity for so doing," they admitted "this seldom happens." Though conceding that Le Jau had had some success, South Carolina's ministers listed numerous obstacles to converting slaves. Enslaved people, they claimed, were only available for instructions on Sundays, when the ministers were otherwise occupied with their regular duties. Assembling enslaved people was difficult because they lived on widely dispersed plantations; it was dangerous because it gave them an "opportunity of knowing their own strength and superiority in point of number," which might lead them to attempt to "recover their liberty, though it were the slaughter and destruction of the whole colony." Ministers were also hampered by most masters' opinion that "a slave grows worse by being a Christian." The colony's legislature did not support the work, they protested, because the conversion of slaves was thought "inconsistent with the planters' secular interest and advantage." Some masters were guilty of greedily "pretending" that slaves, and "the negroes especially" were "a wicked stubborn race of men, and can never be true converts." Finally, the clergymen noted that many masters gave slaves parts or all of Saturdays and Sundays to work for themselves, which meant that enslaved people were often not available for instruction even then. Carolina's ministers primarily blamed masters for these difficulties, but their conclusion that "if any-one should think that the clergy can [convert slaves] without the Government's countenance and the help of itinerant catechists he is greatly mistaken" was also a careful exercise in self-justification to their superiors.[90]

Despite these difficulties, many Society supporters continued to exhibit a real interest in the religious lives of enslaved people. Leading members and the Society as a matter of organizational policy repeatedly advocated the work. Given the frequency, spread, and duration of missionaries' complaints, it seems clear that the hostility of masters played a part in limiting the conversions achieved in the Society's first decades. These reports, in turn, made winning the support of masters the centerpiece of those efforts that originated in London. As David Humphreys put it in his 1730 history, "The Society have always been sensible, the most effectual Way to convert the Negroes, was by engaging their Masters, to countenance and promote their Conversion."[91] Calls on slave owners became a regular feature of SPG annual sermons, as did rebuttals of claims that Christian-ized slaves made less obedient servants. The membership devoted comparatively less effort to the development of new missionary strategies or materials designed to appeal to the specific spiritual, social, or cultural needs of African and African American people. While the Society encouraged the publication of the Book of Common Prayer in the Mohawk language, for example, Elias Neau's efforts to translate prayers into African languages were not repeated for many decades. Instead, the Standing Committee's 1715 resolution to ask a "member of the Society to draw up a small Treatise to encline and encourage the masters of the Negroe Slaves to promote their conversion &c" was representative of how the SPG approached Christianizing black people. The member the committee tapped, the future bishop Samuel Bradford, declined, but not because he dis-agreed with focusing on slave owners. Rather, he doubted such exhortations would do much and advocated "obtaining some Legal Declaration" that slaves were "never the less Servants for being Christians," a measure that "has been sometimes proposed" with the Society, as more likely to prove effective.[92]

Although the difficulty of the task was gradually becoming clearer, interest remained strong in London, and several new initiatives emerged in the 1720s. In 1725 the Society ordered any clergymen that "have Negroes of their own to instruct them in the Principles of the Christian Religion in order to their being baptized." In the same period William Fleetwood's 1711 annual sermon, which strongly urged masters' cooperation, was reprinted so that it could be dispersed in the colonies.[93] In 1726 the SPG refocused on the religious condition of the people it owned on Codrington plantation by appointing a new catechist and ordering the estate's manager to aid him.[94]

The 1727 pastoral letters advocating slave conversion issued by Edmund Gibson were particularly significant manifestations of the zeal members showed in this period. Gibson, who served as bishop of London from 1720 until his death in 1748, was committed to exercising his authority over the colonial church and a dominant figure in the SPG, which he had joined by 1712. In 1723, attempting to gain a clearer picture of the state of the church overseas, Gibson circulated a set of questions to all colonial Anglican clergymen. Among these was "Are there any Infidels, bond or free, within your Parish; and what means are us'd for their Conversion?"[95] When responses arrived in London they revealed that transatlantic Anglicanism's efforts to convert enslaved people were not keeping pace with the growth of slaveholding in the colonies. In 1727, equipped with this information and the experiences of the SPG, Gibson wrote two public letters, one directed to masters and mistresses, and the other to Anglican ministers, in order to encourage the conversion of slaves and to answer potential objections to the work.[96]

Gibson's letters expressed the principles that underpinned missionary Anglicanism's program among slaves. Masters were urged to consider enslaved people "not barely as Slaves, and upon the same Level with labouring Beasts" but as "*Men*-Slaves and *Women*-Slaves, who have the same Frame and Faculties with your selves" and "Souls capable of being made eternally happy." While labeling cruelty sinful, Gibson also noted that "Christianity takes not out of the Hands of Superiors any Degrees of Strictness and Severity, that fairly appear to be necessary for the preserving Subjection and Government." The letters assumed that masters could and should control the religious lives of the people they owned. Gibson urged slave owners to think of themselves "not only as Masters, but as *Christian* Masters" who were "oblig'd by your Profession to do all that your Station and Condition enable you to do" to break "the Power of Satan" and enlarge "the Kingdom of Christ."[97]

Gibson's letters also reflected how a coalescing SPG analysis of the situation in the colonies was leading some of its key supporters to make further efforts to harmonize Christianity and slavery. Before his elevation to the episcopate, Gibson's reputation rested primarily on his work as a compiler and interpreter of secular and canon law concerning the Church of England, including his comprehensive 1713 *Codex Juris Ecclesiastici Anglicani*.[98] His *Codex* included a section addressing the legal implications of slave baptism, which noted it had been debated but not determined in English courts "whether by Baptism, a Negroe-Slave acquires Manumission." Gibson observed that it was said that if

Figure 9. Edmund Gibson (c. 1669–1748). Bishop of London (© Trustees of the British Museum.)

manumission occurred "it would very much endanger the Trade of the Plantations." Yet he also noted:

> At the same time, it seemed to be taken for granted, that if he had been Baptized with the Master's consent, Manumission would have followed; which I gather from the manner of stating the Question, Whether Baptism, *without the privity of the Lord*, will amount to a Manumission.[99]

Gibson's 1713 analysis reached no definite conclusion, leaving open the possibility that manumission might result if a master consented to baptism. This

assessment suggests that Gibson, like some other early Anglican commentators, may have regarded slavery as a troubling institution in this period. By
1727, however, after several years as bishop of London and an SPG leader, Gibson was more certain and doctrinaire about the legal relationship between
slavery and Christianity, and more focused on winning the support of planters.
He wrote in his pastoral letters that "the embracing of the Gospel, does not
make the least Alteration in Civil Property, or in any of the Duties which
belong to Civil Relations" but "continues Persons just in the same State as it
found them."[100] In this way Gibson's letters both encouraged the baptism of
enslaved people and gave slaveholding the public sanction of a key transatlantic Anglican leader and the Society. In 1727 the Society paid to print ten thousand copies of Gibson's letter to masters and five hundred copies of his letter to
missionaries for distribution in the colonies.[101] In March 1729, at Gibson's suggestion, the Society created a fund dedicated to supporting catechists to be
employed solely in slave conversion.[102] A second edition of the letters published in 1729 included Gibson's "Address to Serious Christians" to "Assist the
Society for Propagating the Gospel."[103] To extend their reach, Gibson's letters
were quickly translated into French and included in their entirety in the Society's 1730 official history.[104] In some cases the letters had the desired effect and
masters allowed baptisms after reading them, but many missionaries reported
continuing planter hostility.[105]

Another illustration of the SPG's focus on slave owners was provided by a
critic. Robert Robertson of Nevis was a plantation owner and Anglican clergyman but not supported by the SPG. In a string of writings in the 1730s and
1740s, Robertson defended the interests and reputations of West Indian sugar
planters. In 1730 he published a combative response to Gibson's letters in which
he argued, "your Lordship had been misinform'd in almost every Particular of
the Case." Robertson's doubts about how Anglican leaders were thinking about
slave conversion had first been produced by his reading of the SPG's proceedings
for 1714 and 1715, the latter of which included a "Remarkable Passage" that
Robertson quoted: "It has been often represented from the press, and in Conversation almost every where, that the great Obstruction to the Conversion of the
Slaves lies at the door of their Covetous, Atheistical, and Ungodly Masters."
Robertson viewed this statement and Gibson's similar sentiments as defaming
colonial planters. They led him to delineate the difficulties involved in converting slaves: the profusion of languages spoken by them, the bad morals and fears
of white men common among them, the huge numbers of enslaved people on
islands like Jamaica and Barbados, the widespread practice of "polygamy," the
habit of slaves using Sundays for their own work and marketing, and, among
many other things, the fact that "the Sense of their Slavery seems to lie deep in

the Minds of many of them."[106] Robertson argued these factors were much more to blame for slaves' continued heathenism than any obstructionism by planters. The masters of the Leeward Islands had not, he claimed, actually prevented a single slave from being converted and, in a swipe at the Society, he suggested that what the islands really lacked were books and missionaries dedicated to the work. Let any man in Holy Orders "come to the West-Indies; he will find he may baptize every Negro-Infant every where without Opposition" and "he may have Five Hundred or a Thousand adult Slaves every Day in the Year to teach and instruct, unless he should obstruct it himself by pretending to take them off unseasonably from their Labour." His own plan for converting slaves, which he advanced in his work, called for sending boys and girls from English charity schools to the colonies as catechists.[107]

Throughout his text Robertson was at pains to defend Caribbean planters, and he argued that since slavery was of proven economic value to Britain and other countries, it was unlikely to be abolished in the near future. Robertson's argument was fueled by resentment at the suggestion that colonists were uniquely morally culpable for slavery or enslaved people's heathenism. "Our Countrymen at Home must not think to shake off the stupendous Load of Guilt that is contracted by this Affair, and throw it upon the White People of the Colonies." In a notable irony given the subsequent criticism leveled against the SPG by British abolitionists, it was also the proslavery, West Indian apologist Robertson who first publicly commented on the Society's own growing entanglements with Atlantic slavery. Robertson took aim at what he viewed as the Society's hypocrisy on slavery, suggesting sarcastically that if it needed better information on the real situation on the islands, it could seek the advice of its own treasurer, at the time the West Indian merchant William Tryon, or "any other noted Sugar Factor in London."[108] Robertson's defense of his fellow planters can certainly be seen as hypocritical, but it highlighted how the regular invocation of masters' hostility could be interpreted as providing cover for other failures in missionary methodology or commitment.

Initiatives like Gibson's letters reflected the ongoing commitment of the SPG to Christianizing black people, but the Society's program was also increasingly affected by slaveholding within the organization itself. One significant element in this development was the Society's assumption of ownership of Codrington plantation in 1710. The Society signaled its acceptance of the legitimacy of slavery by taking ownership of the plantation and the people attached to the estate without any recorded debate. However, this taking of control was couched in a strongly reformist language and infused with hope that Codrington would be the foundation of wider missionary success. William Fleetwood used his 1711 annual

sermon to make the SPG's first public acknowledgement of the receipt of the gift
and to consider how little most masters had done to covert their slaves. He noted:

> It would be as hard for them [masters], to give an Account of what they
> think of those unhappy *Creatures*, whom they use thus cruelly: They see
> them equally the Workmanship of God, with themselves; endued with
> the same Faculties, and intellectual Powers; Bodies of the same Flesh
> and Blood, and Souls as certainly immortal: The People were made to
> be as Happy as themselves, and are as capable of being so; and however
> hard their Condition be in this World, with respect to their Captivity
> and Subjection, they were to be as Just and Honest, as Chast[e] and
> Virtuous, as Godly and Religious as themselves.[109]

Like Morgan Godwyn's earlier text, Fleetwood's sermon mixed an acceptance of
slavery with an impassioned reformism that challenged how slavery was actually
operating. It is a measure of the impact of this early reformist zeal that the Barbados clergyman Charles Irvine reported to the bishop of London in the summer
of 1711 that Fleetwood's sermon "hath been very ill taken" in Barbados and that
he "doth the Colonies injustice."[110] Fleetwood's sermon was reprinted and frequently distributed by the Society, but despite such early rhetoric the SPG long
ran Codrington much like any other sugar estate and had only sporadic success
in Christianizing its enslaved population.

It was also the case that, like other European settlers, many individual SPG
ministers owned people. By 1725 slave ownership was sufficiently common
within its ranks for the Society to write to all its missionaries ordering them to
instruct and baptize any people they owned.[111] In places where slaveholding was
widespread, such as South Carolina, most SPG ministers appear to have owned
people.[112] William Tredwell Bull noted in 1715 that "I have very lately purchased
a Woman Slave an Indian, & two small Children, with a Boy of about 15 years of
age." Francis Le Jau owned at least three people. Brian Hunt, complaining about
his own poverty, noted that since he had only one slave he could not plant crops
"as other Missionaries do" and that most of the single men who served the SPG
"save up money & purchase slaves." When the philosopher and future bishop
George Berkeley, who subsequently became an SPG member, traveled to Rhode
Island in 1729 he quickly followed the example set by his local clerical colleagues
and bought people. At Clement Hall's death in 1759, the North Carolina missionary's estate included a library of 628 books and the enslaved men Henry,
Moses, Jeremiah, Benjamin, Lewis, and London; the women Sarah, Grace, and
Lucy; and the children Virgil, Lucy, Tumea, Easther, and Cloe.[113]

Even in areas where slave-based agriculture was not predominant, SPG missionaries owned people as household servants. George Pigot, a missionary in Marblehead, Massachusetts, owned a woman named Mary Celia in 1728. Robert Jenney, who served the SPG between 1714 and 1742, reported from Long Island that among the people he baptized in 1726 was a "Negroe Infant of my own."[114] The possibility of slave ownership by Anglican clergymen also spread to the European side of the Atlantic. In 1727 Henry Newman, the American-born, long-serving secretary of the SPCK, sought to pay tribute to Edmund Gibson through the gift of an enslaved boy. Newman wrote to Gibson that, "Having a present made me of a good natured little black boy native of Jamaica a beauty of his kind but not christened I have accepted of him upon condition I may have leave to make a present of him to your Lordship in acknowledgement of your great tenderness to the souls of the whole race of negroes."[115] In the 1740s, the SPG's own secretary Philip Bearcroft actually accepted another young enslaved boy, Toby, from the missionary Thomas Thompson of South Carolina, apparently as a gift for his wife.[116]

As missionaries' slaveholding became more common, the SPG accepted it as part of the normal course of affairs and sanctioned it through its policies. For example, in 1726 it decided to financially compensate the missionary William Guy for the death of an enslaved boy of his who drowned while traveling with Guy on Society business.[117] In other cases, particularly in South Carolina, parishes provided missionaries with the use of enslaved labor as part of their salary, or attached enslaved people to the glebe as part of an endowment for ministers. Brian Hunt told the Society in 1725 that his parishioners had spent £150 purchasing five people for his use after he convinced them of "the necessity" of the minister having slaves.[118] In 1753 the parishioners of the newly appointed South Carolina missionary William Langhorne "purchased two Negroes for his Service." A Goose Creek parishioner of James Harrison made "a present of a Negroe girl for the Use of the minister of that Parish as a small encouragement to him for his endeavouring to propagate the gospel among the slaves of the Parish."[119] Property in people also became a means for the Society's donors to support its missionary efforts. In 1720 the SPG's secretary thanked Mr. Salmon of Riglington, Somersetshire, for his charitable gift to them of "a young Negroe Man for the Service of their Plantations in Barbados," and asked that he be shipped to Codrington at the first available opportunity. When missionary Richard Ludlam died in 1728, he left the SPG his estate, including twelve enslaved people, to be sold off and used to fund a charity school in his Goose Creek parish.[120]

The growth of slaveholding within the organization meant that SPG missionaries and the Society as a whole were increasingly pulled in two directions over how slavery should function in the colonies. Society supporters wanted to encourage and enable enslaved people to accept Christianity, and they wanted to benefit economically from slaveholding. Brian Hunt was anxious to own slaves and quite hopeful about the prospects for the conversion of enslaved people, including his own, when he began to serve in St. John's, South Carolina, in 1723. Yet, by 1728 Hunt lamented that two of the four people he held were "in a manner useless to me." While he thought his successors might benefit from the labor of these people, who were attached to the glebe, he complained that they were "unfaithful as well as unhappy wretches: two diseased and two thievish." Hunt complained that his own lenient treatment was part of the reason that these enslaved people were not proving valuable to him, observing "I cannot be as cruel as some here to slaves, from whose wounds they extract their estates."[121] Hunt may or may not have been less abusive than other masters, but his claim that his economic interests and moral duties were in conflict is revealing.

Some ministers complied willingly with the Society's instructions regarding instructing and baptizing their own enslaved people. William Tredwell Bull told the Society that he "shall not fail" to prepare his slaves "as soon as ever I can make them understand English which I hope will be in a very Little time." James Honyman informed the Society that he had not only instructed and baptized the people he owned but also sent them to school to learn to read.[122] Others were more skeptical. Robert Jenney, whose long career as an SPG missionary and then as rector of Christ Church, Philadelphia, and Pennsylvania's Commissary marked him as an influential colonial clergyman, wrote a detailed letter to the Society in 1725 in which he expanded at length on the many obstacles to slave conversion. At that point, stationed in Rye, New York, he held three enslaved people. While he had baptized the child he owned and the two adults were "oblidge[d] constantly" to attend household prayers and church services, his efforts "have not had so good success as to influence me to give them the benefit of Baptism as yet." Jenney cited masters' obstructionism and other common obstacles to the wider conversion effort, but he also observed, in what seems a more personal reflection, that some claimed that baptism gave enslaved people "better notions of themselves than is consistent with their state of slavery." Dr. Timothy Cutler, a former head of Yale College and SPG minister in Boston from 1723 to 1764, reported that he could not baptize the people he owned because of their continuing moral unfitness for the sacrament, but he did claim them as an economic necessity. "I must acknowledge to my Grief, that I have two Negros unbaptiz'd. . . . I know it is a Scandal that my house is in this instance examplary to my Parish, but the difficulty of parting with them, & of getting help in this Country in lieu of them will I hope in some Measure excuse me."[123]

The tensions inherent in slave ownership by the Society and its clergymen can also be seen in the ways missionary-minded Anglicans simultaneously criticized and participated in the forms of repression and violence that were endemic to Atlantic slavery. In his 1712 annual sermon, White Kennett criticized "the Severity of some Masters to their Slaves" that "we hope will be redres'd, as Christianity, by our Care."[124] Hopes for making Atlantic mastership less cruel were also expressed early on in connection with Codrington. In 1711, the SPG member Sir John Philipps proposed that "Instructions shou'd be give to the Society's Attorneys and Manager in Barbados to use the Slaves belonging to the two plantations late of Gen. Codrington with greater humanity and tenderness than is commonly practised by planters." This notion seems to have had some wider support within the membership. The secretary informed the newly appointed Barbados attorneys that "it has been proposed to the Society to think of some means to cause the Negroes to be better & more humanly treated by their Masters the Planters, & as to our own, I believe the Society will take care they shall be all Instructed & baptised into our Holy Faith as soon as possible," and asked for their opinion on the matter.[125] That such a policy never took hold on Codrington is another indication of how the Society's early hopes were altered by immersion in slaveholding, but the sentiment never disappeared entirely. In 1730 John Denne argued in his annual sermon that colonial settlers "should be Christian Masters, treating their Heathen Slaves not as Beasts of Burden, but as Fellow-Creatures." Critiques of planter cruelty could be found in SPG sermons even decades later.[126]

SPG clergymen in the field also protested against the brutalization of enslaved people. No missionary did this more strongly than Francis Le Jau. Most Society supporters talked in euphemistic generalities about the violence that underpinned slavery, but Le Jau, like Morgan Godwyn had, used gut-wrenching specificity. He first wrote to the Society protesting "the cruel burning alive of a poor Negroe woman which all of us thought to be innocent of a Crime she was accused of." Though himself a slave owner, Le Jau seems to have risked angering his congregation by protesting such atrocities. In 1712 he wrote to the Society of the "Barbarous usage of the poor slaves," which he aimed to improve by urging "the dutyes of mercy towards them as much as I am able." Although his preaching was "contradicted by Several Masters," Le Jau also "oppose[d] with all my might" a "very inhumane Law" concerning the punishment of runaways, which sanctioned the "amputation of Testicles" for men and "Ears if a woman." Le Jau said that he "openly declared against such punishment" and, citing Exodus 21, based his preaching on "the Law of God, which setts a slave at liberty if he should loose an Eye or a tooth when he is corrected." When people did run away, Le Jau claimed it was "immoderate labour and want of Victualls and rest" that made them do so. With a similar forthrightness, Le Jau detailed a brutal method of torture invented by a local overseer to punish "small faults." Enslaved people were chained in "a coffin where they are crushed almost to death" and kept in that "hellish Machine for 24 hours." This man by Le Jau's estimate had killed five enslaved people within the last two or three years, "yet he pretends to go to Church." Other masters, he noted, "hamstring, maim, and unlimb those poor Creatures for small faults."[127]

Le Jau hoped such information would "inspire the Honourable Society my most Illustrious Patrons to consider those things so that they may be remedied for the Encouragement of those poor Creatures."[128] However, slave ownership involved the Society and its missionaries in the coercion and violence upon which Atlantic slavery relied. Unsurprisingly, this is not detailed in the missionaries' letters to their London superiors, but it does emerge from other sources. The Rhode Island clergyman James MacSparran's diary records that he whipped the enslaved people he owned to punish and control them, and there is no reason to think that he was unique in this.[129] It is also suggestive that enslaved people evidently had reasons for running away from their clerical masters. Timothy Millechamp, a Goose Creek minister between 1732 and 1746, advertised in the *South-Carolina Gazette* in 1736 that he would pay forty shillings for the return of a missing horse and his runaway "Negro Man named Braveboy, this Country born, who speaks very good English, and has lately lost the first joint of his middle Finger on the left Hand." An enslaved pair, Dick and Sabina, decided to risk running away from their master, the missionary Daniel Dwight, in 1746. Alexander Garden Jr., the long-serving rector of South Carolina's St. Thomas parish, twice advertised in 1747 to offer a reward for the return of an enslaved Igbo man named March, who had run away from the parsonage house. Likewise Pompey, a "new negro man" ran away from Garden in 1752.[130] Charles Inglis, a minister in New York, offered a reward in 1773 for the capture of his slave Dick, "a likely, well-made Fellow," whom Inglis suspected "has been seduced by bad Company during the late Holydays."[131]

Codrington Plantation provides the clearest example of how the Society's immersion in slave ownership entailed its involvement in violent coercion. Despite Le Jau's explanations for why enslaved people ran away, the Society gave Codrington's manager permission in the 1720s to counter escapes by shipping recalcitrant slaves to Virginia for sale.[132] Between 1724 and 1732, enslaved people on Codrington had "SOCIETY" branded on them to suppress their running away. The Barbados minister Arthur Holt complained to the Society and the bishop of London that branding was "a thing noted to be done only by the severest Masters or to the worst of slaves," and a practice "very discouraging to those poor Creatures."[133] Like other Barbados slaves, Codrington's people worked its fields in gangs under the compulsion of whip-wielding drivers. Well into the nineteenth century, public whippings were also used to punish rule-breaking by enslaved people there.[134]

Most enslaved people who encountered the Society's missionaries were not owned by them, but tensions and entanglements between missionary Anglican-ism's religious message and the practices used to maintain colonial slavery also existed within the context of parish life. What constituted sinfulness and what constituted resistance by enslaved people in their districts often blurred in mis-sionaries' accounts. Likewise, missionaries' desire to affect moral reform could become entangled with the mechanisms for control and coercion inherent in the slave system. Francis Le Jau, always concerned about the sexual behavior of enslaved people, complained to the Society that one of his students "has deceived me, and the unclean Spirit of Lust has given much trouble to his Master and to me." The man had "vowed to keep to his Lawfull wife, but thro' love for another Man's wife he has been quite distracted and furious." Le Jau reported he could "find no remedy but to take care that the Adultress shou'd not come near him" and hoped that this enforced separation and time would "blot out that Criminal affection." Le Jau evidently thought that controlling the movements of slaves might lessen their sexual sinfulness, but his ability to do so rested on the coercive power of masters. Notably, in the same letter in which he laid out this plan, which relied on combining his authority with that of the man's owner, he lamented the fact that his hopes "to promote a Reformation of Manners" more generally in his parish did not look promising because "the Evil cannot be stop't for want of au-thority to repress it; and we of the Clergy have hardly the liberty to speak and our Chief Men are little inclin'd to compell Men to be less scandalous." Le Jau's letter distinguished between the ways he thought about preventing immorality among the different residents of his parish. Enslaved people could be subjected to direct control, while the means for ending other, free parishioners' sinfulness were much more circumscribed. Given his limited power over local whites, Le Jau rued that in aiming to reform their behavior "We must content ourselves" to "pray and Edify and exhort one another as we have opportunitys."[135]

Enslaved people responded to the SPG's efforts in diverse ways of their own choosing—ranging from outright rejection to enthusiastic attention or co-option. Assuming that their responses were or should have been uniform would be repeating an error the Society frequently made. Many were simply not inter-ested in the Society's message. Peter Stoupe in New Rochelle, New York, claimed in 1725 that some slaves "will kindly receive Instructions & Baptizm, but others also will hardly be convinced of its advantage & necessity." In 1727 John Holbrooke in Salem, New Jersey, jointly attributed his lack of success to "the remissness of their Masters" and "the Stupid unconcernedness of the Negroes."[136] If the inability of SPG missionaries to convert enslaved people en masse was partly attributable to planters' antagonism and the inadequacy of the resources dedicated to the task, it was also due to the fact that relatively few enslaved people made becoming Anglican a priority in their lives.[137] When masters told a South Carolina missionary that when an enslaved person became a Christian "all other slaves do laugh at them," they were probably accurately reflecting the skepticism of many within colonial black communities to the SPG's program.[138]

For other enslaved people, Anglican Christianity might have been appealing for one or more of a host of reasons including its doctrine's promises, the communal fellowship it entailed, the social status it afforded, and the access it might provide to literacy. For enslaved people who had prior experiences with Roman Catholicism in Africa or elsewhere, like some of the Kongolese slaves brought to South Carolina, the Church of England may have provided a way to continue to live as Christians. Le Jau reported in 1710 that four enslaved men who had "been born and baptized among the Portuguese" asked to be admitted to communion.[139] We can often only surmise the intense, multisided intrapersonal dynamics that surrounded many missionary encounters. In some cases, pressure from masters and a desire to win their confidence may have been part of the calculations made by enslaved people. Timothy Cutler reported favorably in 1736 about the baptism of an enslaved man who had "discovered to all the impressions of religion in the reformation of his temper and carriage, his fidelity in his business, and abandoning all loose and dangerous conversation."[140] Others pursued Anglicanism despite their masters' opposition. In 1708, Elias Neau noted that "unfortunately" it was those enslaved people owned by the most anti-conversion masters that had been "best fitted for Instruction" and "had their heart touched by those truths which they know."[141] John Usher in Bristol, Rhode Island, had "sundry Negroes make application for Baptism" who "were able to render a very good account of the hope that was in them," but Usher was "forbid by their Masters" from granting their requests.[142]

Such cases blended with those in which enslaved people used Anglican Christianity to resist slavery or seek freedom. Neau and the Society as a whole worked hard to quash the idea that Christian slaves might be less obedient in the aftermath of New York's slave rebellion. However, there were some reports that belied missionary Anglicanism's propaganda. In 1723 Edmund Gibson received an appeal from a literate, mixed-race enslaved person in Virginia, who noted there were in the colony "molatters which are Baptised and brouaht up in the way of the Christian faith and followes the wayes and Rulles of the Chrch of England" and asked that England's rulers "Releese us out of this Cruell Bondegg."[143]

George Ross, a missionary in Delaware and Pennsylvania for nearly fifty years, told the Society that the failure to convert slaves en masse was regrettable but "very much owing to the Conduct of those Slaves who after their Initiation grew turbulent & boisterous aiming at Freedome, which though no part of their Christian Priviledge, it appeared they had most at heart."[144] An alleged slave conspiracy in Virginia in 1730 was attributed by some to the effects of Christianization efforts.[145] The *South-Carolina Gazette* printed a report from Antigua in 1737 that claimed that an attempted rebellion there had been led by enslaved people who had been educated and Christianized in conformity with Bishop Gibson's letters. The writer's suggestion that this was an example of "what may be expected from Converting Negroes" was refuted by a South Carolinian, probably Commissary Alexander Garden, who countered that it was actually bad treatment and the lack of religion that made slaves rebel.[146]

Try as they might, SPG supporters could not stop enslaved people from interpreting the meaning and implications of conversion for themselves. Before baptizing them, Francis Le Jau had his enslaved catechumens pledge before God and the assembled congregation that "you do not ask for the holy baptism out of any design to free yourself from the duty and Obedience you owe to your Master while you live, but merely for the good of Your Soul and to partake of the Graces and Blessings promised to the Members of the Church of Jesus Christ." But even when enslaved people did not overtly use their Christian status to claim freedom, baptism or participation in Christian education and ritual could enable the exercise of new forms of autonomy and authority within their communities. In 1710 Le Jau requested the Society's guidance on an extraordinary incident, reporting that "the best scholar of all the Negroes in my parish and a very sober and honest Liver" was "thro[ugh] his learning" likely to "create some Confusion among all the Negroes in this Country." The enslaved man could read, and he had "a Book wherein he read some description of the several judgm[en]ts that Chastise Men because of their Sins in these latter days." Reading this prophetical literature had "made an Impression upon his Spirit" and led him to use his knowledge to criticize his own master. "He told his master abruptly there would be a dismal time and the Moon would be turned into Blood, and there would be dearth of [*sic*] darkness and went away." The incident troubled Le Jau considerably and he sent for the man, "who ingeniously told me he had read so in a Book." His defense impressed Le Jau, but he "advised him and Charged him not to put his own Constructions upon his readings after that manner, and to be Cautious not to speak so, which he promised to me." Despite this promise, Le Jau noted the enslaved man "yet would never shew me the Book."[147]

Whether he learned of it through direct reading of the Bible or through an intermediate work, the text that ultimately seems to have inspired this man was one that probably had particular meaning for enslaved people. He appears to have been quoting Joel 2:31 to his master, with Le Jau subsequently noting that he had put "his own Construction upon some words of the Holy Prophets."[148] The relevant section of Joel promised deliverance through the Lord:

> And it shall come to pass afterward, [that] I will pour out my spirit upon all flesh; and your sons and your daughters shall prophesy, your old men shall dream dreams, your young men shall see visions: And also upon the servants and upon the handmaids in those days will I pour out my spirit. And I will shew wonders in the heavens and in the earth, blood, and fire, and pillars of smoke. The sun shall be turned into darkness, and the moon into blood, before the great and the terrible day of the Lord come. And it shall come to pass, [that] whosoever shall call on the name of the Lord shall be delivered: for in mount Zion and in Jerusalem shall be deliverance, as the Lord hath said, and in the remnant whom the Lord shall call. (Joel 2:28–32)

Le Jau's "best scholar" appears to have known his Bible, drawing on a passage that mixed a dire warning for society with a promise that God would bestow special favor on "servants" and "handmaids."[149] It also contained the images of Zion and Jerusalem that subsequently would have continuing power within African American Christianity and the antislavery movement. Le Jau's fears over the uses that enslaved people might make of such scriptural material were probably well founded.

Le Jau's attempt to constrain his prophet-quoting catechumen suggests again how close contact with slavery, including witnessing acts of resistance and self-assertion by enslaved people, could affect how missionaries approached their work. The event had wider implications in part because it became well known in the area. Le Jau reported that "when he spoke those few words to his Master, some Negroe overheard a part." As a result "it was publickly blazed abroad that an angel came and spake to the man," that "he had seen a hand that gave him a Book," and that "he had heard voices, seen fires &c." The incident shook Le Jau, who "took care to undeceive those who asked me about it."

The incident also made Le Jau fear the consequences of teaching enslaved people to read. Aware that the Society was dedicated to distributing religious literature and promoting literacy, he chose his words carefully:

> I fear that those Men have not judgment enough to make a good use of their Learning; and I have thought most convenient not to urge too far that Indians and Negroes shou'd be indifferently admitted to learn to

read, but I leave it to the discretion of their Masters whom I exhort to examine well their Inclinations. I have often observed and lately hear that it had been better if persons of a Melancholy Constitution or those that run into the Search after Curious matter had never seen a Book: pardon me if I disclose my thoughts with too much freedome.[150]

Le Jau's anxiety was shared by others. The long-serving New York missionary John Bartow told the Society in 1725 about an enslaved man whom he owned and baptized and who could "read English." The man had "got a trick of marrying slaves with the office in the Common Prayer Book." Bartow thought this was a "desecration of the holy Rite" and put a stop to it. He also thought "this shews that they are ambitious of being free but I fear their freedom would be unsafe & dangerous as well as very chargeable to the Inhabitants."[151] As a self-consciously Protestant body, the Society took the promotion of literacy and the distribution of the Bible, the Book of Common Prayer, and other religious literature as one of its fundamental purposes.[152] While some parochial SPG ministers and catechists, encouraged by the metropolitan membership, continued to teach small numbers of enslaved people to read, others like Le Jau came to see oral instruction as more amenable to masters and more suited to the conditions of enslaved people. This meant one of the keystones of missionary Anglicanism's religious program was eroded by contact with Atlantic slavery. As incidents like the ones Le Jau and Bartow reported suggest, missionary Anglicanism's message was also continually subject to reinterpretation and refashioning by enslaved people.

A sense of reformist zeal was notable in the SPG's first years and many of the Society's supporters envisioned a more paternalistic and Christian form of slavery emerging in Britain's colonies. Encouraged by the SPG's metropolitan membership, many missionaries in widely dispersed locations worked to catechize and baptize enslaved people and to bring them into the Church of England. The resources allocated to this work were never equal to the growth of the British Empire's slave population, but the SPG's early efforts contributed to the development of black Protestant Christianity in the Atlantic world. Elias Neau's mission in New York both suggested that the religious education and conversion of enslaved people was possible, and revealed the social and political risks that the Society would run in pursuing this part of its program. As a result, in an effort to Christianize slaves while underlining its commitment to upholding the colonial social order, the SPG put appealing to masters, rather than to enslaved people themselves, at the center of its circum-Atlantic policy.

    The immersion of clergymen in communities economically and politically dominated by planters, the growth of slaveholding among the Society's own missionaries, and the Society's corporate exploitation of slave labor contributed to this developing propensity to identify with masters. This would have far-reaching implications for missionary Anglicanism and for the wider position of slavery within the British Atlantic world. While the SPG pioneered efforts to bring enslaved people into the church, and often advocated for their better treatment, its growing desire to win the support of slave owners led it to engage in political lobbying intended to reassure masters by explicitly stating that the conversion of slaves would not lead to their temporal freedom. More generally, the Society increasingly stressed that its religious message and slavery, not just as a theoretical status but as a concrete reality, could be harmonized. The severing of the older link between an individual's religious condition and their suitability for enslavement, and its replacement by an increasingly racial form of slavery, was a gradual process that was already underway when the SPG began its operations. However, this transformation was not completed when missionary-minded Anglicans began to attempt to remake life in the colonies. The SPG's hopes for winning slaveholders' sympathy led it to produce arguments and pursue policies that helped strengthen slavery's moral and political legitimacy within the British Empire.

Missionary work always took place within the context of the dynamics of the local communities in which SPG clergymen and enslaved people lived. The Society's message resonated differently in various settings and enslaved people responded to the Society's missionaries in many ways. Anglicanism had a presence among some enslaved people in the eighteenth century because individuals found it appealing for a variety of spiritual, social, and cultural reasons. More enslaved people were either disinterested or resistant to the SPG's efforts. Because the Society's ministers in many locations identified with planters and were themselves often slave owners, the lines between Anglican Christianity and other pillars of the colonial social order were not always sharp. Glimpses into the dynamics of the exchanges between enslaved people, their masters, and SPG clergymen between 1701 and 1740 suggest how missionary Anglicanism's deepening connections to slavery frequently compromised its appeal even as the Society and its missionaries worked sincerely to effect conversions.

4

Masters and Pastors

Anglicanism, Revivalism, and Slavery, 1740–65

A member of the Associates of Dr. Bray, a Georgia Trustee, and a supporter of the SPCK and the SPG, Stephen Hales believed in the conversion of enslaved people. Best known as a celebrated example of an English type, the clerical natural philosopher, Hales combined his passion for philanthropy with a penchant for experimentation that produced inventions like his ventilator, which was used to introduce fresh air into confined spaces including prisons and below decks on ships. Like other Anglicans of his era Hales was also sure that both human law and scripture sanctioned slaveholding.[1] In late 1742, Hales and his fellow Associates of Dr. Bray considered his friend Dr. Thomas Wilson's suggestion that their organization and the SPG, of which Wilson was a member, jointly petition the Crown about "obliging the planters to have the negroes instructed." Wilson's idea that missionary-minded Anglicans should seek governmental assistance for the conversion of slaves was one that had been raised repeatedly within the Society's membership since 1701. The Associates agreed with Wilson's proposal and they "conferred with a Committee of the Incorporate Society, in which we desired they would join us in addressing his Majesty that he would earnestly recommend it to the planters." To the consternation of Hales, "the Society rejected our proposal, though so very reasonable a one, which has ever since been matter of great surprise to me."[2] Though the SPG and other like-minded Anglicans had sought a variety of similar measures in earlier decades, by 1742 the Society had decided it would not support legally compelling masters. This could have been partly a tactical decision; the membership may have believed that such measures would only stir up opposition in the colonies or that their own experiences demonstrated that such an enactment was unobtainable. However, the surprise that Hales expressed about the Society's refusal to cooperate also reveals how closely the SPG as a body had come to identify its own interests with those of slaveholders by this time. While pious hopes for the conversion of slaves remained, by the early 1740s the SPG as a body was no longer willing to challenge colonial masters. Instead, conciliation and cooperation with slave-holders had become increasingly common.

Although most of the first generation of SPG members and missionaries accepted slavery, many hoped to reform it so that it was less sinful for slaveholders and the enslaved. The SPG never ceased working among slaves and its missionaries continued to incorporate black people into their congregations in small and sometimes larger groups, but the strong reformist spirit that initiated that program faded over time. Instead, a growing desire to harmonize missionary outreach with a slave system seen as sanctioned by scripture, a range of Anglican opinion, and colonial elites altered the SPG's missionary approaches. The emergence of Francis Le Jau's concerns about teaching enslaved people to read are an example of how this pattern could play out in the course of an individual clergy-man's mission, but he was not the only one affected by it. This process began almost as soon as the Society began operating in the colonies and these developments were gradual, but by 1740 some important changes were visible. The Society's charter generation hoped to change slavery through its missionary program; by mid-century it was the organization's religious program that had been transformed.

Several factors contributed to the changes that became increasingly apparent after 1740. By then an early cohort of particularly zealous missionaries had passed from the scene. Francis Le Jau died in 1717, Elias Neau in 1722, and Francis Varnod in 1736. None of their replacements were as full-throated in their advocacy of slave conversion. Likewise, the energy that the Society's English supporters had devoted to the conversion of enslaved people in the 1720s ebbed as that decade's push failed to result in mass conversions. Slave ownership among the Society's employees had become more entrenched, and its missionaries more integrated into settler society. As colonial Anglicanism became better established and colonial communities matured socially and economically, service in the SPG's ranks appealed to a wider range of clergyman. While this probably helped improve the collective qualifications of those the SPG was able to employ, it also meant that comparatively fewer missionaries were drawn to its service out of a particular desire to convert "heathens."

The circum-Atlantic religious environment in which the Society operated was also changing. While prior to the 1730s Anglicans led efforts to covert enslaved people to Christianity around the British Empire, the waves of religious revivals collectively known as the Great Awakening spread new forms of religious practice, intensified intra- and interdenominational rivalries, and appealed to enslaved people in new ways.[3] In 1742, for example, the Society's annual abstract reported that recent letters from its missionaries in New England "abound with the wild doings of Enthusiasm." The preaching of George White-field, who though a Church of England minister was scathingly critical of the colonial Anglican clergy, was particularly troubling. Whitefield's first tour of the colonies, from November 1739 to January 1741, brought him into conflict with several Anglican clergymen. The New England commissary Roger Price noted "the strange effects produced by the doctrines of Mr. Whitefield and his followers" while letters from New Hampshire requested "Tracts against this new Phrenzy." Reports from New York recorded that colony had also seen "Trouble from Methodism and the new Light."[4] The SPG's supporters had long been concerned about what its members saw as the disorderliness and heterodoxy of colonial societies, but new forms of evangelical religion magnified their concerns about the strength of Dissent in the colonies, deepened many Anglicans' commitments to upholding political and social hierarchy, and offered enslaved people new choices on how to integrate Christian practices and beliefs into their own lives.

This chapter explores these changes and their ramifications in the period between 1740 and 1765 by considering the Society's activities among enslaved people from three successively widening perspectives. It begins narrowly, by examining everyday tensions within the household of a long-serving, slave-owning SPG minister, James MacSparran of Narragansett, Rhode Island. It then widens to consider the impact of evangelical revivalism on missionary Anglicanism's program for slave conversion through exchanges between George Whitefield and the Reverend Alexander Garden of Charleston, South Carolina. As Garden and transatlantic Anglicans attempted to counter Whitefield's influence, a new initiative began: a Charleston school for catechizing enslaved people set up by Garden and funded by the SPG. The history of this venture illustrates how the Society's supporters, in the context of new, unsettling competition from revivalism, came to hold that slavery could be a positive good and imported it into the very center of the organization's religious program. Finally, the perspective widens again to consider the circum-Atlantic implications of these developments through a key missionary text, Thomas Wilson's *The Knowledge and Practice of Christianity Made Easy*, which the SPG dispersed extensively from the 1740s to further the conversion of slaves. In the same period as the Charleston school signaled the Society's new relationship to slavery, Wilson's text was revised to make its message more palatable to masters. By disseminating such works, the Society spread its increasing sympathy towards slavery throughout the British Empire.

For some affiliated with the Society, the concerns of masters came to seem so pressing because they knew slavery intimately and as a part of their daily lives.

The implications of missionaries' ownership of enslaved people are most evident in the diary of James MacSparran (1693–1757), an SPG missionary to Narragansett, Rhode Island, for thirty-seven years. In 1727 MacSparran reported that there were already about two hundred enslaved people in his parish, and his ensuing years in southern Rhode Island coincided with the development of the "Narragansett Plantations," large-scale farms worked by sizeable numbers of enslaved people.[5] MacSparran ministered among these people and, like many lay neighbors and clerical peers, came to own slaves, whom he employed as domestic servants and farm laborers.

MacSparran's diary, covering the years 1743–45 and 1751, provides a more personal perspective on missionary Anglicanism's encounter with slavery than the letters preserved in the Society's archive, primarily written from employees to their superiors. The diary, while no doubt shaped by the conventions of its genre too, mingles references to MacSparran's running of his household, which centered on the management of his enslaved people, with expressions of piety, accounts of his pastoral duties, and episodes from his dealings with his neighbors. It also provides rare glimpses of the individual lives of a few of the enslaved people who interacted with the Society's missionaries. Better than any other source, it captures the way that slave ownership became blended with attempts to convert enslaved people in the day-to-day lives of SPG clergymen.

MacSparran was born, probably in Ireland, to a Scottish Presbyterian family with clerical connections. He emigrated to America and was appointed as a Congregational minister in Bristol, Rhode Island. His prickly personality and disputes with his parishioners and other New England ministers (including Cotton Mather) ultimately resulted in his leaving Bristol. He went to England where he was ordained as an Anglican priest in 1720. In this period he may have become attached to SPG member Francis Nicholson, whom he called his "great friend and patron."[6] In 1721 MacSparran returned to Rhode Island as a Society missionary and married Hannah Gardiner, a local woman from a well-connected family. Disputes with New England's non-Anglican clerical establishment became a long-running theme in MacSparran's life. For decades he unsuccessfully pursued a legal case to wrest control of Rhode Island lands set aside for church use away from a Congregational minister. He also shared the Society's antipathy to Quakerism, which was politically powerful in Rhode Island, noting that wherever Quakers predominated there "you shall never fail to find immoralities and disorders prevail."[7] MacSparran, always self-conscious about the dignity of the clergy, signaled his disapproval when he recorded that "Caesar, the Negro" had preached to local Quakers and that his wife's brother-in-law, the colony's deputy governor William Robinson, had been present at those meetings.[8] He was skeptical too of new forms of evangelical religion, noting his

Figure 10. James Macsparran (1693–1757). SPG Missionary to Narragansett, Rhode Island (Bowdoin College Museum of Art, Brunswick, Maine, Bequest of Charles Edward Allen, Esq., Class of 1835.)

encounters with "New Light" people and Whitefield's visit to Rhode Island in the mid-1740s.[9]

MacSparran worked diligently to Christianize enslaved people as part of his wider parochial duties. In 1741, for example, he presided over a catechizing session attended by some one hundred slaves.[10] His diary has many entries like that for Sunday, September 25, 1743, when he "Catechized the negro's, read Prayers, catechized the white children, gave notice of the Communion next Sunday and preached the Second Part of my Sunday Sermon." In that same year, MacSparran recorded a prayer for one of his enslaved catechumens, Cujo, who was considering baptism. "Prepare him, Good Lord," MacSparran wrote, "for such an entrance into the church, your Kingdom here, as shall terminate in his free and welcome Admittance into the church triumphant, thy glorious Kingdom above." Another prayer, asking for God's blessing on his Sunday services, suggests that MacSparran saw ministering to his parish's black population as integral to his responsibilities. "Give me thy presence, my God, at thy house, in Instructing the negro's, in preaching, praying & praising."[11] Such apparently heartfelt commitment was a continuing feature of MacSparran's long ministry and he endeavored to incorporate enslaved people more fully into parish life. In 1737 he baptized an enslaved woman named Rose after her own declaration of faith. When Rose died in 1749, MacSparran presided over her burial in St. Paul's churchyard and reported that she was a communicant and a person who had "lived & died a good [Christia]n."[12] In 1756, shortly before his death, MacSparran accepted Caesar Gardiner and Phillis, who were owned by parishioners related to him, as communicants for the first time.[13]

While he was promoting the Christianization of Narragansett's black population, MacSparran was also directing the labor of his own slaves, and his diary is replete with references to the work performed by them. These people—including the men Harry, Stepney, Bolico, and Hannibal, and the women Moll, Emblo, and Maroca—spent much of their lives toiling to maintain MacSparran's family. At his orders, they dug potatoes, picked beans and apples, harvested wheat, husked corn, built stone walls, made baskets, and ran multitudes of errands large and small. MacSparran, in conformity with the instructions of the Society and Bishop Gibson of London, and his own convictions, baptized the people he owned. Maroca, who appears to have been African-born (her name was recorded as "Maroca african a negro girl" in the parish register) was baptized in February 1726 at age thirteen "upon her personal Profession of her own faith." Emblo, also apparently African, was baptized as a child in 1730, as was Stepney in 1736. Harry was baptized as an adult in 1742. Whether their being baptized affected how their master treated them is impossible to say. When Stepney drowned in 1745, MacSparran mourned the loss of "my first, best and most principal Servant" and "preached his Funeral Sermon to a great Assembly of negro's." Subsequent references to the "poor Boy" and his "dear Servant" suggest MacSparran valued and had affection for Stepney. When Emblo had a son in 1751, MacSparran named him Stepney.[14] MacSparran clearly believed that an enslaved person's Christianity did not limit his property rights. In 1748 MacSparran baptized Phillis, a daughter of his slave Moll, shortly before selling her to a new owner.[15]

MacSparran's slaves may or may not have embraced Christianity entirely of their own volition; the pressure on them to do so was probably intense. Regardless, the man who saw himself as responsible for the care of their souls remained their master. MacSparran's simultaneous commitment to their conversion, material and moral interest in their behavior, and the authority he wielded over them must have been powerful forces in these peoples' lives. In 1751 MacSparran suspected Maroca and Harry of stealing food. His diary recorded the prayer "Gracious God, give my Servants Grace to live in a holier manner, that my Peace & Property mayn't be invaded by their evil doings, and that their own Guilt mayn't be increased."[16] As MacSparran's fears about theft suggest, enslaved people found ways to resist the mastership of the SPG clergymen who owned them.

MacSparran's simultaneous position as master and minister clearly produced tensions within his own household. Like other missionaries, MacSparran wanted to alter and control the sexual behavior of enslaved people and this, in particular, produced domestic conflict. In 1732 MacSparran baptized Mary, the daughter of "Maroca his slave," who was "wife to Richard african his slave likewise."[17] In October 1743 MacSparran recorded that Maroca "was bro't to bed of another Girl" and prayed "Good God do thou direct me what to do with her." Richard, who seems to have died or been sold by this point, was evidently not the baby's father. MacSparran worried about Maroca's relationship with "Col. Updike's negro" and fretted that though "she is a [Christia]n" she seemed "not concerned about her soul, nor minds her promise of chastity, which she has often made me." In February MacSparran baptized the child, whom the parish register noted had "been given to Mr. Benjamin Mumford by Doctor MacSparran." Whether this separation of mother and infant was intended as a form of punishment or not, it was a clear assertion of MacSparran's power. Ministers' concerns about the sexual morality of enslaved people were common, but MacSparran's authority as Maroca's master shaped the way he responded to her behavior. In June 1745 MacSparran gave "Maroca one or two Lashes for receiving Presents from Mingo" because he thought "it was my Duty to correct her." His whipping of Maroca upset his wife, for he recorded wishes that "whatever Passion between my wife and me on that occasion, Good Lord forgive it."[18] MacSparran's efforts to regulate Maroca's sexual activity seem to have failed. In 1749 MacSparran baptized another of Maroca's children, Jane, who he then gave to his niece.[19]

Some of MacSparran's ugliest confrontations with the people he owned were with Hannibal. In late August 1751, MacSparran found that Hannibal "had been out" during the night "a whoring I suppose."[20] Hannibal's actions seemed to have both angered MacSparran as a master who desired to control his slaves' movements and as a clergyman who was troubled by sexual sinfulness within his household and cure. MacSparran "stript [him] and gave him a few Lashes till he begged" as punishment. Hannibal's misbehavior angered Harry, another enslaved man in MacSparran's household, so much that he also gave Hannibal "a lash or two." Hannibal ran away after being whipped and was recaptured after having fled to Block Island. After this escape MacSparran had a metal collar, "what is called Pothooks," put around Hannibal's neck and prayed that "God would give my Servants—the Gift of chastity."

A few weeks later, MacSparran recorded that Hannibal's "Disobedience yesterday and malpert Behaviour to his Mistress this Morning exposed him to the whip," and he ran away again. MacSparran evidently had a reputation for his temper, and when a neighbor again returned Hannibal, he also carried a note to the clergyman from a mutual friend urging Macsparran "to Spare him, which I did upon his Promise of better Behaviour." Within a week, though, having been told that Hannibal was "concocting another escape," MacSparran sent him to work on his friend William Martin's farm on the nearby island of Conanicut, while Martin sent a slave of his to MacSparran. Six weeks latter, MacSparran recorded without ceremony that he had written Martin to instruct him to sell Hannibal.[21]

MacSparran's ministry to slaves, his relations with the fellow masters who made up the most influential members of his parish and community, and his coercion of the enslaved people in his own household were inseparable. While we know less about how other Anglican clergymen controlled and disciplined the people they owned, occasional references in their letters reveal that doing so was an ongoing issue for many of them. MacSparran's diary confutes any facile assumptions that clergymen were necessarily benevolent masters. MacSparran beat and whipped the people he owned, recaptured runaways, used punishment instruments, separated enslaved children from their mothers, and sold people for both his own gain and as a form of discipline. The experiences of Maroca and Hannibal reveal that, for some enslaved people, having a clergyman as a master entailed the hardship of having their behavior subject to expanded inspection and correction. MacSparran used his power as a master, his diary suggests, not only to control the labor of the people he owned but also to compel them to conform to his religiously inspired moral code. These dynamics would have been visible to MacSparran's white and black parishioners; they were inescapable for Hannibal, Maroca, and the other people he owned. MacSparran's diary, with its routine mixtures of piety and violence, demonstrated how a missionary's immersion in slaveholding belied the Society's vision of paternalistic, benevolent mastership and suggests some of the wider, longer-term effects that common slave ownership had on the Society's representatives in the colonies.

MacSparran worried about disorderly enslaved people within his own household. The rise of evangelical religion in the Atlantic world raised much wider fears about the stability of the colonial social order, which affected how the SPG's missionary program developed in the years after 1740. Alexander Garden served as the bishop of London's commissary to South Carolina in the mid-eighteenth century. While not himself an SPG missionary—he was rector of the wealthy St. Philip's Church in Charleston—Garden had long cooperated with the Society in superintending the clergymen in the colony and in 1740 become more involved with it when the Society began to support a school for slaves in his parish. Revealingly, in Garden's case, concerns about the religious condition of enslaved people were closely linked to fears of social turmoil that emerged out of the confrontation between colonial Anglican ministers and proponents of the religious revivalism associated with the Great Awakening.[22]

The Society's supporters were not universally hostile to evangelicalism or the efforts that revivalists would make to bring enslaved people into the church. Like the revivalists, devout Anglicans had long hoped for a multifaceted spiritual rebirth in the colonies. Prior to the new evangelicalism's emergence, few SPG ministers believed that their parishioners were as religious or moral as they ought to be in any respect, including their support for the conversion of "heathens." Many affiliated with the SPG had also argued that far more catechists, which the Great Awakening seemed likely to provide, would be needed to effectively convert the large numbers of enslaved people in the colonies. Reflecting on the "grand impediments" to slave conversion on the verge of Whitefield's arrival on the religious scene, the Massachusetts commissary Roger Price told the Society in 1739 that the problems were "the want of ministers qualified" for the job by "an uncommon share of humility and Zeal for the glory of God" and the "low ebb of Christianity at this day throughout the world."[23] Moreover, because some key evangelical leaders including John and Charles Wesley and Whitefield were Anglican clergymen, they had many ties to the Society's supporters. Sir John Philipps, an early supporter of the Oxford Holy Club where the Wesleys and Whitefield began their spiritual transformations, was for years one of the Society's most active lay members. John Wesley himself served an unsuccessful stint as an SPG missionary in Georgia before he returned to England and began the itinerant preaching that transformed him into the founder of Methodism. Several Anglican clergymen in the colonies initially cordially received Whitefield. One SPG missionary, Edward Ellington of Georgia, ultimately resigned his position "through the Solicitations of the Reverend Mr. Whitefield" to work at his Bethesda Orphan House.[24] Nor was it the case that the Society's supporters were unanimously opposed to the ecumenism that became a conspicuous feature of circum-Atlantic revivalism. Protestant internationalism had been popular among the Society's founding generation and Huguenots like Elias Neau and Francis Le Jau had been prominent in the SPG's project among slaves for decades.

However, most clergymen associated with the Society on both sides of the Atlantic soon became opposed to the new evangelicalism. They were not alone in this, and their attitudes resembled those of some Congregationalists and Presbyterians who became hostile to the disruptive impact revivalism had on their own churches. Many colonial Anglican clergymen were antagonized by Whitefield's and other preachers' attacks on their dedication and methods. Whitefield's uncompromising Calvinism and insistence on the necessity of "new birth" also raised difficult theological issues. When he preached that any Church of England minister who would not embrace justification by faith alone "belongs only to the *Synagogue of Satan*" it made it hard for even sympathetic Anglican clergymen to support him openly.[25] More broadly, the revivalists' promotion of heartfelt religion appeared to many on both sides of the Atlantic as dangerously irrational enthusiasm. There were unmistakable differences between the Society's attempts to promote Christianity through the creation of a well-educated and episcopally ordained colonial clergy, the provision of traditional ritual, and the distribution of sound religious literature, and the openness of the revivalists to ministry by anyone moved by the spirit, their new and emotional forms of preaching and worship, and their disdain for dry-as-dust rationalistic Christianity.

These differences affected how traditionally oriented Anglicans and revivalists approached ministering to enslaved people. From the first stirrings of revivalism in the mid-1730s, evangelical preachers throughout the mainland colonies were noting slaves among those who listened to their preaching and experienced the "new birth."[26] Whereas Anglicans typically saw the baptism of adult enslaved people as the culmination of an often-lengthy period of religious instruction, revivalists were less concerned with proof of a convert's knowledge of Christian doctrine. While Anglican communal worship carefully modeled and upheld the social hierarchy through practices such as having enslaved people sit or stand at the back of the church, revivalist gatherings were less careful to preserve such gradations. The power of emotional preaching, extemporaneous prayers, and worshippers being brought to laugh, yell, or gesticulate through the urgings of the Spirit attracted people of all sorts to revivalism, but many Anglican clergymen thought these practices destroyed proper decorum. Especially because of the absence of a colonial episcopate to settle clerical disputes, churchmen were likewise concerned about the destabilizing effects that itinerant preachers, even Anglicans, could have on relations between a parish clergyman and his flock. While many SPG missionaries traveled to meet the needs of communities that lacked local ministers, the Society always aimed to permanently settle clergymen. Revivalists' willingness to stir up religious enthusiasm and then move on was disconcerting.

Revivalism also gave enslaved people, those with little or no formal education, women, and others opportunities to preach, lead prayers, and otherwise exercise religious authority. Because missionary Anglicanism was premised on the necessity of properly trained and episcopally ordained clergymen, this attitude toward ministry posed a fundamental challenge to the Society's program. As the Massachusetts missionary Charles Brockwell saw it in 1742, the "whole Country" was thrown into "convulsions" by a "set of Enthusiasts that strole about harangueing the admiring Vulgar in *extempore* nonsense." Worse, it was not "confined to these only, for Men, Women, Children, Servants, & Nigros are now become (as they phrase it) Exhorters." Brockwell decried "the tragic scene" performed by those "entering into the pangs of the New Birth," which was marked by "groans, cries, screams, & agonies" from some and "the ridiculous & frantic gestures of others." "The Eye never beheld," he complained, instances of "such confusion, disorder, & irregularity."[27]

As such hostility coalesced, Alexander Garden emerged as the most outspoken colonial Anglican opponent of revivalism. Angered by Whitefield's itinerant preaching in South Carolina, which he characterized as a violation of "the canons and Ordination vow," in 1740 Garden tried to use his Commissarial authority to convene an ecclesiastical court and bring Whitefield to heel. Whitefield refused to recognize the proceedings' legitimacy or Garden's authority, and the effort to silence him failed. The encounter made the two men bitter opponents, and the wide attention the incident received publicly exposed the growing rift between the established colonial Anglican leadership and the new revivalism.

If Garden resented Whitefield's lack of respect for ecclesiastical hierarchies, the specter of disorder had been raised in South Carolina in an even more dramatic way by the recent events of the Stono Rebellion. In September 1739 at the Stono River near Charleston, a group of enslaved people had risen up, seized weapons, and killed more than twenty whites before their uprising was crushed. The rebels were largely Kongolese people and their Roman Catholic Christianity seems to have been an element in their collective identity.[28] Both these recent events and Whitefield and Garden's antagonism lay behind their splenetic 1740 exchange of pamphlets touching on slavery. *Three Letters from the Reverend Mr. G. Whitefield* initiated the controversy by attacking colonial Anglicans like Garden on multiple fronts. Two letters condemned rationalist Anglican theology, while the third criticized the failure of colonial masters to convert their slaves.[29] Whitefield did not advocate an end to slavery, but he mixed a commitment to converting slaves with a willingness to chastise colonial masters and clergymen for their failings. Just as importantly he was prepared to continue calling for slave conversion in the aftermath of Stono. The arguments that emerged from Whitefield's attack and Garden's response revealed links between churchmen's concerns about the maintenance of order and the conversion of slaves, and how missionary Anglicanism had been affected by its connections with the slave system.

Whitefield's critique focused on the spiritual and physical treatment of enslaved people, which he portrayed as so bad as to merit retribution. He observed that "perhaps it might be better for the poor Creatures themselves, to be hurried out of Life, than to be made so miserable, as they generally are in it. And indeed, considering what Usage they commonly meet with, I have wondered, that we have not more Instances of Self-Murder among the Negroes, or that they have not more frequently rose up in Arms against their Owners." Whitefield even speculated, with memories of Stono still fresh in the colony, that slave revolts might be divine punishment for the failure to convert slaves, writing, "tho' I heartily pray God they may never be permitted to get the upper Hand; yet should such a Thing be permitted by Providence, all good Men must acknowledge the Judgment would be just."[30]

Whitefield's criticisms of masters echoed points that had been long advanced by some affiliated with the Society. In 1718 Philip Bisse had used his annual sermon to warn that opposition to slave Christianization by masters meant that "all the Wealth obtain'd under so open a defiance of GOD and Religion, will, I fear, prove a Curse, even to our National Interests, instead of a Blessing." In 1719 Edward Chandler noted that converting Indians and slaves was the best way to secure their loyalty but warned "may it not be feared, if no Reformation follow, that God will suffer those Barbarians to drive us quite from their Coasts, whose Manners we might have civilized with Religion, but did not? And deliver your Plantations to another Nation, that will bring forth better Fruits?" In 1740, just as Whitefield and Garden's pamphlets were published, SPG member Bishop Thomas Wilson wrote that "it would be a terrible, but just Judgment, if God should suffer those Heathens to revenge *his Quarrel* upon such Christians" who opposed slave conversion.[31]

For Garden, however, these comments were as unacceptable as Whitefield's other critiques of the failings of Anglican clergymen and the irreligion of South Carolina society. Garden's response in *Six Letters to The Rev. Mr. George Whitefield* included not only the predictable defense of rationalist theology but also a defense of slaveholding as it was practiced in the southern colonies. Garden singled out Whitefield's comments on slave rebellions for particular censure:

> *And perhaps*, you say, *it might be better for the poor Creatures themselves to be hurried out of Life, than to be made* so miserable, *as they generally are in it. And indeed, considering what Usage they commonly meet with, &c.*—I suppress the remainder of this, and the next following *Paragraph* of your Epistle, as judging it both sinful, and dangerous to the publick

Safety to reprint them. More Virulence and Falshood cannot be contained in so few Lines.

In the aftermath of the Stono Rebellion, for Garden the prospect of slave rebellion was so dangerous that it could not even be mentioned. Whereas strong criticisms of slaveholders had been made by other supporters of the SPG in previous decades, Garden now stressed the benevolence of masters and identified more critical statements as a particular manifestation of Whitefield's dangerous religious enthusiasm. Most revivalists of the mid-eighteenth century, including Whitefield, were not antislavery. Indeed Whitefield would advocate for the introduction of slavery into the new Georgia colony and the orphanage he founded there became financially reliant on slave labor. However, while prior to 1740 figures associated with the SPG and colonial Anglicanism had been at the forefront of those chastising masters, the onset of the Great Awakening contributed to a realignment in the way slavery was discussed in circum-Atlantic religious circles. The voices of more traditional Anglicans like Garden and many others affiliated with the Society, while not silenced, became muted when it came to slave owners' abusiveness and impiety. Proponents of evangelical religion, less concerned about antagonizing elites, became the more public and vociferous critics of colonists' continuing neglect of enslaved people's earthly and spiritual needs.

Garden also lent his considerable authority to the idea that chattel slavery was not only licit, but actually a benevolent institution. He could "dare confidently vouch and affirm, and partly on my own Knowlegdge" that far from being miserable, the lives of colonial slaves were in general "more happy and comfortable in all temporal Respects (the Point of Liberty only excepted)" than those of "three fourths of the hired *farming* Servants and Day Labourers" in Scotland, Ireland, and many parts of England. British servants had to "labour *harder,* and fare *worse*" and worry about how to provide for their children, while slaves did not.[32] Garden's arguments, which anticipated later defenses of slaveholding in the era of abolitionism, presented a paternalistic fantasy and went beyond asserting slavery's permissibility to extol it as a positive good.

Proslavery rhetoric like Garden's was echoed in new programs undertaken by the SPG. These programs were premised on the growing belief that slavery, if properly managed, could help the Society's religious aims. The Society's ownership of a sugar plantation encouraged this development. Its most revealing manifestation, though, occurred not in Barbados, where the Society inherited its initial property in people, but in a new initiative in South Carolina. Alexander Garden's critique of Whitefield had included a rosy portrait of colonial slave holding. In 1741 the Society lent support to such views, and signaled its allegiances in the controversies sparked by Whitefield's evangelizing, by cooperating with Garden in opening a new school for slaves in Charleston. The crux of Garden's novel plan was that teaching would be done by young enslaved men who were trained to serve as catechists to their fellow slaves. The SPG authorized Garden to use its funds to purchase two young men who were to be chosen "with the Advice and Assistance" of its missionaries Thomas Hasell and William Guy and then educated under Garden's supervision. The Society included an enthusiastic full description of the plan in its annual report.[33]

In some ways Garden's plan was a bold one, especially because the Charleston school taught reading in addition to the fundamentals of Christianity. However, the school also demonstrates how the Society's relationship with slavery had changed. Garden used SPG funds to purchase two young, Carolina-born slaves—Andrew and Harry—from the estate sale of the recently deceased Alexander Skene, whose family had been prominent in promoting the conversion of enslaved people. The boys, aged fourteen and fifteen, had been baptized and could say the church catechism, but they could not yet read. Garden supervised the boys' education and, in 1743, the school was opened with Harry as the teacher.

Garden hoped that black catechists would have particular success with slaves, but cultural affinity was not the sole or even the primary benefit he anticipated. It was essential to Garden's plan that the catechists, like their students, be enslaved. As he put it in a May 1740 letter to the Society, the work of converting enslaved people must be undertaken "by Negro Schoolmasters, Home-born, & equally Property as other Slaves, but educated for this Service, & employed in it during their Lives, as the others are in any other Services whatsoever."[34] In describing the plan to the Society, he stressed the expected productivity of the enslaved people who would labor in its service. As Garden noted with enthusiasm, within a few years the school could be expected to "annually turn out" thirty or forty enslaved children who could read the scriptures and who had been instructed in the basics of religion. At that rate, Garden estimated, in twenty years half of the slave population of Charleston could be taught at the school. In a revealing further piece of calculus, Garden computed the Society could expect between thirty and forty years of service, with little future expense, from "a young healthy slave" like the ones it had bought.[35] A key to the scheme was that slaveholding provided a cost-effective, long-term means of securing missionary labor. The Society's membership, aware of the perennial problem of how to support enough workers to convert the colonies' thousands of slaves, appreciated that while other catechists required annual salaries and could leave their posts, Harry and Andrew would not cost the Society anything after their initial purchase and could not quit SPG service. In the 1740 annual report, where Garden's plan was detailed, it was noted that the boys to be purchased at the "Expence of the Society" would be educated so "that they may be employed afterwards during their Lives, as Schoolmasters to instruct their Fellow-Negroes, and chiefly the Children in the same Way." In 1743, the SPG's annual report echoed Garden's view that through the school "the Society hath opened a Door . . . by which the Light of the blessed Gospel will speedily and abundantly pour in among the poor Negroes of Carolina, and that without the least further Charge to the Society for some Years, (that of a few Books only excepted) which the Society is most ready to furnish."[36] The SPG's enthusiasm for this use of slavery was underlined in Secretary Philip Bearcroft's 1745 annual sermon, which noted the "Society hath lately fallen upon an happy Expedient for their Service by the Purchase of two young *Negroes*" for use as "School-masters to their Fellow-Negroes."[37] The school flourished for several years, with Garden reporting that many enslaved people were successfully instructed in Christianity and reading.

Garden's school also presented transatlantic Anglicanism's response to the rise of evangelical religion among enslaved people. Just as Garden's plans developed, South Carolina was experiencing the aftershocks of Whitefield's 1740 tour in the colony. Whitefield's preaching and attention to slaves had deeply touched the planter Hugh Bryan and his family.[38] While inspired by Whitefield, Hugh Bryan previously had been active in his Anglican parish, which was manned by the SPG missionary Lewis Jones, and had been interested in slaves' religious condition before revivalism hit South Carolina. In 1734 Bryan had received books in support of the work from the Associates of Dr. Bray. In 1736 Jones reported that he had fourteen black communicants at Easter and that he had baptized twenty-one black people in his parish.[39]

The Bryans were initially the sort of religiously minded masters that the Society aimed to encourage, but their experiences illustrate how the Great Awakening altered the Atlantic world's religious landscape. Bryan, his wife, Catherine, and his brother Jonathan became some of Whitefield's most fervent supporters, and they and a few other families in their parish of St. Helena heeded Whitefield's message by beginning to instruct local enslaved people more extensively. In 1740 Whitefield persuaded Jonathan Bryan to begin a school for black people in St. Helena under a lay, revivalist-minded catechist he had recommended.[40] What was different about the Bryans' new efforts is that the "frequent and great Assemblies of Negroes" they encouraged in St. Helena were infused with evangelicalism and brought enslaved people from different plantations together in large groups. Lewis Jones complained to the SPG that the slaves there were "taught rather Enthusiasm, than religion" and that they, as followers of Whitefield, pretended to "see visions, and receive Revelations from Heaven and to be converted by an Instantaneous Impulse of the Spirit."[41] By early 1742 the Bryans' evangelizing among slaves had attracted the hostility of authorities.

The colony's General Assembly designated a committee to investigate what was happening. Once again, post-Stono fears of rebellion appear to have been powerful. The committee concluded that the Bryans' meetings brought too many slaves together "to the Terror of some, and to the Disturbance of many" whites in the district and that "however commendable" it was for so-inclined masters to instruct slaves "in the Principles of Religion or Morality, in their own Plantations," encouraging such sizeable assemblies threatened the colony's security and should be punished. In the aftermath of the report, the South Carolina assembly called on the colony's lieutenant governor to enforce laws prohibiting large gatherings of enslaved people. In response, Hugh Bryan appeared before the assembly. The pages he presented into evidence from his own journal revealed that, in an echo of George Whitefield's inflammatory warnings, he had prophesied that slaves would rise up and destroy much of South Carolina in an act of divinely inspired retribution for the colony's sinfulness.[42] While others had previously claimed that irreligious planters invited God's wrath, the promulgation of such notions by an enthusiastic lay preacher and slave owner shook the colony's political establishment and self-consciously orthodox Anglicans.

The denouement of the Bryans' story probably reinforced the growing trend toward associating passion for the conversion of slaves with irrational enthusiasm. It emerged that after foreseeing a bloody future rebellion, Hugh Bryan, in the midst of a deep spiritual episode, had attempted a Moses-like parting of a river's waters with a stick. The attempt failed. Chastened by his failure to perform a miracle, and now subject to investigation and public ridicule, he denounced his prior actions and apologized. Nevertheless, accusations circulated that he had even helped arm slaves for a rebellion, and a grand jury alleged that he had made "sundry enthusiastick Prophecies of the destruction of Charles-Town, and Deliverance of the Negroes from their Servitude." The grand jury urged that the Bryan brothers and others implicated in their evangelization effort should be punished by law.[43]

The legal proceedings against them eventually petered out and the Bryans retired from the public eye, but Hugh Bryan's story circulated in several colonial newspapers as a lesson in the dangers of Whitefieldian enthusiasm. For all the hostility they attracted, the Bryans never rejected slaveholding. It continued to be the source of their wealth, and they aided Whitefield in his turn to slave labor as a source of financial support for his colonial projects, but they also kept up religious efforts among enslaved people on their own plantation. Unsurprisingly, in 1743 the Bryans and like-minded neighbors broke away from the Church of England and founded their own Presbyterian church, which prominently accepted enslaved people as members. Andrew Bryan, a man owned by Jonathan

Bryan who later became free, subsequently became a prominent black Baptist leader in his own right.[44]

It is revealing that in the press coverage surrounding the Bryan affair, supporters of evangelicals' efforts among the enslaved claimed that they were merely attempting to do what Bishop Gibson had previously urged colonists to do. A riposte in the *South-Carolina Gazette*, however, now articulated a distinction between acceptable "regular Attempts" to convert slaves made by masters within their own households and by "Missionaries, or School-masters, lawfully thereunto authorized" and unacceptable efforts by "every idle or designing Person that pleases," which were really "gathering Cabals of Negro's about him, without public Authority, at unseasonable Times, and to the Disturbance of a Neigbor-hood." Rather than teaching enslaved people proper Christianity, such efforts filled "their Heads with a Parcel of Cant-Phrases, Trances, Dreams, Visions, and Revelations," and, even worse, the idea of rebellion, a concept "which Prudence forbids to name."[45] Whitefield, like the Society, claimed that Christianization would make enslaved people better servants, but the forces unleashed by evangelicalism in South-Carolina seemed to fly in the face of his assurances. The Society hoped Garden's school would support the existing social order by acting as an antidote to these new, dangerous forms of religiosity. In 1744, for example, it supported the school by sending a shipment of books that added works like Edmund Gibson's *Observations upon the Conduct and Behaviour of . . . the Methodists*, the anti-Dissenter *The Englishman Directed in the Choice of His Religion*, and *The Rational Communicant* to the usual mix of Bibles, Common Prayer Books, Spelling Books, and Annual Sermons.[46]

In this context, while Garden's school signaled that Anglicans would not abandon the conversion of enslaved people, it also underlined the depth of their commitment to protecting existing colonial hierarchies. Whereas the Bryans' meetings had assembled many adult enslaved people in a dangerously undersurveilled rural setting, Garden's school brought smaller classes of urban slaves, primarily children, together under the auspices of the town's assuredly orthodox Anglican minister. The gatherings in St. Helena were perceived as challenges to order and masters' supremacy; the Charleston school was premised on the legitimacy and continuation of slavery. As South Carolina's political elite mobilized to silence Bryan, Garden's school was allowed to begin operating. When Garden solicited donations for it in 1744, four local slave traders were among the original sixteen donors to the school.[47]

What Andrew and Harry though of their roles in Garden's scheme is unrecorded. Andrew's fate underlined the logic of slaveholding at the plan's heart. Garden had concluded in 1744 that the SPG's investment in Andrew was a poor one as he had shown himself to be of "so weak of an understanding" as to be unfit for teaching school. Garden wanted to sell Andrew and purchase another young man "of better Genius." The Society directed that Garden send Andrew to Codrington, where he presumably would have been put to work as a household servant or field laborer, and use SPG funds to purchase another young man for use as a schoolmaster. Andrew was baptized and had long been associated with supporters of missionary Anglicanism, but the instruction was a stark demonstration that the SPG fundamentally regarded Andrew as a slave whose worth lay in his labor, which was its to command. There was no recorded consideration paid to how traumatic being shipped to Barbados almost certainly would have been for him. Apparently considering the SPG's directive too cruel, Garden instead requested permission to sell Andrew locally. The Society consented, specifying that he be sold for "the best price that can reasonably be gotten." Andrew was sold in 1750. Garden evidently decided not to replace him as the proceeds were remitted to the SPG.[48]

Because the Society operated as a circum-Atlantic institution, this approach to the conversion of slaves had wider resonances. The Society's members thought so highly of Garden's school that they ordered that "the same Experiment" be tried on Codrington, where "the two most promising Negroe-Boys" were to be selected for training as catechists.[49] The Society's Barbados attorneys accordingly selected John Bull and Willoughby (also known on Codrington by his "plantation name," Bacchus) for special instruction by the Society's catechist, Sampson Smirk.[50] In 1746 Garden traveled to England and appeared before the Society to discuss the Charleston school, telling members that he was "now convinced by Experience, that the same Method will answer in other Places," and "humbly recommends it to Practice."[51] When the Society's first missionary to Africa, Thomas Thompson, proposed in 1753 that some local boys be sent to London for education, the Society agreed and ordered that if young men "were only to be had by way of Purchase," then Thompson should "be careful in choosing out the most promising ones." Thompson found local families willing to cooperate voluntarily, so the Society did not repeat the scheme in West Africa, but there too the SPG would attempt to capitalize on Atlantic slavery as it sought the conversion of black people.[52] Some voices within the Society would continue to criticize masters for failing to aid slave conversion in the 1750s, but these calls did not cause the Society to examine its own turn to deploying slaveholding as a missionary methodology.[53]

Garden, "disabled thro' infirmities," resigned from his position as rector of St. Philip's in 1754, but the school continued under his successors Richard Clarke and Robert Smith, and the SPG continued to support it with books.[54] Harry continued teaching until 1768, when the school was permanently closed after the St. Philip's vestry ordered "that Harry, the Negroe that keeps

School at the Parsonage (for Repeated Transgressions) be sent to the Work house, and be put into the Mad house, there to be kept till Orders from the Vestry to take him Out."[55] The nature of his "transgressions" was not recorded. Given the school's roots in Anglicanism's response to the enthusiastic disorders unleashed by the Great Awakening, Harry's confinement in an asylum seems a poignant ending to his twenty-five years of labor. Parish records contain no report of his release.

It has been suggested that Garden's plan for the Charleston school, which was "grounded so firmly in humanitarian ideas," was "a commentary on the curious combination of practicality, vision and courage, characteristic not only of Garden, but of the entire program of the S.P.G."[56] Such a characterization misses how the Charleston school embodied Anglicanism's response to the threat of the new evangelicalism and how far support for slaveholding had permeated the Society's activities by the 1740s. On Barbados, the Society had long operated under the premise that the profits from slave labor could be used to fund bringing enslaved people into the church. In the Charleston school the Society and its supporters attempted to provide directly for the religious welfare of black people by harnessing the economies of slave labor. There, they brought slave labor from the background into the very center of their religious program, the actual education and conversion of people. In doing so, they exhibited the extent to which the Society and its supporters had become enamored with the power and profits that slaveholding promised.

Because of the SPG's circum-Atlantic profile, its rapprochement with slavery had wider cultural and intellectual ramifications. Thomas Wilson's *The Knowledge and Practice of Christianity Made Easy* was the most important instructional work for "heathen" conversion produced in association with the SPG's missionary work in the eighteenth century. Bishop Wilson (1663–1755) was an influential member of the SPG from the time he joined the organization in 1707 until his death in 1755. He had collaborated with Thomas Bray in promoting parochial libraries, proposed the establishment of a school for training missionaries in his diocese on the Isle of Man, and generally shared in the zeal for missionary outreach that united the Society's first generation. An ardent defender of the Church's interests, Wilson nevertheless had a strong ecumenical streak, and his contacts with the Moravians, as well as with James Oglethorpe, further stimulated his interest in converting "heathens."[57] Wilson's decades of affiliation with the Society also meant he was present as attitudes within it developed over time. The history of his text therefore reveals elements of the Society's early ambition and motivations, and the corrosive effects that a deepening connection to slavery had on the organization's work.

Figure 11. Thomas Wilson (1663–1755). Bishop of Sodor and Man (© Trustees of the British Museum.)

In 1740, Wilson published *Essay Towards An Instruction For The Indians, Explaining the most Essential Doctrines of Christianity,* which would become enduringly known through subsequent editions as *The Knowledge and Practice of Christianity Made Easy.*[58] Appearing when Wilson, at age seventy-seven, was already well known as the author of several religious works intended for mass lay audiences, it marked the culmination of his decades of work to promote practical piety and personal devotion. Reflecting his long-standing commitments to missionary Anglicanism, the book was "inscribed" to the archbishop of Canterbury and the members of the SPG and SPCK.[59] The work quickly came to be seen as the Church of England's standard handbook for promoting the conversion of black and Native American people. From the first edition on, the close identification of the text with the Society was underlined by the frequent insertion of extracts from SPG annual sermons into its introductory material.[60]

Wilson's book was intended as a guide for teaching the fundamentals of Christianity and preparing adults for baptism. In a preface, Wilson explained the necessity of missionary work among Native American and black people. The main text presented religious lessons through fictional dialogues between an "Indian" and a "Missionary" on topics such as "The Proofs of the Christian Religion," "Objections against the bad Lives of Christians answered," and "The Commandments of God, practically explained." Reflecting an underlying commitment to the essential unity of all humankind, the book was not solely a handbook for converting "heathens" but was also intended, in the words of its subtitle, as one "which may be of use to all such who are called Christians, but have not well considered the Meaning of the Religion they profess; Or, who profess to know God, but in Works do deny Him." This positioning of the book helps explain its translation into other European languages, the publication of an edition for use in Irish Protestant charity schools, and its simultaneous presence in the hands of missionaries in America and religiously minded people in Britain.[61]

The work circulated for decades. Between 1741, when a second edition was published under its enduring title, and 1787, fourteen editions were printed. The book was reissued periodically into the mid-nineteenth century, with a twentieth edition published in 1848.[62] The book's reach was furthered by its distribution by the SPG and its inclusion in the catalog of the SPCK, which made it available easily at a reduced price.[63] Likewise, publishers discounted copies if they were bought in quantity by "charitable Persons" who intended to distribute them "at Home amongst poor Families, Children, and Servants, or to disperse in our Plantations in America."[64]

Wilson's text had influential boosters among London's Anglican activists. The promotional efforts of Wilson's son, the clergyman Dr. Thomas Wilson (1703–84), who himself became an SPG member in 1733, were partly responsible for the book's speedy success.[65] Other supporters of the book included Stephen Hales, who deemed it likely to "be the means of spreading true Christianity" in the colonies "in an extraordinary manner." The SPG noted that it had received a donation of 850 "copies in Sheets" of the book in 1742 from an anonymous donor through the younger Wilson and an additional 125 copies from an anonymous donor through Hales, who also urged its distribution by the Associates of Dr. Bray. Hales recorded that his continued lobbying on behalf of the work was enough to lead one unnamed SPG member to tell him in 1743 that the "book had been too much puffed already."[66] By 1744, more than two thousand copies of the work had quickly been distributed in the colonies.[67] Wilson and

Hales continued to promote the book's use in ensuing years, sending fifty copies to the Harvard College library in 1758.[68]

The Society encouraged its own employees and others to use the book. In December 1741 the SPG's secretary wrote to Codrington's catechist, Sampson Smirk, and recommended that he employ Wilson's text "for it is calculated for Negroes, as well as Indians" and "will be a great additional help." At the same time, Secretary Philip Bearcroft told Codrington's manager, Abel Alleyne, that simply "changing the words Indians for Negroes" made the book useful for the instruction of the enslaved. The Society sent Alleyne 100 copies along with 120 copies of Bishop Gibson's 1727 letters and a parcel of William Fleetwood's 1711 annual sermon, matching Wilson's text with two of the other most important pro-slave conversion works in the Society's repertoire. Observing that "a Treatise may Instruct the Teachers, as well as the Scholars," Bearcroft asked Alleyne to disperse them to "all the Clergy and Schoolmasters, and such Planters to whom they will be acceptable, upon the Island." In 1744 Alleyne reported using the book in classes he led for Codrington's slaves, in which he would first "Catecizeth" and then read "a Dialogue out of the Bishop of Man's Essay towards the Instruction of the Indians."[69]

Under SPG auspices, copies of the book were quickly and widely distributed elsewhere. The missionary William Guy reported handing out a dozen copies to his South Carolina parishioners in 1742. Alexander Garden received a shipment for distribution in the same year. Copies were sent to William Vesey in New York City and to the clergyman Henry Barclay in Albany. It was subsequently used by SPG missionaries in western New York to catechize Native Americans and may even have been translated into Mohawk.[70] The Society continued including Wilson's text in parcels of books for decades. Samuel Frink reported in 1767 that Wilson's work was among the collection of SPG-provided books and tracts that he distributed to the people of Savannah, Georgia. In the same year, Christian Frederick Post, whom the Society sponsored as a missionary to the Mosquito Coast of modern Nicaragua and Honduras, thanked the Society for copies sent to him.[71] In 1770, thirty years after its first publication, Samuel Auchmuty, the rector of New York's Trinity Church who had served for sixteen years as the SPG's catechist to the town's black population, requested that the Society send "Bibles, prayer Books, & Tracts; especially the late pious Bishop of Soder & Man's Instruction for the Indians, which have been the means of bringing many of these poor Slaves to a true sense of their Duty."[72]

The reach of the book extended far beyond those directly employed by the SPG or instructed by its missionaries. The Society sent many copies to Governors William Shirley of Massachusetts and Benning Wentworth of New Hampshire for them to distribute as they saw fit. Wentworth told the Society he had distributed the one hundred copies sent to him "in the most publick manner thro' his Government."[73] The Society also circulated it in those colonies outside its regular operations, sending copies to Antigua's commissary and Commissary James Blair and Governor William Gooch of Virginia for them to disperse.[74] In 1744 Commissary William Dawson recommended the book, which "has been so well received, and recommended, both at Home and Abroad" to Virginia's ministers and asked that they "would be a Means of putting One of Them into the Hands of every Schoolmaster, Scholar, and Person that can read, in your Parish."[75] In 1745 the book was being "read over again" at the College of William and Mary to an assembled group of "negroes, men, women, and children; and some white servants."[76] In 1760, the Maryland minister Henry Addison requested copies.[77] It is a measure of the book's reach and continuing high status that Olaudah Equiano received it on two separate occasions fifteen years apart: once from the clergyman who baptized him in London in 1759 and again from a silk-weaver during his deeper conversion to Christianity in 1774. Reflecting on his 1774 experience, Equiano reported that the book was "of great use to me, and at that time was a means of strengthening my faith."[78]

The book became a global missionary classic. In 1773 the SPG and SPCK member Charles Walter Congreve offered to underwrite translating it into Tamil.[79] In 1788, the Barbados clergyman Henry Evans Holder proposed "a compendious abridgement" of the text "divested of the form of Q. and A. and digested into short and easy lectur[e]s for use of the Negroes."[80] In 1808 Beilby Porteus recommended the use of an abridged version in the parochial schools for the instruction of slaves that he hoped to found in every parish in the West Indies.[81] By 1819 the book had even reached one of the most isolated outposts of British influence in the world, Pitcairn Island in the Pacific, where it was reportedly a great favorite of the last surviving mutineer from the HMS *Bounty*.[82]

The work's ultimately worldwide distribution and close association with missionary Anglicanism illustrate how the SPG functioned as a network for the transference of ideas about slavery and human difference. In the book, Wilson conceptualized British missionary work as building on biblical precedents. For example, just as God had sent Joseph and Jacob into Egypt to give the Egyptians the opportunity to gain religious knowledge, so "special Providence" had placed Christians near "Heathens" in "latter days" so that they might be converted.[83] Like several other works produced by Anglicans interested in missionary work, Wilson's book was rooted in ethnic theology and emphasized peoples' spiritual equality in the eyes of God, thereby stressing the fundamental unity of humanity. Mankind could only rise or fall together, for "all Men being Sinners, God must either suffer Sin to be in the World, or destroy the Sinners; that is all the Race of Men."[84]

Wilson's text also captured the way that Anglican ethnic theological exegesis could provide intellectual support to slavery, serving as a vehicle for the wide circulation of the association between Noah's curse and black people's enslavement. Moreover, it promoted the interpretation that black slavery was a fulfillment of scriptural prophecy, which imbued the existence of that chronologically and geographically specific form of slavery with apologetic importance. As Wilson noted in his preface:

> As to the Negroes, the Descendants of *Ham* and *Canaan*, who, according to one of the most ancient Prophecies, (*Gen.* ix. 25) for such it really was, are become Servants or Slaves to Christians, the Descendants of *Japheth*,—surely the only righteous Recompence that can be made for them for their being forc'd from their native Country into a strange Land, and for their Labours there, will be to endeavour to bring them to the Knowledge and Worship of the true God, *the God of the Spirits of all Flesh,* that they may have a full Reward in the next World for the Hardships they meet with in this.[85]

Wilson sympathized with the plight of slaves, but black slavery's roots in biblical prophecy entailed both heavenly sanction for the institution and posited an exchange of earthly toil for eternal salvation between heathen slave and Christian master. In Wilson's view, while a failure to convert slaves would make it "very difficult to justify" the trade in them, bondage could be the mechanism through which black people would be saved.[86] Wilson's work encouraged the baptism of enslaved people, but it also brought the argument that black chattel slavery should be understood as part of God's deliberate plan for the world to a global readership.

The cumulative influence of slavery as a functioning institution on the SPG is also suggested by the revision of Wilson's work after its first edition. By 1741 the book was incorporated into the lists of books approved for distribution by both the SPCK and the SPG.[87] In adopting Wilson's text, these groups treated it, like many other works they distributed, as tools that could be altered to fit the needs of their religious agendas. Wilson probably encouraged this. As he stated in the first edition, the book had "so many Defects so easy to be seen in it, that he could almost wish, that it had not gone abroad so imperfect as it is," except for the fact that "those Defects may set some better Hands at work, to perfect what hath been here attempted."[88] While it might be tempting to view Wilson's statement as stock authorial modesty, he was taken precisely at his word. In subsequent editions, among other changes, the dialogues were reorganized, the excerpts from SPG sermons in the preface altered, and printed versions of letters urging the use of the book attached.

Bishop Wilson's direct involvement in these revisions is uncertain. Wilson did not leave the Isle of Man after 1735, and for many years his son, Dr. Thomas Wilson, who was resident in London, was primarily responsible for shepherding his father's works through publication and republication. Whether Bishop Wilson superintended the publication of the editions of *The Knowledge and Practice of Christianity Made Easy* published during his lifetime, it seems likely the changes made to it reflected the concerns of a wider group of supporters of missionary Anglicanism. In what may have been a broadly typical practice, in 1733 the younger Wilson and Sir John Philipps met together to review Bishop Wilson's *Short and Plain Instruction for the better Understanding of the Lord's Supper*, and the two of them "altered a few words of it" before it was published and included on the list of the SPCK's approved books.[89] The younger Wilson circulated the manuscript for the original *Essay Towards An Instruction For The Indians* before it was first published, seeking the comments of SPG members and others, including the dissenting minister Isaac Watts, in the hopes of gaining a wide circulation for the book. Likewise, the younger Wilson probably supervised the revision and publication of the second edition in 1741 after "a great many thousand of the last edition [had been] sent all over our plantations in the West Indies," and again sought the input of others.[90] This deliberate revision process did not lead to major changes to Wilson's exposition of the basic principles of Christian doctrine, but it did lead to alterations that reveal how Anglican attitudes toward slavery were developing.

Between the first and second editions of Wilson's book, sections of the introduction treating the conversion of slaves were changed. On the most basic level, the second edition subtly underlined the identification of black people with a rigorous slavery by replacing the first edition's statement that "Negroes" had become "Servants or Slaves to Christians" with the more rigid assertion that "Negroes" were "Slaves to Christians."[91] Other more sweeping changes were also made. In the first edition of his book, Wilson emphasized the reciprocal obligations slavery imposed on master and servant. Like Whitefield also did in 1740, Wilson initially suggested that masters who did not try to convert their slaves risked divine retribution in the form of a slave rebellion:

> And it would be a terrible, but just Judgment, if God should suffer those Heathens to revenge *his Quarrel* upon such Christians, for the great Dishonour they do him, and for the Injustice they do their Fellow Creatures, not only neglecting, but sometimes even opposing their Conversion; and by their unchristian Lives, provoking God to pour down his Judgments upon their ungrateful Heads, who have been so greatly favour'd by the Light of the Gospel, and are neither thankful for, nor better'd by it.[92]

Even more forcefully, Wilson claimed that recent acts of violence and rebellion around the British Atlantic should be interpreted as a warning by those who had prevented the conversion of slaves. He argued that "surely some Attempts of this Kind, which have been already made, should awaken such Christians as are concern'd with that People, and be look'd upon as gracious Intimations, of what God may suffer them to do, if their Masters should either oppose or neglect their Instruction." Wilson elaborated on this theme, noting the dire results that were produced by, and could be expected from, denying African Americans' full humanity:

> Now to prevent these Judgments, it will not be proper to tell these Negroes, as they say many foolish or profane Wretches do, whether in Jest or Earnest, *That they have no Souls:*—For if they should be brought to believe THAT, they may be tempted to hazard their Bodies, in order the sooner to free themselves from Slavery, as many of them have done.[93]

Wilson may have had the recent Stono Rebellion in mind when he referenced "attempts of this kind," and Antigua had experienced what was seen as a near rebellion in 1736. White New Yorkers, who had turned hostile to Elias Neau's mission following the rebellion of 1712, were driven to a murderous panic by another supposed slave conspiracy there in 1741. Fears of slave uprisings swept the colonies in the face of these events.[94]

All of Wilson's ominous references to slave rebellions and divine vengeance were omitted from the introduction of the book's second edition.[95] These changes imported transatlantic Anglicans' and masters' fears about the spread of slave rebellions into one of the Society's central missionary texts. It is unclear whether the revisers of Wilson's text were specifically mindful of the ongoing controversies over Whitefield's presence in South Carolina and the proselytizing and dire prophecies of Hugh Bryan, but the rise of revivalism also provided an important context for these changes. Wilson's warnings echoed Godwyn and a tradition of missionary Anglican writings frankly critical of slaveholders, but, as the exchange between Whitefield and Garden indicated, such dire prophecies were becoming seen as dangerous and unsuitable expressions of Anglican views on slavery. What *was* kept in the second edition were those sentences that stressed the positive benefits that would accrue to benevolent masters. As was printed in both the first and second editions, "the true way, which all wise and good Masters will take with their Slaves" is to "endeavour that their Slaves may have Ties of Religion and Conscience, to oblige them to be *faithful, peaceable,* and *contented* with their Condition."[96] These changes remained in the many subsequent and widely circulated editions of the book.

The emending of Wilson's book shows that by the early 1740s, orthodox Anglicans were becoming unwilling to speak too forcefully to masters. In an environment in which both many individual ministers and the Society as a whole were owners of slaves and the Society's missionary strategy centered on winning the support of other slaveholders, rebel slaves could no longer be safely invoked as even rhetorical instruments of divine justice. These changes, no doubt, made the work more palatable to many settlers in the colonies. Yet, they were probably also observed by enslaved people. In catering to masters' sensibilities, one of the Society's key missionary tools was stripped of its most strident critiques of slavery as it was actually functioning in the Atlantic world.

By mid-century, fifty years of close contact with slavery had transformed the Society from a body often critical of slaveholders to one committed to upholding slavery as integral to colonial societies. Although much of the early passion for converting enslaved people waned, the SPG continued to work among enslaved people. The Great Awakening increased the reach of evangelical religion and began bringing black people into Christian churches in larger numbers, but it did not change the colonial religious situation overnight. It was not until after the American Revolution that black Christians represented more than a very small minority of the enslaved population of plantation societies, and it was probably not until after 1815 that Christianity was a large presence in the religious lives of enslaved people in the United States and Britain's Caribbean colonies.[97] While the emergence of a distinctive African American Christianity was a gradual process, the growth of evangelical religion around the Atlantic world seemed early on to many Anglicans to be a threat to proper patterns of religious and social subordination. Frederick Cornwallis, a future archbishop of Canterbury, reflected a powerful ethos when he began the Society's 1756 annual sermon by reminding his hearers of Christ's injunction "to *render to Caesar the Things that were Caesar's,* and to pay Obedience to the Powers that were established in the World."[98] When, beginning in the 1760s, the Society first began to encounter abolitionist sentiments at home and in the colonies, many of its members and the SPG as an institution proved hostile.

The commitment of Atlantic communities to the exploitation of unfree labor put local ministers and the SPG and its missionaries under considerable pressure to sanction slavery as a social and economic system. Those colonial elites to whom SPG missionaries often looked for political, financial, and intellectual support were often the people most heavily committed to slavery's perpetuation and growth. The Society did more than passively accept slavery: as an organization it came to embrace slaveholding and employ it first as a financial support and then directly as a means of making converts. This more overtly proslavery

stance provided further intellectual and institutional support to colonial masters. In an era when racial, anti-biblical justifications for slavery still remained
beyond the pale for most people, the deepening embrace of slavery by the SPG
and leading members of the Church of England served to bolster slavery's moral
acceptability around the British Atlantic world.

PART THREE

SITES OF MISSIONARY ENCOUNTER

5

"A Sett of Possitive Obstinate People"

Missionary Encounters on Codrington Plantation

In 1710 Christopher Codrington, former governor-general of the Leeward Islands, died and left the SPG a valuable possession—his working Barbadian sugar plantation with all its slaves. Codrington's vision was that the property would continue to operate and provide ongoing revenue for the construction and maintenance of a college for training missionaries. The SPG would own and run the Codrington estate as a sugar plantation—manned by hundreds of enslaved people—for more than a century. The Society made only sporadic progress during the eighteenth century in establishing Codrington's college, but the estate became a key site in the Society's circum-Atlantic program for Christianizing slaves. There the Society's initially optimistic ideas about reforming slavery and converting enslaved people collided most directly with the routine brutalities of plantation slavery.

The missionary encounters that occurred at Codrington in the eighteenth century were primarily shaped by two forces. As in all situations where SPG clergymen tried to make "heathens" Christians, there was a meeting and interaction of cultures and religions on the estate. More uniquely, the Society's religious program was deeply affected by its attempts to run the plantation profitably and its position as an institutional master. This chapter begins by considering the mechanisms that the Society used to manage the estate, the origins of people who lived and worked there, and the ways that high mortality and low birth rates affected the population that the SPG's missionaries hoped to Christianize. This social history of the estate provides a platform for considering the cultural and religious encounter that occurred there in new ways. As the second part of this chapter examines, the religious program on the estate was repeatedly undermined by efforts to maximize the plantation's profitability. Confronted with pervasive death and a punishing work routine, enslaved people on Codrington, as elsewhere, found ways to resist their masters. Paradoxically, however, it was when the Society was most interested in converting the estate's slaves that the implication of this resistance for its religious program became most apparent. Because mastership and missionizing frequently became entangled on the plantation, resisting Anglicanism became a way for enslaved people there to assert their autonomy.

One effect of Codrington's prevailing demographic regime was that its population remained largely African-born throughout the eighteenth century. In consequence, as a third section analyzes, African-derived cultural and religious practices such as obeah long remained potent forces on the estate, and for many decades they proved more appealing to Codrington's people than membership in the Church of England. Jointly, these people's efforts to resist slavery and retain ties to their West African roots and religious beliefs explain why the SPG was persistently unable to achieve mass conversions on the plantation, even at moments when its members were focused on and committed to that cause. The final part of this chapter examines how the Society's religious program on Codrington was affected by the increased pessimism about "heathen" conversion that emerged within the organization after 1740. On the Society's plantation, the growing sense that Africans and Europeans were separated by a wide, perhaps impassable, divide had practical implications. Several decades of effort had failed to produce mass conversions on the estate, and for long stretches in the second half of the eighteenth century the Society effectively abandoned attempts to convert enslaved people on Codrington, even as it continued to use their labor.

The Society owned people on Barbados until the legal ending of slavery in the British Empire in 1834. Gradually, but especially after 1790, the sometimes perilous state of the estate's finances, changing West Indian plantation management practices, and external pressure led the SPG to ameliorate the living and working conditions of its slaves. Ultimately, in the nineteenth century a more creolized enslaved population on Codrington also received more extensive Christian instruction and began to accept Anglicanism in larger numbers. The estate's history has often been recounted through narratives emphasizing these changes and culminating in enslaved people's emancipation. One of the two principal works on Codrington characterized it as "an Experiment in Anglican Altruism on a Barbados Plantation."[1] Even when the SPG's management of the estate has been considered more critically, the reforms enacted in the late eighteenth and early nineteenth centuries have been stressed in ways that suggest that the freeing of Codrington's people was preordained.[2] For almost all the eighteenth century the SPG operated the plantation as an ongoing concern, with much more attention paid to the profitability of the estate than to any long-term plans for bettering enslaved people's material conditions, much less preparing for some future emancipation. The Society wanted those it owned to become Christians, but it bought hundreds of people not for their benefit but in order to profit from their labor. Before slavery was legally abolished, the Society showed no inclination to free its slaves or divest itself of its plantation.

The prevailing belief within the Society for decades was that slavery, Christianity, and profits could co-exist on its plantation and many of its supporters thought that exhibiting this to other masters was of circum-Atlantic importance. This view persisted until the very end of slavery on the estate. J. H. Pinder, Codrington's catechist between 1819 and 1826, claimed that in that late period the Society's plantation could still show "in what harmony Religious Institutions and Flourishing Agriculture subsist."[3] For more than a century the Society intended Codrington to demonstrate this, not the idea that enslaved people would be happier, healthier, or holier if eventually freed. Emancipation can now seem to be an inevitability, but it did not appear so to the eighteenth-century Society. Moreover, for the generations of people who toiled unwillingly on Codrington but who died, in old age or youth, before emancipation, freedom was not a reward for their labors. Codrington's eighteenth-century history starkly reveals how the Society's program intersected with the bitter reality of slavery and the ideas and actions of enslaved people themselves.

Christopher Codrington was a member of the minority of West Indian masters who favored the conversion of enslaved people, and his interest in that cause seems to have been part of the reason he left his estate to the Society. In 1699 he had proposed supporting efforts to convert enslaved people, if the work was undertaken by "Apostolical men who are willing to take much pains for little reward."[4] Codrington also had connections to members of the SPG's founding generation. Francis Le Jau knew Codrington before he became an SPG missionary. In 1699 and 1700, when Le Jau served for a short, difficult period as a priest on the island of St. Christopher, Codrington was "his great friend" and financial benefactor.[5] George Smalridge, dean of Carlisle, later bishop of Bristol, and an influential early SPG member, was Codrington's Oxford tutor.[6] Bishop Smalridge's brother, John Smalridge, was Codrington's plantation manager and remained in this position for twenty years under the SPG.[7]

In 1711 William Fleetwood, bishop of St. Asaph, used his annual sermon to acknowledge Codrington's gift, reflect on what it meant for the Society, and urge masters to aid in Christianizing their slaves. Fleetwood noted that it meant the Society had "become the *Patrons* of at least *Three Hundred Slaves.*" In this financially valuable donation, Fleetwood could "see and cannot but adore the gracious Hand of God, in thus supplying our Necessities, by casual unexpected

Charitable Benefactions." But Fleetwood also insisted the gift gave the SPG a special responsibility: "If all the Slaves throughout *America*, and every *Island* in those Seas, were to continue *Infidels* forever, yet *ours alone must needs be Christians*." For Fleetwood, converting Codrington's people would not only benefit them but would also be "preaching *by Example*" to other colonists, which was "the most effectual way of recommending Doctrines, to a hard and unbelieving World, blinded by Interest, and other Prepossessions."[8] Fleetwood's hope that Codrington would be a financial boon and a model for other slaveholders also captured the mixed motives that were the hallmark of the SPG's involvement with the estate.

Codrington's bequest clearly envisioned the continuation of slavery on the estate and the creation of an educational institution, but it was less clear whom he hoped would ultimately benefit from the missionaries produced by his college. His will was ambiguous on the point:

> Item: I give and Bequeath my two Plantations in the Island of Barbados to the Society for propagation of the Christian Religion in Forreighn parts, Erected and Established by my Late good master, King William the Third, and my desire is to have the Plantations Continued Intire and three hundred negros at Least Kept always thereon, and A Convenient number of Professors and Scholars Maintained there, all of them to be under the vows of Poverty Chastity and obedience, who shall be oblidged to Studdy and Practice Physick and Chyrurgery as well as divinity, that by the apparent usefulness of the former to all mankind, they may Both indear themselves to the People and have the better oppertunitys of doeing good To mens Souls whilst they are Takeing Care of their Bodys. But the Particulars of the Constitution I Leave to the Society Compos'd of good and wise men.[9]

William Gordon, a Barbados clergyman, told the Society that "The Design of the Bequest was the Maintenance of Monks and Missionaries, to be employed in the Conversion of Negroes and Indians, which Design He took from his Conversation with a Learned Jesuite of St. Christophers, between whom and him, there passed several letters about ye Antiquity, Usefulness, and Excellency of a Monastic Life."[10] It is possible this priest was the celebrated Jean Baptiste Labat— author, missionary, and sugar plantation manager—whom Codrington had met on St. Christopher's in 1701.[11] This Roman Catholic tie was probably not welcome to the Anglican hierarchy or the SPG membership, which showed no interest in using the plantation to create British colonial monasticism.[12] Though slave conversion was not made explicit in Codrington's will, his intentions likely contributed to the SPG considering such work part of its responsibilities on the estate from the start.

Codrington's Catholic connections highlight the fact that plantation and slave ownership were common among religious groups operating in the eighteenth-century Atlantic world. While the SPG owned one plantation cultivated by two hundred to three hundred enslaved people, the Jesuits and other Roman Catholic orders held hundreds of such estates and owned thousands of men, women, and children. By 1760 the Jesuits owned more than 17,000 people in South America, and until their expulsion from Spanish America in 1767 they owned more slaves than any other person or organization in the Western Hemisphere.[13] Nor was Catholic slaveholding limited to Latin America. Between 1717 and 1838, Maryland Jesuits used slave labor on farms that supported endeavors such as their college at Georgetown. In 1765 there were eight such farms, where thirteen Jesuits and 192 enslaved people lived and worked.[14] Roman Catholic orders also owned sugar plantations in the Caribbean.[15] There particularly, slaveholding proved too tempting for even the most avowedly reformist religious communities. Moravians on St. Croix, Jamaica, and Barbados, for example, simultaneously owned enslaved people and worked for their conversion.[16] As was the case on Codrington, slaveholding by religious groups often blended an intention to make converts with economic self-interest.

The SPG was anxious to accept its Barbadian inheritance. The estate consisted of two parts operated as a single unit. The upper plantation contained 270 acres, three-quarters of which were prime sugar-growing land. The lower plantation, sometimes called Consett, abutted the sea on the island's east coast. It was larger than the upper plantation, but its rocky soil was less ideal for sugar cultivation. The estate was well equipped with windmills, boiling houses, a distillery, a pothouse and other buildings, and had a small harbor, which eased the shipment of crops and allowed operation of a small coastal sloop.[17] When the Society took possession of the property, which followed two years of legal wrangling after Codrington's death, there were 276 enslaved people living on it.[18] It was, all told, a large and valuable operation.

In the 1720s the SPG succeeded, at considerable pains and expense, in erecting a large building for the proposed college.[19] However, Codrington's educational plan developed fitfully, largely because the plantation's income alone was insufficient to build and maintain the institution he envisioned. Moreover, operating a true college was largely unrealistic on an island where primary schooling was in short supply and English universities continued attracting elites. In the 1740s, in order to prepare the way for a college, a school for white boys opened. Its fortunes varied; it was closed during some periods of financial difficulty, but the terms of Codrington's will, the interest of some prominent Barbadians in the

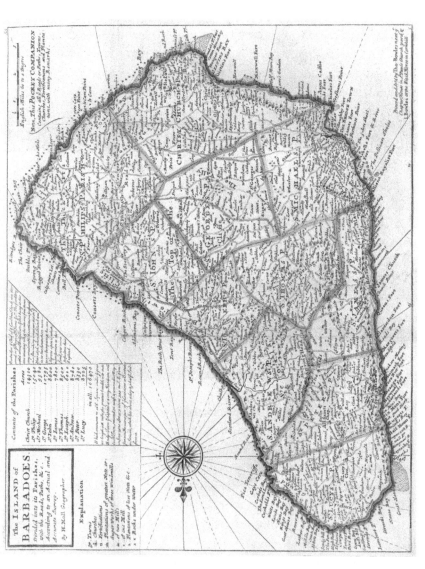

Figure 12. "The Island of Barbadoes" by Herman Moll (1732). Codrington College, the SPG's sugar estate, here labeled as "The Society," and Conset's Bay are in St. John's Parish on the island's east coast, at the top center of this map. (Courtesy of the David Rumsey Map Collection, www.davidrumsey.com.)

school, and the Society's considerable investment meant that it was never permanently abandoned. A college granting secondary degrees began functioning on Codrington in the late 1790s, and this became, in the nineteenth century, a seminary for training West Indian clergymen.

The SPG quickly adapted existing West Indian absentee management practices to suit its particular institutional position and agenda. A manager, experienced in sugar cultivation, lived on the estate and was responsible for its day-to-day operation. One or more missionaries were also resident on the estate, tasked with ministering to enslaved people and with running the school. In London a Barbados Committee was created, which met regularly to review accounts and reports, approve expenditures, issue instructions, and prepare important matters for consideration by the SPG's full membership. This committee, which was open to any SPG member, typically included several clerics and lay members with experience with plantations in the Caribbean or elsewhere. Answerable to the committee were the Society's attorneys—planters and parish clergymen resident in Barbados—who provided local supervision over the estate. The SPG also relied on the services of merchants in both Barbados and London, who acted as its agents in handling the shipping and selling of the Society's sugar, and in keeping the plantation supplied with manufactures and foodstuffs.

The management of Codrington intersected with the Society's general operations. The London merchant brothers Rowland and William Tryon, for example, served in succession as both "Treasurer of the Society and Factor for the Affairs in Barbados," in the 1710s and 1720s, positions that gave them responsibility for the stewardship of the organization's general operating funds and saw them earn commissions for supplying Codrington and selling its sugar.[20] Because of the specific nature of Codrington's bequest, the Society kept its Barbados account separate from that for general operations. At points, however, money was borrowed from the Barbados account to fund the Society's general operations and—much more frequently—money was loaned to the Barbados account from general funds to keep the plantation running or enable long-term investments.[21]

Just as significantly, given the active parts many Society supporters played in the intellectual and political life of the imperial capital, ownership of Codrington brought many SPG members into intimate contact with plantation management. Prominent figures such as Archbishop Thomas Tenison, Bishop Charles Trimnell, and the future bishops White Kennett and George Smalridge were among the early members involved in securing the estate from Christopher Codrington's heirs and then served on the Barbados Committee.[22] These patterns continued throughout the century. The Society's archive records the SPG membership superintending Barbados business, including the buying and selling of enslaved people. In November 1744, for example, the Society was informed that in accordance with its instructions to "fill up the number of negroes on those estates to 300" its Barbados representatives had purchased "20 New Negroes on 18 January last." That meeting was chaired by the archbishop of Canterbury John Potter and the assembled members included the bishops of Rochester (Joseph Wilcocks), Exeter (Stephen Weston), Lincoln (Richard Reynolds), St. Davids (Nicholas Claggett), Bangor (Thomas Herring), Chichester (Matthias Mawson), and Lichfied and Coventry (Richard Smallbrooke), and the future bishops Richard Terrick, Zachary Pearce, and John Thomas (1696–1781).[23] Bishop Robert Hay Drummond, who was elevated to archbishop of York in 1761 and chaired a special committee on Codrington in the 1760s, was immersed enough in plantation business to develop an opinion about renting slaves versus buying them, observing that "A negro of your own not only gives you his labor but is your property & part of your Capital" while "Negro-hire must always be a great expence, & your property is not encreased."[24] These arrangements contributed to the Society's growing collective sympathy for its fellow slave owners.

In addition to the manager and resident clergymen, Codrington was home to a few dozen other white people at any one point. The manager was assisted

Figure 13. "Codrington College" from Robert H. Schomburgk, *The History of Barbados . . .* (London, 1848). This view, from the upper portion of the estate, shows the college, lower plantation buildings, and Consett's Bay. (Courtesy of the Rare Book and Manuscript Library, University of Pennsylvania.)

by a small group of white employees—overseers, bookkeepers, sailors, apprentices, tradesmen working on the college—and this population blended with that of perhaps a dozen or so poor, white, tenant-farming families, who were resident on the estate when the Society took possession.[25] At least one free person of color also lived on the estate over the course of the century.[26] This small white and free population was always dramatically outnumbered by the typically several hundred enslaved people living on the plantation. These enslaved people primarily defined the Codrington community, and the cadences of their work structured life on the estate. Cultivating sugar required both "brute field labor and skilled artisanal knowledge," and Codrington's labor force was organized accordingly.[27] On the estate, in keeping with Caribbean norms, enslaved people were generally divided into three field gangs, with others serving as domestic servants, staffing the boiling house, acting as teamsters, and minding livestock. The first gang was the largest and undertook the most laborious and critical work: holing the ground, planting and harvesting canes, and carrying canes to the mills. The second gang, made up mainly of adolescent boys and girls, but which sometimes included older people deemed unequal to the rigors of first-gang work, was responsible for jobs such as planting corn, fertilizing, and weeding the cane fields. From the age of about seven or eight, children labored in the third gang, which undertook simpler tasks such as gathering fodder and weeding.[28] The annual work cycle culminated in the harvesting and processing of the cane, a period of intense labor that could last five to six months.[29] In addition to cultivating sugar, Codrington's people also worked to produce food and other necessities. As a result, almost all the enslaved people on Codrington worked for the Society for nearly all their lives. In the eighteenth-century Caribbean approximately 90 percent of all enslaved people worked, "probably one of the highest labour participation rates anywhere in the world."[30] A 1712 summary provided by Codrington's manager deemed 84 percent of the enslaved people living on the estate as fit for field labor.[31]

By the terms of Christopher Codrington's will, the estate was to have been continuously tended by a force of three hundred slaves. The Society's agents in Barbados similarly thought that at least three hundred laborers were necessary for the estate to be operated most profitably. However, in most years Codrington's enslaved population was well short of this number, primarily because of the appalling death rate for enslaved people on the estate, which mirrored the wider Caribbean experience.[32] In the period between the Society's takeover and 1748, deaths outnumbered births among enslaved people on Codrington by a ratio of six to one. The health effects of the Middle Passage across the Atlantic from West Africa and the susceptibility of African immigrants to disease led to particularly high mortality for newly imported people. Nutritional deficiencies and a punishing work regimen took further tolls.[33]

To keep the plantation running, Codrington's managers and attorneys frequently hired others' slaves at daily rates, an expensive and unreliable option, and continued to purchase enslaved people. They bought people with the explicit permission and support of the SPG's Barbados Committee, which had to approve the requisite expenditures. Between 1712 and 1761 the SPG bought approximately 450 people, an average of about nine per year. Despite these purchases and the birth of children on the estate, Codrington's enslaved population declined from 292 to approximately 190 over that period.[34] In 1761 the SPG decided to stop buying people from the Barbados slave market, but this decision was not born of altruism. Instead, the Society looked for other options because of how financially draining those purchases of newly imported people had proved to be. The SPG and its Barbados surrogates remained fully committed to the use of slave labor. In 1767, in a risky gambit to permanently solve its labor problem, the Society made a massive, long-term investment in the slave system when it purchased another Barbados plantation so that it could incorporate its enslaved people into Codrington's work gangs.[35]

These mortality rates had dramatic effects on the character of the community that the Society hoped to Christianize. Because Codrington's enslaved population was in near continuous rapid decline, managers incessantly fell behind in their efforts to keep the plantation "well stocked." At no point did they buy enough people to meet their labor demands once mortality rates were taken into account. So, managers overwhelmingly purchased those that they believed would quickly provide the most work: young men. Of the 162 enslaved people purchased during John Smalridge's twenty-one years as manager, 136 were male.[36] Similar practices continued under other managers. In 1741 the estate purchased twenty-one "New Negroes": twenty were "Boys from 16 to 20 years of age" and one was a girl of similar age.[37] In a self-perpetuating cycle, low birth rates and high death rates led to labor crises, which led to overwhelmingly male purchases, which further skewed sex ratios and hurt birth rates. A snapshot of Codrington's enslaved population in this period is provided by a detailed 1745 inventory. At that time, 236 enslaved people lived on the estate, and there were approximately two males for every female. Sex ratios were even more skewed for those people considered of prime working age. Among adults up to age forty, men outnumbered women 91 to 27.

This grim demographic regime meant that African-born people formed the major part of Codrington's slave population for most of the eighteenth century. Shortly before his death, Christopher Codrington had purchased approximately one hundred "new negroes," that is African transplants, and this group made up a large percentage of the estate's population when the Society took possession. Likewise, the approximately 450 people the Society purchased before 1761 were primarily Africans. In most years, a new group of African people was introduced onto the estate, and a large percentage of the total population at any given time was African-born. This trend remained unchallenged until at least 1761, when the Society committed to only buying Creole or "seasoned" slaves.[38] Enslaved people transported to the colonies brought with them, preserved, and adapted many elements of their own African cultural and religious lives, and in doing so shaped wider patterns in their new homes.[39] Recent studies of the slave trade have suggested that contrary to what was once thought, most slaving voyages probably did not result in jumbled human cargoes drawn from across West Africa, but in the transportation of relatively discrete and often identifiable groups of people drawn from specific regions in Africa. The distribution of Africans in the Americas may have been no more random than the distribution of Europeans.[40] While the relative influence of African cultures and the shared experience of enslavement in the colonies on the long-term development of African American and Afro-Caribbean culture continues to be debated, for much of the eighteenth century Codrington is notable for the continuing, direct, and regular contact the estate's community had with African life.[41]

The prevailing patterns of the slave trade to Barbados provide a framework for considering the origins of Codrington's population. Between 1688 and 1761 enslaved people sold on the island were drawn primarily from three adjacent areas on the central west African Coast: the Gold Coast (modern Ghana), the Bight of Benin (modern Togo, Benin, and western Nigeria), and the Bight of Biafra (from modern Nigeria south through to northern Gabon). These three regions accounted for nearly 80 percent of the people shipped from Africa to Barbados in the period.[42] These three regions provided nearly equal numbers of enslaved people to the Barbados market in total, but there were fluctuations in which region predominated. People from the Bight of Benin were particularly prevalent among those shipped to Barbados in the period before 1725, while those exported from the Bight of Biafra were the largest group imported into Barbados from around the mid-1740s. People from the Akan states that made up the Gold Coast were shipped to Barbados steadily throughout the period, with a particularly large number being sent there in the period between 1701 and 1725.[43]

In the years before SPG ownership of the plantation, the Codrington family favored the use of Akan or "Corramante" people from the Gold Coast on their plantations.[44] This preference for Akan people appears to have been shared by the SPG's agents. In 1725 John Smalridge reported that he had purchased "20 Callamantee Negro men" in the previous year.[45] The Barbados clergyman Griffith Hughes, who served as a Codrington attorney and had previously served

Table 1: **Enslaved People on Codrington Plantation, 1745**

Age	N	% of Total Population
Men		
19–40	91	38.6
41–65	40	16.9
Total Men	131	55.5
Boys		
0–10	6	2.5
11–18	19	8.1
Total Boys	25	10.6
Total Males	156	66.1
Women		
17–40	27	11.4
41–65	26	11
Total Women	53	22.5
Girls		
0–10	8	3.4
11–18	19	8.1
Total Girls	27	11.4
Total Females	80	33.9
Total Population	236	100

Source: SPG–L, "List of the Negroes, Cattle, Horses and Asses Living the 31st of December, 1745," C/Win/Bar8/126. This table repeats the source's categorization of individuals as "men" or "women." Males were considered "men" when they were estimated to be nineteen. In the case of females, some were listed as "women" at seventeen, while some eighteen-year-olds were still listed as "girls." Percentages affected by rounding.

as an SPG minister in Pennsylvania, observed in 1750 that on Barbados the "Coromantee" were "looked upon to be the best for Labour, being, in some measure, inured to it in their own country."[46] Enslaved Akans also had a reputation in several areas of the British Atlantic as being proud and particularly prone to revolt.[47] Christopher Codrington claimed that "Not a man of them but will stand to be cut to pieces without a sigh or groan, grateful and obedient to a kind master, but implacably revengeful when ill-treated."[48]

It also seems that the SPG joined other Barbados planters in buying people who were exported from the Bight of Benin. In 1741, the manager Abel Alleyne reported to the Society that "most of the Negroes are Guinea Negroes" of "the Caramantine & Papaw Country."[49] Enslaved people from the "Papaw Country" were shipped or drawn from the region around the two ports of Little Popo and Grand Popo (on either side of the modern Togo/Benin border respectively).[50] People from this region, also known as the Slave Coast, broadly shared a common culture and tended to speak one of a related group of languages.[51] "Papaws" too enjoyed a high reputation among many slaveholders in the British Atlantic. They were seen as accustomed to work, "skilled, complacent, and obedient," and particularly as more even-tempered than "Coromantees."[52] There are also indications that Codrington's managers may have reluctantly participated to some extent in the broader turn to people from the Bight of Biafra made by Barbados's planters from the 1740s on. In 1746 the manager John Payne reported to the Society that shortly after his arrival on the plantation, the attorneys had purchased "Tenn New Negro Men." Payne questioned the policy of purchasing so many new African-born people—he favored the purchase of much more expensive seasoned slaves—in part because "the Negros that are Brought here of late years are of Wild & Bad Countrys."[53]

Additional clues to the African origins of the people of the plantation are provided by documents that record them by name. Among those listed in a 1731 inventory was "Johnno Cutt face," probably a man with obviously distinctive "country marks" signaling his African birth.[54] A few people listed in such documents were recorded with particular ethnonyms attached to their names. For example, a man named Callamantee Sam was reported to have died on the estate soon after the SPG came into possession of it in 1712, and Jack Pawpaw was recorded as living on the estate in 1741.[55] Fanty Cuffey was living on the estate in 1742, likely a person from the coastal Akan state of Fante. Both Curram[an]te Quashey and Shantey Quashey, who was probably from the Gold Coast kingdom of Asante, were living on the estate in 1745.[56] Finally, there are also hints in these types of records that there were at least some representatives of other ethnic groups besides those of the Gold Coast and the Slave Coast on the estate. For example, "Johnno Congo," a fifty-year-old man living on the estate in 1745, was probably from the west central African kingdom of Kongo.[57]

There was also a smaller group of Creole enslaved people living on the estate. They included Codrington-born children and, more rarely, other Barbados-born people purchased on the island market. Given that the Africans purchased were overwhelmingly male, women living on the estate were more likely to be Barbados-born than were men. Because a higher percentage of the estate's women were Creole, they were less likely to succumb to the diseases that attacked African migrants particularly hard and more likely to reach relatively old age. In 1745, despite the fact that men outnumbered women on the estate by a two-to-one margin overall, women outnumbered men by twelve to eleven among those over the age of fifty. Among these Creoles were also some enslaved people of mixed race. "Mallatoe Robin" appeared on a 1731 inventory.[58] In 1750 the attorneys ordered that an inventory of "Negroes and Near kind" be taken.[59] In 1783 "Quasheba Mulatto" was reported to have run away.[60] In a significant long-term transformation, and one which mirrored wider trends in Caribbean demographics, Creole people gradually became the predominant group on the estate. This required both a cessation of the buying of Africans and a slave community in which birth rates outpaced death rates. This transformation took place slowly, beginning perhaps with the switch to buying only "seasoned" people in the 1760s and becoming notable after 1793, when annual natural increases in Codrington's population finally became the rule. By 1822 all but one of the enslaved people living on the estate was Barbados-born.[61]

Understanding the missionary encounter that took place on Codrington requires taking these demographic, work, and cultural dynamics into account. Soon after obtaining possession of the estate, the Society sent Joseph Holt, who was Cambridge-educated, proficient in both theology and medicine, and had lived for many years in the colonies, to act as catechist.[62] Holt's salary was by SPG standards a large one, £100 per year, and he was equipped with a chest of medicines so that he, in conformity with Codrington's wishes, could minister to the bodies and souls of those he encountered.[63] Despite these preparations, Holt's work among Codrington's slaves was from the first a dismal failure. Enslaved people were dying at a rapid rate on the plantation, and Holt's medicine was largely unable to stop it.[64] In June 1713, soon after arriving on the estate, Holt reported an "abundance of Negro's infirm and diseased, some blind, Sundry dimsighted, others have the Yaws, Ulcers, Tumors, Lameness, besides common Sicknesses which are the daily infirmities."[65] John Smalridge rated the summer of 1713 the sickliest in his experience on Barbados, but death and disease continued to be rampant on Codrington in the 1710s and 1720s.[66]

Holt's religious labors met with no better results than his medical interventions. He felt strongly that without a chapel on the estate, religious services could not be conducted with regularity and decency. His insistence on propriety was poorly suited to his station. The death of a Barbadian clergyman meant a vacancy in a local parish, and Holt began serving as interim minister. The Society refused him permission to hold the position permanently but learned a short time later that Holt had abandoned his mission and "gone to Pensilvania or Maryland on his Own Private Affairs."[67] By the 1720s he was back in Barbados serving as a parish clergyman, but experience had left him pessimistic and skeptical about most enslaved people's fitness for Christian education. In 1724 he noted that on the island "Free Negro's are commonly Baptized, So are some Natives, which are capable of Instruction but Transported Slaves are Stupidly ignorant, and it's a long time before they understand any thing of Our Speech."[68] The Society's inability to effect conversions at Codrington in this period cannot be attributed solely to Holt's failings. Some of his immediate successors died soon after their arrival in Barbados; none of them made much impression. By 1726, sixteen years after the death of Christopher Codrington, not one of the Society's slaves had even been baptized. Given its stated commitment to Christianizing enslaved people on the estate and elsewhere, this was a serious failure of duty on the Society's own terms.

In 1726, with the membership focusing attention on the conversion of slaves around the Atlantic, the SPG named Thomas Wilkie as catechist and schoolmaster. From then until the mid-1740s, under the direction of several committed catechists and with the support of SPG attorney and Barbados parish clergyman Arthur Holt (Joseph Holt's son), there were real and sustained efforts to convert enslaved people on Codrington.[69] Unlike his predecessors, Wilkie was a long-term presence on the estate, serving for nearly seven years. He was not ordained, but he received the same salary as Joseph Holt had. The successes of Elias Neau, another lay catechist, may have figured in the Society's decision to appoint Wilkie rather than another clergyman.[70]

Wilkie's appointment coincided with more hardship on the plantation. Between 1723 and 1725, seventy-three enslaved people died but only seven were born. Sugar production fell in tandem with the slave population, declining from 179 hogsheads in the good year 1722 to 113 in 1724 to only 89 in 1726. In response, Smalridge and the attorneys stepped up their purchases from the Bridgetown slave market, buying forty men in the period between 1724 and 1726, and twenty-four men in 1727 alone.[71] This placed large groups of people just arrived from Africa on the estate exactly as Wilkie began working. Marking the start of a nearly twenty-year hiatus in efforts to achieve Christopher Codrington's educational vision, the Society decided to "defer finishing the college because they think it most necessary to purchase a number of Negros before they make further expences in Building."[72] Despite recent purchases, there were only 215 enslaved people on the plantation at the start of 1728, a number seen as dangerously low.[73]

The situation became desperate for those who remained on the estate. Enslaved people ran away from Codrington throughout the eighteenth century, but they were running at a particularly rapid rate in the mid-1720s. Twice in 1724, the plantation paid the standard reward of two and a half shillings for the return of runaways. It paid five such rewards between January and July 1725. In August 1725, there was a particularly large breakout, and Codrington paid rewards for the recapture of five escapees in one month. Smalridge responded to this turmoil by cracking down. On November 13, 1724, the estate paid for "a Silver mark to mark ye Negros Society" which appears to have been the beginning of the human branding that was common on the estate until 1732, when Arthur Holt's complaints seem to have put a stop to it.[74]

The branding of enslaved people with the word "Society" was the most infamous effort to control Codrington's population, but it was not the only one. Smalridge asked the Society for permission to use the intercolonial slave trade to "sell or ship off such Negroes that prove sickly, Lazy, Runaways or otherwise useless on the Estates, and recruit the like Numbers by purchasing others that are more able and willing to work."[75] Smalridge thought an added benefit would be the terrorizing of other enslaved people into obedience, noting that "I hope the rumor of shipping will make some of them mend there Manners."[76] This mode of coercion was not foreign to the SPG, which had heard Elias Neau's complaints that some of his catechumens had been "threaten'd to be sold to Virginia or into the Countrey if they came any more to School."[77] Some members balked at the moral, or perhaps just public relations, implications of the plan. "At the Committee, that part of the Order relateing to Mr. Smalridge's disposeing of the sickly negroes and Infirm being Inserted in the Abstract of the Society's proceedings the same was Objected to, as being Inconsistent with the pious Designs of the Society." But by 1722 the SPG gave him permission to ship disorderly slaves.[78] Over the next three years, Smalridge separated eleven people from any family and friends they had on the estate and sent them to the Chesapeake for resale.[79]

Smalridge's battles with his largely African, undersized, and overworked labor force affected Wilkie's attempts to convert these people to Christianity. Soon after his arrival on Barbados, Wilkie noted that the Society's younger slaves were "very docile & capable to learn any thing, but that so soon as they are capable of doing they are imployed in looking after the cattle & stock so that they have but very little time to learn in."[80] Smalridge, however, like most other managers the Society employed, seems to have been more concerned with maintaining productivity and discipline on the estate than with Christianizing slaves. In 1729 the SPG, on hearing from Barbados that Wilkie's work was being undermined, reiterated its instructions to Smalridge:

[T]he Society have very much at heart this good work the Instruction of the Negroes, and therefore they do hereby strictly require you to give your best assistance to promote this work; In order thereto the Society would have the Negroes allowed Saturday afternoon for them to work for themselves, to prevent their working on Sundays and that you would order the Negroes on proper times to attend Mr. Wilkie for instruction.[81]

The continuing tensions between making profits and making converts on Codrington were powerful. As the instructions that Smalridge "order the Negroes" to attend the catechist also suggest, even when the Society pushed the Christianization project, the results for Codrington's people could be complex. Like the Society's membership in London, Wilkie thought that Smalridge's disciplinary power should be extended to furthering the conversion of souls. "Mr. Smalridge may be very assisting in this good work in commanding the younger to come to me at such times as they can be spared for they dread his displeasure."[82]

The multisided ramifications of the SPG's interest in conversion can be seen particularly in the ongoing struggles over how Sundays should be spent on Codrington, which the Society's letter to Smalridge also addressed. Enslaved people on Barbados were typically freed from fieldwork on Sundays, and they jealously guarded that time for working in their small personal gardens and attending markets, where the island's black and poor white population mixed and traded. Sunday was also the one day of the week that enslaved people could spend largely as they saw fit. As Thomas Wharton, a Codrington chaplain and later an SPG attorney for the estate, explained, "Sundays in particular they claim to themselves, and to be deprived on that day of their visits and little Traffick one among another would be a Task to them more abundantly cruel than the Labour of a Week."[83]

Most missionary-minded Anglicans believed that, especially for adults, baptism needed to be preceded by a period of education, which would teach people the principles of Christianity and ensure their embrace of Christian morality. They were deeply critical of what they considered the token baptisms achieved by their Roman Catholic rivals and held that doing missionary work properly required time. To the SPG membership in London, Sundays were the obvious time for enslaved people to be instructed in Christianity and to participate in religious services. Moreover, Sunday should be a day of pious rest, not a day for marketing and disorderly social mixing. This was an issue of circum-Atlantic scope for the Society. Elias Neau had complained that slaves in New York would "dance & divert themselves" on Sundays.[84] In 1712 SPG ministers in South Carolina complained that slaves' Sunday work was a major obstacle to religious instruction there.[85] The Society attempted on several occasions to attach a measure to bills regulating the slave trade, which would have required masters to allow their slaves to attend church on Sundays.[86]

In return for spending their Sundays in religious instruction, SPG members thought that Codrington's people should be given Saturday afternoons to work in their gardens and to see to their material needs. When Joseph Holt went to Barbados in 1713, the Society's attorneys and overseer on Codrington were ordered that "they Give Liberty to the Slaves to work for themselves every Saturday in the afternoon To the intent they may have time to attend Instructions in Religion on the Lord's day and in consideration of that permission that they be prevented from working on Sundays."[87] Similar instructions were given to a succession of catechists, attorneys, and overseers well into the nineteenth century.[88]

The Society's instructions pleased almost no one on Codrington and were long resisted. To the managers, it probably appeared that the Society was naive about running a plantation. A half-day's labor, one-twelfth of the workweek, could not be eliminated without affecting profitability.[89] Moreover, it dangerously upset the estate's accepted routine. For Codrington's enslaved people, the change entailed trading one day of relative freedom for a half-day of relative freedom and a day centered around Christian education and worship. While this might presumably mean fewer total hours in the field each week, the plantation was still to be worked by the same number of enslaved people, and this labor loss does not appear to have been incorporated into, for example, deciding how much cane to plant in a given year. Since Sundays were to be dedicated to religious instruction and appropriate Christian rest, Codrington's people would also lose some of the time they were able to spend on their own crops and other affairs. The SPG-advocated system also deprived enslaved people of the social and material benefits of attending the island's Sunday markets, which seems to have been particularly resented. As one commentator noted in 1740, though the slaves were "allowed Saturday afternoon to themselves yet they cant be prevailed on to attend [catec]hising on Sunday morning."[90] In 1745 a catechist complained of "the bad Notions which the Negroes in the neighbouring Plantations endeavour to instil into those of our own: They represent to them the Hardship they labor under by being obliged to appear at the College every Sunday in the Afternoon."[91]

The amenability of enslaved people to the Society's religious message was probably also affected by the fact that its Barbados employees from Smalridge on whipped, jailed, and otherwise punished them over the course of many decades to control them and force them to work. Barbados attorneys reminded the Society's members in 1768 that "to govern upwards of 300 negroes on one plantation is no easy task, it requires a good deal of address, and unless a proper decorum and subordination is kep'd up they will soon become turbulent and unruly, for after all those who know them best must allow that they are a most inconsiderate and thoughtless race of mortals."[92] In 1778, a Barbadian reported to the Society that the "Negroes and Mulatto Slaves upon their plantations" were being "treated in the most inhumane and Cruel manner" by a particularly vicious plantation manager.[93] As both the Society's agents and its slaves realized, the economic system in place on the estate was maintained by the constant threat of violence.

Resolving these tensions would have required a thoroughgoing transformation of Codrington's operations, but the membership continued to expect it to be profitable. While the Society frequently instructed its managers and attorneys to institute free Saturdays, none of these men ever lost his position over the issue. Smalridge, who long thwarted implementation, served as manager for more than two decades. Even when the Society ordered slave conversion to be pressed, the estate continued to function first and foremost as a sugar plantation. As a result, work was the standing order for enslaved people, and children labored in the plantation's third gang from the age of seven or eight. Codrington's accounts tell the tale poignantly. A 1756 list of English manufactured goods requested for use on the plantation included four dozen hoes "Very Small for Children."[94] As long as even young children were put to nearly continuous work, no education program proved very successful. This continued for decades. As one manager succinctly put it as late as 1796, "the Younger Negroes cannot be spared any time during the Week days from their usual & appointed work, the Estates requiring much labour."[95] Making time for religious instruction was almost always subservient to the estate's labor needs.

Resistance by Codrington's enslaved people demonstrates that they did not look on the SPG as their benefactor. Some enslaved people on the plantation found their situation so hopeless that they committed suicide. Three out of ten "new Negroes" purchased as a group by Smalridge in 1714 killed themselves; Jack Smith "Hang'd himself" in 1746.[96] Other enslaved people stole food and other property from Codrington and neighboring plantations.[97] Jack General, "belonging to the Society's upper estate," was hanged by the island's magistrates in 1778 for stealing an ox. A woman owned by the SPG was executed by authorities in 1780 as "an abettor in the murder of a white man."[98] Despite Bishop Fleetwood's 1711 claim that Christopher Codrington's bequest made the Society "patrons" to the plantation's slaves, these acts of desperation, resentment, and self-assertion reveal harder truths about the continuing antagonism that existed on the estate.

Sampson Smirk, another layman, succeeded Wilkie as catechist in 1733, and his decade on the estate saw larger numbers of baptisms than many other periods in the century. Nevertheless, it was at this point that the most serious resistance preserved in the Codrington records occurred. In 1738 the plantation's enslaved population had sunk to under two hundred, and the workload for those still alive must have been particularly intense. In late June the manager John Vaughton reported to the Society that "Extraordinary Disorders amongst the Society's Slaves occured." A group of enslaved people had left the plantation without permission and traveled in a body to Bridgetown. There, they complained to Mr. Johnson (probably the Rev. William Johnson, SPG attorney and rector of St. Michael's parish) of their "hard labour, hard usage, whant of Cloaths, Victual, &c." They made a series of demands including that Vaughton should "part with a Book keeper who is a diligent Watchfull Servant" and "that I should keep no more then One white and One Black Overseer." These complaints about working conditions, deprivation, and the behavior of overseers suggest that despite a then-active conversion program, life on the estate was so intolerable for enslaved people that they were willing to run extraordinary risks to change things.

Codrington's people remained in Bridgetown overnight. How Johnson responded to their demands is not recorded, but it seems they were promised that some reforms would be undertaken. They agreed to return home, "but came thro the Country Singing and Dancing with drawn knives as great as if they had gain'd a conquest." When they arrived back on the estate the situation was tense. Vaughton convinced them to return to work the next day but seems to have reneged on any promises made in Bridgetown. "When I had them all in the field I was Under anxiety to lett them know that the Country would not Submitt to Such Agreements." Vaughton and the Society's attorneys restored discipline. Some people were put "under confinement" on the plantation. While the attorneys did not endorse "any Extream Punishment as the taking of life &c," which the colony's laws allowed, two leaders were sent to Bridgetown jail, and the attorneys approved having them "Publickly whipt Several times in Town" and then receiving "Punishment likewise" when they were brought back to Codrington. Vaughton protested that enslaved people were well treated on the plantation in terms that underlined the ubiquity of violence there—"I am well sattisfied they Never had fewer stripes"—and thought that the protest was especially treacherous because its leaders were favorites who had worked in notably easy jobs.[99] These people's anger, and the extraordinary and dangerous method of protest they adopted, show that they found ways to resist the conditions of their enslavement regardless of the Society's religious goals.

It also appears that the SPG's deepening embrace of slavery, visible elsewhere by the 1740s, affected the way conversion was approached on Codrington. In 1741 the Society's secretary informed its plantation manager, Abel Alleyne, that "moderate correction" could be used against any slaves who refused to attend Sunday services.[100] Later that year, Alleyne noted that, in accordance with those instructions, he had been "forc'd to use a little moderate Correction"—that is people were whipped or beaten—to encourage the slaves to attend catechist Smirk more regularly.[101] Alleyne, who served from 1740 to 1746, was part of a prominent Barbados family and additionally atypical as a manager in that he had previously served as a Codrington attorney and was a member of the SPG.[102] After Smirk's death in 1744, Alleyne took up the catechist's duties himself. As catechist, Alleyne claimed to operate under the principle that "things that are forc'd on a person never digest so well" and therefore said he relied on persuasion rather than force to increase his slaves' attendance. As he reported to the Society, his classes were well attended, with audiences of "about 130 Negroes that understand English tollerably well."[103]

Were Alleyne's catechism classes intrinsically more appealing to the plantation's enslaved people than his predecessors? Perhaps they were, but in any case the "persuasive" power of the overseer to secure their attendance was stronger than that of anyone else on the estate, and attracting his displeasure was dangerous for enslaved people. As one subsequent SPG catechist put it, "The Manager of an Estate in Barbados hath so great Influence over his Negroes, that one threatening Word from him will have greater Effect, than any Thing that can be inculcated to them as a Duty incumbent upon them to perform."[104] Alleyne's efforts did not make all Codrington's people converts, but they did reflect an increasing willingness to use slavery and the power of masters as a vehicle for the delivery of Christianity. The SPG granted Alleyne a gift equivalent to the catechist's salary in recognition of his work.[105]

In slave societies around the Atlantic world, the links between spiritual and temporal power were often apparent.[106] These interconnections were inescapable on Codrington, where employees wielded both the Bible and the whip in the SPG's name. Enslaved people acted accordingly. On the Society's estate not participating in religious instruction could be an act of resistance; not embracing the tenets of Christianity was one of the ways its enslaved people could assert their independence. Thomas Wilkie noted in 1727 that not only did enslaved people have very little free time for religious instruction, they were also "very unwilling to come near me and many times when they see me run away and hide themselves among the bushes."[107] Slaves were so unwilling to spend time in catechism classes in the mid-1740s that Thomas Rotheram thought that whoever ran the plantation "must exert his authority over them in punishing those who neglect or refuse to appear at the Time appointed. For unless he does this, the Chatechist must expect to labour in vain."[108] Even in 1796, the Reverend William Thomas cited young enslaved peoples' "obstinacy & their aversion to restraint at their leisure hours" as obstacles to their instruction.[109] Codrington's people were not just the objects of a badly managed conversion effort. Because

Christian education and plantation discipline frequently merged into one system of slave control on the estate, enslaved people seem to have largely rejected the Society's message.

If tensions between its missionary aims and its slave mastership undermined the Society's proselytizing on Codrington, so too did the existence of religious and cultural alternatives to Anglicanism. Evidence for the continuing cultural influence of West Africa on the plantation is diverse and chronologically broad. African languages were spoken on the estate throughout the eighteenth century. Catechists complained about many slaves' inability to speak English. Sampson Smirk noted in 1741 that "they cannot spake English and what they act and do in the plantation affairs is more by Signes than Speech."[110] Another two decades of SPG ownership of the plantation did not result in the slave community's full adoption of English. John Hodgson, chaplain from 1758 to 1760, reported repeatedly that enslaved people did not understand English and that "their language [is] extremely rude and defective." Probably reflecting the divides between Creole and African-born people and the intense labor requirements placed on field hands, Hodgson said that all he had attempted, and thought that could be attempted, was "the Instruction of those Negroes who are immediately employed about the House" who "were more civilized than the rest."[111] Likewise, the continuing prevalence of African-derived names among the enslaved people living on the estate suggests that they retained connections to Africa recognized by them and the Society's white employees.[112]

West African people brought their own religions with them to the Americas in general and to Barbados in particular, and important elements of African religious practice long continued to exist on the estate.[113] While SPG missionaries hoped to establish Christianity on Codrington, the African and Afro-Caribbean people who lived there decided largely for themselves how religion would operate in their lives. The SPG's agents typically reported that the Africans who lived on Codrington were entirely ignorant of Christianity. There are good reasons to be suspicious of those claims, since Christianity was first introduced to many West African peoples in Africa itself, primarily through the Roman Catholic Church.[114] Any Kongolese people on the estate, such as Johnno Congo, could well have been baptized in Africa, since baptism was particularly important to the Catholic Christianity practiced in that kingdom.[115] In the places from which most of Codrington's people were drawn—the Gold and Slave Coasts—Catholic missionary work was more restricted and less successful, but Portuguese, Spanish, French and Italian priests all made visits to the region in the seventeenth and eighteenth centuries, as did small numbers of Protestant clergymen. There is no direct evidence of Roman Catholicism among Codrington's people, but at least some of them likely encountered it in America. Christopher Codrington seems to have acquired enslaved people connected to the French Caribbean. Likewise, when the estate was under SPG control enslaved people named Franswa (François), French Jone, Deagoe, Margaritta, and French Miah all lived on it.[116]

The SPG's Barbados correspondents were also silent about any influence Islam may have had on the estate, but large numbers of enslaved Muslim people were present in the Americas.[117] Given the West African origins of much of Codrington's population, many of them would have been familiar with Islam, and some may well have considered themselves Muslim.[118] Among the enslaved people living on Codrington in the 1740s were a women and a girl named Fattimore (also spelled "Fattemoor"). Fatima has been noted as an "incontestably Muslim name" that appeared among American slaves. Also among the enslaved people living on the estate in the 1740s were men named Yassan and Hussan, names that also may have had Arabic roots.[119]

In the absence of direct reports, the presence of Roman Catholic or Muslim people on Codrington can only be surmised. However, it is clear that at least some of the estate's people engaged in practices derived from indigenous West African religions. Anglican ministers had long worried that the prevalence of African cultural and religious practices on Barbados prevented the spread of Christianity. Morgan Godwyn had observed that nothing was "more barbarous, and contrary to Christianity" than Barbados slaves' "*Polygamy*, their *Idolatrous Dances*, and *Revels*," in which they would usually spend their Sundays after working in their gardens. This dancing, Godwyn claimed, was used "as a *means to Procure Rain*," while slaves were also guilty of "placing confidence in certain Figures, and ugly Representations," which "they usually enshrine in some stately *Earthen Potsherds*."[120] Especially significant was slaves' continued use of and belief in benevolent and malevolent witchcraft, particularly in the form of obeah, adapted from West African traditions.[121] The presence of obeah on Codrington in the eighteenth century, despite its obvious incompatibility with the SPG's religious aspirations, testifies to the continued commitment of its people to African-inspired cultural and religious traditions.[122]

Arthur Holt noted the existence of obeah on Barbados repeatedly. In 1729 he observed that catechists were needed to "prevent the Slaves from following some bad Practices" such as working on Sundays, meeting together on Sundays "to perform their heathen Sacrifices at the Graves of the Dead," and giving "Encouragement" to "their Oby [obeah] Negroes or Conjurers, to which Multitudes are in Slavery."[123] In the same year, Holt wrote the bishop of London in terms that, though pejorative, underlined the power of obeah not only across Barbados but on Codrington in particular. He wished that "sufficient care was taken to

restrain the Negroes of this island, and especially those on the Society's plantations from what they call their plays (frequently performed on the Lord's Days)"
which featured "horrid music, howling, and dancing about the graves of the
dead." At these "plays," enslaved people would "offer victuals and strong liquors
to the souls of the deceased, to keep them (as they pretend) from appearing to
hurt them." The "Oby Negroes or conjurors are the leaders, to whom the others
are in slavery for fear of being bewitched." Holt thought that "whilst these things
are permitted, Christianity is likely to make but slow advances.[124] The existence
of obeah practitioners on Codrington in the late 1720s meant that there was a
powerful alternative to the religion offered by the SPG's catechists during the
very period when the Society was most committed to undertaking the conversion of slaves there. Despite the efforts of planters and ministers, the practice of
obeah proved impossible to eradicate. In 1750 Griffith Hughes noted that on the
island "The Negroes are very tenaciously addicted to the Rites, Ceremonies, and
Superstitions of their own Countries, particularly in their Plays, Dances, Music,
Marriages, and Burials."[125]

Obeah men and women acted as both spiritual intermediaries and physical
healers.[126] This connection between medical and spiritual power was not
unique to West African religions. Many Christian miracles involved physical
healing, but because of the prevalence in Barbadian slave culture of a strong
belief that sickness and death were the product of malevolent witchcraft, the
dual role of obeah men and women was particularly pronounced.[127] Christopher
Codrington—perhaps based on his experience of living among enslaved West
Africans—wanted his college to produce missionaries with medical training so
they could "Both indear themselves to the People and have the better opportunitys of doeing good To mens Souls whilst they are Takeing Care of their Bodys."[128]
While enslaved people were probably reluctant to let missionaries witness their
practice of obeah, the estate's business records give a fuller sense of what occurred from day to day. Plantation managers—usually more concerned with the
physical fitness of Codrington's people than with their souls—seem to have
believed in the efficacy of black medical practitioners. In 1731 the estate paid 5
shillings to a "Negro Doctor" for curing a sick enslaved person. In 1745 the
estate paid the forty-year-old Codrington man Titus 2s. 6d. for curing his fellow
slave "of the Guinea Worms."[129] Despite his evidently respected position on the
estate, Titus is recorded as unbaptized in two lists prepared in the early 1740s.[130]
The presence of enslaved people in such roles is a further indication that African-
influenced cultural practices had a long-term presence on the estate that was
recognized by the Society's Barbados representatives.

Codrington's catechists operated in a community that had a viable competing
set of spiritual and cultural practices. While they succeed in baptizing some

enslaved people, many remained unbaptized, and missionaries bemoaned what they considered the religious and moral failings of even those who had been initiated into the church. Many of Codrington's people were reluctant to convert or conform to Anglicanism because they continued to find utility and meaning in other traditions. This was evident in conflicts over the marital status and sexual lives of enslaved people. A succession of men connected with the Society complained of the promiscuity of the estate's people and their preference for "polygamy" throughout the eighteenth century. Many Anglican clergymen from around the Atlantic world made similar complaints about black and white parishioners. Arthur Holt, for example, reported to the bishop of London on white Barbadians "who debauch them selves with their Infidel Slaves and inhumanly Subject their unhappy offspring to Bondage."[131] However, the marriage and sexual practices of enslaved people on Codrington were seen by Society members as particularly scandalous because they believed its property should serve as a model of a well-ordered, Christian plantation. As a result, the issue was one the Society often raised with its Barbados representatives.

Typically, the perceived unwillingness of Codrington's people to partner according to Anglo-Christian norms was presented as evidence simply of their lax morality. But the estate's demographics suggest that something more complicated than simple "immorality" was at work. Men outnumbered women on the estate by a two-to-one margin for much of the eighteenth century. Despite this skewed sex ratio, the SPG's missionaries and other agents reported frequently that enslaved men had multiple "wives." Thomas Wilkie took it as a victory when he persuaded three of his catechumens "to content themselves with one wife a piece" in 1727.[132] William Duke noted in 1741 that enslaved men "allow themselves the Liberty of having many Wifes and cannot be restrained in other Vices which if they were well Principled in Religion they must forsake."[133] John Hodgson claimed in 1760 that polygamy was a "perpetual Bar to their Admission of Christianity."[134] If these reports were accurate, some of these relationships probably involved partners living on other plantations, which may also have affected enslaved people's responses to efforts to keep them on the estate and in religious instruction on Sundays.

Abel Alleyne, whose interest in slave conversion made him particularly curious about such issues, reported on the situation in some detail in 1741. In answer to the SPG's concern about the mores predominant on the estate, he reported that not only did some of the estate's unconverted men have multiple wives, so too did some of those who were Christian. He felt the custom was so entrenched that it was "as impossible to prevent as anything in the World." Though other SPG commentators saw only sinfulness, Alleyne was more alive to the multiple meanings of enslaved people's practices. He observed, "whether they take it to be a piece of grand use, or whether 'tis from a Lustfull inclination, or whether 'tis that they are such lovers of their Belly that they may expect more Victuals from having more Wifes I can't say but this I know, it frequently makes them great Villains to equip those Wifes as they call them with finery."[135] As Alleyne suggested, these relationships could involve issues of personal status and material well-being, and as such reflected the continued power and adaptability of African-derived practices on the estate. In concluding his thoughts, Alleyne told the Society that these patterns could be changed only if "they cou'd be brought to a true Sense of the Christian religion and be regularly married to a Christian black, for those that have Wifes, only take them as they like them and so part with them at their pleasure." He would work "as far as I can endeavour to prevent this inconvenientcy and have allways shown the utmost dislike to it."[136] As plantation manager, Alleyne had as much power as anyone on the estate to compel enslaved people, but he thought that such a change could be wrought only by a far-reaching religious and cultural transformation.

The SPG's white employees were a tiny Euro-Christian minority on the estate, and the enslaved population on Codrington responded to Christianity in the context of that cultural dynamic. Enslaved people born on the estate were baptized as children and some adults were baptized after catechetical efforts, but most people remained unincorporated into Christianity at even this most basic of levels. A 1741 list of the 202 enslaved people then living on the estate recorded that 71 of them had been baptized and 131 remained unbaptized.[137] More than this, few enslaved people on Codrington appeared willing to live in ways that the Society's ministers deemed as befitting members of the Church of England. As Abel Alleyne noted in 1741, "I must own they are a Sett of possitive Obstinate People and will frequently relapse into the Neglect of their Duty after many fair promises."[138] The manager attributed these peoples' unwillingness to practice Christianity and accept Christian morality to their "ignorance," but their steadfastness was the expression of the continued attraction that other cultural and religious norms held for them.

In 1745 the missionary Joseph Bewsher provided a telling summary of what had happened on the estate since the 1720s. While he believed Alleyne had accomplished more than other catechists, he still found fewer than twenty enslaved people on Codrington "who could repeat their catechism" and those were not older than "12 or 13 years of age," presumably children who had been born and raised on the estate. As for older people on Codrington, some of whom "have had the Privilidge of Instruction there [for] more than 20 years, they appear'd as ignorant of their Duty to God as if they had arrived from Guinea a month before." Bewsher would not determine whether this was "owing to negligence or want of capacity"—although his raising of the specter of black "capacity" was a harbinger of things to come—but it was largely a reflection of the choices made by enslaved people.[139] Around the Atlantic world, the Society promoted the idea that paternalistic Christian mastership was the key to the conversion of enslaved people. Its own experiences on Barbados in its first four decades reveal that this focus was often a poor substitute for finding ways to appeal to the religious needs of enslaved people themselves.

In the mid-1740s, following Alexander Garden's Charleston example, the Society experimented with having two Barbados-born enslaved people serve as teachers, but this plan did not produce a major religious change on the estate and was soon abandoned. By 1751, when the clergyman John Rotheram arrived as a new catechist, the local and metropolitan commitment to the conversion of Codrington's people had waned considerably while around the Atlantic the SPG's ties to the slave system had deepened. Rotheram's career reflects some of the developments in the Society's efforts to convert enslaved people that had occurred by mid-century. Rotheram later became a noted theologian after his return to England, making him the most intellectually renowned of the people the Society employed as a missionary to Native American or black people in the eighteenth century. His time on Barbados was a period of notable development for the educational institution on the plantation. A grammar school for white children opened in 1745, and besides acting as catechist he taught in it as it flourished under the headmastership of his brother Thomas Rotheram.

The Rotheram brothers' tenure was also a period in which the school's teachers became the dominant force on the estate. Between 1748 and 1753, the SPG appointed the clergymen they sent to Codrington as both missionaries and as the estate's only attorneys, giving them local power not just over religious and educational matters but also over the business of the plantation.[140] Both Rotherams served in this capacity. This arrangement gave the Society's religious emissaries unprecedented, direct control over many aspects of the lives of Codrington's people. It also reflected how comfortable with mastership the Society, as an organization, had become. Theoretically, since this management system considerably lessened the possibility that the Society's religious goals among enslaved people could be undermined by unsympathetic Barbadian agents, this might have seemed to be a time for a renewed push to Christianize the estate's population.

However, while the Rotherams' time as schoolmasters was one of the periods in which "the school achieved its greatest progress," it was not one in which the SPG would be particularly committed to the conversion of the enslaved people it owned on the estate.[141] Both in England and in Barbados the focus in these years was elsewhere, and the period between 1745 and 1760 saw few conversions. Rotheram's service on the estate coincided with a period of "striking decline in the Society's attentiveness to the educational progress of its slaves." Despite the push that the Society had made to convert enslaved people on the estate in the 1720s and 1730s, in this period the SPG "ceased to demand frequent and regular returns from its agents" and "appeared little moved by their passive acceptance of defeat." Although he was personally responsible for the work, Rotheram's letters to the Society between 1751 and 1753 "made no mention of the religious program" to convert enslaved people.[142] Instead, he concentrated primarily on his own theological research and writing. In the words of his entry in the *Dictionary of National Biography*, "his increased leisure time while connected with the college" afforded Rotheram the opportunity to develop his scholarship.[143]

Rotheram's lack of interest in the conversion of enslaved people was not unique in these years. The Reverend Thomas Falcon and the Reverend John Hodgson, who followed the Rotherams on Codrington, sent the Society "a melancholy Account of the difficulties that attend the religious instruction of the Negroes, particularly the field Negroes." The Society's formulaic assessment of their reports, recorded in 1760, spoke volumes about the pessimism that had set in about the prospects for slave conversion. "This cannot be too much lamented, but as we are fully satisfied of the ability and attention of these gentlemen in this pious work, we trust in God that their perseverance will be rewarded with better Success."[144]

Increasingly, the SPG's representatives thought that converting enslaved people was almost impossible. Hodgson, the Society's catechist from 1758 to 1760, believed there were "insuperable" barriers to the conversion of slaves:

> They must be talked to in a Language which they do not understand, they must be talked to upon Subjects, which from their being void of all the Principles to which Application should be made, or filled with such, as render their minds still more inaccessible, cannot take the least Hold of them; and they must be talk'd to, not in a collective Capacity, but one by one, it being absolutely necessary to inculcate upon each Individual, even when they are most civiliz'd the several Particulars that are taught them to a degree of Repetition, which can hardly be conceived.[145]

The antipathy of Hodgson and his successors, combined with the Society membership's declining interest in pushing the conversion project, meant that Christianizing enslaved people was effectively dropped as a program even on the SPG's own property. In 1769 the Society learned that no catechetical work had been undertaken on Codrington since 1760.[146] The enthusiasm of earlier decades had been replaced by manifest apathy.

While profitable in many years, Codrington often failed to produce the large, reliable annual income that the Society hoped it would due to poor crops, the expenses associated with building and running the school, and costly mortality among its enslaved labor force. In an effort to contain costs and improve returns, the SPG made a risky attempt in the mid-1760s to enlarge the plantation's permanent workforce by purchasing another Barbados plantation, bringing its slaves to Codrington, and selling the purchased land. The plan, which involved a massive outlay of cash on the SPG's part, threatened to bankrupt the Society itself when the purchaser of the land defaulted on his payments.[147] The imperial crisis of the American Revolution, which devastated the Barbados economy, exacerbated the estate's problems. The school for white Barbados boys operating on Codrington was closed because of financial difficulties in 1775.

Between 1783 and 1793 the SPG leased the estate to a Barbados planter, John Brathwaite, in order to stop its losses and prevent Codrington from draining the Society's stretched general operating fund. This arrangement precluded the Society from direct involvement in the operation of the plantation. In practice it also meant that the slave conversion project was almost entirely abandoned. After the Society resumed control of a financially more stable Codrington in 1793, it implemented an increasingly thorough policy of improving the living conditions of its enslaved people. Like other masters the Society instituted reforms—better food, housing, and working conditions—in an attempt to more efficiently manage its property and restarted efforts to catechize an increasingly creolized population. In implementing these material and religious reforms, the Society was not acting as a pioneer but largely in response to external criticism and the changing economic and social dynamics on Barbados. As the estate's population became more Creole, its people also had their own reasons for being more interested in educational and religious programs in this period.

In 1770 the catechist Thomas Butcher was ordered, like many of his predecessors, to refocus on converting slaves. The SPG's constant emphasis on the harmony between Christianity and slavery sapped Anglicanism's appeal among many prospective black converts. This was particularly true on Codrington. Butcher grasped this essential:

> Your last letter I have received, and shall comply as punctually as I am able with the Society's injunctions respecting the Negroes. To every humane & benevolent heart, it must undoubtedly be ⌊a⌋ matter of the greatest concern to see the thick cloud of intellectual darkness spread over so great a part of the creation; and that concern must be still

heightened, when it is considered that slavery is at variance with, that it combats every principle of Christianity. Were they free, they would soon be Christians.[148]

As Codrington's population was all too aware, the SPG never took Butcher's point. Presented with a religious message bound up with slavery, the eighteenth-century estate's enslaved people largely rejected missionary Anglicanism, found ways to resist their enslavement, and continued to find meaning in their own religious and cultural practices.

"One of their Own Color and Kindred"

Philip Quaque and the SPG Mission to Africa

By the mid-eighteenth century, the SPG had made a concerted attempt to convert black people to Anglican Christianity at a number of sites—New York, South Carolina, and Barbados—and repeatedly encouraged individual ministers to undertake the work wherever they were stationed. Yet, by this point the ardor that had marked the efforts of some early missionaries and members had given way to deepening ties to slaveholders and a view that slavery could be used to accomplish the SPG's religious aims. These developments had led the SPG to attempt to effect changes in colonial and British laws to ease the conversion of slaves, to condone the ownership of slaves by individual ministers, to own slaves and exploit their labor on the Society's own sugar plantation, and to attempt to use enslaved men as lay catechists to other slaves. The Society's use of enslaved catechists was one of many techniques that the organization experimented with to convert black people around the British Atlantic world. Ministers had tried personal instruction to convert individual slaves that lived in their parishes; lay and clerical catechists had attempted group instruction. Oral teaching had been tried; so had teaching some enslaved people to read and write. All of these efforts had failed to achieve the large-scale conversions for which the Society hoped. In the 1750s the Society began a new effort, and after a half century of work in America and the Caribbean launched its first mission to Africa.

Between 1752 to 1816 two SPG missionaries, Thomas Thompson and Philip Quaque, served at Cape Coast in what is now Ghana.[1] Thompson spent only a few years at Cape Coast, but he began the Society's mission to Africa and was instrumental in bringing the African-born Philip Quaque into the Society's program. Quaque then spent eleven years in England before returning to Cape Coast as a clergyman. In England, Quaque was part of a growing community of Africans and Afro-Britons being incorporated into British culture through evangelical Christianity. The first African ordained in the Church of England,

Quaque returned to Cape Coast and spent fifty years as the Society's missionary there. Reflecting attitudes that had spread within the SPG, Thompson's and Quaque's missions were marked by a particularly close connection to transatlantic slavery. Both men held joint appointments while they served at Cape Coast: through the SPG they were missionaries to the African peoples of the Gold Coast, but they were also chaplains to the local employees of the Company of Merchants Trading to Africa, the organization responsible for facilitating the British slave trade.

Quaque's career provides another illustration of the way that the SPG's ideas about conversion interacted with local cultural and social particularities at a site of extended missionary work. Quaque struggled to plant Christianity and to find his place in Cape Coast's multiracial, multicultural trading community. His relationship with the SPG's leadership also reveals how attitudes within the Society about slavery and human difference changed over time. His lengthy career began when the legitimacy of slavery was rarely challenged in Britain and ended nearly a decade after the abolition of the trade upon which Cape Coast's fortunes depended. Quaque's own connections to slavery reflected the difficult position he occupied as a black employee of both the Society and the Company of Merchants, and also the anomalous position he occupied within Cape Coast society. Like other eighteenth-century SPG missionary efforts to black people, Quaque's mission failed to achieve large numbers of conversions, which had ramifications for the way the SPG conceptualized its work among African peoples. One of the ironies of Quaque's pioneering service was that his perceived failure, which might have raised concerns about the organization's close ties to slavery, instead led the Society to begin to doubt the ability of Africans like him to act as agents of Christianization.

The SPG's mission to West Africa was not the product of a centrally planned strategy. Just as Elias Neau had stimulated the SPG membership's interest in New York's slaves, so too missionary Thomas Thompson initiated the Society's activity in Africa. From 1745 to 1751 Thompson served as an SPG-supported minister in Monmouth County, New Jersey. Like other SPG parochial clergymen, Thompson began to instruct slaves he encountered. This work led him, he reported, to become particularly concerned with "the poor *Negroes*, who wanted enlightening more than any."[2] After five years in New Jersey, Thompson asked that he be sent to the "Coast of Guiney, that I might go to make a Trial with the Natives, and see what Hopes there would be of introducing among them the Christian Religion."[3] Following a successful petition to the SPG leadership in London, in 1751 Thompson was appointed as the first Anglican missionary to Africa.

Thompson's selection of Cape Coast as the primary site for his mission put him at the heart of the English slave trade. The Gold Coast was a region thoroughly enmeshed in Atlantic commercial networks, and after changing hands between European powers several times, in the 1670s Cape Coast's fort became the West African headquarters for England's Royal African Company.[4] Coastal African peoples like those who lived at and around Cape Coast were sophisticated traders, consumers, and members of communities that by the mid-eighteenth century had been in constant contact with Europeans for generations.[5] These contacts included interactions with Christianity. Roman Catholic missionaries had visited the region since the fifteenth century; Protestant clergymen accompanied the Dutch, German, Danish, and English traders who lived on the Coast in the seventeenth and eighteenth centuries.[6] Cape Coast Castle, as the fort was known, existed to further the trade in people. Within its walls were storerooms for supplies and merchandise, workshops for the fort's artisans, apartments for officials and traders, barracks for troops, and, cut into the rock on which the fort sat, a series of underground cells used to hold captives before they were put aboard slave ships. In 1750 these chambers were estimated to be large enough to hold 1,500 people.[7] During the existence of the slave trade, more than 109,000 African people were shipped from Cape Coast to Atlantic colonies.[8]

The fort's main defenses faced the sea, but it also overlooked an African town, which lay in the hilly land just behind the bay. Together the fort and this town, Cape Coast to the English and Oguaa in the local language, constituted the community in which Thompson and Quaque operated. The town had grown from a small settlement to a larger one in the late seventeenth century. It had begun as an offshoot of Efutu, located about ten miles north of Cape Coast, which was the principal town of the small Fetu state in the seventeenth century. Its growth into a sizeable settlement and the building of the European fort appear to have been concurrent, with both facilitating the development of Euro-African trade.[9] It was home to some 8,000 people by 1812.[10]

Thompson's time in West Africa came on the heels of a restructuring of the British slave trade. In 1750 the financially ailing Royal African Company, which since 1672 had operated as a chartered joint-stock trading company, was fully removed from management of the British slave trade. This business was now placed entirely in the hands of private merchants. To organize and facilitate their operations on the African coast, Parliament established the Company of Merchants Trading to Africa, which was not to engage in slave trading as a corporate entity but was established to maintain the necessary, existing network of coastal forts out of an annual government grant.[11] Under the Company of Merchants, the governor of Cape Coast was the senior officer in Africa. He, the heads of other coastal English forts, and a few other Cape Coast–based officials formed

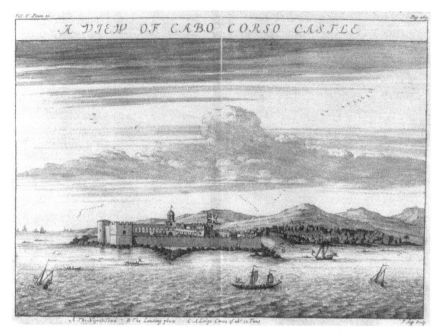

Figure 14. "A View of Cabo Corso Castle" from Awnsham Churchill and John Churchill, comps., *A collection of voyages and travels.*, vol. 5 (London, 1732). The view suggests the close connection between the English fort and the African town at Cape Coast. (The Library of Congress.)

the Council, which was the main body in Africa for administering the Company of Merchant's holdings.[12] These officials were often African traders themselves and typically used their positions to engage in lucrative private trade.

While in Africa, Thompson visited a number of trading forts along the Gold Coast and traveled to Sierra Leone. Through these visits Thompson established relationships with English officials in the region and made contact with several leaders of African communities who did business with the English. He also baptized of a number of the mixed-race children associated with the forts, continuing a tradition that seems to have begun through the chaplains of visiting ships. His health suffered badly on the coast, and in 1756 he returned to England to take up the more relaxed life of a country clergyman and occasional author, initially publishing a pamphlet based on his work in New Jersey and an account of his missionary travels in America and Africa.[13] Thompson's mission did not produce many conversions, but when he left Africa he was hopeful that large-scale Christianization was achievable.[14]

The most important direct result of Thompson's mission was the sending of three young African men—William Cudjo, Thomas Caboro, and Philip

Quaque—to England for education in 1754, and in so doing he continued a long-standing English practice of bringing representatives of the various peoples of the Atlantic world to London. From early in its history, the Society and its supporters sought to use such methods to tie people more closely to the Church of England and, often, to the British Crown. The SPG had participated in the 1710 visit of the four "Indian Kings," who requested that the Iroquois be provided with Anglican missionaries. In 1713 Commissary Gideon Johnston of South Carolina brought "Prince George" of the Yamasee people to England, where he was educated and supported by the Society for several years.[15] Thomas Bray made an abortive effort in 1722 to send two boys, James Macquilan Mussoom and John Chaung Mussoom, taken to London from Delgoa in Mozambique, back to Africa in the company of English missionaries.[16]

More broadly, Quaque's experiences echoed those of other African-born "Atlantic creoles" whose abilities to communicate in European languages positioned them as intermediaries between Africans and Europeans along the West African coast.[17] Under the sponsorship of Britain's successive African companies and individual traders, a stream of young men connected to the Gold Coast's elite traveled to Britain in the eighteenth century. For example, William Ansah Sessarakoo was kidnapped and sold into slavery by a duplicitous trader around 1744 before being redeemed and educated in England by the Royal African Company. He returned to Africa in 1750, later becoming an acquaintance of Thomas Thompson and an employee of the Company of Merchants. Other African and European elites also cooperated in plans that resembled Quaque's education and career in their blending of religious, strategic, and commercial motivations. The West African Jacobus Capitein (1717–47) was trained by Dutch ministers through the efforts of the Dutch West India Company; his Leiden doctoral thesis defended slavery's compatibility with Christianity. The Moravians Frederick Pedersen Svane (1710–89) and Christian Jakob Protten (1715–69), the sons of African mothers and Danish fathers, were educated at the University of Copenhagen. Like Quaque, all three of these men spent time as ministers on the Gold Coast.[18]

Quaque's life was shaped by these wider commercial and religious practices. He and his two companions, William Cudjo and Thomas Caboro, had close ties to the African mercantile and political leaders upon whom the English traders on the Gold Coast depended. Quaque was related to Kwadwo Egyir, known to the English as Cudjoe Caboceer or Birempon Cudjoe. Cudjoe was a powerful figure at Cape Coast and an important English partner.[19] His son and Quaque's relative and associate Frederick Adoy had previously been educated in England before returning to Cape Coast to serve as an intermediary between English and African leaders.[20] African elites like Cudjoe participated in such practices to further their economic and political interests. In 1756 Governor Charles Bell complained that well-connected African youths trained in England and sent back to work for the Company of Merchants were "Quills to suck through, according to the Negroe Phrase; for whatever we allow to maintain them goes half to their Masters."[21] This mutual Afro-European maneuvering for economic and political leverage through the education and employment of African youth was an important element in Quaque's life.[22] Soon after he returned to Cape Coast in 1766, Quaque reported with consternation that he had concluded Cudjoe's support for him had "been Nothing else, but a senister view of getting from Me if possible, the little Income I have from the African Committee into his own Custody, notwithstanding he being a Person of great Repute & Substance."[23]

In England, Quaque and his companions were first enrolled in a school run by Mr. Hickman of Islington. Thomas Caboro died of tuberculosis in 1758. William Cudjo and Quaque were baptized at the Islington parish church in 1759 before being transferred to the care of Rev. John Moore, a member of both the SPCK and the SPG who would become rector of London's St. Bartholomew's parish. Moore had previously cooperated with the Company of Merchants in training other "Atlantic creoles" and the boys lived and studied with him in London for the next six years.[24] William Cudjo's life would end tragically. In January 1766 Moore told the SPG that he had been "put out of the Reach of Instruction by a Lunacy." Details about the nature of this "lunacy" do not appear to exist, but he died at Guy's Hospital in September 1774 after eight years of confinement, with Moore reporting he had proved "incurable."[25]

John Moore was one of those Anglican clergymen who, while remaining within the established church, had sympathies for the emerging Methodist movement, and this probably impacted Quaque's education and religious out-look.[26] Methodism played an important part in the emergence of a distinctive circum-Atlantic black Protestant Christianity in the mid-eighteenth century, and several African-born men of Quaque's generation knew early Methodist leaders personally.[27] Quaque's eventual Anglican ordination makes him unique in the eighteenth century, but his connection through Moore to early Meth-odism resonates with the experiences of other Afro-Britons like Ignatius Sancho and Olaudah Equiano, who had ties both to the established church and to the new movement. Equiano, for example, received Anglican baptism in 1759 and attended services at London parishes before joining a Methodist group in the mid-1770s. Despite his deepening ties to Methodism, in 1779 Equiano reported he was "a protestant of the church of England, agreeable to the thirty-nine arti-cles of that church" and unsuccessfully requested Anglican ordination so that he could take up a mission to Africa.[28] Quaque clearly spent much of his time in London studying and absorbing British culture, as he learned (or improved his ability) to speak, read, and write in English, and his religious studies progressed far enough to make him worthy of ordination. Moore claimed that Quaque "had rewarded my Labours by improving in every Branch of Knowledge necessary to the Station for which he was designed."[29] In 1765 Quaque was ordained a deacon and priest, an event notable enough to include mention in *Gentleman's Magazine*, and he married an English woman, Catherine Blunt.[30] Quaque and his wife soon sailed for Africa, arriving at Cape Coast in February 1766.[31] The cooperation with the Company of Merchants Trading to Africa that led to Quaque's joint appointment as chaplain to Cape Coast's slave traders and missionary to the African people of the Gold Coast should be seen as a concrete expression of mid-century Anglicanism's attitude toward transatlantic slavery. Quaque's London experiences also suggest that he was part of growing community of black people who saw Christianity both as a means of salvation and of entry into English society.

Cape Coast proved a challenging mission station for the young clergyman. African power on the Gold Coast meant that the English were part of a wider regional system in which European traders had to operate within the confines of the existing African social and political structure.[32] Throughout the pre-colonial period, the English at Cape Coast did not hold sovereign power but were in fact tenants of the Dey of Fetu, to whom they paid annual rent. The Company of Merchants also made regular payments to a number of Fetu officials in exchange for their allowing trade at Cape Coast to take place.[33] During the seventeenth century, Fetu independence had allowed it to play the English, the Dutch, and larger African neighbors off each other, but the landscape had shifted by the early eighteenth century as the neighboring state of Fante became the regional power and gradually established its paramountcy over Fetu.[34] As Fante's power grew, the English looked to cooperate with it to create favorable conditions for trade.

Not surprisingly, it was those who could best negotiate interactions between and within the region's African and European communities who wielded economic and political power in this shifting landscape. Cudjoe Caboceer was just such a figure, and between the 1730s and his death in 1776 he exercised effective political power at Cape Coast.[35] A transplant to Cape Coast from a Fante town, Cudjoe rose to a position of great wealth and power partly because he was able to exploit kinship links to both the traditional Fetu rulers of Cape Coast and to the expanding regional power of Fante.[36] In the 1750s Thompson reported that Cudjoe was "the chief Man" of Cape Coast due to his "Wealth and Influence," but that his younger [half-] brother was "the King."[37] Cudjoe, who spoke English, also played an essential role in the local slave trade, and by 1729 he was being paid to act as a company "translator." He solidified his power at Cape Coast during the Seven Years War (1756–63), when he supplied the British garrison with provisions and allowed them to survive a blockade imposed by the French and their African allies. In ensuing decades, a period marked by closer Anglo-Fante ties more generally, Cudjoe became not only the de facto ruler of Cape Coast but also an influential figure across Fante.[38] Quaque's connection to Cudjoe emphasizes his ties to a particular segment of coastal West African society: an elite that was refashioning existing power systems and thriving through the slave trade and European contact.[39]

These political dynamics meant that European officials were anxious to remain on good terms with African rulers and that Christianity could not be imposed on the African population of Cape Coast. Quaque's mission was also shaped by the multiple divisions that existed within local society. Free and unfree Africans of a variety of backgrounds, Europeans, and people of mixed race all lived there. The complex political scene in the eighteenth-century Gold Coast overlay a rich, dynamic mixture of cultural and linguistic groups. The expansion of Fante military and economic power was accompanied by the expansion of Fante cultural influence over the course of the eighteenth century. The predominant cultural group in the region, the Akan, included speakers of a number of related, mutually intelligible dialects. While the Fante, the Asante, and many other peoples of the Gold Coast spoke varieties of Akan, the people of Fetu spoke Efutu, a language from a different family. In the 1750s Thompson noted the gradual growth of Fante influence that had occured in Cape Coast, when he observed that though, "The Langauge of the Coast is very various, each Nation having that which is particularly its own," Fante "is the most extensive in Practice" and "the sole Dialect of the *Cape Coast* Blacks."[40] Nevertheless, trade and population movements meant that cultural and ethnic diversity remained a hallmark of the town. In 1767, for example, Quaque reported that he had preached to "fifty and sixty in number of different country, viz. Fetue[,] Ahunter[,] and Iqwa or Cape Coast people, who behaved considering very orderly and decently, particularly the former people who never saw or beheld such before."[41]

Divisions based on wealth and social status were also important. The permanent population of Cape Coast included various types of unfree people. These included, for example, enslaved people owned by the Company of Merchants. Echoing the way that domestic slaves were treated in local African households, the Company of Merchants prohibited the sale of company slaves off the coast. These people performed a number of specialized tasks, worked set hours, and were paid for their work.[42] They also possessed a cohesive corporate identity. In 1786, for instance, "the whole Body of the Slaves belonging to this Garrison of different occupations" deserted and did not return to Cape Coast for a month.[43]

Their simultaneous connections to the fort and the town had implications for the relationships between Africans and Europeans, as disputes between company slaves and townspeople could come to involve company officials. In 1772 the Council at Cape Coast paid thirty pounds in goods to Cudjoe Caboceer after violence between the townspeople and company slaves broke out when the latter "abused and insulted one of Cudjoe's women."[44] Internal tensions like these would repeatedly hamper Quaque's ability to create a unified Christian community at Cape Coast.

Even the small European community at Cape Coast was notably diverse, with national differences often entailing religious differences that hindered Quaque. In 1766 he lamented the makeup of the Castle's leadership, observing: "I shall have very little or scarce any Pretensions at all with them, they being all Scotch & Irish People, rank Presbyterians." The garrison at various points included men like a Dutch soldier and a French cook, the later "a rank Papist," whom Quaque mentioned in his letters to the Society.[45] Quaque's English wife accompanied him to Cape Coast, but very few other European women resided there. As in other places shaped by the slave trade, sex between European men and African women resulted in a sizeable and long-standing mixed-race population recognized as a distinct part of Cape Coast society. Thompson thought it important to make his SPG superiors aware of the distinctiveness of this "Molatto" population, "a sort of People betwixt a *Negro* and a *White*, the same as we in *England* commonly call *Tawnies*."[46] Mixed-race men formed an important contingent of the company's military garrison at the Castle, and this population too possessed a collective identity that affected SPG missionary efforts. While few Africans accepted Christianity, Thompson reported that the mixed-race population had for the most part been baptized by the chaplains of passing ships or by a previous chaplain to the garrison at the Castle. He observed that they valued "themselves upon their Christian Name, accounting it an honourable Distinction" but that they were largely uninterested in learning more about the religion.[47] In 1768 Quaque baptized "two Mustee Children & two Mullattoes," the former probably the children of European men and mixed-race women.[48] Quaque's ability, as an African, to understand and navigate Cape Coast's internal divisions was probably one of the things about him that initially appealed to the Society.

Yet, paradoxically, Quaque's own local origins and connections made his mission in some ways more challenging, something the SPG did not anticipate or fully understand. Quaque's kinship ties to Cudjoe connected him to a powerful Cape Coast family, but they also enmeshed him in dynastic and political matters. The depth of Quaque's own Anglicization probably further hurt their relations. In 1766 he resisted Cudjoe's efforts to obtain part of his salary. Quaque complained that Cudjoe, "seeing himself with all my numerous Family greatly disappointed in their aim," had "therefore become very careless and thoughtless about us."[49] The unwillingness of Cudjoe and his other African kin to convert was a continuing disappointment to Quaque, who reported they paid little attention to his religious message and treated him "without the least Consideration" and "in no other Light than as one of themselves."[50] Whatever their religious and cultural differences, Quaque remained part of Cudjoe's extended family. When Cudjoe died, his funeral was attended by massive crowds and African leaders from across the Gold Coast. Quaque told the Society that he had been forced to spend over £125 on various funeral gifts and expenses, which he mentioned "to shew them the Difficulties I frequently labor under thro numerous Family Connections whose sole Dependence rests entirely upon me."[51]

At Cape Coast, Thompson and Quaque also confronted a fully functioning African religious system, which had its own carefully maintained rules and rituals, a calendar of festivals that marked community life, and the support of elites and most people. Local Akan religion was also supported by its own well-connected priests, one of whom Quaque disputed with at Cudjoe's house in 1768.[52] Thompson and, perhaps more surprisingly, Quaque viewed Cape Coast religious practices in limited, exclusively pejorative ways as forms of "fetish" worship.[53] They commented particularly on the people of Cape Coast's devotion to ceremonies connected with "Taberah," which Quaque described as a "prodigious high Rock, whereon the better part of the Castle stands, & the remaining Part lanches out into the Sea, and they'll make you believe that this God of Stone is the only support of the Garrison, the Inhabitants therein and the whole Towns People." Sacrifices were regularly offered to Taberah and to other supernatural powers that inhabited natural features around Cape Coast.[54] Content with dismissing them, neither Thompson nor Quaque developed strategies to successfully engage with these beliefs and practices.

Cudjoe's power rested on his abilities as a cultural broker, and his approach to Christianity exhibited his skill at maintaining the middle ground. A 1753 report noted that Cudjoe was "a firm believer" in local religion, "tho he does not chuse to have it thought so."[55] While sometimes willing to have Christian prayers said in his presence, neither Thompson nor Quaque was able to convince him to stop the ceremonies associated with local religious practices. Instead, Christian worship was allowed only insofar as it did not disrupt established community norms. On a number of occasions, Christian worship was cancelled because it would have interfered with the "making of custom" by local people.[56] Thomas Thompson was advised by Cudjoe to switch his preaching to Tuesday if he hoped to have any hearers, as Sunday was a working day for the people of Cape Coast.[57] European traders, dependent on Africans' good will, further underlined the comparative weakness of Christianity at the Coast by participating in many rituals that marked the Cape Coast calendar, providing both food and drink for festivals and encouraging local leaders to swear "fetish oaths" to secure trade and political agreements.[58] Among free and enslaved black people in Britain and its colonies, conversion sometimes gave access to social standing. In contrast, at Cape Coast African leaders remained committed to local religion.

Cape Coast's African population was also unwilling to conform to missionary Anglicanism's cultural and moral prescriptions. Quaque and Thompson complained bitterly about the role alcohol played in local religious ceremonies, and Cape Coast leaders occasionally demanded that their participation in Christian rituals be rewarded with a distribution of liquor.[59] People also resisted Quaque's attempts to change their marriage and sexual practices.[60] In a revealing reversal, Quaque seems instead to have experienced his own difficulties because he violated local marriage norms and kinship obligations. Quaque's English wife Catherine died within a year of their arrival in Cape Coast. He subsequently married two African women (neither of whose names he reported to the Society) and had at least three children with these women, a son Samuel and two daughters. Quaque owned the second woman he married, describing her as "a property of my own." Cudjoe appears to have given her as a gift to Quaque and his first wife so she could serve as Catherine's maid.[61] This second wife died in childbirth in 1770, after she and Quaque had been married less than a year. Quaque reported that her loss was "thro' the bitter hatred & envy held against this [wife?] by my own Relations."[62] In 1811 relations between Quaque and his extended African family were still in a bad state as they quarreled over their future inheritances and Quaque's desire to make a provision for his third wife. He noted then that the Cape Coast people "are all for themselves and wish not that the inferior People should ever rise in equality with themselves."[63]

Quaque remained deeply ambivalent in other ways about the African people he hoped to convert. Although he did not go to England until he was a teenager, Quaque lost—or at least claimed to have lost—the ability to speak Fante, or any other African language, during his time there and had to depend on an interpreter after his return to the Gold Coast.[64] Many of Cape Coast's mixed-race and African inhabitants, including Cudjoe, spoke English but Quaque's inability to speak African languages certainly handicapped his mission. In 1769, the Society urged Quaque "to endeavour to recover his own language," but he was evidently unwilling to doing so.[65] In 1781 he looked to educate his son and eldest daughter in England to give them "a superior Knowledge of Things over their Countrymen" and "to secure their tender minds from receiving the bad impressions of the country, the vile customs and practices and above all, the losing their mother's vile jargon, the only obstacles of learning in these parts."[66] Quaque retained such hostility even after having lived at Cape Coast for decades. His anger over his extended family's efforts to gain control of his property led him to complain more generally about "the avaricious dispos[it]ions of the Blacks" and observed that "the more a man do to these kind of People the more ungrateful and unthankful they seem to be."[67] Despite the SPG's hopes, Quaque was never able to use his connections to Cudjoe Caboceer or Cape Coast's elites to aid his mission. "It is no wonder," he observed, "and too true a saying of our blessed Lord 'that a man's Foes shall be they of his Household and that a Prophet has no honor in his own Country.'"[68]

Quaque's ties to the European administration and traders of the Castle were also difficult. Several governors who presided over the fort during his career were hostile to his mission. Some, though not all, of the local European officials and traders also challenged Quaque's legitimacy because he was an African. In 1767 the trader Richard Brew observed that "He would never come to Cape Coast to be Subservient to, & to sit under the Nose of a Black Boy to hear him pointing or laying out their faults before them."[69] In 1770 Governor John Grossle told another man that Quaque "deserves to be kickt" were it not "a disgrace to a Gentleman to enter into a list with a Negro Priest."[70] Quaque, sensitive to affronts to his status, lamented the unwillingness of various governors to accept him at their table or permit him to perform public worship. Other governors, notably Richard Miles who held office in the mid-1770s, were more accepting and encouraged his public preaching and school. Some white people saw religious worship as impossible in the midst of the slave trade, telling Quaque "that while they are here acting against Light & Conscience, they dare not come to that holy Table."[71] On the whole, few Europeans living at Cape Coast were interested in making Christianity a more integral part of life there.

In some ways, the Cape Coast people that most closely mirrored Quaque's own liminal position were those of mixed race, who often had one foot in the Castle and the other in the town. In 1773 Quaque baptized seven mixed-race soldiers of the fort's garrison, including the "Mulattoe Drum Major."[72] Mixed-race children— either those of European traders and their African or mixed-race "country wives" or of the mixed-race soldiery and their wives—were the main group that Quaque baptized over the decades. Quaque's best, and for many years only, student was a "Mullatoe" young man named Willoughby Senior, who was perhaps the son or other relation of Nassau Senior, a veteran British trader and governor of the fort in the early 1760s. Despite the best efforts of Quaque and Willoughby Senior's "heathen Grandmother," the young man eventually stopped attending school and enlisted as a soldier in the Company's service.[73] In the late 1780s several local employees of the Company of Merchants banded together to form the "Torridzonian Society," an organization that provided Quaque funds for the education of mixed-race children. Although this endeavor survived only into the next decade, several children educated by Quaque in this period apparently resurfaced in the 1820s and 1830s as members of the Anglo-African colonial elite.[74]

Still, Quaque's relations with the mixed-race population could be rocky. As Thompson had noted, these people regarded themselves as a distinct group and prided themselves on their connections to Europe and the fort. While Quaque's own religious and cultural values were probably closer to those of the mixed-race community than those of the African townspeople, of whom he was often critical, both of the women he married at Cape Coast were Africans. In 1767 he noted—in response to suggestions that he should choose a second wife carefully—that "the bettermost sort" at Cape Coast, seemingly a reference to women of mixed race, were unwilling to enter into formal marriages, preferring to preserve a measure of their independence by "consorting" or acting only as "country wives" to Europeans living at the coast. He reported in 1769 that he had married his second wife in part to end a rumor that he had been "disappointed in my Amour of a Mustee young Lady," suggesting that either the mixed-race young woman herself or her family found Quaque somehow unsuitable. His third wife, whom he wed in 1772, was likewise "an adult black girl."[75] These dynamics suggest that members of the mixed-race population may not have entirely accepted Quaque because of his color, origins, or status.

An incident in 1768 reveals other tensions. With the zeal of a still young missionary, Quaque attempted to regularize the mixed-race community's religious practice. He "held a convocation of mullatoe gentlemen and ladies at Cudjoe's Caboceer's house, in order to propose a few questions particularly relative to themselves as they value their se[lve]s preferable to their other native people, calling themselves Christians, because they are of the race of white men." Quaque especially objected to the way they blended Christian and West African religious practices, even as they sought to distinguish themselves from the town's African peoples. Quaque insisted they must give up their "own foolish Traditions" and the "stupid Customs & Rites of those whom you set in Scorn and Contempt." He told those who would refuse to conform not to expect his help when they were sick or needed Christian burial. Quaque proposed that those who wished to be considered Christians must attend Christian services regularly, the unbaptized must attend catechism classes, and those who missed weekly service should pay a fine of £1. Finally, Quaque challenged the mixed-race population's sense of their own distinctiveness and superiority, telling them that "We were by no Means to exclude the black People belonging to our Town or any other without Distinction provided they are willing to join themselves truly and faithfully to this Congregation."[76]

Quaque's efforts to create a color-blind, reformed, and more tightly knit Christian community with membership based on individual religious commitment recalled those of Methodists and other evangelicals in Britain. These proposals upset the status quo at Cape Coast and were met with organized hostility, especially from "the Gentlemen of the Fort" who objected because "their Ladies were concerned." The European men of the fort did not want their mixed-race "country wives" too involved in a religious reform movement. To Quaque's disgust they went "so far as to threaten their Wenches (for so they are here called) with a Divorsement if ever they know 'em [to] attend my Lectures." The men challenged Quaque's authority, asking "what I am that I should pre-scribe laws for the government or reformation . . . of their wenches, without their general consent being asked or sought for?" Such opposition badly under-mined Quaque's plans. He reported that the women were financially dependent on the Europeans, so "for their own Interest sake" they had to "adhere to the voice of their Husbands." When he held services the following Sunday, only four women connected to men at the fort attended. There were another thirteen "Ladies & Gentlemen Inhabitants of Cape Coast" in attendance, a group that appears to have been African since, "the Mullattoe Gentlemen scarce ever . . . attended, as they also judged Me either Mad or else possessed with some Evil Demon or other to think of regulating a Nation that has been the Impossibility of many others before."[77] Ultimately, Quaque was never able to convince the mixed-race population, or any other segment of the Cape Coast community, to fully embrace his missionary aims.

Quaque's mission was also affected by slavery and the slave trade. When he left London in 1765, few British voices were publicly articulating antislavery argu-ments. His return to Cape Coast placed him in a community whose existence and wealth were based on the trade in people and the multiple forms of enslaved labor that existed in the region. People being held in indigenous West African slavery, company slaves, and people destined for the Middle Passage and chattel slavery in the colonies were all present locally. Besides owning his second wife, Quaque benefited from the widespread local use of unfree labor. For example, a 1771 list of company slaves recorded that a man named Adjumacon served as "Chappel Servant."[78] Cudjoe was heavily involved in the transatlantic trade, as were most of the permanent, prominent African residents of Cape Coast.[79] Any challenges to slavery would run up against the entrenched interests of both European and African communal elites, including Quaque's family.

More directly, Quaque was an employee of the Company of Merchants, which intended that all of his religious and educational efforts, like everything else the organization funded, should serve the interests of slave traders. Although he was appointed explicitly as the Company's chaplain at Cape Coast, like other employees of the chronically undermanned organization he was also periodically called on to take up other duties. At several times over the course of his long career, such work involved him more directly in the administration of the Company's efforts to protect and further the trade in human beings and other goods. Quaque's letters record, without any apparent discomfort, that in 1775 he undertook temporary commands at the three minor company forts at Dixcove, Sekondi, and Komenda. In doing so, he participated in the company's efforts to promote the diplomatic and strategic conditions intended to maximize the trade in enslaved people. As other English-literate local Africans did, Quaque also served at times in the bureaucracy that enabled the slave trade to function. In 1789, for example, he was paid by the Company of Merchants as both its chaplain and as a writer, a job that would have involved him in the day-to-day administration of trade.[80] In the late 1780s, the SPG stated that Quaque was more involved in trade than a missionary should be.[81] The reasons for this charge remain obscure, and it was possibly unfair. Like all company officials at Cape Coast, Quaque had to participate in local trade to obtain necessities since his salary was paid in goods not cash.[82] Yet, collectively this evidence suggests that Quaque, like many other residents of Cape Coast, was entangled in the fort's primary business: the facilitation of the transatlantic slave trade.

Quaque also experienced the Company of Merchants' and the SPG's commitments to slavery and their opposition to emerging antislavery activism. In 1769 for example, Governor John Grossle complained to the company's committee in London of "a Spirit of Liberty" that "has crept into the Breast of the African slave as well as the meanest wretch in London Streets, for in all Countries this kind of Liberty is chiefly confined to the lowest class of Men."[83] Throughout Quaque's life the SPG invested prestige, effort, and money in operating Codrington plantation on the premise that profits from enslaved labor and the conversions of enslaved people could be attained simultaneously. In 1768 the SPG turned down the Quaker Anthony Benezet's request that it cooperate with him in advocating abolition.[84] In 1772 Quaque's predecessor, Thomas Thompson, published *The African Trade for Negro Slaves, Shewn to be Consistent with the Principles of Humanity, and with the Laws of Revealed Religion*, which defended the slave trade as a legitimate, beneficial form of commerce.[85] This work, dedicated to the members of the Company of Merchants and published by the man who was directly responsible for beginning Quaque's education and career, was a powerful statement as he contemplated what slavery meant for his mission.

In light of these connections and pressures, it would have been perilous for Quaque to publicly attack slavery or the slave trade. He never appears to have tried to catechize or preach among the captives held at the fort prior to their being shipped across the Atlantic. His correspondence contains few expansive discussions of slavery. Despite the weight of proslavery forces in his life, Quaque seems to have harbored growing doubts about the trade in people largely because he came to believe it undermined his religious endeavors among Cape Coast's permanent population. Quaque's uniqueness as a black Anglican priest and his African posting gave him a degree of notoriety around the Atlantic, and several American clergymen began correspondences with him. In 1767, early in his mission, Quaque responded to a letter from Samuel Johnson, an SPG missionary in Connecticut and later president of King's College in New York. Quaque noted that he had not yet made many converts and reported, "the stir of religion and its everlasting recompense is not so much in vogue as the vicious practice of purchasing flesh and blood like oxens in market places." Quaque argued that African nations were "kept in ignorance for interest and lucre sake, while Christian humanity and fellow-feeling is blinded with profit and loss." In a 1769 letter to Johnson, Quaque agreed with Johnson's sentiment that the "cursed slave trade is the only obstruction to the ministering in these desolate parts." He also lamented the fact that "necessity has driven many promising youths to get their fortune by such way of traffic," a particularly notable regret given his own position as an employee of the Company of Merchants and his multifaceted connections to slavery as a resident of Cape Coast.[86] The Congregational minister and antislavery author Samuel Hopkins of Newport, Rhode Island, was likewise in correspondence with Quaque by 1773. Phillis Wheatley and Hopkins in turn corresponded about Quaque in 1774. Wheatley noted she was "very sorry to hear that Philip Quaque has very little or no *apparent* Success in his mission" and indicated that some negative reports about Quaque were in circulation, adding her hopes that "what you hear respecting him, may be only a misrepresentation."[87] Such letters suggest that Quaque had links to circum-Atlantic evangelical and antislavery networks, even as some in them questioned his commitment or fitness for his work.

Most commonly, as was the case in his 1769 letter to Johnson, Quaque negatively assessed the slave trade in response to prompts from his correspondents. In a 1771 letter to Quaque, Edward Bass, the SPG missionary to Newburyport, Massachusetts, asked if there was any hope for the success of the mission in Africa and "whether that cursed Slave Trade was not the chief Obstruction" to Quaque's work. Quaque evidently felt the need to explain to Bass why his mission was not producing its anticipated results. He reported to the Society that he responded to Bass and "made him to understand, first of the many Obstacles & Difficulties attending the Labours of those who are unfortunately situated here, principally the horrid Slave Trade of which he himself makes a Mention of in his Epistle to me." Quaque believed that his mission could only succeed with the help of a supportive, religious local governor, and that his mission was hampered by European and African attitudes. "Interest or the love of gain and

Ambition on one hand & Superstition and Bigotry on the other is the chief Hindrance," he wrote.[88]

Quaque's reply to Bass comprehensively repudiated the viewpoint within the SPG that underpinned its cooperation with the Company of Merchants in sending missionaries to Cape Coast in the first place: that the business of Atlantic slavery and the growth of Christianity were compatible. Quaque blamed both the slave trade as a whole and the particular involvement of Cape Coast's people in the trade for his failure to achieve large numbers of conversions. Some of Quaque's complaints—about the absence of support from governmental officials and the poor examples set by so-called Christians—were common among SPG missionaries around the Atlantic world. However, Quaque's vehemence reflected a growing sense of frustration at the slave trade as an obstacle to effective Christianization.

Quaque most fully expressed this frustration in a 1775 letter to Bass. The American-born-and-educated Bass was among the relatively small number of SPG clergymen who sympathized with the colonial cause during the American Revolution. In response to a letter evidently expressing Bass's pro-American views on the gathering crisis, Quaque produced his most emotive attack on the slave trade:

> In your Epistle you seem to lament bitterly of your Mother Country for Universal Liberty. You upon whom the light of the Gospel flourishes and . . . as it were advancing daily towards the seat of Bliss find the Hardships of Bondage and Oppression! Good God can this be possible! When I behold with Sorrowful sighing my poor abject Countrymen over whom you without the Bowels of Christian Love and Pity, hold in cruel Bondage. This Iniquitous Practice methinks seems to set Religion aside and only making room for the height of Ambition and Grandeur, the pride of Monarchs &c. to enter. I could wish that the Conviction of this Practice would spring first from the Breast of us all particularly you since we know perfectly well the heinousness of it and may we be diligent to put it in practice by encouraging the Heathen World to partake of the brightness of God's Glory and the precious Promises of the Gospel.[89]

Quaque's letter denounced hypocrisy and argued that slavery prevented the conversion of Africans. He expressed similar sentiments in subsequent correspondence. In 1782 he blamed slavery's local influence for his struggles to obtain the governor's permission to perform public worship. He noted, "that while Countenance is given to the practice of Slavery, Religion will prove to us in these Parts as St. Paul the great Preacher of the Gentiles describes, a stumbling Block, and to the Heathens who we earnestly wish may speedily become the Kingdom of God & of his Christ, Foolishness."[90]

While these passages suggest Quaque believed the slave trade had a negative impact on his community and his mission, he remained entangled in it. Despite his vehement 1775 letter to Bass, that year he assumed temporary command at three English forts on the Gold Coast. In 1781 he was away from Cape Coast and unable to perform services there for "upwards of six Weeks on public Duty," perhaps connected with his work as a writer for the Company of Merchants.[91] It is difficult to reconcile every aspect of Quaque's professional life with his statements, but it appears that like many others in the Atlantic world, his opposition to slavery was becoming more pronounced and public from the 1780s. Quaque's willingness to more openly articulate his opposition to the slave trade may well have been affected by a visit he made to Britain in 1784 to arrange for the education of his children. Almost no information about his time in Britain appears in the SPG's records or in Quaque's correspondence, but this trip placed him in London when the debates that gave rise to the Parliamentary campaign against the slave trade were becoming more heated.[92] Quaque was likely exposed to these debates, especially because they began to involve the SPG directly soon before his arrival. Beilby Porteus, the bishop of Chester and future bishop of London, used his 1783 annual sermon to attack the cruelties of plantation slavery, publicly acknowledge that SPG management of Codrington plantation had not produced large numbers of converts, and lament Britain's leading role in the slave trade.[93] Porteus had relied on a manuscript copy of the Anglican minister James Ramsay's *Essay on the Treatment and Conversion of African Slaves in the British Sugar Colonies* in preparing his sermon. Ramsay published his essay, which would become an influential antislavery tract, at Porteus's urging in 1784.[94] Though Porteus was ultimately unsuccessful in his efforts to persuade the SPG to support abolitionism, his sermon and Ramsay's indictment of West Indian planters raised for the first time the possibility that the Society's stance toward slavery might change.

Quaque was soon back at Cape Coast. In 1785 he purchased a "very old woman slave" at the estate sale of a dead colleague, the only known direct evidence of his personally buying an enslaved person. It is a measure of the complexity of the local and Atlantic contexts in which Quaque lived that his motives in this purchase are impossible to determine and may have been mixed. Perhaps Quaque considered his purchase of the woman, whose low price suggests she was not rated a very valuable slave, as an act of charity; perhaps he hoped to benefit from her labor.[95] A clearer indication of an evolution in his thinking is suggested by his 1786 reaction to the tragic destruction of a Dutch slave ship, the *Neptunus*, on the Gold Coast following a revolt by its human cargo. A European attempt to recapture the vessel led to fighting and an explosion that killed several hundred people, including almost all the slaves aboard and the entire crew. Whereas previously Quaque tended to respond to his correspondents' antislavery statements, this tragedy led him to denounce the slave trade to the SPG without prompting. Quaque blamed "the Captain's brutish Behavior," rather than the slaves, for the revolt because he "did not allow even his own Sailors, much more the Slaves a sufficient Maintenance to support nature." The catastrophe led Quaque to reflect on the conditions that led enslaved people to take such desperate measures in language that suggested his familiarity with Atlantic antislavery arguments. He wondered "can we but help figuring to ourselves the true picture of Inhumanity those unhappy Creatures suffer in their Miserable State of Bondage under the different degrees of austere Masters they unfortunately fall in with in the West Indies."[96]

Though never a public antislavery figure, by the early 1790s Quaque was being cited as a source of information by men who testified before the House of Commons committee that investigated the slave trade. While proponents of the slave trade attempted to portray it as a necessary and humane business in these hearings, antislavery witnesses marshaled by Thomas Clarkson, William Wilberforce, and others attempted to disclose its full horrors. In 1790 the surgeon Alexander Falconbridge testified that when he was last at Cape Coast, the "Rev. Mr. Philip Quackoo" had told him that "the greatest number of slaves were made by kidnapping."[97] Falconbridge had published a damning first-hand account of the slave trade in 1788 as an abolitionist tract. His report of Quaque's information was part of an effort to disprove slave traders' claims that enslaved people were the captives of African wars who were fortunate to have had their lives spared.[98] In 1791 Lt. John Simpson of the Royal Marines, who served aboard a navy ship stationed along the Gold Coast in 1788–89, testified that Quaque had told him "that wars were made in the interior parts" for the "sole purpose" of capturing slaves.[99] In Simpson's testimony, Quaque's evidence was used to argue that European involvement in the transatlantic slave trade was a direct cause of violence in Africa. It is revealing that despite his position in the Company of Merchants, Quaque was willing to provide visitors to Cape Coast with information that was clearly damaging to slave trading interests.

Quaque's changing relationship with company officials also suggests a new willingness to act on his views on slavery in this period. Even though he had previously taken up nonreligious duties on behalf of the company, in 1791 he became engaged in the most serious professional dispute of his career over his refusal to obey an order of the governor of Cape Coast Castle. Governor William Fielde ordered Quaque to accompany him to the English fort at Anomabo and participate in military action against the African people of the town there, an event that resulted in "great slaughter and devestation." Quaque refused on the grounds that his participation would have been "highly inconsistent and injurious to my Profession and the Station I hold in the African Committee's Service." The governor suspended Quaque from the company's service and forced him out of his lodgings in the Castle. Quaque lived for eleven months in Cape Coast town before he was reinstated "as Chaplain only in their Service" by the company's London committee, a designation seemingly designed to clarify that Quaque was no longer obligated to participate in the company's commercial activities. At the same time, the committee ordered that religious worship was to be performed more regularly at the fort.[100] Quaque's unwillingness to participate in the violence on which the Company of Merchants' business depended and his comments on the harshness of the trade suggest that by the early 1790s he had become a firmer opponent of the slave trade.

For the better part of fifty years, Quaque informed the Society that his mission was not going well. He characterized Cape Coast as an "unhappy residence" (1769), an "unfruitful mission" (1777), "desolate parts" (1795), and an "unsuccessful mission" (1811).[101] Quaque provided a number of possible explanations for why his mission had fared poorly, including the problems created by the slave trade, the bad example set by an irreligious European community, and the flaws of Cape Coast's African population. The Society also thought the Cape Coast mission was disappointing, but it stressed Quaque's own failings rather than the circumstances in which he operated. After the 1770s most SPG annual reports simply omitted any mention of Quaque's mission although he remained an employee of the Society. In 1788 the Privy Council asked the SPG to provide information about its missionary efforts among black people in the West Indies and Africa as part of its investigation of the slave trade. The SPG secretary William Morice responded to the Privy Council's request by harshly criticizing Quaque's missionary work:

> He has never been able to fulfil the objects of his mission. After his return he seems to have been intirely disregarded by his own family, with whom he has not the least influence, not even to make a single convert among them. And whether it was from the impossibility of going up the country, or from want of prudence, or from a failure in the due Exertion of his Abilities, such as they were, or from any other Cause, may not be so easy to ascertain; but this is certain, that he has had no Success at all with the Native Blacks; and the Whole of his Mission seems to have been comprized in baptizing a few Mulattoes

and Children of the Garrison: And it is with concern that I may add, that he has of late quite deviated from the Intentions of the Society, and his proper Line of Duty, by paying more Attention to the Purposes of Trade than of Religion.[102]

Morice's letter was published verbatim as part of a parliamentary report and thereby made public.[103] Morice's unabashedly negative assessment, given his official SPG position and the formal nature of the request for information, suggests the depth of members' dissatisfaction with Quaque. Quaque's observations had much in common with the dispirited reports of other SPG clergymen around the Atlantic world—many missionaries found their postings isolated and their charges unresponsive—but the secretary's criticisms of him were markedly different from the Society's typical public defenses of its missionaries. Morice's response indicates the SPG membership had largely given up on Quaque's mission by the 1780s, and though he was to continue at his station for almost another twenty years, Cape Coast came to be considered a backwater.

In another sign of the increasingly poor relationship between Quaque and the SPG, communication between them appears to have declined dramatically over time. While Quaque was extremely regular in his letters to the Society between 1765 and 1795, only one letter from Quaque to the Society survives from the twenty-year period between 1796 and his death in 1816. That letter, written in 1811, makes clear that he had not been in touch with London for several years.[104] The Society may not have written to Quaque at all after 1794.[105] Likewise, the regular payment of his salary appears to have broken down. At the time of his death, the Society owed him several hundred pounds in back pay.[106] Quaque appears to have been largely ignored by supporters of missionary work in nineteenth-century London. When the Reverend William Phillip went out to Cape Coast in 1817 at the behest of the Company of Merchants, he did so unaware that the SPG had supported a missionary there.[107]

Part of the explanation for the Society's lack of support for Quaque may lie in his own changing attitudes. In his letters to the SPG he challenged several of the principles that led to the establishment of his mission in the 1760s, including the compatibility between slavery and Christianity, which probably did not endear him to many within the membership. His own experiences also led him to question whether an African was best suited to convert Africans. In 1780 Quaque wrote, "It was natural and Reasonable to suppose that some probability of Success might be gained in a greater degree thro' one of their own Color and Kindred than any attempt that might be made from another Channel but to my great Sorrow and Astonishment have found it quite the reverse; and am much of

Opinion that Something more than a Human effort must work that effectual Cure of their Bigotry and Superstition."[108]

Quaque's self-doubt was a product of his own difficulties, but it also aligned with the growing pessimism within the SPG about its missionary work among "heathens" and with wider British propensities to increasingly stress the breadth and depth of differences between European and non-European peoples. When Olaudah Equiano sought Anglican ordination in 1779, Bishop Robert Lowth demurred that "the Bishops were not of opinion in sending a new missionary to Africa."[109] In 1783 Quaque asked the SPG to help educate his son Samuel so that he could eventually take up Quaque's mission, but the Society declined.[110] As Quaque aged, the Society made no effort to recruit any other African-born successor to replace him. Despite Lowth's statement, the SPG did not completely abandon African missionary work, but it did stop employing African-born missionaries. The Society became involved, through SPG clergymen in Canada, with the resettlement of "Loyalist" black people in Sierra Leone, but the clergyman assigned to accompany them was European. All of the short-lived missionaries the Society sent to Cape Coast to succeed Quaque were white. By the late eighteenth century, the Society had decided that if Africans were to be Christians, it would be Europeans doing the converting.

There is a particularly poignant coda to Quaque's story that illustrates the direction in which intellectual and cultural trends were moving. Several Victorian authors reported that Quaque had died an apostate. The first printed version of such a story appears to be an 1835 work by Sarah Lee, *Stories of Strange Lands; and Fragments from the Notes of A Traveller*. Lee, who had lived at Cape Coast and traveled elsewhere in Africa, was the widow of T. E. Bowditch, a British official who led an English diplomatic mission from Cape Coast to the increasingly powerful interior Akan state of Asante in 1816. Lee's book presented fictional tales that she augmented with "factual" notes based on her experiences in Africa. It was in one of these notes that Lee observed that "Very excellent people have thought, when a Negro, by dint of application, has been enabled to read the Gospel fluently, they have given him an infallible means of conversion." She disagreed, claiming that "when we consider that the whole of his previous life has been spent in the gratification of sensual feelings, can it be wondered at that the mind must be prepared before any real impression can be made upon it?" The illustration she offered was Quaque:

> In consequence of the rapid mortality which took place at Cape Coast . . . it was suggested that a coloured man should be educated in England for the chaplaincy. . . . He returned to Cape Coast as the Rev. Philip Quawquee, and for some years performed the church service in

his rooms at the Castle; he married a black woman, himself performing the Christian rites; his life was tolerably moral, and he was supposed to have no fear of death, and even to desire it, and he sent to England for a tombstone, properly inscribed with his name and profession. But the hour arrived which proves us all; and he sent for the old fetishwomen of Cape Coast, who smeared his door-posts with blood and eggs, practised every charm ever invented by African pagans, and he died in the midst of their yells and incantations; his greatest consolation being that, according to his request, he should be buried in the spur of the fortress, and every one would see "he had been parson Quawquee."[111]

Lee lived at Cape Coast when Quaque died, and although several biographical details she presented about him appear incorrect, it is possible such reports might reflect that Quaque became more integrated into local African society near the end of his life.[112] There is very little evidence on which to evaluate the truthfulness of Lee's claims, but their existence and repetition is indicative of the depths to which Quaque's reputation had sunk in the nineteenth century.

It is telling that those who repeated the tale of Quaque's apostasy were, like Lee, hostile to African-born men serving as Christian ministers. John Beecham, a secretary for the Wesleyan Methodist Missionary Society, reported in 1841 that "on his death-bed" Quaque "gave evidence that he had at least as much confidence in the influence of the fetish as in the power of Christianity." Beecham, who wrote as Methodists and the SPG competed for permission to establish a mission to Asante, saw Quaque as an example of a failed missionary strategy. He stressed an intrinsic, insurmountable gulf between Europeans and "natives":

> The case of this individual furnishes matter for grave consideration on the part of those who are anxious to promote the enlightenment and elevation of Africa. It yields no support to the plausible theory of Christianizing Pagan lands, primarily or chiefly, by bringing natives to this country for education with a view to their becoming the principal instructors of their countrymen; and shows that if, on their return, they are left to their own resources, it is more likely that they will sink down again to the level of their former state than that they will prove the regenerators of their country. Instructed natives may maintain their consistency, and act a useful part, where they are placed under the eye and direction of European Missionaries; but if they be thrown back into Heathen society without such support, it ought not to excite surprise, should the result prove that the time and care bestowed upon their culture have been expended in vain.[113]

Similarly, Brodie Cruickshank, who wrote in 1853 of Quaque that, "at the approach of death, he had recourse to Fetish practices," noted Quaque's mission only to emphasize the importance of the arrival of European Wesleyan missionaries at Cape Coast in 1835.[114] In attacking Quaque's reputation these authors were signaling, as the SPG's own policies had, new attitudes toward race and the global missionary project.

When the Society's missionaries and supporters found it difficult to convert non-Christian peoples, they often and increasingly stressed a gulf between European and non-European as an explanation. This dynamic can be seen at play in a particularly poignant way in responses to Quaque's mission. At Cape Coast, as at other places around the British Atlantic, the supporters of missionary Anglicanism looked for explanations as to why their work had not resulted in mass conversions of black people. Thompson's short mission to Cape Coast had seemed promising, but Quaque's fifty years of work had not produced the results the Society once thought possible. Quaque was tremendously isolated, a figure not fully accepted by any of the peoples of Cape Coast. Moreover, he operated in Africa alone, without fellow missionaries or the effective support of the Society's London leadership. As Quaque reported that his mission was not succeeding, and as he began to question the possibility of widespread conversion in an environment shaped by the slave trade, the Society came to question Quaque's ability and faithfulness.

Throughout Thompson and Quaque's missions, Christianity remained a minor presence in the life of the African community of Cape Coast. It was only in the mid-nineteenth century, when the imposition of direct British colonial rule reshaped much in the region, that it became widespread among the town's African population. Even then, Anglicanism's place in local life was constrained since, in the colonial context, the Church of England was to many Fante, "*abanmu asor*, the Church of the Castle, the government's Church, a privileged Church."[115] Some commentators have seen Quaque's importance as resting in the fact that his small-scale educational efforts produced a few young men who later in their lives played a role in establishing Methodism in modern Ghana.[116] However, these minor successes are less significant than the overall failure of his mission to achieve large numbers of African conversions. Despite the twentieth-century rehabilitation of Quaque's reputation as a missionary pioneer, his work at Cape Coast was disparaged by the Society and the wider missionary community during and after his life. There were nearly eighty years between Quaque's ordination and the ordination of a second African-born man, the Nigerian-born Samuel Crowther, as a priest of the Church of England. Crowther worked in Africa under the auspices of the evangelical Church Missionary Society and eventually became a bishop, but his own career was likewise marked by disputes over the wisdom of the Church having African-born clergymen.[117]

Rather than marking the beginning of Britain's many nineteenth-century missionary endeavors in Africa, Quaque's career is best understood as an expression of two eighteenth-century ideas that underpinned the SPG's work among the black people of the Atlantic world. First, Quaque's training and appointment reflected the survival into the 1750s and 1760s of a mind-set that downplayed innate differences between human populations and, instead, insisted that all peoples were equally called to and capable of receiving Christianity. This view was beginning to be challenged within the Society by this point, but it never disappeared entirely. It may be that new forms of circum-Atlantic evangelical religion, albeit in a particularly Anglican form, helped keep it viable among some SPG supporters, including Quaque's tutor John Moore. Second, Quaque's appointment embodied the idea that slavery and black conversion were compatible. In posting him to Cape Coast in cooperation with the Company of Merchants, the Society looked to capitalize on the cross-cultural exchanges enabled by the transatlantic slave trade to spread the gospel.

Quaque's long, melancholy mission seemed to challenge the wisdom of posting him to Cape Coast, but the lessons drawn from his difficulties were double-edged. In the aftermath of his career, abolitionism, not cooperation with slave traders, would inspire British missionary work in Africa. While Quaque's failure might have undermined the notion that the slave trade could help Christianity flourish, it also came to be used as a plank in an argument that collapsed and disparaged the abilities of black clergymen. In 1765 it was still possible for an African to be educated in England, ordained, and sent out as a missionary of the established church. By 1816 many believed that Africans were unfit for this work. In this way, changing attitudes about Quaque's mission coincided with two major developments in English society's attitudes toward black people: the growth of antislavery sentiment, and the contemporaneous growth of more critical and essentializing attitudes toward people of African descent.

PART FOUR

RESPONSES TO ANTISLAVERY

7

"Themselves Under this Very Predicament"

The Society and the Antislavery Movement, 1765–1838

Beginning in the 1760s, the context in which the SPG pursued its missionary program among black people was transformed by the emergence of the antislavery movement around the British Atlantic world. Antislavery activists coordinated their activities in the colonies and in Britain, relied on extensive webs of informants and supporters, and widely circulated information and arguments on behalf of their cause. Yet, by the time this movement became influential, the SPG had been sending ministers, religious texts, and funds to Britain's colonies for more than sixty years. When abolitionists began their efforts to awaken Britons to the horrors of the slave trade and slavery, many SPG members already considered themselves well versed in the religious, moral, and material conditions of enslaved people, and viewed their organization as having been at the forefront of efforts to reform slavery and to convert the black population of the Atlantic world.

Religious motivations and networks were central in the campaigns to end the slave trade and slavery itself.[1] However, as the SPG's history shows, religious opinions on slavery were divided in Britain for many decades, and religious networks also produced and distributed proslavery arguments. This chapter considers how the SPG's supporters responded to the antislavery movement in three phases: the period before and during the American Revolution, the period between the American Revolution and the passage of Parliamentary legislation against the slave trade in 1807, and the period between 1808 and the full emancipation of enslaved people around the British Empire in 1838. There were instances where those associated with the Society criticized colonial slaveholders and the slave trade, but SPG supporters also offered a carefully articulated set of counterarguments to abolitionists and emancipationists. The religious "credentials" and Society connections of several proslavery authors have often been ignored, and their works usually have been considered as operating purely in the economic interest of the West India lobby.[2] Examining texts produced by SPG affiliates elucidates how British and Atlantic arguments about slavery were not understood at the time simply as disputes between moral and godly abolitionists and selfish and irreligious planters. Debates about slavery were, in part, intramural contests within sincerely religious circles. These "internal" debates resonated around the Atlantic because the arguments they produced were later picked up and modified by a wider circle of pro- and antislavery authors.

The existence of these debates also suggests that there was no straight line between early SPG efforts to reform slavery and later efforts to abolish the slave trade and free enslaved people. Some of the Society's affiliates were critical of the slave trade, but few became outright abolitionists. Many SPG supporters argued for the reform of slavery, but such advocacy was not typically a way-point on a journey to emancipationism. Instead, many advocates of reform held an alternative vision of the future of colonial societies, one that had a secure place in it for a more paternalistic and Christian form of black slavery. These opinions were articulated in new ways and in more detail in response to the antislavery challenge of the late eighteenth century, but they drew on a long tradition of thought within missionary Anglicanism. SPG reformism was long lasting and often apparently sincere. But characterizing such reformism as a forerunner to abolitionism and emancipationism, which is promoted by scholarly tendencies to search for the origins of British abolitionism and to position the Society as a force for "Anglican humanitarianism," ignores the essentially *proslavery* character of many arguments produced by SPG supporters.[3] The danger is that subsuming such ideas about reform into a history that climaxes in the abolition of the slave trade and ultimately in emancipation makes the antislavery activists' originality and achievements appear less impressive than they were. It also misses the vitality of the debate *within* religious circles about what the future should look like.

In 1767 the Quaker Anthony Benezet sent copies of his antislavery tract, *A Caution to Great Britain and her Colonies with Respect to the Negro Trade*, to the SPG. Benezet began speaking against Quaker slaveholding around 1750, and by later in that decade his campaigning was aimed at a wider audience. The tract he sent to the Society attacked slavery and the slave trade as cruel and contrary to scripture. In a cover letter, Benezet asked SPG members to "seriously consider whether the necessity of at least endeavouring to put a stop to this infamous Traffick is not an Object peculiarly worthy the attention & labour of a Society appointed for the Propagation of the Gospel."[4] Benezet's letter compelled the

Society to consider the legitimacy of slavery in a formal and institutional way. As such, it marked the beginning of the SPG's extended engagement with the antislavery movement at home and in the colonies. The SPG's response to Benezet's challenge was formulated in a meeting of the membership and expressed in a letter that the SPG secretary Daniel Burton was formally ordered to write. Opinion within the SPG was never monolithic on any issue, but this exchange is particularly valuable because, in deciding how to respond, the Society had to identify and articulate a consensus, or at least majority view, on the issues Benezet raised.

While the Society's members "have a great esteem for you on account of the tenderness & humanity which you express for the Negro Slaves," Burton wrote, they could not support his calls for an end to slavery. The Society had decided that, "[T]hey cannot condemn the Practice of keeping Slaves as unlawful, finding the contrary very plainly implied in the precepts given by the Apostle, both to Masters & Servants, which last were for the most part Slaves." Besides arguing that slavery was biblically sanctioned, Burton reflected the sentiments that had grown stronger in the SPG's ranks after 1740. He urged Benezet to consider the religious and public safety implications of advocating an end to slavery, for "if the doctrine of the unlawfulness of Slavery should be taught in our Colonies, the Society apprehend that Masters" will "grow more suspicious & cruel, & much more unwilling to let their Slaves learn Christianity" while enslaved people "will be so strongly tempted by it to rebel against their Masters, that the most dreadful consequences to both will be likely to follow." The SPG's members considered Benezet's challenge so significant that Burton wrote that the Society "must earnestly beg you not to go further in publishing your Notions, but rather to retract them, if you shall see cause, which they hope you may on further consideration."[5]

Benezet's letter may have been more than a pro forma statement of his position because he seems to have hoped the Society was shifting its stance toward slavery. In 1766 Bishop William Warburton delivered the Society's annual sermon, which included, atypically for the period, a radical challenge to the legitimacy of the Atlantic slave trade.[6] Benezet knew of this development as the first 1766 edition of his *Caution and Warning* was printed in Philadelphia with a four-page extract from Warburton's sermon appended to it.[7] In his sermon Warburton called on the Society to use its ownership of Codrington, through which the Society had "become the innocent partakers of the fruits of this iniquitous traf[fic]," as an example for others who held slaves.[8] The Society was in the midst of cooperating with the Company of Merchants Trading to Africa in sending Philip Quaque to Africa, but Warburton also blasted the greed of colonists who employed slave labor and stated unambiguously that "the infamous traffic for Slaves, directly infringes both divine and human Law."[9]

Warburton's sermon went farther in its sustained critique of the slave trade and colonial slavery than previous SPG sermons, demonstrating that by the 1760s there were some people connected to the Society who questioned the way its missionary program had developed. Among these were probably some missionaries, like the New England clergymen Samuel Johnson and Edward Bass who corresponded with Quaque in this same period. This, however, did not lead to substantial change in the Society's institutional posture toward slavery. The rejection of Benezet's calls for a transatlantic abolitionist alliance, more than Warburton's calls for a new direction, guided SPG policy well into the nineteenth century.[10] Moreover, Warburton's sermon and Benezet's letter gave rise to an effort by others within the SPG to clarify its position on slavery and disavow any suggestion that the Society might provide corporate support for antislavery activism.

William Knox's 1768 *Three Tracts Respecting the Conversion and Instruction of the Free Indians, and Negroe Slaves in the Colonies*, which was addressed to the SPG, was a key text in this regard.[11] Knox's pamphlet is important both because of his own involvement with the Society and because, he later reported, he undertook the work specifically at the personal request of Thomas Secker, the archbishop of Canterbury, and the president and most influential figure within the SPG during this period. Secker had been associated with George Berkeley in the late 1720s, and there were clear affinities between Knox's ideas and the vision of a simultaneously more secure and more regulated slavery that underpinned the promotion of the Yorke-Talbot opinion by Berkeley's circle.[12] After a period as a plantation owner in Georgia, Knox returned to Britain in the early 1760s and established a political reputation that led to his appointment in 1770 as an undersecretary of state in the American department, a position he held until 1782.[13] Knox became a member of the SPG in 1765, and through the 1770s he consistently participated in supervising the management of Codrington plantation.[14] Knox's *Three Tracts* is best known for presenting his unique view that enslaved people should be regarded as subjects of the British Crown and because his thoughts on slavery intersected with broader questions about the proper relationship between Britain and its colonies.[15] While it is interesting as part of wider debates about slavery and empire, Knox's text was also intended to articulate a position on slavery and the future of the institution in the colonies that the missionary-minded membership of the Society could support.[16]

In his text, Knox acknowledged the difficulties the SPG had experienced in its decades of missionary work among non-Europeans, but he urged the Society and its supporters to redouble their efforts to convert Native Americans and black people. The first of Knox's tracts addressed the Society's work among

Native Americans; the second and third considered the position of enslaved people. Knox wrote the second tract in the period after Warburton's sermon had been issued but before the SPG had clarified its position on slavery in reply to Benezet's letter.[17] It addressed converting enslaved people in light of legal and social conditions operative in the British Empire.

Knox argued that colonial slavery was the peculiar product of colonial law. He thought the solution to the perennial problems of Christianizing slaves and mitigating planter cruelty lay in closer cooperation between church and government, and the more effective regulation of the colonies by Crown and Parliament. The idea that the imperial government and the established church might cooperate in reforming the colonies was long a dream for many supporters of the Society. Knox claimed that as things stood planters could have no confidence in the intentions behind reformist measures because of circum-imperial legal uncertainties. "The British laws disown perpetual servitude, and the people of these islands have a general antipathy to slavery. The right of the planter to his Negro is only founded on the acts of his provincial assembly, and beyond their jurisdiction he has no power over him." This situation also unsettled enslaved people and, when fueled by incendiary sentiments like Warburton's, increased the likelihood of rebellions. In this volatile environment, planters were hostile to education and Christianization, which they feared could lead to emancipation.[18]

While Knox raised the possibility that abolition or emancipation might theoretically occur, he did so to emphasize the fact that neither Parliament nor the Crown had ever taken advantage of any opportunities to restrict or end the slave trade or slavery. He also offered a historical survey that concluded that slavery was practiced widely throughout history and around the world. Given that slavery and the slave trade were sanctioned by laws and by historical precedents, Knox issued a challenge to Warburton and any other potential supporters of abolition within the ranks of the SPG:

> If the reverend members of the society should be of opinion that this trade is contrary to divine laws, it will surely be proper to apply to government for an act of parliament to prohibit it.... But if on the contrary the opinion should be, that the trade is not a violation of the divine laws, it will be highly proper to transmit that opinion to the colonies, for the satisfaction of conscientious planters, as well as to encourage them to give their Negroes instruction, thereby to avail themselves of such authority for making them contented with their condition.[19]

Of course, it is clear throughout his work that Knox thought slavery was permitted by divine and colonial law. He made the case that the only way forward for the transatlantic conversion project lay in reassuring planters through a statement of SPG principles and clear, imperial law sanctioning slavery.

The third of Knox's tracts, written after the SPG had responded to Benezet's letter, noted that the Society had now admitted "The lawfulness of purchasing negroe slaves, and continuing them and their posterity in perpetual servitude." In light of that welcome decision, Knox offered the Society proposals for better- ing the treatment of enslaved people and accomplishing their conversion on the basis that they were "surely to be deemed subjects of Great Britain in their par- ticular capacity and circumstance" and that consequently colonial laws concern- ing them should be subject to review by the Crown and British courts. In Knox's vision of a more tightly regulated empire, laws should "create reciprocal duties" between masters and enslaved people. Based on this premise, Knox proposed a revived missionary program that would rely on itinerant missionaries and would use music to attract enslaved people to religious services and classes. He also called for specific reforms, emphasizing the oft-stated SPG concern that enslaved people be given Sundays off from fieldwork. Finally, looking to put the central tenet of his tracts into action, Knox advocated the distribution of a "discourse addressed to the owners of Negroes in the colonies, in which the lawfulness of retaining the Negroe slaves in perpetual servitude, should be set forth as the opinion of the society" and "the obligation" of planters to convert their slaves should be "pressed home upon their consciences."[20]

Knox's plan had reformist elements, but this reformism was construed explic- itly as an alternative to early stirrings of the antislavery movement. The Society never embraced all aspects of Knox's missionary proposals nor pushed for slaves to be recognized as subjects. His text reflected his specific concerns with the position of the colonies vis-à-vis imperial law, but many of Knox's ideas echoed themes that had been present in SPG missionary efforts over the previous decades. Likewise, Knox suggested that his vision of the future had more sup- port from the Society's membership than Benezet's calls for collaboration in antislavery activism. Knox underlined his victory over Benezet by including, and thereby publicizing, the Society's previously unpublished rejection of Benezet's overtures as part of the *Three Tracts.*[21]

The vitality of precocious anti-abolitionist thinking within the Society was further demonstrated by Thomas Thompson's 1772 *The African Trade for Negro Slaves, Shewn to be Consistent with the Principles of Humanity, and with the Laws of Revealed Religion.* As a whole, members of the SPG were much less committed to defending the slave trade than they were to protecting slavery itself. Thompson, however, defended both, and his claims to authority rested in large part on his own experiences as the first SPG missionary to Africa. The Society's member- ship had recognized this service on its behalf by electing him a fellow member in 1769.[22] His 1772 pamphlet, dedicated to his other former co-employers, the "Worshipful Committee of the Company of Merchants Trading to Africa," deployed his religious knowledge to defend the slave trade as an economic necessity that existed under the sanction of civil and biblical law. The slave trade, Thompson argued, was "really as vindicable as any species of trade whatever."[23]

The wider context for Thompson's work was the public attention focused on slavery in 1772 by the Somerset case, in which Lord Mansfield, chief justice of King's Bench, ultimately ruled that a person who had been a slave in the colonies could not be forcibly removed from England. The case was widely considered as a test of whether slavery was permitted by English law, and Mansfield's decision, although carefully and deliberately narrow, was widely interpreted as a major antislavery victory. Mansfield was petitioned to issue the writ of habeas corpus around which the case revolved on December 3, 1771.[24] It was more than six months before Mansfield issued a ruling, and in that time a public debate and lobbying effort emerged to which Thompson's pamphlet was a contribution. In this charged atmosphere, Thompson's work received a quick and largely critical review in London's *Monthly Review*. While to the anonymous reviewer Thompson appears "a sensible man, and capable of discussing the argument" ultimately his claims grounding the legitimacy of slavery in Jewish law were "not, in our view of the matter, at all conclusive." Still, the journal conceded Thompson's views might have some merit, noting that though "upon the whole, we must own, this little treatise is not convincing to us" yet "as different persons are differently affected by the same considerations, it may prove more satisfactory to others."[25] Thompson's views, according to the *Monthly Review,* could be disputed but not dismissed.

This helps explain why Granville Sharp produced his 1773 *Essay on slavery, proving from Scripture its inconsistency with humanity and religion,* which was a direct rebuttal to Thompson. Sharp, who had begun aiding enslaved people in Britain in and out of the courts in the mid-1760s, was a prime mover behind the effort to make the Somerset case a test of English law on slavery. Like Thompson, Sharp had a deep personal commitment to the Church of England and a connection to the SPG. His grandfather, the archbishop of York John Sharp, had been a charter member of the Society in 1701. Sharp's correspondence suggests he was motivated initially by fears that Thompson's argument might sway Mansfield's decision in the Somerset case. In the case's aftermath, he remained worried that Thompson's claims could be used to support a Parliamentary bill that might be introduced to undo Mansfield's judgment.[26]

Sharp claimed that Thompson's argument was based on the "false premise" that there was a strict agreement between the Jewish law, which allowed slavery, and natural law. Some laws contained in the Bible, Sharp contended, were intended to be binding always and everywhere while others applied solely to the historical and cultural circumstances of the "Israelitish commonwealth." After citing other biblical laws that were generally understood to apply only to the Israelites, Sharp contended that the gospel, in any case, destroyed "all narrow, national partiality" and required the profession of "universal benevolence" by Christians. Therefore, he argued, no matter how much the slave trade might benefit England and her colonies, they could not profit from the sufferings of others. Sharp revealed how the combination of Thompson's religious credentials and proslavery arguments upset abolitionists through phrases like "For shame Mr. Thompson!" and observations including "Mr. Thompson has notoriously wrested St. Paul's words."[27]

These exchanges reverberated around the Atlantic world. Sharp's essay circulated among British and colonial abolitionists in manuscript and was first published in New Jersey in 1773. Thompson's arguments had also quickly become known in the colonies. The first edition of Sharp's essay included a lengthy editor's introduction, which took note of both Thompson's text and the opinions of it expressed in the Monthly Review. Both the essay and this editorial augmentation in turn re-crossed the Atlantic and were published as an appendix in the first London edition of Sharp's longer 1776 work The Just Limitation of Slavery in the Laws of God.[28] In Sharp's 1777 A Tract on the Law of Nature, and Principles of Action in Man, Thompson was again noted, being pithily though rather misleadingly dismissed simply as "an advocate for the African slave trade."[29] That Thompson's arguments continued to nettle antislavery advocates for many years is underlined by the preface to the 1786 English-language edition of Thomas Clarkson's antislavery Cambridge dissertation, which noted that, "Of all the publications in favour of the slave-trade, or the subsequent slavery in the colonies, there is not one, which has not been written either by a chaplain to the African factories, or by a merchant, or by a planter, or by a person whose interest has been connected in the cause which he has taken upon him to defend."[30] Sharp and Clarkson never fully addressed Thompson's connections to the SPG in print, a striking omission given that he was the first Anglican missionary to Africa. They appear to have wanted to downplay Thompson's remarkable personal missionary history and instead stress his connections to the Company of Merchants Trading to Africa, tying him to the greed of planters and slave traders rather than to a church to which they themselves were deeply attached.

Criticism of the slave trade and masters did not disappear from the Society's ranks. In the aftermath of Mansfield's Somerset decision, Sharp vainly hoped for a time that the aging archbishop of York, Robert Hay Drummond, might mobilize antislavery sentiment in the Society.[31] In 1775 Shute Barrington used his annual sermon to call the slave trade "as inhuman in the mode of carrying it on, as it is unjustifiable in it's [sic] principle." Yet, he claimed that the position of slaves in the West Indies had improved through the good example provided by the Society's management of Codrington. Barrington would later build on this sermon and become an important advocate for abolitionism within the Anglican episcopate.[32] Barrington became a notable voice against the slave trade, but he too failed to bring many other SPG supporters along with him.

Wider events may have had some bearing on this. Barrington's 1775 sermon contained no mention of the building political crisis in America, but it soon became impossible to ignore. The American Revolution played a central part in the development of antislavery into a national political force in the 1780s.[33] Paradoxically, despite this broader transformation, for several years the American Revolution diverted SPG supporters' attention away from more theoretical considerations of slavery and the slave trade. The American war massively disrupted and threatened to totally destroy the colonial Church of England that the Society had helped build.[34] For several years SPG attention and resources were directed primarily toward aiding displaced American clergymen and Loyalist congregations.

The SPG's concern with the religious condition of black people was not completely abandoned during the war. African Americans seized upon the war as an opportunity to claim their own liberty.[35] Virginia's governor Lord Dunmore's 1775 proclamation promising freedom to any person who took up arms on behalf of the Crown led substantial numbers of runaway slaves in the Chesapeake to join British troops. In 1779 the British general Sir Henry Clinton guaranteed "every Negro who shall desert the Rebel Standard" the ability to pursue "any Occupation" they chose, and subsequently tens of thousands of people escaped to behind British lines. Several thousand long free or recently escaped black people, still-enslaved people owned by Loyalist masters, and enslaved people seized by British troops were among those who traveled to Canadian territories during and immediately after the war. In this context, many black people underlined and bolstered their claims to liberty and independence by embracing Christianity in general and Anglicanism in particular. As the Reverend John Breyton of Halifax, who baptized "many hundreds" of black immigrants in the aftermath of the war, reported, "they daily crowd to me for Baptism, and seem happy with their prospects of Religion and Freedom."[36]

However, few British settlers, or the Society's supporters, envisioned those North American colonies that remained loyal to the Crown as particular bastions of freedom for black people. John Wentworth, SPG member, former royal governor of New Hampshire, and future governor of Nova Scotia, brought enslaved people with him to Nova Scotia when he emigrated as a Loyalist. Finding it difficult to continue to profit off their labor in Halifax, he shipped the people he

owned to his cousin's plantation in Dutch Guiana.[37] In a striking repetition of
earlier patterns, the colonists of Prince Edward Island passed a law in 1781 stipulating that baptism would not entail emancipation.[38]

Several SPG ministers who were themselves Loyalists worked among black
and white refugees in these years. Society-supported clergymen cooperated
with the Associates of Dr. Bray in establishing schools for free and enslaved
black children in Nova Scotia.[39] In 1786 the SPG appointed Patrick Fraser as a
missionary to accompany free black people who left England to settle in Sierra
Leone, although he soon left his position. The missionary Jacob Bailey, who
was forced to flee his Maine station and resettle in Nova Scotia, reported in
1784 that about sixty-five black families lived near the town of Digby and were
"heartily disposed to receive any religious instruction which is offered to
them," but were being ministered to by one of the area's "enthusiastic teachers."
Many other SPG missionaries reported with concern about the competition
they faced in these new black communities from Wesleyan and Baptist
preachers, some of whom were black themselves. Bailey reported that both the
Digby people and others near Annapolis had been enslaved in the "Southern
provinces," where their masters "detained them under pagan darkness." He
had baptized several of them and thought their "situation and humanity"
meant they deserved more religious care. Yet, rather improbably given these
peoples' extraordinary quest for freedom, he also claimed that they had "discovered a docility and readiness to embrace the Christian religion which is
highly commendable."[40] The experiences of many SPG clergymen and the
Society's communications network put its supporters in a strong position to
understand how the conflict reshaped the landscape of slavery in the Atlantic
world, but these events seem to have to done little to change attitudes toward
slavery within the organization as a whole. Instead, they were widely interpreted as demonstrating the Society's long-standing claims that correctly inculcated Christianity would instill proper sentiments of loyalty and obedience
in black and white people alike.

The situation on Codrington plantation likewise inhibited any major change
in policy. While the 1750s and 1760s were a profitable period on the estate, a
succession of bad crops pushed its accounts into the red in the early 1770s. In
1775 financial problems led the Society to temporarily close the estate's school
for white children. The coming of war disrupted Barbadian trade, hampering
exports and driving up the price of imported foodstuffs and other supplies.
Most significantly, the Society's risky 1766 decision to invest a huge amount of
capital (£18,000) in the purchase of another entire Barbados plantation had
proven by this time to be disastrous. Under the plan, the Society bought the
Henley plantation as a way to obtain a large number of "seasoned slaves" for use

on Codrington in the hopes of ending the need for making costly purchases of newly imported Africans, who were likely to die soon after arriving in Barbados. The Henley purchase was a massive, long-term economic investment in slavery made in the same year as Warburton's antislavery sermon, and it added 149 "seasoned" enslaved people to Codrington's labor force. However, its financial viability depended on recouping much of the invested money by selling Henley's land and buildings to a third party, and this proved a debacle. The land's purchaser, the merchant Gedney Clarke, failed to make payments to the Society, and his subsequent bankruptcy entangled the SPG in a protracted, expensive legal struggle to obtain payment or at least regain control of Henley so that it could find a new buyer. The estate's losses in the period were so severe that they "would have broken almost any private owner."[41] Natural disaster compounded financial folly. In October 1780 a major hurricane struck Barbados and severely damaged the estate. The combination of insufficient capital reserves, successive poor crops, and the need to rebuild led the Society, already stretched by the crisis in America, to transfer considerable amounts from its general fund to its Barbados account. By 1781 the "debt" owed to the Society's general fund from the Barbados account was over £3,000.[42] The need to right Codrington's finances loomed in the background as SPG members engaged with antislavery activists in the coming years.

Daniel Burton's reply to Benezet, the SPG's decision to invest in slavery for the long-term through the Henley purchase, Knox's tracts, and Thompson's early attempt to counter antislavery arguments collectively show there was a powerful countermovement to antislavery activism within the Society in these years. This led figures like Knox and Thompson to produce some of the earliest defenses of slavery and the slave trade that emerged in the Atlantic world. In Knox's case, the result was the articulation of an agenda the Society had long supported—the reform of slavery and the expansion of efforts to Christianize enslaved people—newly presented as an alternative to the proposals of antislavery activists like Benezet. What was envisioned by Knox, and others in the coming decades, was a continuing Atlantic slave system that was more patriarchal and Christian *and* more stable and secure. In Thompson's case, the weight of his connections to the Society and his own personal history offered a considerable challenge to antislavery activists' efforts to seize the moral high ground. While the role of SPG figures in criticizing slavery has long been recognized, the way that collectively these other early actions and texts formed an influential counterargument often has been missed. If the period between 1766 and 1782 marked the opening of a transatlantic debate about slavery, as far as the Society was concerned it was not clear who was winning it as the American war ended.

The 1783 SPG annual sermon by Beilby Porteus was an important moment in the history of the abolitionist movement. In it Porteus issued a clear, dramatic, and forceful condemnation of the slave trade along with a detailed critique of colonial slavery. While most other sermons that mentioned slavery did so as part of a broader commentary on the Society's work, Porteus devoted nearly his entire text to considering the position of enslaved people. He not only expanded dramatically on the criticisms of the cruelty and impiety of colonial masters offered in other SPG sermons, and characterized the slave trade as an "opprobrious traffic," he also pointed to the gap between the Society's claimed good intentions in its management of Codrington and the poor results that had been achieved there. He called on the Society to make the religious and material plight of enslaved people a priority. Porteus's sermon marked the public accession to the abolitionist cause of an influential politico-religious figure.[43]

Porteus's stance forced the Society's members to again consider their institution's position on slavery. As he promised in his sermon, in March 1784 Porteus submitted to the Society a detailed plan for overhauling Codrington's management and expanding Anglicanism's outreach to West Indian black people. But after considering the matter for only four hours, a committee decided that "his Lordship merited the thanks of the Society for the great pains and trouble he had taken, but that the circumstances of the Society rendered it at that time unadvisable to adopt the plan." It was evident that "the Bishop was both disappointed and hurt by such a hasty rejection."[44] Porteus's subsequent efforts on behalf of enslaved people, which included establishing a new organization to promote conversions in the West Indies, were made outside of the Society.[45]

The Society's quick rejection of Porteus's proposal was probably partly attributable to Codrington's continuing economic problems, which had reached a crisis point. Anxious to stop the estate from sapping the organization's general operating fund, the Society decided in 1783 to lease the plantation out in return for a secure annual rent of £500. One of the Society's Codrington attorneys, the successful Barbados plantation owner John Brathwaite, agreed to this scheme and, in the interests of reviving the now defunct school on the estate, offered to donate any profits made while the plantation was under his management to the Society. Porteus knew about the lease but evidently still hoped the Society would change its policies.[46] However, the Society's decision to entrust the management of Codrington to Brathwaite, who also served as Parliamentary agent for Barbados and a prominent spokesman for West Indian planters in this period, suggests the membership's continuing comfort with slaveholding and its political advocates.[47] In the ten years between 1783 and 1793, when the Society reclaimed direct control, Brathwaite's nonresident management turned Codrington's financial fortunes around.[48] Slave births began to outnumber deaths, and the

Figure 15. Beilby Porteus (1731–1809), Bishop of London (© Trustees of the
British Museum)

plantation was put on a path to consistent long-term profitability. The Society
was grateful—in 1793 Brathwaite was thanked with a piece of silver plate—but
the period highlighted how the control of Codrington always factored into the
Society's responses to proposals advocating changes to Atlantic slavery. Since
the lease removed the Society's Barbados committee from direct involvement in
the estate, it also severely limited the ability of the SPG to dictate how the time
of enslaved people there should be spent. Efforts to convert and educate the
population of Codrington stagnated even as Porteus and others were advocating
a new drive to Christianize the West Indies.

   Porteus does not appear to have been alone in the mid-1780s in hoping that
the Society might have been willing to re-examine its position on slavery.

Granville Sharp became a member of the SPG in 1785, a reflection of his hereditary ties to the Society and his commitment to evangelization. His membership in the Society appears to have been primarily the product of his interest in the American episcopate in the aftermath of the Revolution. Samuel Seabury, the first bishop of the newly independent Protestant Episcopal Church in the United States, was a former SPG missionary consecrated by non-juring Scottish bishops in 1784 after English prelates refused to participate on religious and political grounds. Sharp helped secure the transatlantic political and ecclesiastical settlement that resulted in the next two American bishops, William White and Samuel Provoost, being consecrated by bishops from the Church of England in 1787.[49] In this effort, his interests in ensuring a continuing close relationship between American Episcopalianism and the Church of England aligned closely with SPG members' desires to secure their legacy in the United States.

When it came to slavery, Sharp, like Porteus, faced much more resistance within the Society. In 1786 Sharp successfully promoted SPG support for Patrick Fraser, who accompanied black colonists to Sierra Leone, but he failed in his attempts to swing the membership over to abolitionism.[50] His frustration was reflected in a letter Sharp wrote to John Moore, the archbishop of Canterbury, in August 1786. Sharp had recently intervened to aid a black man who was being shipped against his will to Barbados. The incident, he told Moore, reminded him of the fact that Barbados still retained "abominable, wicked laws" that allowed masters to kill their slaves and that Codrington plantation remained SPG property. The Society's continued ownership of enslaved people, despite the fact that it had "long experienced the extreme impropriety and unprofitableness of that baneful mode of cultivation" distressed Sharp as a committed churchman. His letter also illuminates the difficulties the Society's continuing acceptance of slavery posed for pious Anglican abolitionists like him. He reported that when Codrington "was mentioned in the last meeting of the Society, I could scarcely refrain from the declaring my mind about it; but thought it might be improper to interfere, as the business was already referred to a Committee." Sharp's fear, it seems, was that he might be seen as speaking out of turn within an organization so closely identified with the church he loved and led by bishops whose authority Sharp was committed to upholding.

Sharp also told Moore he continued to be concerned by Burton's reply to Anthony Benezet "many years ago," which he claimed had led to a great deal of his own research on slavery. He was hesitant to air his concerns about Burton directly in print, but he noted that his research had resulted in several antislavery tracts intended "to remove the stigma thrown on our Holy Religion, as if it could be deemed capable of affording any sanction to a complicated system of iniquity." Sharp also pointed out that while he had answered Thomas Thompson, whom in this private context he identified as "their missionary," with a publication of his own, he had "too much veneration for the Society to permit their opinion to be called publicly in question."[51] Sharp's letter reveals how seriously some antislavery activists took the Society's position and how delicately some felt compelled to handle it. While Sharp's reputation as a philanthropist with strong Anglican credentials might have won him a hearing from some SPG members, he too failed in these years to persuade most bishops or the Society to support antislavery activism.

Likewise, while some other SPG annual sermons in the 1780s echoed some of Porteus's themes, none went as far as his did. The 1784 and 1785 preachers avoided controversy by not discussing the Society's work among enslaved people at all. The 1786 sermon by Thomas Thurlow, bishop of Lincoln, sought a delicate middle ground. On the one hand, Thurlow positioned Atlantic slavery as the fulfillment of Noah's prophetic curse and therefore a vindication of the truth of scripture.[52] On the other hand, Thurlow questioned the humanity and lamented the cruelties of the planters.

The 1787 sermon by John Warren, bishop of Bangor, forcefully described the slave trade as "an infamous traffick, which ought not to be suffered under a Christian Government" and admitted with regard to the Society's efforts to convert enslaved people that "this part of our *Design* has not hitherto been attended with much success," but repeated the traditional explanations for these difficulties by attributing them to masters. Rather than criticize the Society's management of Codrington, Warren returned to the idea it was a model to other masters. In light of the poor financial performance of Codrington since the 1770s, Warren suggested that providing this example was "the best, perhaps the only reason for our continuing to execute a *Trust*, which has hitherto proved very burthensome to us, and which will probably never answer in point of profit." This was a new characterization of Codrington, one that would be amplified in some subsequent sermons, but it was not a clear call for the abolition of the slave trade, much less a call for an end to slavery.[53] Moreover, Warren predicted a bright future, noting that "many of the Planters are said now to be not only less rigorous in the tasks they impose" but also more attentive to "the spiritual wants of this unhappy Race." Rather than question the Society's policies, Warren suggested that the change in the planters could be attributed to their "being convinced of the justice and advantage of such a conduct, partly, we hope, by the admonitions from this place, and partly by the useful example, which this Society have held out in the mild treatment of their own *Slaves*."[54] The Yorkshire Anglican clergyman and poet William Mason cited Warburton's 1766 annual sermon and

Warren's text in a 1788 antislavery sermon he produced, but sentiments like Warren's did not amount to a clear endorsement of the abolitionists' political agenda or a dramatic new direction for the Society's views on slavery. Warren, in fact, was among those that the West Indian lobbyist Stephen Fuller counted as political opponents of abolition in 1788.[55]

Abolitionist churchmen's struggles to awaken their co-religionists in this period are well known, but the period between 1783 and 1807 also saw more figures connected with the SPG promote reformism as an alternative to more radical antislavery measures. In response, in the later 1780s, some antislavery authors followed Porteus and began to more openly criticize the SPG. This dynamic led proslavery authors without direct connections to the SPG to identify their cause with a defense of the Society. They highlighted statements on slavery by SPG supporters as counterweights to the religious and moral criticisms of slaveholding disseminated by abolitionists. As a result of these exchanges, the Society's position on slavery stopped being primarily an internal matter and became part of a wider debate about slavery and the slave trade.

A central figure in this period was the antislavery activist and Anglican clergyman James Ramsay. Ramsay's 1784 *Essay on the Treatment and Conversion of African Slaves in the British Sugar Colonies* provided an eyewitness account of the cruelties of West Indian slavery and laid out cautious plans for ameliorating the lives of enslaved people, for their eventual emancipation, and for their religious conversion. Ramsay was a slave owner himself, and he claimed a plan for bettering slaves' lives must "be gentle, slow in its progress, keeping pace with the opening of their minds, and looking forward . . . to a distant period."[56] Ramsay initially stressed that the better treatment of enslaved people and their conversion to genuine Christian belief would benefit masters. Nevertheless, proslavery West Indians looked on Ramsay's detailed criticism of their treatment of slaves as a slanderous betrayal.

As an Anglican clergyman, Ramsay was not a particularly harsh critic of the Church of England in the colonies. Instead, he repeated the common criticisms that masters refused to give their enslaved workers Sundays off and that too many planters were unwilling to give clergymen access to enslaved people. His proposals for achieving more conversions, which Porteus largely adopted in his presentation to the Society in 1784, aimed to ease the minds of masters and win the support of the Anglican hierarchy. Although as a bishop and Society member Porteus was willing to question the Society's efforts to convert enslaved people in his 1783 sermon, the only mention that Ramsay made of the SPG in his long essay was the suggestion that it be given the authority to "examine, select and recommend" potential catechists to be sent to the West Indies as part of the more vigorous missionary program he envisioned.[57]

While SPG annual sermons often noted the cruelty, greed, and impiety of Atlantic slave owners, Ramsay's coupling of similar criticisms with calls for dramatic changes in the slave trade and eventual emancipation elicited virulent responses. The 1784 *An Answer to the Reverend James Ramsay's Essay* contested the veracity of Ramsay's depiction of Caribbean slavery while claiming to reveal his failings as a clergyman.[58] As part of this strategy, the *Answer* also made an explicit effort to counter any idea that Christianity was historically inimical to slavery. Beside citing the typical scriptural quotations, the anonymous author of the *Answer* countered "the feeble attacks of enthusiasts" with references to several SPG sermons and texts from the 1740s, "all which concur in acknowledging the legality of slavery to be expressly allowed by the Holy Scriptures, though they recommend instruction and proper treatment." The *Answer* did not deny that enslaved people should become Christians but insisted "if ever negroes are converted to the profession and practice of Christianity, it must be in their present state" while "the schemes of the Essayist are visionary and impractical" and maybe even "ruinous and subversive of the community."[59]

Ramsay's essay also drew responses from figures with direct ties to the Society. In 1786 the Barbados plantation owner Philip Gibbes first published his *Instructions for the Treatment of Negroes*, one of several texts published by West Indians in this period that laid out plans for the better treatment of enslaved people on economic and humanitarian grounds, in part seeking to undercut abolitionists' charges that planters were unfeeling, greedy, and cruel. Gibbes had a long connection with the SPG, having been elected a member in 1777 and serving as an attorney for Codrington in the years before Brathwaite leased the property. Gibbes claimed that the guidelines he offered for how enslaved people, particularly recent arrivals from Africa, should be housed, fed, worked, and so on had first been offered to a fellow plantation owner in 1771, before antislavery agitation became serious.[60]

In his text, Gibbes argued for a reform of the slave trade, which would, after a considerable period of time, culminate in its abolition—though not in emancipation for enslaved people. Gibbes also looked "to impress every Christian, who thinks himself justified in holding a property in his fellow creatures, that it is his duty to make the lives of his slaves as happy as a state of slavery admits." Masters should promote Christianity, Gibbes claimed, in part because it would increase their plantations' efficiency. Young enslaved people, in particular, should be baptized and provided with religious instruction. Their lessons should start with promoting a belief in God and the message that enslaved converts could demonstrate their belief through good behavior. Such instruction would benefit masters because "a submission to the state, in which it has pleased God to place them, cannot be too early inculcated."[61] As a whole, Gibbes's plan

took converting slaves seriously and, if implemented, would have entailed significant changes in how enslaved people were commonly treated. At the same
time, it was essentially a defense of slaveholding, a vindication of West Indian
planters, and a work that argued for only a very gradual end to the slave trade at
some unspecified future date. As was the case for Thompson's earlier arguments
on the slave trade, Gibbes's commitment to Christianizing the Atlantic world's
black population made it difficult for abolitionists to dismiss his arguments.[62]

Gibbes was a proslavery reformer: he had a history of interest in converting
the Atlantic world's black population and was a planter with an economic interest in perpetuating slavery. By the late 1780s, proslavery authors without similar religious credentials were appealing to the moral and religious cover provided
by the SPG. The Nevis planter James Tobin's anonymously published *Cursory
Remarks upon the Reverend Mr. Ramsay's Essay* presented a page-by-page refuta-
tion of Ramsay's account of West Indian life.[63] Ramsay's subsequent self-defense
elicited a response in which Tobin highlighted the SPG's position to justify
slaveholding. Tobin's *A Farewel Address to the Rev. Mr. James Ramsay* (1788) included an appendix that reprinted the Society's 1768 reply to Anthony Benezet.
Tobin also approvingly reprinted an excerpt from the London newspaper the
Morning Chronicle, which had also recently published the Society's reply to
Benezet. The *Morning Chronicle* printed the Society's letter because of "A great
deal having lately been said, as if the Bench of Bishops, and the Society for the
Propagation of the Gospel in Foreign Parts, had given their countenance to a
present prevailing opinion, that slavery is inconsistent with the natural and
divine rights of mankind."[64] The reappearance of the reply to Benezet in proslavery literature and the London press in the late 1780s shows the continuing
importance attached to the SPG's position. Because of the corporate nature of
the Society's answer, proslavery polemicists aimed to depict it as an official and
even binding expression of the Church of England's views on slavery, even as
many individual clergymen and some bishops were becoming more sympathetic to the abolitionist cause.

Public awareness of the reply to Benezet also illustrates the ongoing problem
the Society's institutional position posed for abolitionists. A telling example of
this is James Ramsay's 1788 *Objections to the Abolition of the Slave Trade, with
Answers*, which provided rebuttals to objections to abolition that Ramsay had
"collected from various persons and writings."[65] In the first edition of his work,
Ramsay considered the fact that "A religious society is possessed of a plantation
in Barbadoes, and employs slaves." Ramsay argued the Society:

> [H]olds the Codrington estate for particular purposes, on condition of
> keeping up a certain number of slaves. Like other absent proprietors, it

has suffered by the mismanagement of servants. It is now in a train to answer both the intentions of the donor, and the wishes of humanity.[66]

It may be that neither proslavery nor antislavery forces considered Ramsay's attempt to distance the Society from Codrington to be sufficient, because in the second edition of his work Ramsay added a second objection to abolitionism connected with the SPG: "Dr. Burton, Secretary to this society, wrote a letter to Mr. Benezet, under the direction of an eminent prelate, which acknowledged the lawfulness of slavery, as mentioned in the bible."

While Ramsay's answer to the first objection was short, his attempt to answer the second objection was much longer and more involved, suggesting he took it as needing careful handling. First, he attempted to contextualize Burton's response, writing, "That letter appears plainly to have been written under the impression of an alarm for the consequences of agitating then the question of liberty, for which the slaves were not prepared, nor the times fit." Despite his own emancipationist sympathies, Ramsay further attempted to highlight the crucial distinction between freedom for all slaves and abolition of the slave trade, claiming "the abstract question, 'is slavery lawful?' is not now agitated." What was in dispute, Ramsay said, was whether the modern slave trade, with all its cruelties, should be allowed to continue. Ramsay seems to have been discomfited by the idea that the reply to Benezet was the considered response of the Society and the leading Anglicans who constituted its membership. He attempted to portray the Society's reply to Benezet as the product of sloppy reasoning by Burton acting in his individual capacity, claiming that "the Doctor," in considering whether slavery was lawful, left "it as he found the practice to be in the times of the apostles" and failed to consider the slave trade as it was practiced in modern times. In any case, Ramsay argued, "We are not indeed concerned in the defence of Dr. Burton."[67] Ramsay's text strove, rather unconvincingly, to separate the SPG from its 1768 statement in the hopes of reconciling his abolitionist beliefs with his loyalty to the established church.

Ramsay's circumspection is revealing, but the place the SPG occupied in this period's debates is fully demonstrated by a less inhibited antislavery author. Peter Peckard was a Cambridge vice-chancellor with a record of outspoken, independent thinking on theological matters, which had led him into conflict with leading churchmen, including Thomas Secker.[68] His 1788 abolitionist text *Am I not a Man? And a Brother?* focused on dispelling the idea that people of African descent were less than fully human. In it he disparaged the SPG's decades of work among enslaved people by rhetorically asking, "Has the Society for the Propagation of the Christian Religion ever made any endeavours to convert the African Negroes to Christianity? If they have, on what principles have they done it?" If the Society had failed to make such attempts, was this "because these Negroes are not of the Human race?" Peckard suggested this was indeed the view of some in the Society, claiming "that they are *not* Men the author has heard more than one of that venerable society positively assert."[69] If Peckard was an accurate witness, he suggests that more modern forms of racist thought might have been developing in the Society's ranks.[70] In any case, Peckard's criticism went to the heart of the SPG's sense of its own history. For decades, the Society's sermons and reports had asserted the humanity of the Atlantic world's black population and detailed its efforts to convert them; Peckard dismissed these efforts and attacked the membership. While some figures like Porteus might admit the SPG had not achieved all it had hoped, Peckard suggested that it had not even tried.

The first Parliamentary campaign to end the slave trade, led by William Wilberforce, came to a head in 1789. Ultimately, Wilberforce's political opponents managed to prevent a vote being taken on abolitionist motions during that year's Parliamentary session by arguing that the House of Commons should hear evidence itself about the slave trade, but the legislative maneuvering by both sides was accompanied by a swirling public debate that again involved and invoked the Society. A new edition of William Knox's 1768 *Three Tracts* was published in 1789, reasserting his views at this critical juncture.[71] The anonymous pamphlet *No Abolition* presented excerpts from Parliamentary reports and other sources to prove the economic value and legality of the slave trade. Its appendix quoted extensively from the SPG reply to Benezet and pointed the interested reader to the new edition of Knox's work for more information.[72] While these texts drew on previously published works, this was also a moment when figures associated with the Society produced new arguments. In an attempt to counter Parliamentary abolitionism, several texts explicitly aligned the Society's position on slavery with a defense of the status quo.

In the years since Porteus's 1783 annual sermon, no bishops speaking before the Society had gone as far as he did, but several had characterized the end of the slave trade as something to be wished for. The 1789 sermon by Samuel Hallifax, bishop of St. Asaph, responded to the debates of the late 1780s and revealed the extent to which some within the Church of England and the Society felt bound to follow the SPG precedents recently stressed by proslavery authors. Hallifax's sermon contained calls for reform and characterized the slave trade as "a commerce disgraceful to the human species." Reflecting Codrington's growing place in public debates, Hallifax characterized it as a "*damnosa hereditas*" that had proved financially burdensome to the Society. Characterizing the abolitionist campaign in strikingly contorted terms, he observed that "the genius of Christian Charity" was "already active in prosecuting the scheme, not simply of restricting, but of abolishing a commerce, which, however protected by custom and sanctioned by law, is not, I fear, in its origin to be defended on the rigid principles of natural justice."[73]

While tying himself into knots over the abolition of the slave trade, Hallifax was clearer and more critical in analyzing the tendency of antislavery authors to commingle calls for emancipation with calls for abolition. It is here that the weight of SPG precedents was particularly important. Several recent speakers before the SPG, like Porteus, had criticized the slave trade, but they tended to restate, also like Porteus, the old argument that there were biblical sanctions for slavery itself. These sentiments were not advanced only as defenses of slavery but, in keeping with SPG tradition, were couched as assurances to masters in the context of calling for reforms. Wary of antislavery activism, Hallifax developed this position in a new way that offered fresh support to beleaguered planters. He claimed the notion that "Christianity and Slavery are incompatible, and cannot subsist together, is more than the authority of Scripture will warrant us to affirm," and referenced biblical passages in concluding "we find it no where declared in Scripture that the institution of Slavery is unlawful." Since "slavery in Christian kingdoms is not repugnant to the precepts of holy Scripture," Hallifax warned that "to represent it as such to a deluded public, is injuring the cause we mean to serve by an imprudent manner of defending it, and is both impolitic and unjust."

Hallifax also seems to have feared the effects of the rhetoric of revolution in the Atlantic world, suggesting that "tumults and insurrections of slaves" might result if they believed "they have the same unalienable right to liberty with their masters, and are under no restraints either from religion or justice to assert that liberty."[74] SPG sermons did not explicitly address either the French or Haitian revolutions, but the old arguments that the Christianization of enslaved people would provide the best defense for planters took on a new resonance in light of them. If, as many churchmen claimed, revolutionary principles were imbued with godlessness, the SPG continued to promote orthodox Christianity and the preservation of the existing social order. While reformist and somewhat sympathetic to the antislave trade campaign, Hallifax's sermon marked a carefully developed and clear restatement of the Society's acceptance of slavery itself. It garnered wide attention and was interpreted as a blow against the antislavery movement at an important political juncture.

The West Indian planter Gilbert Francklyn, who had been a member of the SPG since 1776, likewise published two proslavery tracts in 1789 that are notable for the lengths they went to associate the Society with the defense of slavery.[75] In one of them, Francklyn responded to the antislavery writings of the Anglican clergyman Robert Nickolls, who had suggested that the SPG could vouch for the fact that most Caribbean masters were not solicitous of enslaved peoples' religious welfare. In reply he attempted to defend the reputations of his fellow colonials while also vindicating the SPG's efforts. He attributed any failures that the Society had experienced on Codrington not to the hostility of planters but "to the want of diligence and zeal" in the catechists the Society had appointed and likewise defended in similar terms the ongoing absentee management of Codrington by John Brathwaite. In doing so Francklyn looked to support the membership of the SPG, Brathwaite, and other nonresident proprietors against abolitionists by shifting blame for plantation cruelty and the failure of conversion efforts onto underlings. Francklyn's defense of the Society's record on Codrington, therefore, helped defend Caribbean slavery by suggesting that any problems were not fundamental but isolated and correctable through reform rather than through abolition or emancipation.[76]

Francklyn's second proslavery tract of 1789, a reply to Thomas Clarkson's *Essay*, sought to undercut Clarkson's efforts to assert the moral and religious superiority of abolitionism and did so through repeated references to the Society and authors associated with it. Francklyn cited the Society's reply to Benezet and observed, "We do not hear that the opinion of that corporation is changed at present," a claim bolstered by a citation of Hallifax's recent sermon.[77] Most strikingly, Francklyn used the involvement of leading churchmen in the Society's ownership of enslaved people on Codrington to counter what he viewed as slanders against planters. Clarkson had criticized purchasers of enslaved people as receivers of stolen goods. Francklyn wondered that Clarkson "should venture to call the gentlemen who purchase negroes . . . by the odious name of *Receivers*—forgetting, sure, that among such purchasers are my Lords the Archbishops, Bishops, Noblemen, and Gentlemen, who are members of the Society for Propagating the Gospel in Foreign Parts?"[78] It became an important part of antislavery activists' political strategy to distinguish between abolishing the slave trade and the more radical idea of ending slavery itself. Francklyn claimed the Society's ownership of Codrington gave its imprimatur to slavery *and* the slave trade within the British Empire.

Other authors without Francklyn's ties to the Society adopted a similar strategy. Liverpool ship captain Robert Norris deployed the SPG's ownership of Codrington to defend his fellow slave traders, arguing that "the adventurers in this trade" had seen "for near a century past the Society for propagating Christianity, composed of the Archbishop of Canterbury, the Bishop of London, and many pious doctors of the established church, deriving, as masters, a yearly income from the labor of their Negro slaves in the West Indies, which is appropriated to the increase of Christianity in the world." In Norris's view, this meant slave traders could not consider their business "as contrary to the spirit of the

Scriptures, or to the principles of morality."[79] These patterns continued in ensuing years. The Scottish and Antiguan physician James Makittrick Adair contrasted the position of the "enthusiastic Quaker" Benezet with the much more reasonable views of the SPG, "that wise and respectable society" that did not "deem slavery unlawful" but did advocate that enslaved people be treated better and "instructed in the duties of obedience and subordination."[80] In 1790 the proslavery politician John Holroyd (later first Earl of Sheffield) persuaded Bristol's electors to send him to Westminster largely through his *Observations on the Project for Abolishing the Slave Trade*, which was published the same year. In it, he cited Hallifax's sermon as evidence of the good sense of the bulk of the Anglican leadership on slavery.[81] John Stanley, the agent for Nevis, cited Hallifax to "refute the many false and vicious calumnies" issued against planters in the House of Commons debates over the 1791 bill to abolish the slave trade.[82] Such references to the SPG became part of the arsenal that proslavery authors and politicians wielded as they fought the abolitionist movement to a standstill in Parliament through the 1790s. These arguments were never as prominent as assertions of the slave trade's economic and strategic importance, but they provided some cover against claims that the slave trade must be abolished, whatever the cost, because of its immense immorality.

At the same time, it is clear that many SPG supporters were becoming more critical of the slave trade. When SPG preachers decried its cruelties, as several did in this period, they often tended to couple this with defenses of slave ownership that offered considerable aid to other slave owners. In 1793 Bishop John Douglas called the slave trade a "disgraceful Traffic, founded on the Misery of a great Part of Mankind" in his annual sermon. Douglas also, though, repeated the traditional arguments that Codrington could serve as a model for other planters and demonstrate that Christianization was "the most effectual Means of insuring the Fidelity and Diligence of their Slaves." Douglas also mounted a defense of the SPG's fellow slaveholders, claiming that he had "been informed, upon the most respectable Authority" that on Barbados the "Planters in general have, of late, treated their Slaves with much Humanity; –that less Work is required; – more indulgences given; –and Instruction in the Principles of Christianity encouraged; and that, in consequence of this happy Change, many Negroes upon other Plantations, besides that of the Society, regularly attend Public Worship with Devotion, and some even join in the Communion."[83] Douglas's arguments criticized the slave trade, but they offered succor to planters by highlighting reforms and aligning the Society's running of Codrington with the plantation management practices of other slaveholders.

The cumulative weight of such repeated pronouncements was significant. Public interest in the SPG's position and its continuing control of Codrington probably made some fearful of embroiling the Society in controversy. Samuel Horsley, bishop of Rochester and then St. Asaph, became an SPG member in 1777. Horsley became, next to Porteus, the most prominent abolitionist on the episcopal bench and, though on personally poor terms with Wilberforce, an abolitionist speaker in the House of Lords in the later 1790s and 1800s. Like Porteus, Horsley was careful to distinguish between abolishing the slave trade, which he favored, and threatening slavery itself, which he saw as "impolitic and even mischievous to attack," even if he may have personally opposed it.[84] Horsley's abolitionist views had developed by at least 1794, but when he delivered the 1795 SPG annual sermon he avoided all mention of the subject in his text. It is telling that in a widely publicized speech he made during a Parliamentary debate on the slave trade in 1799, he devoted considerable effort to arguing that the SPG sermon given by his old friend Bishop Hallifax, which had been quoted by a pro–slave trade speaker in the debate, was not actually a defense of slavery. He worked to marshal his own Bible passages characterizing the slave trade as "man-stealing" and "sinful in a very high degree."[85]

Other SPG speakers continued to support slaveholders. The High Church clergyman Charles Manners-Sutton, a personal favorite of George III who in 1805 became the archbishop of Canterbury and thereby the president of the SPG, argued in 1797 that the Society had done much good among enslaved people in the colonies over the previous century. Among its accomplishments, he claimed, was dispelling the planters' previous view that their material interests were "at variance with the mental Improvement of their Slaves." Ignoring decades of antislavery campaigning, Manners-Sutton treated the legitimacy of slaveholding itself as a settled issue, arguing that another benefit of SPG work was that it would not "any longer be objected, that the Principles and Duties of Christianity are hostile to the Existence of Slavery, however modified." Instead, he argued that Christianity left "all temporal Governments as it found them" and only went so far as instilling in the "the Minds of Governors and Governed the Love of Order, of Justice, of Mercy, of Forgiveness, of mutual Good-Will, of universal Charity." If slavery made holding such views impossible, Manners-Sutton noted, than it was indeed irreconcilable with Christianity, but this point simply underlined, in his view, the need for masters to cooperate in the conversion of the people they owned.[86]

In the next year, Edward Venables-Vernon, who would rise to become archbishop of York in 1808, offered another robust defense of slaveholding. In Venables-Vernon's view, slave owning by Christian masters could help achieve conversions. While in relations "with great and established nations, we must take them, such as they are already, with their ideas, their prejudices, their opinion, their habits and the dispositions, already formed," slavery made things "widely different" in Britain's own colonies. "There," he argued in a reassertion of the position that slavery could be a positive good, "the Christian Master will have it certainly in his power (if he will take the pains to do it) to form, himself, the habits and dispositions of his Slaves." Codrington, he argued, gave the Society the power "to exhibit the example" of Christian mastership that he believed held the key to the civilization and conversion of enslaved people.[87]

It is worth noting how linkages between the SPG and the proslavery movement were deployed by one of the most able advocates for the West Indian planters, Bryan Edwards.[88] Edwards was a wealthy planter, a leading political figure in Jamaica, a successful West India merchant in England, and a spokesman in the Westminster Parliament for the "'moderate' group of West Indians who supported the slave trade with certain restrictions and the amelioration of colonial slavery."[89] He was also his era's most important historian of the British Caribbean. His two-volume *History, Civil and Commercial, Of the British Colonies in the West Indies*, published in 1793, capitalized on the SPG's public position in debates over slavery to win sympathy for planters.

Edwards claimed there were "many persons" in Britain who "find themselves possessed of estates in the West Indies which they have never seen, and invested with powers over their fellow creatures there, which however extensively odious, they have never abused." Edwards argued that such men initially might be "misled by the popular outcry" into considering freeing their slaves but would then become convinced that such emancipation could not be effected "consistently even with the happiness of the Negroes themselves." Edwards rhetorically embodied these sensitive but ultimately wise absentees not through the example of a representative individual nonresident plantation owner but through the SPG, who "are themselves under this very predicament." In Edwards's hands the SPG's atypical, institutional ownership of Codrington became the quintessence of the reluctant proprietors' dilemma. He went on to use what he characterized as the Society's benevolent intentions to provide a humanitarian argument for the continuation of the slave trade as a protection for those already enslaved. "They [the SPG] have found themselves not only under the disagreeable necessity of supporting the system of slavery which was bequeathed to them with the land; but are induced also, from the purest and best motives, to purchase occasionally a certain number of Negroes, in order to divide the work, and keep up the stock." In a final move, Edwards used the Society's slave ownership to make the case not just for the necessity of the system, but for slavery as a positive good. The Society, he claimed, "well know that moderate labour, unaccompanied with that wretched anxiety to which the poor of England are subject, in making provision for the day that is passing over them, is a state of comparative felicity: and they know also, that men in savage life have no incentive to emulation: persuasion is lost on such men, and compulsion, to a certain degree, is humanity and charity."[90] Using the SPG, Edwards argued that reluctant though they might be, planters had a moral responsibility to continue owning people.

Arguments like those of Francklyn and Edwards reveal the place occupied by the SPG in debates about abolition. Proslavery authors were, of course, interpreting and publicizing the SPG's history for their own ends, just as abolitionist authors who cited Warburton and Porteus were. What is noteworthy is the close connection that some of these proslavery authors had with the Society. Knox, Thompson, and Francklyn drew directly on their experiences with and connections to the SPG to articulate defenses of the status quo that reached around the Atlantic world.

Initially, religiously motivated antislavery activists like Benezet, Sharp, and Porteus hoped to persuade the Society and the Church to adopt institutional stances in favor of abolitionism. Notoriously, that change in official posture never came. Some individual bishops and many individual Anglican clergymen voiced opposition to the slave trade, but neither the SPG nor the Church as a whole swung its institutional weight solidly behind abolitionism. Because they retained strong loyalties to the Church of England, figures like Sharp, Clarkson, and Ramsay were loath to openly criticize the SPG even as they worked to circumvent it. Moreover, because they sought to position abolition as a religious crusade, antislavery activists tended not to acknowledge the existence of counterarguments emanating from within religious circles. It would have been impolitic for abolitionists to stress the SPG connections of some of their proslavery opponents, so they usually did not do so. Relying too heavily on abolitionists' own accounts of their struggle risks unwittingly perpetuating these omissions. Doing so would be to miss the full scope of the antislavery movement's achievement in the period before 1807.

Ultimately at least thirteen bishops voted for the abolition of the slave trade in 1807.[91] Abolition's passage was a testimony to the long public campaigns of antislavery activists, which raised awareness of the horrors of the slave trade, and to the clever political strategies its advocates deployed. The most prominent antislavery activists—Anthony Benezet, Granville Sharp, Thomas Clarkson, William Wilberforce, and others—opposed the transatlantic slave trade and the perpetuation of slavery. While much of the pro- and antislavery literature produced in the period between the American Revolution and 1807 intermingled arguments about slavery with arguments over the slave trade, antislavery activists were ultimately successful in splitting abolition and emancipation as political questions.

Most supporters of missionary Anglicanism were much more committed to slavery than they were to the transatlantic slave trade. As SPG sermons demonstrate, many associated with the Society became aware of the horrors of the African trade, no doubt thanks to abolitionist campaigning. For these reasons, the bishops grew increasingly willing to accept Parliamentary restrictions on the slave trade. At the same time, most bishops were unwilling to challenge the legitimacy of slavery and their support for ending the slave trade could be lukewarm, with few willing to put all their political weight firmly behind the cause. When the abolition bill of 1807 was introduced, it came on the heels of the 1806 abolition of British slave trading with foreigners, which had been successfully positioned as in the nation's wartime strategic self-interest. Besides benefiting from popular agitation on behalf of abolition, the 1807 bill was also introduced with the strong support of most of the newly formed cross-party government, the "Ministry of All the Talents" under the leadership of Lord Grenville, and many bishops were reliable government votes in the House of Lords.[92] Like others in Britain's political class, bishops were brought to support abolition through a combination of circumstances, moral awakening, public pressure, and Parliamentary strategy.

It is instructive, however, that Porteus, the most prominent abolitionist bishop, was one of the relatively few antislavery activists who distinguished between abolition and emancipation not just on tactical grounds but on the basis of principle. Likewise, abolition did not lead the Society's supporters to embrace emancipationism en masse. The depth of the support for slavery within the SPG is underscored by the re-emergence of the Society's policies as a source of controversy several decades later, during the push to emancipate all enslaved people within the British Empire. Many changes occurred in Britain's political, social, and religious landscapes in the years between abolition and emancipation, but there was a surprising resilience to the support for slavery within the Society's ranks. For decades after the abolition of the slave trade, many SPG members continued to consider slavery as part of the long-term future for the British Empire and as a mechanism for effecting positive religious and moral change.

The SPG's understanding of what had happened on Codrington in recent decades was important in this respect. John Brathwaite's lease of Codrington had turned the financial position of the estate around. When he returned the plantation to SPG control in 1793, its enslaved population was growing naturally for the first time and it was producing sizeable, steady profits. It has been calculated that between 1750 and 1783 Codrington produced average annual net profits of £806, but there was a notable mixture of good and bad years in this period. Between 1784 and 1823 annual net profits were steadier and averaged £2083. Moreover, the trend seemed upward: the decade between 1814 and 1823 saw average annual profits soar to £4042.[93] The Society used this stream of revenue to finally achieve Christopher Codrington's vision of a college on the estate and to fund increasingly ambitious catechetical and educational efforts among its enslaved people. This, combined with the increasing creolization of the estate's population as the demographic situation on the plantation improved, saw more enslaved people on the estate accepting Christianity. For some SPG members, this combination of profits, population growth, and increasing Christianization was evidence of the wisdom of the Society's moderate reformism.

In the aftermath of Parliamentary abolition, British antislavery activists shifted their attention to ending slave trading by other European nations. While there were some efforts after 1815 to reform colonial slavery, there was not initially a drive by figures like Wilberforce to free those still enslaved, and political antislavery in the period was largely a "dormant force."[94] A new phase in antislavery activity was sparked by abolitionists' realization that the end of the slave trade had not stopped planter cruelty nor led to slavery gradually dying out. In 1823 Wilberforce and others founded the Society for Mitigating and Gradually Abolishing the State of Slavery throughout the British Dominions and started a new round of investigations, public campaigning, and legislative maneuvering aimed at emancipation.[95] Antislavery was multivocal in this period, with gradualists and typically younger, more radical immediate emancipationists vying for influence and sparring over tactics. Emancipationist efforts were met by a new public defense of slavery mounted by West Indian planters and their British supporters. Whereas in the 1780s and the 1790s most evangelical antislavery churchmen had been careful not to criticize the SPG too vehemently, by the 1820s Anglican evangelicals were more powerful and assertive. They controlled their own institutions like the Church Missionary Society, established as an evangelical counterpart to the SPG, and several journals for promoting their opinions on religious and social issues. Against this background, Codrington reemerged as a point of contention between antislavery activists and the SPG's supporters.

In 1827 the evangelical Anglican clergyman John Riland published the *Memoirs of a West Indian Planter*. His preface lamented "the apathy, and even the impatience and irritability" about antislavery activism shown in recent years "by numbers of the Christian philanthropists of these busy times." Riland called for a reinvigoration of the commitment displayed in the 1780s and 1790s, and argued that "the Slave Trade and Slavery are identical." His text also took aim at the SPG and its management of Codrington. Riland attacked the cruelty of the enduring Caribbean practice of forcing enslaved people to work in gangs under whip-wielding drivers. He observed that a slave driver was still used on the Society's estate and decried Bryan Edwards's "extraordinary apology for the retention, by a Christian corporation, of an estate worked under the whip." Riland argued that it "is a question of some importance" whether the SPG "is justified in putting into its treasury the fruits of slave labour." Noting Porteus's failure to spur the Society to action "about fifty years ago," Riland claimed the SPG "has always been under a cloud." Riland also called attention to the "very unsatisfactory" last annual report of the SPG, which he said failed to provide adequate details about how Codrington's enslaved people were being treated.[96] Whereas Bryan Edwards had used the Society's ownership of Codrington to represent and thereby defend planters, Riland seized upon the estate to highlight Caribbean slavery's continuing abusiveness and to shake the public out if its self-satisfied post-abolition complacency.

Codrington likewise began attracting attention from the evangelical press. The May 1827 issue of the Claphamite *Christian Observer*, reporting on the SPG's annual meeting in February 1827, noted with "regret" that "no allusion was made to the society's proceedings in Barbados" at the meeting, an omission archly attributed to the Society's probable realization that its slaveholding was unlikely to "interest the British public in behalf of the institution." The *Christian Observer* wished "that another Porteus will be found to advocate the cause of the society's bondsmen" and claimed that many otherwise pro-missionary members of the public could not support the SPG because they would "not cast in their mite to a fund contaminated by the produce of extorted slave labor." The journal extended its criticism to the Society's members, who it suggested "incur the guilt of being willing slaveholders" whose "example should be pleaded by others, or rest as an incubus on the efforts" of those who sought to emancipate the enslaved.[97]

These criticisms sparked a controversy carried out in the Anglican press over the ensuing year. A correspondent calling himself S.H.P. published an extended reply to the *Christian Observer* and to Riland's criticisms of the Society in the *Christian Remembrancer*, a journal associated with High Church opinion.[98] The correspondent expressed his "grief at the uncharitable" and almost "insidious" opinions about Codrington and contended that contrary to the criticisms, "corporal punishment is abolished on the estate." Less reassuringly, he also argued that even if corporal punishment was still occurring, it was "splitting hairs" to distinguish between the way that the poor in England were treated in workhouses and giving "a man a stripe across the back for idleness in the West Indies." He insisted that any profits on Codrington were spent on the estate and school there and not incorporated into the Society's general revenues, and that, therefore, "the husbandman is, in the fullest sense, partaker of the fruits of his labour." Reviving an oft-repeated SPG argument, S.H.P. claimed that slavery remained a means for doing good, noting that the *Christian Observer* "would seem to advise the Society to set free their slaves, and to sacrifice at the altar of liberty all the power, which the present condition of the slaves affords, of making them disciples of Christ, and communicating to them the word of salvation."

S.H.P. also called on the scriptural literalism that had long underpinned the Society's acceptance of slavery. He observed that while he found many passages in the Bible that noted the duties of slaves, "I find not any intimation that the master is bound to the release his slaves from their duty." Moreover, he argued, the Society's recent reports on Codrington had recorded the many efforts made by the organization to improve the health, education, and religious lives of the people it owned. Such information, he claimed, must tend "to convince persons, that whatever the slaves on other estates may be, the Society's slaves cannot be an unhappy people." S.H.P. not only defended the SPG's good intentions, he associated the Society fully with slavery's continued practice on Barbados and endorsed, even in the late 1820s, slavery as a valuable means for furthering the institution's missionary program.

This defense elicited a response from Riland that questioned a host of practices on Codrington, and by extension, challenged the West Indian lobby's contention that slavery in the Caribbean had been reformed into a more humane and Christian institution since the abolition of the slave trade. Riland called on the Society to clarify its policies and practices on a wide range of issues including punishment, the treatment of women, the introduction of wages onto the plantation as a system of rewards, and record-keeping on enslaved peoples' treatment.[99] The Society, as Riland knew, had not systematically instituted these reforms, and his criticisms challenged not only the way the Society had run the estate recently but the totality of its nearly 120 years of control of Codrington.

Other mouthpieces of the evangelical emancipationist movement took up Riland's theme. Zachary Macaulay's *Anti-Slavery Reporter* published a lengthy piece in February 1829 that juxtaposed references to reformist comments made in SPG annual sermons between 1711 and 1783 with evidence of how little had actually been accomplished in reforming the moral and religious lives of Codrington's enslaved people. The piece criticized the Society for failing to encourage the marriages of its enslaved people and for the resulting sexual immorality it claimed was rampant on Codrington as a result.[100] The familial relationships and sexual behavior of enslaved people had long concerned the Society's missionaries on Codrington and elsewhere, so this criticism was one that turned the SPG's own avowed interests back on its membership. These attacks elicited further defenses of the morality and benevolence of the Society's ownership of Codrington by contributors to the *Christian Remembrancer* and another journal associated with High Church opinion, the *British Critic*.[101] Riland capped his participation in these exchanges by publishing an open letter to the archbishop of Canterbury pushing the prelate, in his capacity as president of the Society, to effect speedy emancipation on Codrington.[102]

The Society's official response to these criticisms was in keeping with its history. In 1829 the Society issued *A Statement Relative to Codrington College*, which presented extracts from its annual reports and missionary correspondence designed to show that it was actively working to better the lives of its enslaved people. The *Statement* called for adopting a system of management of Codrington that sought to convert enslaved people and improve their material conditions while being "in every way coincident with the colonial interest: a system, which, while it effectually secures progressive amelioration in the dispositions, understandings, and habits of the Slaves, may afford a model for other Proprietors to follow."[103] Rather than conceding that the slave regime on Codrington needed to be changed, the *Statement* claimed that it was enslaved people who were still in need of reform. It was a program that fit perfectly with the Society's traditions and one that envisioned the open-ended continuation of slavery. Its critics were unimpressed, and subsequent issues of the *Anti-Slavery Reporter* in 1829 and 1831 continued the attack and pressed for evidence that enslaved people were really being treated as well as SPG-produced texts suggested they were.[104]

In 1831 the SPG issued an official "Report from the Committee of the Codrington Trust," which sought to vindicate the Society's management of the property and describe a plan for the future running of the estate. Obviously conscious of recent public criticism, the authors positioned the Society carefully as "*Trustees* for the Codrington Estates in Barbados," attempting to dissociate the plantation from its other activities. In response to the repeated calls for evidence of its commitment to reform, the document contains a detailed list of "Resolutions" that had been adopted by the Society's membership and were designed to regulate the work patterns, health, education, and sexual morality of its enslaved people.

The report also considered the future of slavery on the estate, claiming that the Society was faced with three choices. It could relinquish its trusteeship, "but it is not difficult to shew that the interests of humanity and religion would be rather impeded than promoted by such a measure." The report admitted the Society could "enfranchise" the people it owned immediately, but that is "a step which they believe would be followed by more suffering and crime than have ever yet been witnessed under the most galling bondage." Or, the Society could "make provision for their gradual emancipation; and by the introduction of free labour into the colonies, afford an example which may lead to the abolition of slavery without danger to life or property."[105] The Society's members, the text reported, had adopted the last option because "they firmly believe that the circumstance of slave-property being held in trust by a great religious corporation may be made the means of conferring the most essential benefits upon the Negro population of the West Indies, and of promoting their ultimate enfranchisement."

The Society, the report claimed, would now take the lead in "systematic emancipation."[106] But this "systematic emancipation" was envisioned as gradual, and the SPG committed itself to no dates. Repeating a long-dominant claim, the report's authors argued that with Codrington, "They can shew that the Negro is capable of instruction, for they have instructed him. They can shew that he is susceptible of the same devotional feelings as ourselves, and may be brought under the controlling influence of the same divine laws." Through continued mastership the Society could "combat the prejudices of the Negro on the spot" about marriage through "the arguments of religion and the influence of temporal advantage." Most importantly, on "the question of Emancipation," Codrington meant the Society was "able not only to suggest a course, but to make the trial themselves, for the satisfaction of others; and to shew the planters how they may gradually enfranchise their Slaves without destruction to their property."[107]

Such gradualism was closely in line with positions adopted by spokespeople for the West India interest in the face of the growing national support for emancipation. For example, an April 1831 address "To the People of Great Britain and Ireland" signed by forty-one West Indian proprietors responded to emancipationist petitioning with the following sentiments:

> [W]e assert, in the face of our country, our well-founded conviction that the "Speedy annihilation" of slavery would be attended with the devastation of the West India Colonies, with loss of lives and property to the White Inhabitants, with inevitable distress and misery to the Black Population, and with a fatal shock to the commercial credit of this Empire.[108]

The Society's emancipationist critics, like abolitionists a generation earlier, never managed to convince a majority of the membership to change its views on slavery. Even in the 1830s, in a testimony to the depth and weight of the proslavery tradition within the Society, arguments defending the existing social order and calling for cooperation with masters remained predominant. It was Parliamentary emancipation, not self-imposed gradualism, that led to freedom for the Society's slaves.

Looking back from the 1850s and recounting the history of the antislavery movement, the abolitionist MP and activist Sir George Stephen recalled that "Next to the Quakers, the dissenters were foremost in the Anti-slavery battle; next to the West Indian committee, the most hostile to emancipation were the bishops, and the Society for the Propagation of the Gospel, themselves among the largest of our slaveholders."[109] In Stephen's view, far from serving as a well-spring of humanitarian sentiment upon which antislavery campaigners could draw, the Society operated as a powerful institutional opponent to their efforts. Stephen was not a dispassionate chronicler. Unlike some other abolitionist leaders who preferred quiet persuasion, Stephen was known to be exceedingly blunt. On one occasion, he reportedly sarcastically referred to the Society as the "The Honourable Bench of Bishops and Board of Slaveholders, Inc."[110] A second-generation abolitionist, Stephen had inherited his antislavery principles from his Claphamite father James Stephen, who was Wilberforce's close ally in the abolitionist cause from 1789 on. George Stephen himself was a fierce partisan in the fights of the late 1820s and 1830s to obtain emancipation, when as a leading figure in the Anti-Slavery Society he helped lead a public-pressure campaign that helped secure passage of the 1833 law that ended slavery. He was also involved in later internecine feuds over who should be credited for the abolitionists' victories. Stephen was, however, in a position to understand how key figures within the antislavery movement perceived the Society's position over many decades. An evangelical Anglican, Stephen saw the church's episcopate and the SPG leadership as a consistent opponent in the lengthy struggles over slavery. Reflecting, for example, on the situation preceding the final push to enact emancipation, Stephen wrote that "the pulpits too were closed" to the advocates for emancipation, because Church of England ministers, "excepting those of the evangelical class," were "taking their cue from the episcopal bench."[111]

The Society had to consider and articulate its position on slavery repeatedly over the nearly seventy years that the antislavery movement actively campaigned in Britain. There were many figures associated with the SPG who criticized how colonial masters treated the people they owned and, especially, the limited enthusiasm planters showed for converting slaves. While the Society never corporately supported the abolition of the slave trade, some individual members, including some bishops, became increasingly willing to criticize its cruelty and support its ending. However, neither reformism nor abolitionism ever persuaded the Society as a whole to disavow slavery or its own slaveholding. As multiple public statements and SPG policy toward Codrington reveal, many members continued to see slavery as sanctioned by scripture and even, if properly regulated, as a positive good. Such views proved remarkably durable, withstanding decades of attack by antislavery activists and persisting through wider political and cultural changes.

Despite its claims that it would take the lead in "gradual emancipation" and even as pressure to free the enslaved grew intense, the Society retained the people it owned until the bitter end. In May 1838 the Barbados legislature—tired of outside agitation and already committed to gradual emancipation through the apprenticeship system that the Emancipation Act of 1833 had mandated—voted to end slavery entirely on the island on August 1, 1838. To preempt the embarrassment of being legally obliged to free the "apprentices" on its estate two months later, the Society unilaterally emancipated Codrington's population on May 30. Like other planters, the SPG applied for compensation from the British government following emancipation, receiving £8,823 8s. 9d. for the loss of its human property.[112] Reconstructing the powerful tradition of support for slavery within the Society's ranks between 1765 and 1838 suggests that, as antislavery activists themselves came to realize, there was no straight line connecting reformism to abolitionism and emancipationism.

Conclusion

The SPG dispatched missionaries and texts around the Atlantic world, confident that the Church of England was suited not just to English people but to all those who lived in the nation's growing empire. Despite its roots in England's unique cultural, political, and religious history, Anglicanism as promulgated by the Society proved to be an adaptable and vigorous faith as it spread to new peoples and territories. The SPG's missionaries and literature defended orthodoxy, looked to reconcile reason and revelation, promoted the benefits of episcopacy and a properly trained and ordained clergy, defended and strengthened social hierarchy, and emphasized the need for cooperation between church and Crown. These ideas, closely associated with Anglicanism at home, and justified primarily on religious, not secular, grounds, had major implications for the SPG's efforts to convert Native American and black peoples. By the nineteenth century, the Society was able to point to many successes in making the Church of England a much larger presence among European settlers in Britain's colonies and former colonies than it had been before 1700. As many SPG supporters also conceded, the Society's record was more mixed among other peoples.

While in the eighteenth century the Society was a quintessentially Atlantic institution, by the mid-nineteenth century the SPG had completed a significant transformation.[1] The origins of this change lay in the cataclysmic impact of the American Revolution on the Society's program. It produced major hardships for the many Anglican clergymen who remained loyal to the British Crown, and the American victory ended the SPG's operations in the colonies that became the United States. Among other effects, this ended missionary Anglicanism's work among African Americans in places, like South Carolina, where it had operated for decades. In the conflict's aftermath the Society shifted large amounts of its financial and manpower resources to caring for people it considered loyalists— both black and white—in Britain's remaining North American colonies and elsewhere. Charles Inglis, a former SPG missionary, was consecrated as the first bishop of Nova Scotia in 1787, marking the initial step in the creation of a long-wished-for colonial Anglican episcopate. Between 1813 and 1833, the SPG administered Parliamentary grants for supporting Anglican clergy in what became Canada. These developments in North America were the beginning of a process that saw the SPG realign its missionary program to fit the new contours and altered politics of the British Empire, including the development of major initiatives in other parts of the world. The SPG began directly supporting missionaries in India in 1818 and focused much of its attention there during the nineteenth century.

In the Caribbean there were also significant changes. The creation of the independent diocese of Jamaica and diocese of Barbados and the Leeward Islands, whose first bishop William Hart Coleridge was consecrated in London in 1824, changed the political and ecclesiastical conditions under which the Society operated in that part of the world. So too did emancipation of the enslaved people of the British Empire. By the time of the passage of the Emancipation Act of 1833, the Society had been subject to antislavery criticism for decades. The act mandated the formal end of slavery throughout the British Empire on August 1, 1834. However, only young children were to be fully free immediately; any enslaved person over age six had to serve a period of unpaid "apprenticeship" that, depending on the type of work they performed, kept them tied to their owners for several years. This plan for gradual emancipation was widely recognized as marking the start of a period of major transformation for West Indian society, and its passage spurred British and colonial discussions about the economic, political, and religious future of the islands. Although the Society had opposed dramatic changes to the status quo in the West Indies for decades, the passage of the 1833 law helped spur a renewed interest in missionary outreach to the region's black population.

In 1835 the Society established a "Negro Education Fund." The SPG had first attempted to create a dedicated fund for paying catechists to black people in the late 1720s, but that effort had quietly faded in the mid-eighteenth century. Its re-establishment in the wake of emancipation's passage marked efforts to adjust to a dramatically new context. Reflecting the fact that the social and cultural position of the black population of the Caribbean was now firmly on the British imperial agenda, this new fund was supported not only by private donors and old allies like the SPCK but also by a dedicated national collection and by grants from the British Parliament. Between 1835 and 1850 the SPG used this money to pay the salaries of a fresh wave of missionaries, catechists, and schoolmasters, and to build churches and schools on a number of Caribbean islands. The social and cultural environment was transformed by emancipation, and the Society was no longer hamstrung by the ties to slavery that had existed earlier, but the Church of England still faced challenges among the black population in the region. The Society achieved more success in bringing black West Indians into the Church of England in this period than it had in the eighteenth century, but Anglicanism faced significant new competition in the Caribbean from independent churches, which were seen as less closely allied with the islands' planter elites.[2]

Elsewhere too, the social and political foundations of eighteenth-century SPG activity were swept away. In Africa, Philip Quaque's death in 1816 marked the effective end of the missionary presence that the Society had supported at Cape Coast since the 1750s. It sent a series of very short-lived British-born ministers to Cape Coast in the years up to 1824, but the Society then ceased sending missionaries to the region. The SPG approached things differently when it re-engaged in missionary activity in West Africa in 1851, providing financial support to missionaries but not selecting or supervising them. Instead, missionaries were dispatched by the Barbados Church Society, an Anglican organization formed in the now independent diocese of Barbados. These missionaries, who were both black and white West Indians, were trained at Codrington College. Additionally, whereas in the eighteenth century the Society's presence in Africa was limited to the West African coastal regions most closely integrated into the Atlantic economy, imperial expansion led to new fields of mission. In 1820 the first SPG missionaries in southern Africa were sent to minister to English settlers in Cape Colony, and the region was subsequently the site of much SPG activity.

In the Pacific, the SPG began providing salaries to schoolmasters in Australia in the 1790s, though the comparatively speedy creation of an Australian episcopate meant that the SPG was never as prominent a presence there as it was elsewhere. This points to a larger change. In the nineteenth century, new British colonies were provided with Anglican bishops relatively quickly after imperial control was established, so the colonial ecclesiastical context in which the Society operated was often very different from what had prevailed in the eighteenth century, when the absence of colonial bishops magnified the importance of the SPG. The Society continued to provide colonial churches with funds and other aid, but with resident bishops able to ordain and supervise local clergymen, the patterns of ongoing close supervision from London that existed in the eighteenth century gradually faded. At home too, the Society's membership and leadership found themselves operating in a radically different context by 1850. The repeal of the Test and Corporation Acts, Catholic Emancipation, and Parliamentary reform all altered the political and ecclesiastical conditions that had shaped the eighteenth-century Society's operations. Likewise, a host of new voluntary missionary organizations within and outside the Church of England emerged beginning in the 1790s. As a result, by 1850 the SPG was a different organization than it had been in the eighteenth century. Bigger in the scope of its operations but probably smaller in its national influence, it had become one missionary organization among many operating in Britain's now global empire.

By the admission of those who led the Society through these changes, in its first century the SPG had not accomplished as much among "heathen" peoples as the organization's founding generation had hoped, but there were achievements. Based on a religiously grounded understanding of humanity that emphasized commonalities over differences, the SPG made sincere and sustained attempts to convert Native Americans and African and African American people in a number of locations. The Society maintained a long-lasting presence among the Iroquois, and its missionaries helped bring a community of Mohawks into the Church of England. The three-sided relationship between the Mohawks, the Church of England, and the British state proved an enduring one, able to adapt to political and cultural change in the eighteenth century and beyond.

The Society's work among enslaved people in the British Atlantic was pioneering. Begun in a period when few other Protestant voices were advocating for the conversion of enslaved people, the Society's missionaries and membership repeatedly called attention to what they regarded as those peoples' troubling spiritual plight. The SPG stressed that enslaved people, like all human beings, were capable of inclusion into the church. While individual missionaries and members varied in their level of commitment, the Society as a body never stopped arguing that enslaved people deserved the opportunity for salvation and more Christian treatment from their masters. In some cases, the Society's missionaries offered enslaved people education in reading and writing. In several locations, Anglicanism became a means for more fully incorporating black people into colonial communal life. This sustained commitment to black people's inclusion in the Church of England and calls for more paternalistic slaveholding led to the baptism of thousands of free and enslaved people in the eighteenth century. The Society's proselytizing was an early and important stage in the emergence of black Protestantism as a major cultural and religious force around the Atlantic world.

Nevertheless, as the Society's inability to convert most of the colonial black population demonstrates, enslaved people had no uniform reaction to the Society's missionaries in the eighteenth century. Missionary Anglicanism's message was variously accepted, modified, and rejected by people and communities throughout the Atlantic world. Individuals could shape missionary encounters in significant ways. Elias Neau's charisma was critical to establishing the New York mission as a long-lasting site of SPG endeavor. Philip Quaque's complex, often painful relationships with his London mentors and his African family were important for the way his mission unfolded. Some people gratefully accepted the ministers, teachers, and books placed in their communities by the SPG's efforts. Some enslaved people used Anglicanism to assert their own status and autonomy. The Bible-quoting catechumen who frightened Francis Le Jau took religious instruction and used it to challenge masters. In other cases, such as at Codrington and Cape Coast, Anglicanism was long rejected or ignored. Local political, social, and cultural conditions were often important in determining these responses. Everywhere the Society's missionaries operated there was an interplay between their religious aims and the needs and desires of the people they hoped to Christianize.

The SPG's first generation of members accepted slavery as biblically sanctioned. More than this, the Society's supporters often believed their religious aims required defending the social order against the irreligion and disorder that they saw as prevalent in Britain's colonies. While the Society consistently advocated for the reform of multiple facets of colonial life, including slavery, neither its missionaries nor their London-based backers challenged the legitimacy of slaveholding itself. Instead, in pursuit of making colonial societies more godly and well ordered, the Society adopted a number of strategies for converting enslaved people, which, while religiously reformist, provided cultural, intellectual, and political support to slave masters. The Society's ownership of a plantation and the people who lived and worked there was central to this development. Codrington committed the Society to the principle that benevolent and Christian mastership was possible. Despite decades of evidence to the contrary, the SPG continued to insist (until the passage of emancipation) that Codrington could provide other masters with an example of a plantation that was profitable and run on Christian and paternalistic principles. It is an accurate reflection of the prominent place that the plantation occupied in the Society's program—and a telling example of how dramatically perceptions of the Society's involvement with the estate have changed in recent years—that Codrington was at the center of an apology for participation in slavery issued by the Church of England's General Synod in 2006.

Codrington was not an anomaly in the eighteenth century. Rather, it was one expression among many of the Society's acceptance of slavery, and one manifestation among several of its willingness to deploy slavery in pursuit of missionary objectives. Given that local political, social, and cultural circumstances helped determine how enslaved people responded to SPG clergymen, it also mattered to missionary Anglicanism's conversion program that large numbers of these men were themselves slave owners. More broadly, the consensus within the SPG that the key to converting enslaved people lay in appealing to their masters shaped its missionary program in significant ways. The clergymen who delivered annual sermons before the Society regularly appealed to masters. Missionaries in the field used these sermons, Edmund Gibson's pastoral letters, and their own arguments to persuade slaveholders of the charitableness, safety, and benefits of converting their slaves. Colonial clergymen regularly stressed that Christianity would make enslaved people more obedient, more loyal, and more content and, to further assuage slave owners, often stripped teaching in reading and writing from their missionary methodology. In seeking to make their religious message as nonthreatening to masters as possible, the Society's backers also repeatedly created and disseminated arguments that stressed the legality and morality of slaveholding. Correspondingly, this multidimensional emphasis on masters probably weakened missionary Anglicanism's appeal among enslaved people.

This focus on masters intersected with a quintessentially eighteenth-century Anglican belief in cooperation between church and state. This is an area in which the Society's activities had a particularly significant impact on the wider history of Atlantic slavery. The SPG as a body and the influential churchmen who supported it used their extensive political contacts to lobby for laws in the colonies and the metropole that made it explicit that baptism did not result in freedom for enslaved people. This campaign reflected a wider Anglican ethos—most prominently displayed in the better-known efforts of churchmen to establish a colonial episcopate—that obtaining the support of the law and the government in the pursuit of transatlantic religious aims was legitimate and advisable. In New York, where Elias Neau secured a change in colonial slave law, and in London, where the Society advocated for similar changes throughout the empire and where George Berkeley's circle of supporters obtained the 1729 Yorke-Talbot opinion, these efforts strengthened slavery as an institution and made slaveholders more secure in their property in people. While several SPG missionaries and the Society's metropolitan supporters continued to call for more paternalistic, godly mastership, the reformism associated with the Society was premised on the idea that properly ordered slaveholding could be a moral and Christian practice. Missionary Anglicanism may have sometimes afforded enslaved people opportunities for education and provided some with religious succor, but the Society's rhetoric and actions also provided significant support for the system that kept these people in bondage.

The SPG's early push to convert enslaved people had reached a high point by around 1730, but the Society had still proven unable to effect mass conversions. At Codrington, the litmus test for the Society's approach, African cultural and religious practices provided a genuine counterweight to missionary Anglicanism, and slavery fatally undermined religious outreach, even when it was pursued by committed missionaries with strong backing from London. In the ensuing decades, the Society came to embrace slavery more fully as not just permissible but as a useful tool that could be wielded in support of its religious goals. Deploying enslaved people as catechists in Charleston and on Codrington in the 1740s brought slavery from the background to the foreground of its program. In the same period, the Society's zealous founding generation of supporters was being replaced by a new cohort who were more comfortable with slavery as an integral feature of Britain's empire and less likely to share early hopes for speedy mass conversions of heathen peoples. While the SPG's collective enthusiasm for slave conversion ebbed, the Great Awakening gave enslaved people new religious choices. It also challenged the colonial social hierarchy, which exacerbated the Society's propensity to avoid measures that might unsettle its fellow slaveholders.

By mid-century, the ramifications of these developments were increasingly apparent. Few members now expected the "Great Harvest" of souls that Elias Neau had envisioned when he opened his school. The lack of commitment to converting enslaved people shown by several Codrington catechists after 1750, and the fact that the Society did little to remedy this situation, reflects how pessimism and apathy had grown. Thomas Thompson's mission to Africa and Philip Quaque's education and posting to Cape Coast show that the Society had not abandoned its interest in converting black people and that it was willing to try new missionary strategies. However, the SPG's cooperation with the Company of Merchants Trading to Africa highlighted how enmeshed with Atlantic slavery its religious program had become.

The eighteenth century saw not only the rise of antislavery thought but also the development and dissemination of arguments that supported a long dominant, proslavery ideology. Missionary Anglicanism contributed to that ideology, and the SPG's participation in slaveholding put the weight of a powerful institution with considerable moral and political influence behind slavery. The responses of many SPG supporters to the antislavery movement from the 1760s is a powerful indication of how the attitudes toward slavery that had developed within the organization affected the wider culture and politics of the British Atlantic world. Some figures associated with the SPG came to support abolitionism, but they repeatedly failed to alter the organization's corporate position. The Society frequently asserted that its management of Codrington was a model for other masters in the Atlantic world, a view many of its supporters continued to proclaim even as the conversion program there flagged. When a figure like bishop of Exeter Frederick Keppel used his annual sermon in 1770 to claim in reference to Codrington that "It is with great satisfaction also that we observe the humane and tender treatment of those negro slaves, who are become our possession, and we may reasonably hope that our good example will have its proper effect upon other masters," he was helping to make the case that benevolent mastership was a real possibility.[3] In the late eighteenth and early nineteenth century, debates about the Society's position on slavery and the SPG's management of Codrington were hotly contested because they were recognized by pro- and antislavery partisans as emblematic of wider disputes over the past and future of slavery in the British Empire. Unwilling to admit that its management of Codrington had failed to advance its religious agenda, influential voices within the Society continued right up until the moment of emancipation to argue that slaveholding was moral and that slavery, because it could serve as a vehicle for Christianization and civilization, could be a positive good in the lives of enslaved people.

The Society did not change its collective position on slavery before it was legally ended in the British Empire, but some within the organization did come to stress the differences that separated black people from the white population among whom the Society had more success. The Society's evident desire by the 1780s to disassociate itself from Philip Quaque, its decision to not provide for an African-born replacement for him, and the fate of Quaque's posthumous reputation suggest how perceptions of human difference hardened within the organization over time and how that change resonated in British culture. The SPG's supporters did not abandon a biblically based belief in the essential unity of humankind. The Society, for example, continued to maintain that Christian, properly ordered mastership could improve enslaved people on Codrington, marking their attitude as significantly different from later expressions of "scientific" racism. However, SPG members were increasingly likely to frame the process of "civilizing" and Christianizing black people as one that would be indeterminately long and difficult.

In 1811 Philip Quaque wrote his final preserved letter to the Society's secretary in London. During his extraordinary fifty years of service as an Anglican missionary, he had lived to see the beginning of the changes that remade the SPG in the nineteenth century, but his career was firmly rooted in the ethos of the eighteenth-century Society. Late in his life, living in a community turned upside down by the abolition of the slave trade, and in conflict with his African family and neighbors, a disheartened Quaque told the Society that his years at Cape Coast had been an "unsuccessful mission." Where formerly he had "some hopes of its growth," he now thought "the face of things bears but an indifferent aspect." More conversions would not happen "unless a new change would take place for the better."[4]

In pursuit of converting "heathens," the Society's members and missionaries made sustained and often pioneering efforts, including Quaque's own training, ordination, and posting, to bring Protestant Christianity to African and African American peoples around the British Empire. As Quaque knew as a convert and rued as a missionary, those peoples responded to the SPG's efforts in many ways. The hope for mass conversions that led to the establishment of his mission in Africa and the disappointment he felt when they failed to materialize replicated a trajectory experienced by many missionaries and the Society as a whole. The attitudes toward slavery that led to Quaque's posting at Cape Coast undermined his mission and many others. The increasing doubts that the Society's London-based leadership had about a black man serving as its missionary also reflected how the Society's thinking about human difference evolved over time and shaped its religious outreach. Quaque's career, with its internal contradictions and cultural complexities, exemplifies the mixed history of the SPG's efforts to convert the black population of the eighteenth-century British Atlantic world.

ABBREVIATIONS

Primary Sources

SPG–L Society for the Propagation of the Gospel in Foreign Parts (SPG) *Letters.* A, B, and C Series

SPG–J SPG *Journal*

SPG–SC SPG *Standing Committee Minutes*

SPG–X SPG *X-Series* (Documents relating to Codrington Plantation). All in the *Archives of the United Society for the Propagation of the Gospel in Foreign Parts*, Bodleian Library of Commonwealth and African Studies at Rhodes House, Oxford, England. Segments available on microfilm.

Fulham Papers *Fulham Papers.* Lambeth Palace Library, London, England and microfilm.

RAC *Records of the African Companies.* National Archives, Kew, England.

Secondary Sources

ANBO *American National Biography*, Online edition

HMPEC *Historical Magazine of the Protestant Episcopal Church*

WMQ *William and Mary Quarterly*

ODNB *Oxford Dictionary of National Biography*, Online edition

NOTES

Introduction

1. George Stanhope, *The early Conversion of Islanders, a wise Expedient for propagating Christianity. A Sermon Preached before the Incorporated Society for the Propagation of the Gospel in Foreign Parts . . . On Friday the 19th of February, 1713/14* (London: Joseph Downing, 1714), 24.

2. On the New England Company, see William Kellaway, *The New England Company, 1649–1776: Missionary Society to the American Indians* (New York: Barnes and Noble, 1962).

3. John Williams, *A Sermon Preached before the Society for the Propagation of the Gospel in Foreign Parts . . .* [on] *February 15, 1705/6* (London: Joseph Downing, 1706), 20–21.

4. Robin Blackburn, *The Making of New World Slavery: From the Baroque to the Modern, 1492–1800* (London: Verso, 1997), 371–400.

5. The SPG became owners of at least 276 people when it received Codrington plantation. Between 1712 and 1761 it purchased approximately 450 people from Barbados slave markets. In 1767 it made a one-time purchase of 149 enslaved people. Between 1712 and 1748, the period for which figures are available, 69 enslaved people were born into slavery on Codrington. It purchased 2 enslaved people in South Carolina. These figures, which do not include enslaved people born on Codrington after 1748, suggest that the Society owned significantly more than 946 individuals in the eighteenth century. See J. Harry Bennett Jr., *Bondsmen and Bishops: Slavery and Apprenticeship on the Codrington Plantations of Barbados, 1710–1838* (Berkeley: University of California Press, 1958), 46, 52–53. According to one recent estimate the Society sent "just over 410 ordained missionaries" to the colonies in the eighteenth century. See Daniel O'Connor et al., *Three Centuries of Mission: The United Society for the Propagation of the Gospel, 1701–2000* (London: Continuum, 2000), 27; and chap. 1.

6. For definitional statements about Atlantic history, see David Armitage, "Three Concepts of Atlantic History," in *The British Atlantic World, 1500–1800,* ed. David Armitage and Michael J. Braddick, 2nd ed. (New York: Palgrave Macmillan, 2009), 13–29; Bernard Bailyn, *Atlantic History: Concept and Contours* (Cambridge, MA: Harvard University Press, 2005); Nicholas Canny, "Writing Atlantic History; or, Reconfiguring the History of Colonial British America," *Journal of American History* 86, no. 3 (Dec. 1999): 1093–114; and Jack P. Greene, "Beyond Power: Paradigm Subversion and Reformulation in the Re-Creation of the Early Modern Atlantic World," in *Interpreting Early America: Historiographical Essays* (Charlottesville: University Press of Virginia, 1996), 17–42. For assessments of how Atlantic History has developed, see Jack P. Greene and Philip D. Morgan, eds., *Atlantic*

History: A Critical Appraisal (New York: Oxford University Press, 2009). A valuable recent overview of religion in the British Atlantic world is Carla Gardina Pestana, *Protestant Empire: Religion and the Making of the British Atlantic World* (Philadelphia: University of Pennsylvania Press, 2009).

7. S. C. Bolton, "South Carolina and the Reverend Doctor Francis Le Jau: Southern Society and the Conscience of an Anglican Missionary," *HMPEC* 40, no. 1 (Mar. 1971): 64.

8. John Venn and J. A. Venn, comps., *Alumni Cantabrigienses . . . Part I. From the Earliest Times to 1751*, 4 vols. (Cambridge: Cambridge University Press, 1927), 4:228; Thomas Thompson, *An Account of Two Missionary Voyages. . . .* (1758; repr., London: SPG/SPCK, 1937).

9. Nicholas M. Beasley, *Christian Ritual and the Creation of British Slave Societies, 1650–1780* (Athens: University of Georgia Press, 2009). John Frederick Woolverton's work comes closest to providing a comprehensive overview of the SPG's eighteenth-century activities but does not address the Caribbean and West Africa, and favors "select lives, ideas, episodes, and contemporary comments" over an attempt at overall assessment. Woolverton, *Colonial Anglicanism in North America* (Detroit: Wayne State University Press, 1984), 9. For an assessment of the SPG's work among slaves within the wider context of the religious world of the British Atlantic, see Pestana, *Protestant Empire,* 171–76.

10. John K. Nelson, *A Blessed Company: Parishes, Parsons, and Parishioners in Anglican Virginia, 1690–1776* (Chapel Hill: University of North Carolina Press, 2001). S. Charles Bolton, *Southern Anglicanism: The Church of England in Colonial South Carolina* (Westport, CT: Greenwood Press, 1982). Nancy L. Rhoden, *Revolutionary Anglicanism: The Colonial Church of England Clergy during the American Revolution* (New York: New York University Press, 1999). James B. Bell, *The Imperial Origins of the King's Church in Early America, 1607–1783* (New York: Palgrave Macmillan, 2004). On SPG agitation for a colonial episcopate and the American Revolution, see, among others, Arthur Lyon Cross, *The Anglican Episcopate and the American Colonies* (New York: Longmans, Green, and Co., 1902); Carl Bridenbaugh, *Mitre and Sceptre: Transatlantic Faiths, Ideas, Personalities, and Politics 1689–1775* (New York: Oxford University Press, 1962); and J. C. D. Clark, *The Language of Liberty 1660–1832: Political Discourse and Social Dynamics in the Anglo-American World* (Cambridge: Cambridge University Press, 1994). On the SPG's place in educational history, see John Calam, *Parsons and Pedagogues: The SPG Adventure in American Education* (New York: Columbia University Press, 1971).

11. David Humphreys, *An historical account of the incorporated Society for the Propagation of the Gospel in Foreign Parts . . .* (London: Joseph Downing, 1730); C. F. Pascoe, *Classified Digest of the Records of the Society for the Propagation of the Gospel in Foreign Parts, 1701–1892* (London: SPG, 1893); Pascoe, *Two Hundred Years of the SPG. . .., 1701–1900* (London: SPG, 1901); H. P. Thompson, *Into All Lands: The History of the Society for the Propagation of the Gospel in Foreign Parts, 1701–1950* (London: SPCK, 1951); and O'Connor, *Three Centuries of Mission.*

12. Klingberg's work includes: Frank J. Klingberg, *The Anti-Slavery Movement in England, a Study in English Humanitarianism* (1926; Hamden, CT: Archon Books, 1968); Klingberg, ed., *The Carolina Chronicle of Dr. Francis Le Jau, 1706–1717* (Berkeley: University of California Press, 1956); Klingberg, ed., *Carolina Chronicle: The Papers of Commissary Gideon Johnston, 1707–1716* (Berkeley: University of California Press, 1946); Klingberg, *An Appraisal of the Negro in Colonial South Carolina: A Study in Americanization* (Washington, DC: Associated Publishers, 1941); Klingberg, *Anglican Humanitarianism in Colonial New York* (Philadelphia: Church Historical Society, 1940); Klingberg, "The Efforts of the SPG to Christianize the Mosquito Indians, 1742–1785" *HMPEC* 9 (1940): 305–32; Klingberg, "The Indian Frontier in South Carolina as Seen by the S.P.G. Missionary," *Journal of Southern History* 5, no. 4 (Nov. 1939): 479–500; Klingberg, "Philip Quaque: Pioneer Native Missionary on the Gold Coast, 1765–1816," *Journal of Negro Education* 8, no. 4 (Oct.

1939): 666–72. For a review of Klingberg's scholarship and its focus on humanitarianism, see Samuel Clyde McCulloch, "Professor Frank J. Klingberg (1883–1968): Historian of British Humanitarianism," *HMPEC* 38 (1969): 93–107. Klingberg's students continued his investigations and produced influential scholarship on the SPG and the colonial Church of England. See Klingberg, ed., *Codrington Chronicle: An Experiment in Anglican Altruism on a Barbados Plantation, 1710–1834* (Berkeley: University of California Press, 1949); Samuel Clyde McCulloch, ed., *British Humanitarianism: Essays Honoring Frank J. Klingberg* (Philadelphia: Church Historical Society, 1950); McCulloch, "Dr. Thomas Bray's Commissary Work in London, 1696–1699," *WMQ*, 3rd ser., 2, no. 4 (Oct. 1945): 333–48; McCulloch, "Dr. Thomas Bray's Trip to Maryland: A Study in Militant Anglican Humanitarianism," *WMQ*, 3rd ser., 2, no. 1 (Jan. 1945): 15–32; McCulloch, "Dr. Thomas Bray's Final Years at Aldgate, 1706–1730," *HMPEC* 14 (1945): 322–36; McCulloch, "The Importance of Dr. Thomas Bray's Bibliotheca Parochialis," *HMPEC* 15 (1946): 50–59; McCulloch, "A Plea for Further Missionary Activity in Colonial America. Dr. Thomas Bray's Missionalia," *HMPEC* 15 (1946): 232–45; McCulloch, "The Foundation and Early Work of the Society for Promoting Christian Knowledge," *HMPEC* 18 (1949): 3–22; and McCulloch, "The Foundation and Early Work of the Society for the Propagation of the Gospel in Foreign Parts," *HMPEC* 20 (1951): 121–35. Another Klingberg student, J. Harry Bennett, produced the key monograph on Codrington: Bennett, *Bondsmen and Bishops*. His other works included Bennett, "The S. P. G. and Barbadian Politics," *HMPEC* 20 (1951): 190–206; Bennett, "The Problem of Slave Labor Supply at the Codrington Plantations," *Journal of Negro History* 36, no. 4 (Oct. 1951): 406–41; and Bennett, "The Problem of Slave Labor Supply at the Codrington Plantations," *Journal of Negro History* 37, no. 2 (Apr. 1952): 115–41.

13. For recent work sharing this view, see Rowan Strong, *Anglicanism and the British Empire, c. 1700–1850* (Oxford: Oxford University Press, 2007), 100–103; and Jeffrey Cox, *British Missionary Enterprise Since 1700* (New York: Routledge, 2008), 36–40.

14. On the importance of Protestantism and Anglicanism to British and English culture, see Linda Colley, *Britons: Forging the Nation, 1707–1837* (New Haven, CT: Yale University Press, 1992); J. C. D. Clark, *English Society 1660–1832: Religion, Ideology and Politics during the Ancien Regime*, 2nd ed. (Cambridge: Cambridge University Press, 2000). For assessments stressing the vitality of the eighteenth-century Church of England at home see William Gibson, *The Church of England, 1688–1832: Unity and Accord* (London: Routledge, 2001); and John Walsh, Colin Haydon, and Stephen Taylor, eds., *The Church of England c. 1689–c. 1833: From Toleration to Tractarianism* (Cambridge: Cambridge University Press, 1993). On colonial Anglican ministers, see Patricia Bonomi, *Under the Cope of Heaven: Religion, Society, and Politics in Colonial America* (New York: Oxford University Press, 1986), 41–61, 119–23. See also Bonomi, *Under the Cope of Heaven: Religion, Society, and Politics in Colonial America*, rev. ed. (New York: Oxford University Press, 2003). On the importance of the Church of England to the development of colonial American Christianity, see Jon Butler, *Awash in a Sea of Faith: Christianizing the American People* (Cambridge, MA: Harvard University Press, 1990), 98–128, 291. Such work in religious history connects with more general studies of colonial American culture that have sought to de-emphasize New England, the least Anglican of colonial British America's regions, as representative of the wider American experience. See especially Jack P. Greene, *Pursuits of Happiness: The Social Development of Early Modern British Colonies and the Formation of American Culture* (Chapel Hill: University of North Carolina Press, 1988), 28–54. On the global relationship between missions and empire, see Andrew Porter, *Religion versus Empire? British Protestant Missionaries and Overseas Expansion, 1700–1914* (Manchester: Manchester University Press, 2004). On the relationship between religion and empire in colonial America, see Eliga H. Gould, "Prelude: The Christianizing of British America," in *Missions and Empire*,

Oxford History of the British Empire Companion Series, ed. Norman Etherington, (Oxford: Oxford University Press, 2005), 19–39; and Pestana, *Protestant Empire.*

15. Sylvia R. Frey and Betty Wood, *Come Shouting to Zion: African American Protestantism in the American South and British Caribbean to 1830* (Chapel Hill: University of North Carolina Press, 1998), 79.

16. On the difficulty of uncovering black attitudes toward early Anglican missionary efforts, see Annette Laing, "'Heathens and Infidels'? African Christianization and Anglicanism in the South Carolina Low Country, 1700–1750," *Religion and American Culture* 12 (2002): 197–228. Robert Olwell attempted to estimate the number of black Anglicans in eighteenth-century South Carolina, a population created primarily through SPG efforts, by sampling parish reports. He put the number of baptized black Anglicans at between 3 and 5 percent of the colony's total enslaved black population, which would have meant there were about 2,500 baptized enslaved black people in South Carolina alone in 1750. Robert Olwell, *Masters, Slaves, and Subjects: The Culture of Power in the South Carolina Low Country, 1740–1790* (Ithaca, NY: Cornell University Press, 1998), 117–19.

17. See entries for "Anglican," "Anglicanism," and "church," *Oxford English Dictionary*, online edition; J. Robert Wright, "Anglicanism, *Ecclesia Anglicana*, and Anglican: An Essay on Terminology," in *The Study of Anglicanism*, ed. Stephen Sykes et al., rev. ed. (London: SPCK, 1998), 477–82.

18. On the usefulness of "religion as a category of analysis in the construction of race and slavery" in early America, see Rebecca Anne Goetz, "Rethinking the 'Unthinking Decision': Old Questions and New Problems in the History of Slavery and Race in the Colonial South," *Journal of Southern History*, vol. 75, no. 3 (Aug. 2009): 610–12. On religion's impact on the development of ideas about human difference see, for example: Colin Kidd, *British Identities before Nationalism: Ethnicity and Nationhood in the Atlantic World, 1600–1800* (Cambridge: Cambridge University Press, 1999); Kidd, "Ethnicity in the British Atlantic World, 1688–1830," in *A New Imperial History*, ed. Kathleen Wilson (Cambridge: Cambridge University Press, 2004), 260–77; Dror Wahrman, *The Making of the Modern Self: Identity and Culture in Eighteenth-Century England* (New Haven, CT: Yale University Press, 2004), 199–202, 278–82; Roxanne Wheeler, *The Complexion of Race: Categories of Difference in Eighteenth-Century British Culture* (Philadelphia: University of Pennsylvania Press, 2000), especially 14–21, 61–77; and Kathleen Wilson, *The Island Race: Englishness, Empire and Gender in the Eighteenth Century* (London: Routledge, 2003), 80–84.

Chapter 1

1. SPG–L, Edward Bishop to Secretary, Feb. 16, 1710/11, A6/11.

2. Shelley Burtt, "The Societies for the Reformation of Manners: Between John Locke and the Devil in Augustan England," in *The Margins of Orthodoxy: Heterodox Writing and Cultural Response, 1660–1750*, ed. Roger D. Lund (Cambridge: Cambridge University Press, 1995), 149–69; Tony Claydon, *William III and the Godly Revolution* (Cambridge: Cambridge University Press, 1996), 111–21; T. C. Curtis and W. A. Speck, "The Societies for the Reformation of Manners: A Case Study in the Theory and Practice of Moral Reform," *Literature and History* 3 (1976): 45–64; Eamon Duffy, "Primitive Christianity Revived; Religious Renewal in Augustan England," in *Renaissance and Renewal in Christian History: Papers Read at the Fifteenth Summer Meeting and Sixteenth Winter Meeting of the Ecclesiastical History Society*, Studies in Church History 14, ed. Derek Baker (Oxford: Basil Blackwell, 1977), 287–300; Tina Isaacs, "The Anglican Hierarchy and the Reformation of Manners, 1688–1738," *Journal of Ecclesiastical History* 33, no. 3 (1982): 391–411; M. G.

Jones, *The Charity School Movement: A Study of Eighteenth Century Puritanism in Action* (Hamden, CT: Archon Books, 1964); Craig Rose, "Providence, Protestant Union and Godly Reformation in the 1690s," *Transactions of the Royal Historical Society*, 6th ser., 3 (1993): 151–69; Gordon Rupp, *Religion in England 1688–1791* (Oxford: Clarendon Press, 1986), 289–322; W. M. Spellman, *The Latitudinarians and the Church of England, 1660–1700* (Athens: University of Georgia Press, 1993), 144–46; John Spurr, "The Church, the Societies and the Moral Revolution of 1688" in *The Church of England c. 1689–c. 1833: From Toleration to Tractarianism,* ed. John Walsh, Colin Haydon, and Stephen Taylor (Cambridge: Cambridge University Press, 1993), 127–42; and John Walsh, "Religious Societies: Methodist and Evangelical 1738–1800," in *Voluntary Religion: Papers Read at the 1985 Summer Meeting and the 1986 Winter Meeting of the Ecclesiastical History Society,* Studies in Church History 23, ed. W. J. Sheils and Diana Wood (Worcester: Ecclesiastical History Society, 1986), 279–83.

3. [Josiah Woodward], *An Account of the Societies for Reformation of Manners, In England and Ireland. . . .* (London: B. Aylmer, 1699); Burtt, "The Societies for the Reformation of Manners," 152–53.

4. C. F. Pascoe, *Two Hundred Years of the SPG . . ., 1701–1900* (London: SPG, 1901), 3.

5. Thomas Bray, *A course of lectures upon the church catechism in four volumes* (Oxford: Leonard Litchfield, 1696). See also Thomas Bray, *A Short Discourse Upon the Doctrine of our Baptismal Covenant. . . .* (London: E. Holt, 1697).

6. Craig Rose, "The Origins and Ideals of the SPCK 1699–1716," in Walsh, Haydon, and Taylor, *Church of England c. 1689–c. 1833,* 172–90. See also W. O. B. Allen and Edmund McClure, *Two Hundred Years: The History of the Society for Promoting Christian Knowledge, 1698–1898* (London: SPCK, 1898); W. K. Lowther Clarke, *Eighteenth Century Piety* (London: SPCK, 1944), 96–100; Clarke, *A History of the SPCK* (London: SPCK, 1959), 5–10; Leonard W. Cowrie, *Henry Newman: An American in London, 1708–1743* (London: SPCK, 1956), 21–26; and Samuel Clyde McCulloch, "The Foundation and Early Work of the Society for Promoting Christian Knowledge," *HMPEC* 18, no. 1 (Mar. 1949): 3–22.

7. William Kellaway, *The New England Company, 1649–1776: Missionary Society to the American Indians* (New York: Barnes and Noble, 1962); and J. A. de Jong, *As the Waters Cover the Sea: Millennial Expectations in the Rise of Anglo-American Missions, 1640–1810* (Kampen: J. H. Kok, 1970), 34–78.

8. Samuel Clyde McCulloch, "Dr. Thomas Bray's Commissary Work in London, 1696–1699," *WMQ*, 3rd ser., 2, no 4 (Oct. 1945): 334–48; Bernard C. Steiner, ed., *Rev. Thomas Bray: His Life and Selected Works Relating to Maryland* (Baltimore: Maryland Historical Society, 1901). On commissaries and the colonial authority of the bishops of London, see William Wilson Manross, *The Fulham Papers in the Lambeth Palace Library: American Colonial Section Calendar and Indexes* (Oxford: Clarendon Press, 1965), xiv–xxii; and James B. Bell, *The Imperial Origins of the King's Church in Early America, 1607–1783* (New York: Palgrave Macmillan, 2004), 58–73.

9. See, for example, the focus on Quakerism in Thomas Bray, *A Memorial, representing the present state of religion, on the continent of North-America* (London: John Brudenell, 1701).

10. Thomas Bray, *Apostolick Charity, Its Nature and Excellence. . . .* (London: W. Downing, 1698), ix–x.

11. Ibid.

12. Samuel Smith, *Publick Spirit, Illustrated in the Life and Designs Of the Reverend Thomas Bray, D.D. . . .* (London: J. Brotherton, 1746), 17–19. On the Roman Catholic organization, see J Metzler, ed, *Sacrae Congregationis de Propaganda Fide Memoria Rerum . . ., 1622–1972* (Rome: Herder, 1971); and A. D. Wright, *The Counter-Reformation: Catholic Europe and the Non-Christian World* (London: Weidenfeld and Nicolson, 1982), 30–39.

13. See, for example, William Dawes, *A Sermon Preach'd before the Society for the Propagation of the Gospel in Foreign Parts ... On Friday February 18. 1708/9* (London: Joseph Downing, 1709); Edward Waddington, *A Sermon Preached before the Incorporated Society for the Propagation of the Gospel in Foreign Parts ... On Friday the 17th of February, 1720* (London: J. Downing, 1721); John Thomas, *A Sermon Preached before the Incorporated Society for the Propagation of the Gospel in Foreign Parts.... On Friday, February 20, 1746* (London: Edward Owen, 1747); and Robert Hay Drummond, *A Sermon Preached before the Incorporated Society for the Propagation of the Gospel in Foreign Parts ... On Friday, February 15, 1754* (London: Edward Owen, 1754).

14. Clarke, *History of the SPCK*, 11–12.

15. Pascoe, *Two Hundred Years of the SPG*, 1–7.

16. Richard R. Johnson, "Growth and Mastery: British North America, 1690–1748," in *Oxford History of the British Empire*, vol. 2, *The Eighteenth Century*, ed. P. J. Marshall (Oxford: Oxford University Press, 1998), 280–81; Philip D. Morgan, "The Black Experience in the British Empire, 1680–1810," in ibid., 468.

17. Pascoe, *Two Hundred Years of the SPG*, 939.

18. On SPG/SPCK ties, see Thomas Secker, *A Sermon Preached before the Incorporated Society for the Propagation of the Gospel in Foreign Parts ... On Friday, February 20, 1740–41* (London: J. and H. Pemberton, 1741), 29.

19. H. P. Thompson, *Into All Lands: The History of the Society for the Propagation of the Gospel in Foreign Parts, 1701–1950* (London: SPCK, 1951), 38–39; Pascoe, *Two Hundred Years of the SPG*, 4–7; Clarke, *History of the SPCK*, 8. On the division of responsibility between the SPG and SPCK see *A Letter From a Member of the Society for the Propagation of Christian Knowledge in London, to a Correspondent in the Country* (London[?], 1702[?]). One important exception to the division of labor between the two societies was to be found in India, where the SPCK directly supported missionary activity because the chartered SPG was precluded from operating there. See Clarke, *History of the SPCK*, 59–76; Pascoe, *Two Hundred Years of the SPG*, 468–72; Penelope Carson, "An Imperial Dilemma: The Propagation of Christianity in Early Colonial India," *Journal of Imperial and Commonwealth History* 18, no. 2 (May 1990): 169–90; and Philip Lawson, *The East India Company: A History* (London: Longman, 1993), 149–56.

20. Pascoe, *Two Hundred Years of the SPG*, 932–33.

21. Edward Carpenter, *Thomas Tenison, Archbishop of Canterbury: His Life and Times* (London: SPCK, 1948), 344–47.

22. Burtt, "The Societies for the Reformation of Manners," 154.

23. Daniel O'Connor, et al. *Three Centuries of Mission: The United Society for the Propagation of the Gospel, 1701–2000* (London: Continuum, 2000), 10.

24. Eamon Duffy, "*Correspondence Fraternelle:* The SPCK, the SPG, and the Churches of Switzerland in the War of Spanish Succession," in *Religious Motivation: Biographical and Sociological Problems for the Church Historian: Papers Read at the Sixteenth Summer Meeting and the Seventeenth Winter Meeting of the Ecclesiastical History Society*, Studies in Church History 15, ed. Derek Baker (Oxford: Basil Blackwell, 1979), 251–80; O'Connor, *Three Centuries of Mission*, 10.

25. Charles Trimnell, *A Sermon Preached before the Society for the Propagation of the Gospel in Foreign Parts ... Friday the 17th of February, 1709/10* (London: Joseph Downing, 1710), 9.

26. Bell, *Imperial Origins of the King's Church*, 210.

27. Membership numbers compiled from SPG Annual Reports; Pascoe, *Two Hundred Years of the SPG*, 939.

28. Craig Rose, "The Origins and Ideals of the SPCK 1699–1716," 173–77. Daniel O'Connor has identified the SPG more closely with particularly High Church Anglicanism. See O'Connor, *Three Centuries of Mission*, 8. Laura Stevens has noted that the SPG's annual sermons were given by "divines whose positions ran the gamut from High to Low Church,

although the organization's emphasis on widespread moral education, voluntary association, and active participation by the laity marked it to some degree as a Low Church enterprise." See Laura M. Stevens, *The Poor Indians: British Missionaries, Native Americans, and Colonial Sensibility* (Philadelphia: University of Pennsylvania Press, 2004), 98–99.

29. Frederick R. Goff, "Introduction" in [White Kennett], *The Primordia of Bishop White Kennett, the First English Bibliography on America.* Introductory Study by Frederick R. Goff (Washington, DC: Pan American Union, 1959), x; G. V. Bennett, *White Kennett, 1660–1728, Bishop of Peterborough: A Study in the Political and Ecclesiastical History of the Early Eighteenth Century* (London: SPCK, 1957), 190–92. Kennett was particularly active in the early years of the Society, serving regularly on the Standing Committee and in 1706 publishing an early account of the organization: [White Kennett], *An Account of the Society for the Propagating the Gospel in Foreign Parts . . .* (London: Joseph Downing, 1706).

30. Stuart Handley, "Fleetwood, William (1656–1723)," *ODNB*.

31. Richard Sharp, "Smalridge, George (1662–1719)," *ODNB*; William Gibson, "Altitudinarian Equivocation: George Smalridge's Churchmanship," in *Religious Identities in Britain, 1660–1832*, ed. William Gibson and Robert G. Ingram (Aldershot: Ashgate, 2005), 44.

32. Norman Sykes, *Edmund Gibson Bishop of London, 1669–1748: A Study in Politics and Religion in the Eighteenth Century* (Oxford: Oxford University Press, 1926), 30–53.

33. Rowan Strong, "A Vision of an Anglican Imperialism: The Annual Sermons of the Society for the Propagation of the Gospel in Foreign Parts, 1701–1714," *Journal of Religious History*, 30, no. 2 (June 2006): 180–81.

34. Pascoe, *Two Hundred Years of the SPG*, 823–25; Thompson, *Into All Lands*, 36–37.

35. SPG-J, Mar. 6, 1715/16, vol. 3, 126–27.

36. See SPG-X, X784 (Annual Accounts 1701–1737) and the Table of SPG Income and Expenditure in Pascoe, *Two Hundred Years of the SPG*, 830–31.

37. W. M. Jacob, *Lay People and Religion in the Early Eighteenth Century* (Cambridge: Cambridge University Press, 1996), 155–85.

38. [Kennett], *Account of the Society for Propagating the Gospel in Foreign Parts*, 86; David Humphreys, *An Historical Account of the Incorporated Society for the Propagation of the Gospel in Foreign Parts. . . . to the Year 1728* (London: Joseph Downing, 1730), 18–19.

39. Philip Stubbs, *The divine mission of gospel-ministers; with the obligations upon all pious and rich Christians to promote it . . .* (London: R. and J. Bonwicke, 1711), 18.

40. SPG-J, Mar. 6, 1701/2, vol. 1, 39–40.

41. This aspect of the SPG's activity, and the environment of religious competition out of which it grew, is analyzed in Alison Gilbert Olson, *Making the Empire Work: London and American Interest Groups, 1690–1790* (Cambridge, MA: Harvard University Press, 1992), 54–56, 61–75.

42. As an example of the attention given to the Church of England's legal position, see the statutory collection compiled by the SPG member, Anglican partisan, and South Carolina jurist Nicholas Trott, *The laws of the British plantations in America, relating to the church and the clergy, religion and learning* (London: B. Cowse, 1721).

43. John A. Schutz and Maud E. O'Neil, "Of the Plantations Intire . . .," in *Codrington Chronicle: An Experiment in Anglican Altruism on a Barbados Plantation, 1710–1834*, ed. Frank J. Klingberg (Berkeley: University of California Press, 1949), 55; SPG-L, John Pownall to Secretary, Mar. 13, 1764, C/Am/8/26.

44. Richard Willis, *A Sermon Preach'd before the Society for the Propagation of the Gospel in Foreign Parts . . . On Friday February the 20th. 1701/2* (London: Matt. Wotton, 1702), 17–18.

45. Gilbert Burnet, *Of the Propagation of the Gospel in Foreign Parts. A Sermon Preach'd . . . Feb. 18. 1703/4* (London: D. Brown, 1704), 20–21.

46. See, for example, Thomas Wilson, *An Essay Towards An Instruction For The Indians, Explaining the most Essential Doctrines of Christianity* (London: J. Osborn, 1740), xiv–xv.

47. [Philip Stubbs], "An Account of the Propagation of the Gospel in Foreign Parts" (London: Joseph Downing, 1704), printed in James S. M. Anderson, *The History of the Church of England in the Colonies and Foreign Dependencies of the British Empire*, 3 vols. (London: Francis and John Rivington, 1845–56), 2:767.

48. Trimnell, *Sermon Preached before the Society*, 17, 20.

49. SPG–J, Apr. 28, 1710, vol. 1, 478–81.

50. George Stanhope, *The early Conversion of Islanders, a wise Expedient for propagating Christianity. A Sermon Preached before the Incorporated Society for the Propagation of the Gospel in Foreign Parts . . . On Friday the 19th of Feb. 1713/14* (London: Joseph Downing, 1714), 28.

51. SPG–J, Mar. 21, 1706/7, vol. 1, 277–80.

52. SPG–J, vol. 5, 200–202, 211, 220, 226, 236. This fund was periodically discussed in Abstracts of Proceedings until it was joined back with the Society's general account in 1752. See Abstract of Proceedings printed with Edward Cressett, *A Sermon Preach'd before the Incorporated Society for the Propagation of the Gospel in Foreign Parts . . . On Friday, February 16, 1753* (London: Edward Owen, 1753), 57–58.

53. Bell, *Imperial Origins of the King's Church*, 43–73, 125–41.

54. John K. Nelson, *A Blessed Company: Parishes, Parsons, and Parishioners in Anglican Virginia, 1690–1776* (Chapel Hill: University of North Carolina Press, 2001), 218–19.

55. Bell, *Imperial Origins of the King's Church*, 143.

56. Ibid., 137.

57. "An Account of Dr. L'Jaus Papers Relating to the Condition of the Clergy, and other Material Things in the Leeward Caribee Islands, offered to the consideration of the Society pro propaganda fide &c.," SPG–J, Appendix B, Doc #67.

58. SPG–L, Samuel Auchmuty to Secretary, Apr. 13, 1765, B2/9.

59. Olson, *Making the Empire Work*, 58.

60. *An Abstract of the Proceedings of the Society for the Propagation of the Gospel in Foreign Parts, In the Year of our Lord 1715* (London: Joseph Downing, 1716), 8–11, 35–36; and Abstract of Proceedings printed with John Thomas, *A Sermon Preached before the Incorporated Society for the Propagation of the Gospel in Foreign Parts . . . On Friday, February 15, 1750* (London: Edward Owen, 1751), 37–41.

61. O'Connor, *Three Centuries of Mission*, 27; Pascoe, *Two Hundred Years of the SPG*, 849–929; Thompson, *Into All Lands*, 102.

62. For his account of his SPG mission, see George Keith, *A Journal of Travels from New-Hampshire to Caratuck, on the Continent of North-America* (London: Joseph Downing, 1706). See also Ethyn Williams Kirby, *George Keith, 1638–1716* (New York: American Historical Association, 1942).

63. For Talbot, see SPG–L, Edmund Gibson to Secretary, Dec. 18, 1724, A18/15–16; Anonymous to Secretary, July 29, 1724, A18/17–18; and John Talbot to Secretary, July 18, 1725, A19/172–73. See also Robert William Duncan, "A Study of the Ministry of John Talbot in New Jersey, 1702–1727: On 'Great Ripeness,' Much Dedication and Regrettable Failure," *HMPEC* 42, no. 3 (Sept. 1973): 233–56; Edgar Legare Pennington, *Apostle of New Jersey, John Talbot, 1645–1727* (Philadelphia: Church Historical Society, 1938); and John Frederick Woolverton, *Colonial Anglicanism in North America* (Detroit: Wayne State University Press, 1984), 132–35. For Neau, see J. Morin, *A short account of the life and sufferings of Elias Neau. . . .* (London: John Lewis, 1749), 76–78; SPG *Letters*, Elias Neau to Secretary, Aug. 29, 1704, A2/19; William Vesey to Secretary, Oct. 26, 1704, A2/26; William Vesey to bishop of London, Oct. 26, 1704, A2/40; Elias Neau to John Hodges, Dec. 20, 1704, A2/67.

64. See, for example, Samuel Auchmuty accusing fellow SPG missionary Charles Inglis of "adopting the principles & Cant of the Methodists." SPG–L, Samuel Auchmuty to Secretary, Apr. 13, 1765, B2/9.

65. Bell, *Imperial Origins of the King's Church*, 142–47.

66. See for example, SPG–SC, vol. 1, Feb. 1, 1703/4, which notes "the 3 Scotch Ministers recommended to the Society by the Ld. Bp. of London."

67. SPG–L, Church Wardens and Vestry of St. James, South Carolina to Secretary, Oct. 29, 1717, A12/153–54.

68. O'Connor, *Three Centuries of Mission*, 28; Pascoe, *Two Hundred Years of the SPG*, 851–52; SPG–L, Thomas Pardo to Secretary, May 10, 1732, A24/82–83; and Mary Clement, ed. *Correspondence and Records of the S.P.G. Relating to Wales, 1701–1750* (Cardiff: University of Wales Press, 1973).

69. Bell, *Imperial Origins of the King's Church*, 143. The American-born clergymen of the SPG prominently included a group of New Englanders associated with Yale College who conformed to the Church of England in 1722. See SPG–L, Rev. Samuel Johnson's Representation, Jan. 18, 1722, A16/42–44; Francis Nicholson to Secretary, Jan. 11, 1722, A16/95–99; George Pigot to Secretary, Aug. 20, 1722, A16/298–300; and George Pigot to Secretary, Oct. 3, 1722, A16/302–303a; Pascoe, *Two Hundred Years of the SPG*, 44; O'Connor, *Three Centuries of Mission*, 28.

70. Studies of individual clergymen and particular colonies give a sense of the range of local activity. See, for example, S. Charles Bolton, *Southern Anglicanism: The Church of England in South Carolina* (Westport, CT: Greenwood Press, 1982); Howard E. Kimball, "Gideon Johnston, the Bishop of London's Commissary to South Carolina, 1707–1716," *HMPEC* 42 (1973): 5–36; Frank J. Klingberg, ed., *The Carolina Chronicle of Dr. Francis Le Jau, 1706–1717* (Berkeley: University of California Press, 1956); Klingberg, ed., *Carolina Chronicle: The Papers of Commissary Gideon Johnston, 1707–1716* (Berkeley: University of California Press, 1946); Edgar Legare Pennington, "The Reverend Francis Le Jau's Work among Indians and Negro Slaves," *Journal of Southern History* 1 (1935): 442–58; Pennington, *Apostle of New Jersey: John Talbot*; and Henry Caner, *Letter Book of the Rev. Henry Caner, S.P.G. Missionary in Colonial Connecticut and Massachusetts until the Revolution*, ed. Kenneth Walker Cameron (Hartford, CT: Transcendental Books, 1972).

71. For the SPG mission in Africa, see F. L. Bartels, "Philip Quaque, 1741–1816," *Transactions of the Gold Coast and Togoland Historical Society* 1 (1952–1955): 153–77; Frank J. Klingberg, "Philip Quaque: Pioneer Native Missionary on the Gold Coast, 1765–1816," *Journal of Negro Education* 8, no. 4 (Oct. 1939): 666–72; Margaret Priestley, "Philip Quaque of Cape Coast," in *Africa Remembered. Narratives by West Africans from the Era of the Slave Trade*, ed. Philip D. Curtin (1967; Prospect Heights, IL: Waveland Press, 1997), 99–139; and Ty M. Reese, "'Sheep in the Jaws of So Many Ravenous Wolves': The Slave Trade and Anglican Missionary Activity at Cape Coast Castle, 1752–1816," *Journal of Religion in Africa* 34, no. 3 (2004): 348–72.

72. For the SPG school in New York, see Frank J. Klingberg, *Anglican Humanitarianism in Colonial New York* (Philadelphia: Church Historical Society, 1940), 121–86; For the SPG school in South Carolina, see Frank J. Klingberg, *An Appraisal of the Negro in Colonial South Carolina: A Study in Americanization* (Washington, 1941), 101–22; and Robert Olwell, *Masters, Slaves, and Subjects. The Culture of Power in the South Carolina Low Country, 1740–1790* (Ithaca, NY: Cornell University Press, 1998), 119–21. For Philadelphia, see "An Abstract of the Charter and of the Proceedings of the Society for the Propagation of the Gospel in Foreign Parts" attached to Samuel Lisle, *A Sermon Preached before the Incorporated Society for the Propagation of the Gospel in Foreign Parts; At their Anniversary Meeting in the Parish-Church of St. Mary-le-Bow, On Friday, February 19, 1747* (London: Edward Owen, 1748), 61–62.

73. For the schools run by the Associates of Dr. Bray, see *An Account of the Designs of the Associates of the late Dr Bray; with an Abstract of their Proceedings* (London: n.p., 1763); Edgar Legare Pennington, "Thomas Bray's Associates and Their Work Among the Negroes," *Proceedings of the American Antiquarian Society* 38 (1938): 311–403; John C. Van Horne, "Impediments to the Christianization and Education of Blacks in Colonial America: The Case of the Associates of Dr. Bray," *HMPEC* 50, no. 3 (Sept. 1981): 243–69; and Van Horne, ed., *Religious Philanthropy and Colonial Slavery: The American Correspondence of the Associates of Dr. Bray, 1717–1777* (Urbana: University of Illinois Press, 1985). For examples of the involvement of SPG ministers in these schools, see SPG–L, Samuel Auchmuty to Secretary, Sept. 19, 1761, B2/2; Marmaduke Brown to Secretary, Jan. 9, 1763, C/Am/9/61.

74. O'Connor, *Three Centuries of Mission*, 32.

75. For the SPG efforts among the Iroquois see, William B. Hart, "'For the Good of Our Souls': Mohawk Authority, Accommodation, and Resistance to Protestant Evangelism, 1700–1780" (PhD diss., Brown University, 1998); and John Wolfe Lydekker, *The Faithful Mohawks* (Cambridge: Cambridge University, 1939). For SPG efforts in Caribbean Central America, see Frank J. Klingberg, "The Efforts of the SPG to Christianize the Mosquito Indians, 1742–1785," *HMPEC* 9 (1940): 305–21. For assessments of SPG work among Native Americans, see O'Connor, *Three Centuries of Mission*, 30–34; Gerald J. Goodwin, "Christianity, Civilization, and the Savage: The Anglican Mission to the American Indian," *HMPEC* 42, no. 2 (June 1973): 93–110; and Stevens, *Poor Indians*, 111–37.

76. See especially Bell, *Imperial Origins of the King's Church*.

77. The debates over the creation of an American episcopate, and their possible connection to the outbreak of revolution, have generated significant study. Most of this work was sparked by Carl Bridenbaugh's argument that an "Anglican plot" precipitated the crisis of the revolution: Bridenbaugh, *Mitre and Sceptre: Transatlantic Faiths, Ideas, Personalities, and Politics, 1689–1775* (New York: Oxford University Press, 1952). Responses include Peter M. Doll, *Revolution, Religion, and National Identity: Imperial Anglicanism in British North America, 1745–1795* (Madison, NJ: Fairleigh Dickinson University Press, 2000); Donald F. M. Gerardi, "The Episcopate Controversy Reconsidered: Religious Vocation and Anglican Perceptions of Authority in Mid-eighteenth-century America," *Perspectives in American History*, n.s., 3 (1987): 81–114; David L. Holmes, "The Episcopal Church and the American Revolution," *HMPEC* 47, no. 3 (Sept., 1978): 261–91; William H. Hogue, "The Religious Conspiracy Theory of the American Revolution: Anglican Motive," *Church History* 45, no. 3 (Sept. 1976): 277–92; and Frederick V. Mills, *Bishops by Ballot: An Eighteenth-Century Ecclesiastical Revolution* (New York: Oxford University Press, 1978). A catalog of works treating the issue is provided in Frederick V. Mills, "The Colonial Anglican Episcopate: A Historiographical Review," *Anglican and Episcopal History* 61, no. 3 (Sept. 1992): 345. Nancy L. Rhoden has delineated the religious, as opposed to purely political, reasons why Anglicans desired American bishops: Rhoden, *Revolutionary Anglicanism: The Colonial Church of England Clergy during the American Revolution* (New York: New York University Press, 1999), 37–63.

78. In a work primarily focused on nineteenth-century missionary movements, Andrew Porter has made a similar call for a focus on the religious, as opposed to exclusively imperial aims of British missionaries, including the SPG, more generally: Porter, *Religion versus Empire? British Protestant Missionaries and Overseas Expansion, 1700–1914* (Manchester: Manchester University Press, 2004), 6–11, 20–28.

79. Olaudah Equiano, *The Interesting Narrative and Other Writings*, ed. Vincent Carretta (New York: Penguin Books, 1995), 183–93.

80. Nelson, *Blessed Company*, 267.
81. Nicholas Beasley, *Christian Ritual and the Creation of British Slave Societies, 1650–1780* (Athens: University of Georgia Press, 2009), 30–33. On the role of black people in Anglican congregations, see also Robert A. Bennett, "Black Episcopalians: A History from the Colonial Period to the Present," *HMPEC* 43, no. 3 (Sept. 1974): 231–45; and Denzil T. Clifton, "Anglicanism and Negro Slavery in Colonial America," *HMPEC* 39, no. 1 (Mar. 1970): 29–70.
82. Van Horne, "Impediments to the Christianization and Education of Blacks in Colonial America: The Case of the Associates of Dr. Bray," 268; and Olwell, *Masters, Slaves, and Subjects*, 117–19.
83. Thomas Newton, *On the imperfect Reception of the Gospel. A Sermon Preached before the Incorporated Society for the Propagation of the Gospel in Foreign Parts . . . On Friday, February 17, 1769* (London: E. Owen, 1769), 23–27.
84. On the cultural influence of social networks in the Atlantic world, see Marcy Norton, "Tasting Empire: Chocolate and the European Internalization of Mesoamerican Aesthetics," *American Historical Review*, 111, no. 3 (June 2006): 670.
85. James MacSparran, *A Letter Book and Abstract of Out Services*, ed. Daniel Goodwin (Boston: Merrymount Press, 1899), 5, 51; Philip Quaque to Samuel Johnson, Nov. 26, 1767 and Apr. 5, 1769, in *Samuel Johnson President of King's College: His Career and Writings*, ed. Herbert Schneider and Carol Schneider, 4 vols. (New York: Columbia University Press, 1929), 1:424–30.
86. [Kennett], *Account of the Society for the Propagating the Gospel in Foreign Parts,*67.
87. Humphreys, *An Historical Account of the Incorporated Society*, iii.
88. Philip Bearcroft, *A Sermon Preached before the Incorporated Society for the Propagation of the Gospel in Foreign Parts . . . On Friday, February 15, 1744* (London: Edward Owen, 1744/5), 5.
89. Thomas Bray, *An Essay Towards Promoting all Necessary and Useful Knowledge, both Divine and Human, in all the Parts of His Majesty's Dominions, Both at Home and Abroad* (London: E. Holt, 1697), i.
90. SPG–SC, Mar. 31, 1702.
91. SPG–L, "A Catalogue of Books Left on the Societie's Plantation at the Death of Mr. Smalridge," June 29, 1732, C/Win/Bar 11/135; "A Catalogue of the Library at Codrington College Barbados," 1798, C/Win/Bar 11/138; Pascoe, *Two Hundred Years of the SPG*, 775, 798–99.

Chapter 2

1. Linda Colley, *Britons: Forging the Nation, 1707–1837* (New Haven, CT: Yale University Press, 1992); David Hempton, *Religion and Political Culture in Britain and Ireland: From the Glorious Revolution to the Decline of Empire* (Cambridge: Cambridge University Press, 1996); and Tony Claydon and Ian McBride, eds., *Protestantism and National Identity: Britain and Ireland, c. 1650–c. 1850* (Cambridge: Cambridge University Press, 1998). J. C. D. Clark, *English Society 1660–1832: Religion, Ideology and Politics during the Ancien Regime*, 2nd ed. (Cambridge: Cambridge University Press, 2000) provides the most sweeping argument for Anglicanism's importance.
2. Jeremy Gregory, "Christianity and Culture: Religion, the Arts and the Sciences in England, 1660–1800," in *Culture and Society in Britain, 1660–1800*, ed. Jeremy Black (Manchester: Manchester University Press, 1997), 105. On the largely religious and clerical nature of the English Enlightenment, see B. W. Young, *Religion and Enlightenment in Eighteenth-Century England: Theological Debate from Locke to Burke* (Oxford: Clarendon Press, 1998), 3, 85–86, 99; J. G. A. Pocock, "Clergy and Commerce: The Conservative

Enlightenment in England," in *L'Età dei Lumi: Studi Storici sul Settecento Europeo in Onore di Franco Venturi*, 2 vols. (Naples: Jovene Editore, 1985), 1:523–62; Roy Porter, "The Enlightenment in England," in *The Enlightenment in National Context*, ed. Roy Porter and Mikuláš Teich (Cambridge: Cambridge University Press, 1981), 1–18; James R. Jacob and Margaret C. Jacob, "The Anglican Origins of Modern Science: The Metaphysical Foundations of the Whig Constitution," *Isis* 71, no. 2 (June 1980): 265; and Margaret C. Jacob, *The Newtonians and the English Revolution, 1689–1720* (Ithaca, NY: Cornell University Press, 1976).

3. David Spadafora, *The Idea of Progress in Eighteenth-Century Britain* (New Haven, CT: Yale University Press, 1990), 85–132.

4. Colin Kidd, *British Identities before Nationalism: Ethnicity and Nationahood in the Atlantic World, 1600–1800*, (Cambridge: Cambridge University Press, 1999); in *A New Imperial History*, ed Kathleen Wilson (Cambridge: Cambridge University Press, 2004), 260–77; and Kidd, *The Forging of Races: Race and Scripture in the Protestant Atlantic World* (Cambridge: Cambridge University Press, 2006); Neil C. Gillespie, "Natural History, Natural Theology, and Social Order: John Ray and the 'Newtonian Ideology,'" *Journal of the History of Biology* 20, no. 1 (Spring 1987): 1–49.

5. William Gibson, *The Church of England, 1688–1832: Unity and Accord* (London: Routledge, 2001), 52–63.

6. Ivan Hannaford, *Race: The History of an Idea in the West* (Washington: Woodrow Wilson Center Press, 1996), 191, 203, quote 187. See also Nicholas Hudson, "From 'Nation' to 'Race': The Origin of Racial Classification in Eighteenth-Century Thought," *Eighteenth-Century Studies* 29, no. 3 (1996): 247–64.

7. Kidd, *British Identities before Nationalism*, 10–11.

8. La Peyrère's work was translated into English by 1656. Isaac de La Peyrère, *Men before Adam* … (London: n.p., 1656). See also Richard H. Popkin, *Isaac La Peyrère (1596–1676): His Life, Work and Influence* (Leiden: Brill, 1987).

9. On the rise of biblical literalism and reading Genesis as history in the wake of the Reformation, see Peter Harrison, *The Bible, Protestantism and the Rise of Natural Science* (Cambridge: Cambridge University Press, 1998), 121–47.

10. Stephen R. Haynes, *Noah's Curse: The Biblical Justification of American Slavery* (New York: Oxford University Press, 2002), 23–27. See also Don Cameron Allen, *The Legend of Noah: Renaissance Rationalism in Art, Science, and Letters* (Urbana: University of Illinois Press, 1949); H. Hirsch Cohen, *The Drunkenness of Noah* (University: University of Alabama Press, 1974), 13–19, 29–30; William McKee Evans, "From the Land of Canaan to the Land of Guinea: The Strange Odyssey of the 'Sons of Ham,'" *American Historical Review* 85, no. 1 (Feb. 1980): 15–43; and J. David Pleins, *When the Great Abyss Opened: Classic and Contemporary Readings of Noah's Flood* (Oxford: Oxford University Press, 2003), 129–44. The importance of the Noachian curse to nineteenth-century American proslavery arguments has received attention from Haynes and Thomas Peterson. See Thomas V. Peterson, *Ham and Japheth: The Mythic World of Whites in the Antebellum South* (Metuchen, NJ: American Theological Library Association, 1978). For the continued power of such conceptions into the twentieth century, see Edith R. Sanders, "The Hamitic Hypothesis: Its Origin and Functions in Time Perspective," *Journal of African History* 10, no. 4 (1969): 521–32.

11. Benjamin Braude, "The Sons of Noah and the Construction of Ethnic and Geographical Identities in the Medieval and Early Modern Periods," *WMQ*, 3rd ser., 54, no. 1 (Jan. 1997): 133. See also Peter Harrison, *"Religion" and the Religions in the English Enlightenment* (Cambridge: Cambridge University Press, 1990), 105–12.

12. Braude, "The Sons of Noah," 134, 141–42. Quote, 142.

13. Kidd, *British Identities before Nationalism*, 45.

14. Richard Kidder, *A Commentary on the Five Books of Moses* … 2 vols. (London: J. Hepinstall, 1694), 1:45–50.

15. Simon Patrick, *A Commentary upon the first book of Moses, called Genesis* (London: Ri[chard] Chiswell, 1695).

16. W. M. Spellman, *The Latitudinarians and the Church of England, 1660–1700* (Athens: University of Georgia Press, 1993), 11–13.

17. Patrick, *Commentary*, unnumbered pages of preface.

18. Ibid., 164–65.

19. For the connection between the fight against deism and rhetoric concerning the conversion of the heathen in early SPG sermons, see Laura M. Stevens, *The Poor Indians: British Missionaries, Native Americans, and Colonial Sensibility* (Philadelphia: University of Pennsylvania Press, 2004), 117–27.

20. Richard Cumberland, *Origines gentium antiquissimæ; or, attempts for discovering the times of the first planting of nations* . . . (London: W. B., 1724), 142–89.

21. On Prideaux as a moderate, see Norman Sykes, *From Sheldon to Secker; Aspects of English Church History, 1660–1768* (Cambridge: Cambridge University Press, 1959), 48–49; and M. Jacob, *Newtonians and the English Revolution*, 92.

22. Humphrey Prideaux, *The Old and New Testament connected in the history of the Jews and neighboring nations* . . . 2 vols. (London: R. Knaplock, 1716–18). On Cumberland's and Prideaux's places within the history of ethnic theology, see Kidd, *British Identities before Nationalism*, 45–48.

23. Edward Maunde Thompson, ed., *Letters of Humphrey Prideaux Sometime Dean of Norwich to John Ellis Sometime Under-Secretary of State 1674–1722* (Westminster: Camden Society, 1875), 86; Lambeth Palace Library, *Gibson Papers*, MS 933/2; and SPG–J, vol. 1, 82.

24. Morgan Godwyn, *The Negro's & Indians Advocate, Suing for their Admission into the Church.* . . . (London: Printed for the author, by J. D., 1680). Godwyn, *A Supplement to the Negro's & Indians Advocate* . . . (London: J. D., 1681) sought to refute objections. Godwyn's sermon, *Trade preferr'd before Religion* . . . (London: B. Took, 1685), blamed greedy planters and merchants for slaves' continued heathenism.

25. Thomas Bray, *De Enunciando Evangelio* . . . (London: W. Roberts, 1728), [2]; White Kennett, *The Lets and Impediments in Planting and Propagating the Gospel of Christ. A Sermon Preach'd before the Society for the Propagation of the Gospel in Foreign Parts* . . . *On Friday the 15th of February, 1711/12* . . . (London: Joseph Downing, 1712), 15; and [White Kennett], *The Primordia of Bishop White Kennett, the First English Bibliography on America.* Introductory Study by Frederick R. Goff (Washington, DC: Pan American Union, 1959), ix.

26. Details of Godwyn's biography are from *ODNB*; *DNB*; and Joseph Foster, *Alumni Oxonienses: The Members of the University of Oxford, 1500–1714* . . ., 2 vols. (Nendeln, Lichtenstein: Kraus Reprint Limited, 1968), 2:585. Maurice Cranston, *John Locke: A Biography* (New York: Macmillan, 1957), 71. My thanks to David Armitage for pointing out the connection between Locke and Godwyn. See also Alden Vaughan, *Roots of American Racism: Essays on the Colonial Experience* (New York: Oxford University Press, 1995), 55–81.

27. Godwyn, *Negro's & Indians Advocate*, 104 (misnumbered as p. 104, actually p. 120). Page references to this work hereafter cited in text.

28. See also Winthrop Jordan, *White Over Black: American Attitudes Toward the Negro, 1550–1812* (Chapel Hill, NC: University of North Carolina Press for the Institute of Early American History and Culture, 1968), 229–31.

29. Godwyn, *Negro's & Indians Advocate*, 14–15. Page references to this work hereafter cited in text.

30. Michael Anesko, "So Discreet a Zeal: Slavery and the Anglican Church in Virginia, 1680–1730," *Virginia Magazine of History and Biography* 93, no. 3 (July 1985): 253; Charles F. Irons, *The Origins of Proslavery Christianity: White and Black Evangelicals in Colonial and*

Antebellum Virginia (Chapel Hill: University of North Carolina Press, 2008), 39–40. It has been suggested Bray had a hand in Virginia's 1667 law. See Edgar Legare Pennington, "Thomas Bray's Associates and their Work Among Negroes," *Proceedings of the American Antiquarian Society* 48 (1938): 345.

31. David Armitage, "John Locke, Carolina, and the "Two Treatises of Government," *Political Theory* 32, no. 5 (Oct. 2004): 609. On English legal reform efforts in this period, see Ruth Paley, Cristina Malcolmson, and Michael Hunter, "Parliament and Slavery, 1660–c. 1710," *Slavery & Abolition* 31, no. 2 (June 2010): 257–81.

32. Godwyn, *Negro's & Indians Advocate*, 129.

33. David Brion Davis, *The Problem of Slavery in Western Culture* (New York: Oxford University Press, 1966), 291–332.

34. George Fox, *To the Ministers, Teachers, and Priests . . . in Barbadoes* (London[?], 1672). See also G[eorge] F[ox], *Gospel family-order being a short discourse concerning the ordering of families, both of whites, blacks, and Indians* (London[?], 1676); and Davis, *Problem of Slavery in Western Culture*, 304. Larry Gragg noted how seventeenth-century English migrants to Barbados sought to create an "orderly society," which affected attitudes toward Quakerism and slave conversion. Gragg, *Englishmen Transplanted: The English Colonization of Barbados, 1627–1660* (Oxford: Oxford University Press, 2003), 152–67. See also Gragg, *The Quaker Community on Barbados: Challenging the Culture of the Planter Class* (Columbia, MO: University of Missouri Press, 2009), 121–41.

35. Jean D. Soderlund, *Quakers and Slavery: A Divided Spirit* (Princeton: Princeton University Press, 1985), 3–4; and Davis, *Problem of Slavery in Western Culture*, 305–9. See also J. William Frost, ed., *The Quaker Origins of Antislavery* (Norwood, PA: Norwood Editions, 1980); and Thomas E. Drake, *Quakers and Slavery in America* (Gloucester, MA: P. Smith, 1950).

36. Godwyn, *Negro's & Indians Advocate*, 4–6.

37. Ethyn Williams Kirby, *George Keith, 1638–1716* (New York: American Historical Association, 1942), 35–38.

38. SPG–J, Appendix B, Doc #3.

39. Jon Butler, "'Gospel Order Improved': The Keithian Schism and the Exercise of Quaker Ministerial Authority in Pennsylvania," *WMQ*, 3rd ser., 31, no. 3 (July 1974): 431–52; Kirby, *George Keith*; and J. William Frost, *The Keithian Controversy in Early Pennsylvania* (Norwood, PA: Norwood Editions, 1980).

40. George Keith, *An exhortation & caution to Friends concerning buying or keeping of Negroes* (New York: William Bradford, 1693); and Kirby, *George Keith*, 88–90. Keith may have been inspired by the similarly framed 1688 petition of some German-speaking Quakers living in Germantown, Pennsylvania. See Carla Gardina Pestana, *Protestant Empire: Religion and the Making of the British Atlantic World* (Philadelphia: University of Pennsylvania Press, 2009), 104; and Gary B. Nash and Jean R. Soderlund, *Freedom by Degrees: Emancipation in Pennsylvania and Its Aftermath* (New York: Oxford University Press, 1991), 43–44.

41. Davis, *Problem of Slavery in Western Culture*, 310.

42. Anthony Hill, *Afer Baptizatus: Or, the Negro turn'd Christian . . .* (London: Charles Broome, 1702).

43. Foster, *Alumni Oxonienses, 1500–1714*, 2:709.

44. Hill, *Afer Baptizatus*, 21.

45. Ibid., 29–41.

46. Ibid., 50.

47. Andrew Pyle, "Introduction" in *A Defence of Natural and Revealed religion: Being an Abridgment of the Sermons preached at the Lecture Founded by Robert Boyle*, ed. Gilbert Burnet, 4 vols. (1737, repr. Bristol: Thoemmes Continuum, 2000), 1:viii.

48. Boyle supported the New England Company's missionary work and aided the translation of scriptures into languages including Irish, Scots, Welsh, and Massachusett. See Joyce Chaplin, *Subject Matter: Technology, the Body, and Science on the Anglo-American Frontier, 1500–1676* (Cambridge, MA: Harvard University Press, 2001), 287–93.

49. M. Jacob, *Newtonians and the English Revolution*, 143–200.

50. See also Anita Guerrini, "The Tory Newtonians: Gregory, Pitcairne and their Circle," *Journal of British Studies* 25, no. 3 (July 1986): 288–311; Geoffrey Holmes, Review of *The Newtonians and the English Revolution*, by Margaret C. Jacob, *British Journal for the History of Science* 11 (1978): 164–71. On SPG-connected Boyle Lecturers focused on revelation, see the lectures by John Williams, Richard Kidder, and Josiah Woodward, in Burnet, *Defence of Natural and Revealed Religion*, 1:121–93, 1:69–119, 2:371–405.

51. James Henry Monk, *The Life of Richard Bentley, D.D.* (London: C. J. G. & F. Rivington, 1830); and R. J. White, *Dr. Bentley: A Study in Academic Scarlet* (London: Eyre & Spottiswoode, 1965).

52. SPG–J, vol. 1, 545–49.

53. Samuel Clarke, *The scripture-doctrine of the Trinity....* (London: James Knapton, 1712); Larry Stewart, "Samuel Clarke, Newtonianism, and the Factions of Post-Revolutionary England," *Journal of the History of Ideas* 42, no. 1 (Jan.–Mar. 1981): 53–72.

54. Thomas Bray, *Bibliotheca Parochialis...* (London: E. H., 1697).

55. Patrick Gordon, *Geography Anatomized, Or, A Compleat Geographical Grammar...* (London: J. R, 1693), 206–7.

56. Gordon, *Geography Anatomized*, 4th ed. (London: S. J. Sprint, 1704), unnumbered "Epistle Dedicatory"; SPG–J, vol. 1, 46–47, 88–90; SPG, *Letters*, John Meers to Secretary, July 13, 1713, C/Am/14/72. See also O'Connor, *Three Centuries of Mission*, 5–6; and W. K. Lowther Clarke, *Eighteenth Century Piety* (London: SPCK, 1944), 91–95.

57. Two useful guides to natural religion's place in eighteenth-century British intellectual life are Peter Byrne, *Natural Religion and the Nature of Religion* (London: Routledge, 1989) and Gerald R. Cragg, *Reason and Authority in the Eighteenth Century* (Cambridge: Cambridge University Press, 1964).

58. John Williams, *A Sermon Preached before the Society for the Propagation of the Gospel in Foreign Parts ... [on] February 15, 1705/6* (London: Joseph Downing, 1706), 17. See also Thomas Sherlock, *A Sermon Preached before the Incorporated Society for the Propagation of the Gospel in Foreign Parts ... On Friday the 17th of February, 1715* (London: J. Downing, 1716), 18–19; and Stevens, *Poor Indians*, 120–22.

59. *A Collection of Papers Printed by Order of the Society for the Propagation of the Gospel in Foreign Parts....* (London: Joseph Downing, 1712), 24. This work was issued in six successively revised editions in the eighteenth century: 1706, 1712, 1715, 1719, 1741, and 1788.

60. Ibid. (J. Downing, 1719), 29–30.

61. Ibid. (E. Owen, 1741), 13–14.

62. See Pyle, "Introduction," and Harris's Boyle lecture in Burnet, *Defence of Natural and Revealed Religion*, 1:xii, 1:255–94; John Harris, *Remarks on some Late Papers, Relating to the Universal Deluge: And to the Natural History of the Earth* (London: R. Wilkin, 1697), 64–67; Kidd, "Ethnicity in the Atlantic World," 266; and Larry Stewart, "Harris, John (ca. 1666–1719)," *ODNB*. Harris's *Remarks* responded to skeptical criticism of John Woodward's claims that the fossil record proved that the Noachian flood had occurred. Woodward's critic had emphasized the diversity of human populations and advocated a theory of polygenesis. See L. P., Master of Arts [pseud.], *Two Essays Sent in a Letter from Oxford, to a Nobleman in London. The first concerning some Errors about the Creation, Flood, and the Peopling of the World ...* (London: R. Baldwin, 1695), 15–28; and John Woodward, *An Essay toward a natural history of the earth ... with an account of the universal deluge: and of the effects that it had upon the earth* (London: Ric. Wilkin, 1695).

63. John Harris, *Navigantium atque Itinerantum bibliotheca: Or, A Compleat Collection of Voyages and Travels: Consisting of above Four Hundred of the most Authentick Writers*, 2 vols. (London: Thomas Bennet, 1705).

64. Ibid., 1:i.

65. Ibid., 1:viii.

66. SPG–J, vol. 3, 16. Goff, "Introduction" in [Kennett], *Primordia*; G. V. Bennett, *White Kennett. 1660–1728*, 19–21; and Charles Deane, *An Account of the White Kennett Library of the Society for the Propagation of the Gospel in Foreign Parts* (Cambridge, MA: John Wilson and Son, 1883).

67. David Armitage, *The Ideological Origins of the British Empire* (Cambridge: Cambridge University Press, 2000), 99.

68. [Kennett], *Primordia*, iv.

69. Goff, "Introduction," in [Kennett] *Primordia*, xxiv. The original collection was sold to libraries and private collectors. The British Library, the John Carter Brown Library, and others now hold several of the volumes, often identifiable through Kennett's signature on the title page.

70. *A Collection of Papers Printed by Order of the Society for the Propagation of the Gospel in Foreign Parts. . . .* (1712), 18.

71. Samuel Purchas, *Purchas his Pilgrimage, or Relations of the World and the Religions Observed in all Ages and places Discovered, from the Creation unto this Present. . . .* 4th ed. (London: William Stansby, 1626), 723. On Purchas see Loren E. Pennington, ed., *The Purchas Handbook: Studies of the Life, Times and Writings of Samuel Purchas, 1577–1626, with bibliographies of his books and of works about him*, 2 vols. (London: Hakluyt Society, 1997), 1:73–76; and Hannaford, *Race*, 171. For the evolving treatment of black people in successive editions of Purchas, see Braude, "The Sons of Noah," 135–38.

72. [Kennett], *Primordia*, ii.

73. For example, *England and East India Inconsistent in their Manufacturers: Being an Answer to a Treatise Intituled An Essay on the East-India Trade* (1697); *An Answer to the Reasons against an African Company* (1711); and Charles Lockyer, *An Account of the Trade in India Containing Rules for good Government in Trade, Price Courants and Tables* (1711).

74. [Kennett], *Primordia*, viii.

75. Kidd, *British Identities before Nationalism*, 14.

76. Thomas Thorowgood, *Jewes in America, or Probabilities That the Americans are of that Race. . . .* (London: W. H., 1650); Giles Fletcher and S[amuel] L[ee], *Israel Redux: Or the Restauration of Israel . . .* (London: S. Streater, 1677).

77. On Acosta and Horn, see Kidd, *British Identities before Nationalism*, 15.

78. The SPG member John Williams, for example, thought connections between Native Americans and Jews to be unproven. See Williams, *A Sermon Preached before the Society for the Propagation of the Gospel in Foreign Parts . . .* [on] *February 15, 1705/6*, 25.

79. [Kennett], *Primordia*, ix.

80. Edward Stillingfleet, *Origines Sacrae: Or a Rational Account of the Grounds of Christian Faith . . .*(London: R.W., 1662); Kidd, *British Identities before Nationalism*, 40; Bray, *Bibliotheca Parochialis*, 34–35; and SPG–J, Appendix B, Doc. #27.

81. M. Jacob, *Newtonians and the English Revolution*, 32. See also Richard Popkin, "The Philosophy of Bishop Stillingfleet," *Journal of the History of Philosophy* 9 (1971): 303–19.

82. For these lists, see SPG–J, Appendix B, Doc. #27; *A Collection of Papers Printed by Order of the Society for the Propagation of the Gospel in Foreign Parts* (1741); and *A Collection of Papers Printed by Order of the Society For the Propagation of the Gospel in Foreign Parts . . .* (London: T. Harrison, 1788).

83. SPG–J, Appendix B, Doc. #137, Doc. #128.

84. On Le Jau's interest in "heathen" conversion, see Frank J. Klingberg, ed., *The Carolina Chronicle of Dr. Francis Le Jau, 1706–1717* (Berkeley: University of California Press, 1956); Gerald J.

Goodwin, "Christianity, Civilization and The Savage: The Anglican Mission to the American Indian," *HMPEC* 62, no. 3 (June 1973): 93–110; Peter H. Wood, *Black Majority: Negroes in Colonial South Carolina from 1670 through the Stono Rebellion* (New York: Alfred A. Knopf, 1974), 131–66.

85. SPG–L, Francis Le Jau to Secretary, Jan. 4, 1712, A7/391–95.
86. Ibid., Sept. 11 and 18, 1708, A4/126.
87. Ibid., Mar. 19, 1715/16, A11/130–35.
88. Ibid., June 13, 1710, A5/120. Braude has identified Purchas as a particularly revealing text in the history of interpreting human difference: Braude, "The Sons of Noah," 132–38.
89. SPG–L, Robert Maule to Secretary, Aug. 2, 1711, A7/363–65; Thomas Haliday to Secretary, July 13, 1715, A10/191–92; Francis Varnod to Secretary, Jan. 15, 1723, A17/120–12; Francis Varnod to Secretary, Jan. 13, 1723/24, A18/69–75.
90. Larry Tise, *Proslavery: A History of the Defense of Slavery in America, 1701–1840* (Athens: University of Georgia Press, 1987), 115. See also William Sumner Jenkins, *Pro-Slavery Thought in the Old South* (Chapel Hill University of North Carolina Press, 1935), 206; and Elizabeth Fox-Genovese and Eugene D. Genovese, *The Mind of the Master Class: History and Faith in the Southern Slaveholders' Worldview* (Cambridge: Cambridge University Press, 2005), 473–504.
91. Philip Bisse, *A Sermon Preach'd before the Incorporated Society for the Propagation of the Gospel in Foreign Parts . . . On Friday the 21st of February, 1717* (London: Joseph Downing, 1718), 29–30; William Marshall, "Bisse, Philip (bap. 1666, d. 1721)," *ODNB*.
92. Philip Bearcroft, *A Sermon Preached before the Incorporated Society for the Propagation of the Gospel in Foreign Parts . . . On Friday, February 15, 1744* (London: Edward Owen, 1744), 21–22.
93. Thomas Newton, *Dissertations on the Prophecies, Which have remarkably been fulfilled, and at this time are fulfilling in the world*, 3 vols. (London: J. and R. Tonson, 1754–56).
94. Ruth H. Bloch, "The Social and Political Base of Millennial Literature in Late Eighteenth-Century America," *American Quarterly* 40, no. 3 (Sept. 1988): 385–87.
95. Newton, *Dissertations on the Prophecies*, 1:23.
96. Ibid., 1:29. Newton likewise devoted his 1755 Boyle lectures to the argument that the fulfillment of prophecies provided evidence for the truth of Christianity. In his 1769 SPG annual sermon, Newton argued that the Society was an instrument for the fulfillment of the prophecy that all the world would ultimately be converted to Christianity. See Thomas Newton, *On the imperfect Reception of the Gospel. A Sermon Preached before the Incorporated Society for the Propagation of the Gospel in Foreign Parts . . . On Friday, February 17, 1769* (London: E. Owen, 1769), 3, 16–18.
97. Haynes, *Noah's Curse*, 38–39; and Peterson, *Ham and Japheth*, 43, 61, n. 40.
98. SPG–J, Appendix B, Doc. #48.
99. David Humphreys, *An Historical Account of the Society for the Propagation of the Gospel in Foreign Parts . . . to the Year 1728* (London: Joseph Downing, 1730), 306.
100. Henry Stebbing, *A Sermon Preached before the Incorporated Society for the Propagation of the Gospel in Foreign Parts . . . On Friday, February 19, 1741–42* (London: E. Owen, 1742), 19–20.
101. Stevens, *Poor Indians*, 126–27.
102. Samuel Lisle, *A Sermon Preached before the Incorporated Society for the Propagation of the Gospel in Foreign Parts . . . On Friday, February 19, 1747* (London: Edward Owen, 1748), 22–23.
103. John Thomas, *A Sermon Preached before the Incorporated Society for the Propagation of the Gospel in Foreign Parts . . . On Friday, February 15, 1750* (London: Edward Owen, 1751), 13. See also John Hinchcliffe, *A Sermon Preached before the Incorporated Society for the Propagation of the Gospel in Foreign Parts . . . On Friday, February 16, 1776* (London: T. Harrison and S. Brooke, 1776), 13.

104. Abstract of Proceedings printed with Edmund Keene, *A Sermon Preached before the Incorporated Society for the Propagation of the Gospel in Foreign Parts . . . On Friday, February 18, 1757* (London: E. Owen and T. Harrison, 1757), 52. For similar sentiments, see also Drummond, *A Sermon Preached before the Incorporated Society . . . 1754*, 16–18; Frederick Cornwallis, *A Sermon Preached before the Incorporated Society for the Propagation of the Gospel in Foreign Parts . . . On Friday, February 20, 1756* (London: Edward Owen, 1756), 18–19.

105. Wahrman, *Making of the Modern Self*, 116.

106. B. W. Young, *Religion and Enlightenment in Eighteenth-Century England*, 168–212; Robert G. Ingram, "William Warburton, Divine Action, and Enlightened Christianity," in Gibson and Ingram, *Religious Identities in Britain*, 97–117; Arthur William Evans, *Warburton and the Warburtonians: A Study in Some Eighteenth-Century Controversies* (Oxford: Oxford University Press, 1932); and P. J. Marshall and Glyndwr Williams, *The Great Map of Mankind: British Perceptions of the World in the Age of Enlightenment* (London: J. M. Dent, 1982), 92–93.

107. Frank J. Klingberg, *Anglican Humanitarianism in Colonial New York* (Philadelphia: Church Historical Society, 1940), 37–40, 237–49.

108. William Warburton, *The Divine Legation of Moses Demonstrated, on the principles of a religious deist. . . .* 3rd ed. 2 vols. (London: Executor of the late Mr. Fletcher Gyles, 1742), 1:317–20. When *The Divine Legation* was first published between 1738 and 1741, it did not mention Native Americans. Compare the 3rd edition with Warburton, *A Sermon Preached before the Incorporated Society for the Propagation of the Gospel in Foreign Parts . . .On Friday, February 21, 1766* (London: E. Owen and T. Harrison and S. Brooke, 1766), 16–25.

109. Warburton, *Divine Legation*, 3rd ed. (1742), 1:317–18.

110. B. W. Young, "Warburton, William (1698–1779)," *ODNB.*

111. Warburton, *A Sermon Preached*, 20–23.

112. John Ewer, *A Sermon Preached before the Incorporated Society for the Propagation of the Gospel in Foreign Parts . . . On Friday, February 20, 1767* (London: E. Owen and T. Harrison, 1767), 4.

113. These calls coincided with the increasing European importance of "four stages theory," which postulated a tight correlation between a society's means of subsistence and the level of its civilization. Four stages theory was secular and essentially descriptive; the growth of the notion within the Society that Indians should be transformed into agriculturalists was religious and prescriptive. On four stages theory see Roxann Wheeler, *The Complexion of Race: Categories of Difference in Eighteenth-Century British Culture* (Philadelphia: University of Pennsylvania Press, 2000). For SPG calls for the introduction of settled agriculture among Native Americans, see the annual sermons by John Green (1768), Thomas Newton (1769), Frederick Keppel (1770), and Robert Lowth (1771). For the long-term influence of Warburton's sermon on this question, see Samuel Hallifax's 1789 SPG sermon.

114. Jonathan Shipley, *A Sermon Preached before the Incorporated Society for the Propagation of the Gospel in Foreign Parts . . . On Friday, February 19, 1773* (London: T. Harrison and S. Brooke, 1773), v–vi; and Edmund Law, *A Sermon Preached before the Incorporated Society for the Propagation of the Gospel in Foreign Parts . . . On Friday, February 18, 1774* (London: T. Harrison and S. Brooke, 1774), xiv–xv, xx–xxi.

Chapter 3

1. SPG–L, Elias Neau to Mr. Hodges, July 10, 1703, A1/106. Neau wrote to the Society in his native French. His letters were typically translated into English by the SPG secretary for

members' use and entry into the Society's records. This and subsequent English quotations attributed to Neau are taken from these translations.

2. On Neau's mission see Patricia Bonomi, *Under the Cope of Heaven: Religion, Society, and Politics in Colonial America* (New York: Oxford University Press, 1986), 121; Jon Butler, *Awash in a Sea of Faith: Christianizing the American People* (Cambridge, MA: Harvard University Press, 1990), 161, 169; Leslie M. Harris, *In the Shadow of Slavery: African Americans in New York City, 1626–1863* (Chicago: University of Chicago Press, 2003), 34–40; and Graham Russell Hodges, *Root and Branch: African Americans in New York and East Jersey, 1613–1863* (Chapel Hill: University of North Carolina Press, 1999), 55–68.

3. SPG–L, George Muirson to Secretary, Jan. 9, 1707/9, A3/138; John Thomas to Secretary, June 21, 1709, A5/4. [White Kennett], *An Account of the Society for Propagating the Gospel in Foreign Parts* ... (London: Joseph Downing, 1706), 59. David Humphreys, *An Historical Account of the Incorporated Society for the Propagation of the Gospel in Foreign Parts* ... (London: Joseph Downing, 1730), 236–44.

4. Elias Neau, *An Account of the Sufferings of the French Protestants, Slaves on board the French Kings Galleys* ... (London: Richard Parker, 1699); J. Morin, *Histoire abrégée des souffrances du sieur Elie Neau sur les galères et dans les cachots de Marseille* (Rotterdam: A. Archer, 1701); J. Morin, *A short account of the life and sufferings of Elias Neau,* ... (London: John Lewis, 1749); David C. A. Agnew, *Protestant Exiles from France* ..., 3rd ed., 2 vols. ([Edinburgh: Turnbull and Spears], 1886), 2:62.

5. Humphreys, *Historical Account of the Incorporated Society*, 237.

6. SPG–L, Elias Neau to Secretary, [June 25, 1715], A10/195–96.

7. Ibid., July 5, 1710, A5/134.

8. Ibid., Oct. 3, 1705, A2/124.

9. Ibid., Elias Neau to Josiah Woodward, Sept. 5, 1704, A2/48; Elias Neau to Secretary, July 24, 1707, A3/128; Elias Neau to Secretary, June 9, 1709, A4/155.

10. Ibid., "Memorial [on] behalf of Mr. Elias Neau," n.d. (1718?), A13/44–48. See also Jon Butler, "Les 'Hymnes ou cantiques sacrez' d'Elie Neau: Un nouveau manuscrit du 'grand mystique des galères,'" *Bulletin de la société de l'histoire du protestantisme français* 124 (1978): 416–23.

11. SPG–L, Elias Neau to Secretary, n.d., A6/87.

12. Ibid., Apr. 2, 1722, A16/196–97.

13. Ibid., Oct. 3, 1705, A2/124; Nov. 15, 1705, A2/125.

14. Ibid., Feb. 27, 1708/9, A4/121.

15. [Kennett], *An Account of the Society for Propagating the Gospel in Foreign Parts*, 59.

16. SPG–L, Elias Neau to John Hodges, Apr. 15, 1704, A1/178.

17. Marcus W. Jernegan, "Slavery and Conversion in the American Colonies," *American Historical Review* 21, no. 3 (Apr. 1916): 506.

18. Herbert S. Klein, *Slavery in the Americas: A Comparative Study of Virginia and Cuba* (Chicago: University of Chicago Press, 1967), 47, 117. On the reconciliation of Virginia's Anglican establishment to the slave system, see Michael Anesko, "So Discreet a Zeal: Slavery and the Anglican Church in Virginia, 1680–1730," *Virginia Magazine of History and Biography* 93, no. 3 (July 1985): 247–78.

19. Helen Tunnicliff Catterall, ed., *Judicial Cases concerning American Slavery and the Negro*, 5 vols. (Washington: Carnegie Institution of Washington, 1926), 4:1; and John Codman Hurd, *The Law of Freedom and Bondage in the United States*, 2 vols. (1858–62; repr., New York: Negro Universities Press, 1968), 1:297, 1:300–1. For other colonies and wider discussion of the issue, see Hurd, ibid., 1:250–52; David Brion Davis, *The Problem of Slavery in Western Culture* (New York: Oxford University Press, 1966), 208–11; and Winthrop Jordan, *White Over Black: American Attitudes Toward the Negro* (Chapel Hill, NC: University of North Carolina Press for the Institute of Early American History and Culture, 1968), 179–87.

20. *English Reports*, vol. 83, 518. [83 E.R. 518].

21. These various cases are analyzed in Catterall, *Judicial Cases*, 1:1–12; Davis, *Problem of Slavery in Western Culture*, 207–11; William M. Wiecek, "Somerset: Lord Mansfield and the Legitimacy of Slavery in the Anglo-American World," *University of Chicago Law Review* 42:1 (Autumn, 1974), 89–95; A. Leon Higginbotham, *In the Matter of Color. Race and the American Legal Process: The Colonial Period* (New York: Oxford University Press, 1978), 313–29; James Oldham, "New Light on Mansfield and Slavery," *Journal of British Studies* (Jan. 1988): 45–68; and George Van Cleve, "Somerset's Case and Its Antecedents in Imperial Perspective," *Law and History Review* 24 (Fall 2006): 601–24.

22. Ruth Paley, Cristina Malcolmson, and Michael Hunter, "Parliament and Slavery, 1660–c.1710," *Slavery & Abolition* 31, no. 2 (June 2010): 257–81.

23. Winthrop Jordan, *White Over Black*, 92–93; John C. Van Horne, ed. *Religious Philanthropy and Colonial Slavery, The American Correspondence of the Associates of Dr. Bray* (Urbana: University of Illinois Press, 1986), 27. Compare with the printed version of the Duke's Laws in *Collections of the New York Historical Society, For the Year 1809*, vol. 1 (New York: I. Riley, 1811), 322–23, which does not contain the proviso.

24. *The Colonial Laws of New York from the Year 1664 to the Revolution . . .*, 5 vols. (Albany, NY: James B. Lyon, 1894–1896), 1:484.

25. Ibid., 1:519–21.

26. SPG–L, Elias Neau to Mr. Hodges, July 10, 1703, A1/106.

27. SPG–L, Elias Neau to Josiah Woodward, Sept. 5, 1704, A2/48.

28. SPG–J, vol. 1, 122, 125, 129; Lambeth Palace Library, *Gibson Papers*, MS 941/72. On Hooke, see Stuart Handley, "Hooke, John (1655–1712)," *ODNB*.

29. SPG–L, Elias Neau to Secretary, Oct. 3, 1705, A2/124.

30. Ibid., Mar. 1, 1705/6, A2/159.

31. Ibid., Apr. 30, 1706, A2/167. On Neau's role in these events, see also Thelma Wills Foote, *Black and White Manhattan: The History of Racial Formation in Colonial New York City* (New York: Oxford, 2004), 124–29.

32. John Williams, *A Sermon Preached before the Society for the Propagation of the Gospel in Foreign Parts . . . February 15, 1705/6* (London: Joseph Downing, 1706), 20.

33. Bruce T. McCully, "Governor Francis Nicholson, Patron 'Par Excellence' of Religion and Learning in Colonial America." *WMQ*, 3rd ser., 39, no. 2 (Apr. 1982): 310–33; Stephen Saunders Webb, "The Strange Career of Francis Nicholson." *WMQ*, 3rd ser., 23, no. 4 (Oct. 1966): 513–48; Ruth M. Winton, "Governor Francis Nicholson's Relations with the S.P.G.," *HMPEC* 17, no. 3 (Sept. 1948): 274–86; and Kevin R. Hardwick, "Nicholson, Sir Francis (1655–1728)," *ODNB*.

34. SPG–J, vol. 1, 235. For the Extracts of Laws given to the Committee by Nicholson, see SPG–J, Appendix B, Doc #79 and William Manross, *S.P.G. Papers in the Lambeth Palace Library. Calendars and Indexes* (Oxford: Clarendon Press, 1974), 91, 152, 156. The Society touted these efforts in its own early promotional literature. See [Kennett], *Account of the Society for Propagating the Gospel in Foreign Parts*, 60–61.

35. On the long-term failure of the British state to comprehensively regulate imperial slavery see Christopher L. Brown, *Moral Capital: Foundations of British Abolitionism* (Chapel Hill: University of North Carolina Press for the Omohundro Institute of Early American History and Culture, 2006), 240–45; Jonathan A. Bush, "The British Constitution and the Creation of American Slavery," in *Slavery and the Law*, ed. Paul Finkelman (Madison: Madison House, 1997), 379–418; and Eliga H. Gould, "Zones of Law, Zones of Violence: The Legal Geography of the British Atlantic, circa 1772, *WMQ*, 3rd ser., 60, no. 3 (July 2003): 503–7.

36. SPG–L, Elias Neau to Secretary, Nov. 28, 1706, A3/17. In 1709 Neau reported to the SPG that Cornbury was scandalously cross-dressing. See Patricia Bonomi, *The Lord Cornbury*

Scandal: The Politics of Reputation in British America (Chapel Hill: Omohundro Institute of Early American History and Culture, 1998), 70–76, 148–65. If Neau's reports were rooted in political animosity, it is noteworthy that the law concerning slave conversion could engender support from multiple factions in the colony's political landscape. Cornbury, having succeeded as Earl of Clarendon, became a member of the SPG in 1712.

37. SPG–L, Elias Neau to Secretary, July 22, 1707, A3/80; July 24, 1707, A3/128.
38. *Colonial Laws of New York*, 1:597–98.
39. Ibid., 1:598.
40. SPG–L, Elias Neau to Secretary, Nov. 28, 1706, A3/17; July 22, 1707, A3/80.
41. SPG–L, "Proclamation of Gov. Robert Hunter," Jan. 12, 1711/2, C/Am/1/13.
42. *Documents Relative to the Colonial History of the State of New York*, 15 vols. (New York: Weed, Parsons and Company, 1853–1887), 5:341–42.
43. On the 1712 New York slave rebellion, see Harris, *In the Shadow of Slavery*, 37–40; Hodges, *Root and Branch*, 63–68; Edgar J. McManus, *A History of Negro Slavery in New York* (Syracuse, NY: Syracuse University Press, 1966), 121–126; Kenneth Scott, "The Slave Insurrection in New York in 1712," *New-York Historical Society Quarterly* 45 (1961): 43–74; and Herbert Aptheker, *American Negro Slave Revolts* (New York: Columbia University Press, 1943), 172–74.
44. Humphreys, *Historical Account of the Incorporated Society*, 241. Humphreys's account of the rebellion and its aftermath is a near verbatim repetition of: SPG–L, John Sharpe to Secretary, June 23, 1712, A7/214–17.
45. Scott, "The Slave Insurrection in New York in 1712," 65–66.
46. SPG–L, John Sharpe to Secretary, June 23, 1712, A7/214–17. Sharpe told the SPG that he visited Robin on the third day that he hung in chains and that it was then, in what must have been extreme distress, that he admitted his knowledge of the conspiracy but denied personally killing Hoghlandt.
47. Humphreys, *Historical Account of the Incorporated Society*, 241; and SPG–L, Elias Neau to Secretary, Dec. 15, 1712, A7/226–27.
48. *Documents Relative to the Colonial History of the State of New York*, 5:356–57; and Scott, "The Slave Insurrection in New York in 1712," 69–74. Provisions outlawing slave gatherings and sanctioning corporal punishments strengthened previous laws. See McManus, *History of Negro Slavery in New York*, 80–81.
49. SPG–L, Elias Neau to Secretary, Dec. 15, 1712, A7/226–27.
50. Humphreys, *Historical Account of the Incorporated Society*, 241–42; *Documents Relative to the Colonial History of the State of New York*, 5:341–42; and Scott, "The Slave Insurrection in New York in 1712," 64–65.
51. SPG–L, "A List of the Slaves taught by Mr. Neau since the year 1704," Nov. 6, 1714, A10/220–23; Elias Neau to Secretary, Nov. 22, 1715, A11/283–86; Elias Neau to Mr. Taylor, Dec. 6, 1715, A11/293–94; Extract of a Letter from Elias Neau to Dr. Sharpe, Nov. 22, 1715, A11/294–95.
52. SPG–L, Elias Neau to Secretary, Dec. 15, 1712, A7/226–27; "Mr. Neau and Mr. Bondets Representations Transmitted with Mr. Sharps Letter . . .," Feb. 28, 1712/13, A8/292–94.
53. SPG–L, Elias Neau to Secretary, Oct. 8, 1719, A13/479–82.
54. SPG–L, James Wetmore to Secretary, June 24, 1726, A19/395–96; James Wetmore to Secretary, Dec. 3, 1726, A19/190–94.
55. SPG–L, William Huddleston to Secretary, Nov. 24, 1722, A16/212–14; Rector (William Vesey), Churchwardens, and Vestry of Trinity Church to Secretary, Dec. 18, 1722, A16/229–30; Secretary to James Wetmore, Mar. 2, 1723/4, A17/324; Secretary to William Vesey, Mar. 2, 1723/4, A17/325; Churchwardens and Vestry of Trinity Church, New York, to Secretary, Oct. 17, 1726, A19/407–08.

56. Faith Vibert, "The Society for the Propagation of the Gospel in Foreign Parts: Its Work for the Negroes in North America Before 1783," *Journal of Negro History* 18, no. 2 (Apr. 1933): 186–87. Brown, *Moral Capital*, 63. For SPG reports on efforts in 1710 see SPG–J, vol. 1, 465–67, SPG–SC, vol. 1, Feb. 20, 1709/10 and Mar. 6, 1709/10, and John Chamberlayne to Francis Le Jau, Feb. 20, 1710/11, in Manross, *SPG Papers in the Lambeth Palace Library*, 148 (vol. 17, 30). For efforts in 1714, see SPG–J, vol. 2, 382–85, and SPG–L, "Clause concerning the Negro's delivered by Mr. Jennings," [1714], A9/68–69. For the presence of these efforts within the Parliamentary record, see Leo Francis Stock, ed., *Proceedings and Debates of the British Parliaments respecting North America*. 5 vols. (Washington: The Carnegie Institution of Washington, 1924–1941), 3:237 and 3:295–96. Clauses promoting slave Christianization were introduced on March 16, 1709/10 and May 27, 1712. The second of these efforts saw a clause attached to a bill through a vote, but the bill subsequently failed to pass. These Parliamentary efforts tied the SPG's promotion of religious reforms to debates over the protection of the Royal African Company from competition from independent slave traders, a dispute that was ultimately won by free traders in 1714. See Kenneth G. Davies, *The Royal African Company* (New York: Atheneum, 1970), 134–52; and William A. Pettigrew, "Free to Enslave: Politics and the Escalation of Britain's Transatlantic Slave Trade, 1688–1714," *WMQ*, 3rd ser., 64, no. 1 (Jan. 2007): 3–38.

57. SPG–L, Ebenezer Taylor to Secretary, Apr. 23, 1719, A13/212–24.

58. Travis Glasson, "'Baptism doth not bestow Freedom': Missionary Anglicanism, Slavery, and the Yorke-Talbot Opinion, 1701–30," *WMQ*, 3rd ser., 68, no. 2 (Apr. 2010): 279–318.

59. SPG, *A Collection of Papers, Printed by Order of the Society for the Propagation of the Gospel in Foreign Parts* ... (London: Joseph Downing, 1706), 35.

60. SPG–L, Thomas Hasell to Secretary, Mar. 20, 1721/2, A16/60–63.

61. SPG–L, William Guy to Secretary, Jan. 22, 1727/8, A20/110–15. On the SPG's missionary program in the colony see S. Charles Bolton, *Southern Anglicanism: The Church of England in South Carolina* (Westport: Greenwood Press, 1982); Annette Laing, "'Heathens and Infidels'? African Christianization and Anglicanism in the South Carolina Low Country, 1700–1750," *Religion and American Culture* 12 (2002): 197–228; and Robert Olwell, *Masters, Slaves, and Subjects: The Culture of Power in the South Carolina Low Country, 1740–1790* (Ithaca, NY: Cornell University Press, 1998), 103–39, and various works by Frank J. Klingberg. On the development of South Carolina plantation society, see Peter H. Wood, *Black Majority: Negroes in Colonial South Carolina from 1670 through the Stono Rebellion* (New York: Alfred A. Knopf, 1974).

62. SPG–L, Richard Ludlam to Secretary, 1725, A19/66–67; Dec. 12, 1727, A20/98–104.

63. SPG–L, Brian Hunt to Secretary, Nov. 5, 1725, A19/80–82. On Hunt's checkered career see Annette Laing, "A Very Immoral and Offensive Man": Religious Culture, Gentility and the Strange Case of Brian Hunt, 1727," *South Carolina Historical Magazine* 103, no. 1 (Jan. 2002): 6–29.

64. Abstract of Proceedings printed with James Johnson, *A Sermon Preached before the Incorporated Society for the Propagation of the Gospel in Foreign Parts* ... *On Friday, February 24, 1758* (London: Edward Owen, 1758), 50.

65. SPG–L, John Adams to Secretary, Oct. 4, 1709, A5/102; Robert Maule to Secretary, [ca. 1710], A5/133; James Giguillet to Secretary, May 28, 1710, A5/119; John Bartow to Secretary, July 5, 1710, A5/139.

66. SPG–L, Francis Le Jau to Secretary, Feb. 9, 1710/11, A6/58; Sept. 18, 1711, A6/142; Dec. 11, 1712, A7/440–41; Aug. 10, 1713, A8/362–65.

67. SPG–L, William Tredwell Bull to Secretary, Jan. 20, 1714/15, A10/90–92.

68. SPG–L, Francis Varnod to Secretary, Jan. 13, 1723/24, A18/69–75; Feb. 13, 1730/31, A23/230; Richard Ludlam to Secretary, Mar. 22, 1724/25, A19/62–63; John Usher to Secretary, Sept. 28, 1727, B1/226; Samuel Auchmuty to Secretary, Apr. 13, 1765, B2/9. For

Harrison's view, see Frank J. Klingberg, *An Appraisal of the Negro in South Carolina: A Study in Americanization* (Washington, DC: Associated Publishers, 1941), 94. On master's objections to Anglican conversion efforts, see also Albert J. Raboteau, *Slave Religion: The "Invisible Institution" in the Antebellum South*, rev. ed. (New York: Oxford University Press, 2004), 99–104.

69. SPG–L, Extract of a Letter from William Cary to Henry Newman, Jan. 19, 1718/19, A13/88–90.

70. SPG–L, Benjamin Dennis to Secretary, Sept. 3, 1711, A6/143.

71. On colonial Anglican funeral and burial practices, see Nicholas Beasley, *Christian Ritual and the Creation of British Slave Societies, 1650–1780* (Athens: University of Georgia Press, 2009), 109–35.

72. SPG–L, Ebenezer Taylor to Secretary, July 28, 1713, A8/354–58; Extract of Letter from Lilia Haigue, n.d., read at SPG meeting July 15, 1715, A10/81–83. Abstract of Proceedings published with George Stanhope, *The early Conversion of Islanders, a wise Expedient for propagating Christianity. A Sermon Preached before the Incorporated Society for the Propagation of the Gospel in Foreign Parts . . . On Friday the 19th of February 1713/14* (London: Joseph Downing, 1714), 44–45. On Skene's prominence in South Carolina politics, see Klingberg, *Appraisal of the Negro*, 39–45.

73. SPG–L, Francis Varnod to Secretary, Jan. 15, 1723/4, A17/120–22; Clergy of South Carolina to Secretary, Mar. 10, 1723/4, A18/65–67. Francis Varnod to Secretary, July 12, 1724, A18/85–87; Mar. 21, 1725, A19/60; Jan. 4, 1726/7, A19/343–44; May 4, 1727, A20/81; and Apr. 3, 1728, A21/77–87. See also Klingberg, *Appraisal of the Negro*, 55–61. Samuel Wragg, who spent his career primarily in England, and his brother Joseph Wragg played a leading part in the establishment of the slave trade to South Carolina. Elizabeth Donnan, "The Slave Trade into South Carolina Before the Revolution," *American Historical Review* 33, no. 4 (July 1928): 804–28. SPG–J, vol. 5, Aug. 20, 1725.

74. SPG–L, Francis Varnod to Secretary, Apr. 3, 1728, A21/77–87; Klingberg, *Appraisal of the Negro*, 86–88.

75. Klingberg, *Appraisal of the Negro*, 40–41.

76. Abstract of Proceedings printed with Richard Osbaldiston, *A Sermon Preached before the Incorporated Society for the Propagation of the Gospel in Foreign Parts . . . On Friday, February 21, 1752* (London: Edward Owen, 1752), 43, 47–48.

77. SPG–L, James Honyman to Secretary, Sept. 7, 1727, B1/222; Abstract of Proceedings printed with John Gilbert, *A Sermon Preached before the Incorporated Society for the Propagation of the Gospel in Foreign Parts . . . On Friday, February 17, 1743–44* (London: J. and H. Pemberton, 1744), 44.

78. SPG–L, James Greaton to Secretary, Jan. 23, 1771, B3/147.

79. Klingberg, *Appraisal of the Negro*, 62.

80. SPG–L, Richard Ludlam to Secretary, July 2, 1724, A18/83.

81. SPG–L, Thomas Hasell to Secretary, Mar. 12, 1712, A7/400–02.

82. SPG–L, John Thomas to Secretary, June 21, 1709, A5/4.

83. SPG–L, Richard Tabor and Thomas Lloyd to Secretary, Dec. 5, 1707, A3/147. Printed in Frank J. Klingberg, "As to the State of Jamaica in 1707," *Journal of Negro History* 27, no. 3 (July 1942): 288–94.

84. SPG–L, Thomas Standard to Secretary, Nov. 5, 1729, B1/50.

85. SPG–L, John Bartow to Secretary, Nov. 5, 1725, A19/184–85.

86. Ibid., Nov. 30, 1710, A5/179.

87. SPG–L, Robert Jenney to Secretary, Nov. 19, 1725, B1[appendix]/78. On Anglican efforts to regulate marriage and sexual morality in the colonies, see Beasley, *Christian Ritual*, 54–64.

88. SPG–L, Francis Le Jau to Secretary, Nov. 15, 1709, A4/91; Oct. 20, 1709, A5/49.

89. SPG–L, Ibid., Aug. 5, 1709, A5/48; Secretary to Francis Le Jau, Nov. 6, 1712, A7/478–79. On baptism's significance among black and white colonial Anglicans, see also Beasley, *Christian Ritual*, 64–83.

90. SPG–L, "Instructions of the Clergy of South Carolina given to Mr. Johnston . . .," Mar. 4, 1712, A8/423–38.

91. Humphreys, *Historical Account of the Incorporated Society*, 248.

92. SPG–J, vol. 3, 67–68; SPG–L, Samuel Bradford to Secretary, [1715], A10/10.

93. William Fleetwood, *A Sermon Preached before the Society for the Propagation of the Gospel in Foreign Parts . . . On Friday the 16th of February, 1710/11* (London: Joseph Downing, 1711), 20–22; SPG–J, vol. 5, 25.

94. SPG–L, Secretary to Attorneys in Barbados, July 26, 1726, C/Win/Bar2/28; and Secretary to John Smalridge, July 26, 1726, C/Win/Bar2/28. SPG–J, vol. 5, 184.

95. On Gibson's queries to colonial ministers see Patricia Bonomi and Peter Eisenstadt, "Church Adherence in the Eighteenth-Century British American Colonies," *WMQ*, 3rd ser., 39, no. 2 (Apr. 1982): 253–86; William Manross, *The Fulham Papers in Lambeth Palace Library: American Colonial Section Calendar and Indexes* (Oxford: Clarendon Press, 1965), xiii, xxiii.

96. Edmund Gibson, *Two letters of the Lord Bishop of London: the first, to the masters and mistresses of families in the English plantations abroad; . . . The second, to the missionaries there; . . .*(London: Joseph Downing, 1727).

97. Ibid., 14.

98. On the intersection between Gibson's legal scholarship and his wider interests in reforming the Church of England at home, see Stephen Taylor, "Introduction" to "Bishop Edmund Gibson's Proposals for Church Reform," in *From Cranmer to Davidson: A Church of England Miscellany*, ed. Stephen Taylor, 171–86 (Woodbridge, Suffolk: Boydell Press, 1999).

99. Edmund Gibson, *Codex juris ecclesiastici Anglicani. . . .* 2 vols. (London: J. Baskett, 1713), 1:449–50. Gibson's references reveal he was considering "Sir Thomas Grantham's Case," (1686/7) and *Chamberline v. Harvey* (1696/7).

100. Gibson, *Two letters of the Lord Bishop of London*, 10–12.

101. SPG–J, vol. 5, 119, 122–23, 125.

102. SPG–J, vol. 5, 200–02, 211, 220, 226, 236.

103. Edmund Gibson, *Two letters of the Lord Bishop of London: the first, to the masters and mistresses of families in the English plantations abroad; . . . The second, to the missionaries there; . . . To both which is prefix'd, an address to serious Christians among our selves, to assist the Society for Propagating the Gospel, . . .* (London: Joseph Downing, 1729).

104. Humphreys, *Historical Account of the Incorporated Society*, 249–75; and SPG–J, vol. 5, 119, 200.

105. For favorable reports on the effects of Gibson's letters see SPG–L, James Wetmore to Secretary, Feb. 20, 1727, A20/207–20; William Beckett to Secretary, May 29, 1729, A22/322–23; Fulham Papers, James Blair to Edmund Gibson, June 28, 1729, vol. 7, 134–35. For more skeptical responses, see SPG–L, George Ross to Secretary, May 17, 1728, A21/241–43; Thomas Standard to Secretary, Nov. 5, 1729, A22/363–71; Fulham Papers, Marquis Duquesne to Henry Newman, May 15, 1728, vol. 17, 248–57; Christopher Wilkinson to Edmund Gibson, Oct. 18, 1728, vol. 3, 120; and James Wetmore to Edmund Gibson, Nov. 1, 1728; v. 6, 190–91.

106. [Robert Robertson], *A Letter to the Right Reverend The Lord Bishop of London. . . .* (London: J. Wilford, 1730), 5–6 (quote), 5–15. For the text from which Robertson was quoting, see *An Abstract of the Proceedings of the Society for the Propagation of the Gospel in . . . 1715* (London: Joseph Downing, 1716), 12. On Robertson, see Brown, *Moral Capital*, 33–37; and Thomas W. Krise, "True Novel, False History: Robert Robertson's Ventriloquized Ex-Slave

in 'The Speech of Mr. John Talbot Campo-Bell' (1736)," *Early American Literature* 30, no. 2 (1995): 152–64.

107. [Robertson], *A Letter to the Right Reverend The Lord Bishop of London*, 19–26.

108. Ibid., 20, 89.

109. Fleetwood, *A Sermon Preached Before the Society*, 13.

110. SPG–L, Charles Irvine to bishop of London, July 14, 1711, A6/114. See also SPG–L, Dudley Woodbridge to Secretary, Aug. 25, 1711, A6/115.

111. SPG–L, Secretary to All Missionaries, July 30, 1725, A19/113.

112. For representative examples of slaveholding by South Carolina-based missionaries, see SPG–L, John Urmston to Secretary, Feb. 14, 1715/6, A11/85–90; "A Copy of Mr. Maules Will delivered to the Committee by Mr. Bull," Sept. 30, 1719, A13/249–50; "Mr. Boyle's Will attested by Col. Johnson," n.d. (1719?), A13/262; Thomas Morritt to Secretary, Apr. 6, 1726, A19/312–14; Thomas Hasell to Secretary, May 12, 1726, A19/314–15; and "Tax Return for St. James's Parish, Goose Creek, South Carolina," 1745, C/Am/7/149.

113. SPG–L, William Treadwell Bull to Secretary, Jan. 20, 1714/15, A10/90–92; Francis Le Jau to Secretary, Mar. 18, 1716/7, A12/63–67; Brian Hunt to Secretary, May 25, 1724, A18/80–82; Edwin Gaustad, *George Berkeley in America* (New Haven, CT: Yale University Press, 1979), 94; and Inventory of the Estate of Clement Hall, Jan. 17, 1759, in *The Church of England in North Carolina: Documents, 1742–1763*, ed. Robert J. Cain and Jan-Michael Poff (Raleigh: Office of Archives and History North Carolina Department of Cultural Resources, 2007), 188–91.

114. SPG–L, George Pigot to Secretary, Apr. 29, 1728, A21/404–6; Robert Jenney to Secretary, May 1, 1727, A20/182–83.

115. Quoted in W. K. Lowther Clarke, *A History of the SPCK* (London: SPCK, 1959), 18. See also Clarke, *Eighteenth Century Piety* (London: SPCK, 1944), 49.

116. Daniel O'Connor et al., *Three Centuries of Mission: The United Society for the Propagation of the Gospel, 1701–2000* (London: Continuum, 2000), 34. Toby reportedly "died of yaws" soon after his arrival in Britain. See SPG–L, Philip Bearcroft to Thomas Thompson, July 15, 1743, B11/201; Thomas Thompson to Philip Bearcroft, Jan. 30, 1743, B11/214–16; Bolton, *Southern Anglicanism*, 58, 114; and H. P. Thompson, *Into All Lands: The History of the Society for the Propagation of the Gospel in Foreign Parts, 1701–1950* (London: SPCK, 1951), 38.

117. SPG–L, William Guy to Secretary, Nov. 7, 1726, A19/338–39; SPG–J, vol. 6, 44.

118. SPG–L, Brian Hunt to Secretary, May 12, 1725, A19/73–74. See also Churchwardens and Vestry of St. Johns, South Carolina, to Francis Nicholson, Feb. 6, 1721/2, A16/54–56; and Brian Hunt to Secretary, Nov. 24, 1726, A19/339–41.

119. See the Abstract of Proceedings attached to Robert Drummond, *A Sermon Preached before the Incorporated Society for the Propagation of the Gospel in Foreign Parts . . . On Friday, February 15, 1754* (London: Edward Owen, 1754), 63, and to James Johnson, *A Sermon Preached before the Incorporated Society for the Propagation of the Gospel in Foreign Parts . . . On Friday, February 24, 1758* (London: E. Owen and T. Harrison, 1758), 51–52. On the extent of slaveholding by SPG missionaries, see also O'Connor, *Three Centuries of Mission*, 34; and Klingberg, *Appraisal of the Negro*, 52. Slaveholding was also prevalent among the non-SPG Anglican clergyman of Virginia and Maryland. See John K. Nelson, *A Blessed Company: Parishes, Parsons, and Parishioners in Anglican Virginia, 1690–1776* (Chapel Hill: University of North Carolina Press, 2001), 262; and Carol von Vorst, *The Anglican Clergy in Maryland, 1692–1776* (New York: Garland Publishing, 1989), 261–65.

120. SPG–L, Secretary to Mr. Salmon, Jan. 20, 1720, C/Win/Bar 2/17; SPG–X, X/37, 270–71. On Ludlam's bequest, see St. Julien Ravenel Childs, "Kitchen Physick Medical and Surgical Care of Slaves on an Eighteenth Century Rice Plantation," *Mississippi Valley Historical Review* 20, no. 4 (Mar. 1934): 549–54.

121. Klingberg, *Appraisal of the Negro*, 50–54.
122. SPG–L, William Treadwell Bull to Secretary, Jan. 20, 1714/15, A10/90–92; James Honyman to Secretary, Dec. 23, 1725, A19/247–48.
123. SPG–L, Robert Jenney to Secretary, Nov. 19, 1725, A19/187–90; Timothy Cutler to Secretary, Apr. 4, 1726, A19/441–42.
124. White Kennett, *The Lets and Impediments in Planting and Propagating the Gospel of Christ. A Sermon Preach'd before the Society for the Propagation of the Gospel in Foreign Parts . . . On Friday the 15th of February, 1711/12* (London: Joseph Downing, 1712), 26–27.
125. SPG–J, vol. 2, 4; SPG–L, John Chamberlayne to [Dudley] Woodbridge, Mar. 7, 1711, C/Win/Bar 1/7.
126. John Denne, *Want of Universality no just Objection to the Truth of the Christian Religion. A Sermon Preached before the Incorporated Society for the Propagation of the Gospel in Foreign Parts . . . On Friday, the 19th of February, 1730* (London: Joseph Downing, 1730), 63. For a later critique of planter violence, see Robert Lowth, *A Sermon Preached before the Incorporated Society for the Propagation of the Gospel in Foreign Parts . . . On Friday, February 15, 1771* (London: E. Owen and T. Harrison, 1771), 26–27.
127. SPG–L, Francis Le Jau to Secretary, June 13, 1710, A5/120; Feb. 20, 1711/12, A7/395–97; Feb. 23, 1712/13, A8/346–48.
128. Ibid., Feb. 20, 1711/12, A7/395–97.
129. MacSparran is discussed in more detail in chap. 4.
130. Lathan A. Windley, comp., *Runaway Slave Advertisements: A Documentary History from the 1730s to 1790*, vol. 3, *South Carolina* (Westport, CT: Greenwood Press, 1983), 22, 69, 76, 79, 114. Alexander Garden, rector of St. Thomas, was the nephew of South Carolina commissary Alexander Garden and the son-in-law of Francis Le Jau.
131. Graham Russell Hodges and Alan Edward Brown, eds., *Pretends to Be Free: Runaway Slave Advertisements from Colonial and Revolutionary New York and New Jersey* (New York: Garland Publishing, 1994), 167.
132. SPG–X, X36, 3–7; SPG–L, John Smalridge to Secretary, July 25, 1722, C/Win/Bar2/27; SPG–X, X36, 23–25; Secretary to SPG Attorneys in Barbados, Jan. 31, 1721, X37; X37a, 103–11.
133. SPG–X, X37a, which records the purchase of the metal brand. SPG–L, Arthur Holt to Secretary, Apr. 3, 1732, A24/267–70; Fulham Papers, Arthur Holt to Edmund Gibson, Aug. 16, 1732, vol. 16, 31–32.
134. For the nineteenth-century controversy this engendered, see chap. 7.
135. SPG–L, Francis Le Jau to Secretary, July 10, 1711, A6/103.
136. SPG–L, Peter Stoupe to Secretary, Sep. 26, 1725, A19/179; John Holbrooke to Secretary, Nov. 17, 1727, A20/193–98.
137. On this point, see also Beasley, *Christian Ritual*, 137–39.
138. Raboteau, *Slave Religion*, 121.
139. On Anglicanism's potential appeal to slaves, see Laing, Heathens and Infidels," 197–228.
140. Timothy Cutler to Secretary, Sept. 6, 1736, in *Historical Collections Relating to the American Colonial Church*, ed. William S. Perry (1873), 3:315.
141. SPG–L, Elias Neau to Secretary, Aug. 24, 1708, A4/68.
142. SPG–L, John Usher to Secretary, Aug. 4, 1730, A23/124–26.
143. Thomas N. Ingersoll, "Releese us out of this Cruell Bondegg": An Appeal from Virginia in 1723," *WMQ*, 3rd ser., 51, no. 4 (Oct. 1994): 781.
144. SPG–L, George Ross to Secretary, Sept. 1, 1726, A19/372–73.
145. Anthony Parent, *Foul Means: The Formation of a Slave Society in Virginia, 1660–1740* (Chapel Hill: University of North Carolina Press, 2003), 159–62; Frey and Wood, *Come Shouting to Zion*, 69–70; Glasson, "'Baptism doth not bestow Freedom,'" 301.
146. Bolton, *Southern Anglicanism*, 112–13.

147. On the pledge Le Jau instituted, see SPG–L, Francis Le Jau to Secretary, Oct. 20, 1709, A5/49; Frank J. Klingberg, ed., *The Carolina Chronicle of Dr. Francis Le Jau, 1706–1717* (Berkeley: University of California Press, 1956), 60; and Frank Lambert, "'I Saw the Book Talk': Slave Readings of the First Great Awakening," *Journal of Negro History* 77, no. 4 (Autumn 1992): 188. On his Bible-quoting student, see SPG–L, Francis Le Jau to Secretary, Feb. 1, 1709/10, A5/98. For the multiple meanings that Anglican baptism could have for enslaved people in Virginia, see Lauren F. Winner, *A Cheerful and Comfortable Faith: Anglican Religious Practice in the Elite Households of Eighteenth-Century Virginia* (New Haven, CT: Yale University Press, 2010), 38–44.

148. Imagery of the moon turning to blood also appears in Rev. 6:12.

149. James Sidbury has noted the resonances between the book of Joel and the experiences of enslaved people involved in planning Gabriel's Rebellion in Virginia in 1800. See Sidbury, *Ploughshares into Swords: Race, Rebellion, and Identity in Gabriel's Virginia, 1730–1810* (Cambridge: Cambridge University Press, 1997), 69.

150. SPG–L, Francis Le Jau to Secretary, Feb. 1, 1709/10, A5/98.

151. SPG–L, John Bartow to Secretary, Nov. 5, 1725, A19/184–85.

152. On SPG efforts to promote literacy in colonial America, see E. Jennifer Monaghan, *Learning to Read and Write in Colonial America* (Amherst: University of Massachusetts Press, 2005), 143–65, 241–72.

Chapter 4

1. D. G. C. Allan, "Hales, Stephen (1677–1761)," *ODNB*. For his views on slavery see Stephen Hales, *A Sermon Preached before the Trustees for Establishing the Colony of Georgia in America and before the Associates of the late Rev. Dr. Thomas Bray . . . On Thursday, March 21. 1734* (London: T. Woodward, 1734/5?), 12–16. Hales did not join the SPG, but he collected donations for it, corresponded with its secretary on missionary matters, and left it money in his will.

2. John Keble, *The Life of the Right Reverend Father in God, Thomas Wilson, D.D., Lord Bishop of Sodor and Man*, 2 vols. (Oxford: John Henry Parker, 1863), 2:931–32.

3. On evangelical religion's essential role in the development of African American Christianity, see Sylvia R. Frey and Betty Wood, *Come Shouting to Zion: African American Protestantism in the American South and British Caribbean to 1830* (Chapel Hill: University of North Carolina Press, 1998); and Albert J. Raboteau, *Slave Religion: The "Invisible Institution" in the Antebellum South*, rev. ed. (Oxford: Oxford University Press, 2004), 128–50.

4. Abstract of Proceedings printed with Matthias Mawson, *A Sermon Preached before the Incorporated Society for the Propagation of the Gospel in Foreign Parts . . . On Friday, February 18, 1742–3* (London: Somerset Draper, 1743), 40–45.

5. SPG–L, James MacSparran to Secretary, Dec. 14, 1727, B1/235. On the Narragansett Plantations, see Robert K. Fitts, *Inventing New England's Slave Paradise: Master/Slave Relations in Eighteenth Century Narragansett, Rhode Island* (New York: Garland, 1998).

6. James MacSparran, "America Dissected . . .," printed in Wilkins Updike, *History of the Episcopal Church in Narragansett, Rhode Island. . . .* (New York: Henry M. Onderdonk, 1847), 488. This 1753 work presents MacSparran's critical views on America through letters to a fellow Irishman.

7. MacSparran, "America Dissected," 489, 510–14. On MacSparran, see Mary Sarah Bilder, *The Transatlantic Constitution: Colonial Legal Culture and the Empire* (Cambridge, MA: Harvard University Press, 2004), 145–67; Troy O. Bickham, "Macsparran, James (1693–1757)," *ODNB*; and John F. Woolverton, "MacSparran, James," *ANBO*.

8. James MacSparran, *A Letter Book and Abstract of Out Services*, ed. Daniel Goodwin (Boston: Merrymount Press, 1899), 26–27, 128–29.

9. Ibid., 12, 25–26, 55, 58.

10. Wilkins Updike, *A History of the Episcopal Church in Narragansett, Rhode Island . . .* 2nd ed., ed. Daniel Goodwin, 3 vols. (Boston: D. B. Updike, 1907), 1:200. Hereafter Updike and Goodwin, *Episcopal Church in Narragansett*.

11. MacSparran, *Letter Book*, 4, 6, 13.

12. Updike and Goodwin, *Episcopal Church in Narragansett*, 2:519, 2:605.

13. Ibid., 2:552.

14. MacSparran, *Letter Book*, 24, 26–27, 57–58; Updike and Goodwin, *Episcopal Church in Narragansett*, 2:482, 502.

15. MacSparran, *Letter Book*, 78–79, 105; Updike and Goodwin, *Episcopal Church in Narragansett*, 2:538–39.

16. MacSparran, *Letter Book*, 49.

17. MacSparran had baptized Richard in 1728. Updike and Goodwin, *Episcopal Church in Narragansett*, 2:492, 2:509.

18. MacSparran, *Letter Book*, 15, 29; Updike and Goodwin, *Episcopal Church in Narragansett*, 2:532.

19. Updike and Goodwin, *Episcopal Church in Narragansett*, 2:541.

20. Goodwin's edited version of MacSparran's letter book removed such direct references to sex and indelicate descriptions of MacSparran's work as a local medical practitioner. The phrase "a whoring as I suppose" appears in the MS version of the diary. Compare "Diary and Letterbook of James MacSparran," University of Rhode Island Library Special Collections, 6, and MacSparran, *Letter Book*, 52.

21. MacSparran, *Letter Book*, 52, 54–56, 63.

22. For Garden's career and his conflict with Whitefield, see S. Charles Bolton, *Southern Anglicanism: The Church of England in South Carolina* (Westport: Greenwood Press, 1982), 37–62.

23. Roger Price to Secretary, Mar. 2, 1739, in *Historical Collections Relating to the American Colonial Church*, ed. William S. Perry, 5 vols. (Hartford, 1873–78), 3:326.

24. SPG–L, Church Wardens and Vestry of Augusta, Georgia, to Secretary, Feb. 27, 1770, C/Am/8/25.

25. William Howland Kenney III, "Alexander Garden and George Whitefield: The Significance of Revivalism in South Carolina," *South Carolina Historical Magazine* 71, no. 1 (Jan. 1970): 2.

26. Thomas S. Kidd, *The Great Awakening: The Roots of Evangelical Christianity in Colonial America* (New Haven, CT: Yale University Press, 2007), 19, 35–37, 53, 98–99, 114, 128, 133–39, 152, 181, 213–33, 239–42, 249–51.

27. Extract from Charles Brockwell to Secretary, Feb. 18, 1741/2, in Perry, *Historical Collections*, 3:353.

28. John K. Thornton, "African Dimensions of the Stono Rebellion," *American Historical Review* 96, no. 4 (Oct., 1991): 1101–13.

29. G[eorge] Whitefield, *Three Letters from the Reverend Mr. G. Whitefield . . .* (Philadelphia: B. Franklin, 1740).

30. Ibid., 13–14.

31. Philip Bisse, *A Sermon Preach'd before the Incorporated Society for the Propagation of the Gospel in Foreign Parts . . . On Friday the 21st of February, 1717* (London: Joseph Downing, 1718), 17; Edward Chandler, *A Sermon Preached before the Incorporated Society for the Propagation of the Gospel in Foreign Parts . . . On Friday the 20th of February, 1718* (London: Joseph Downing, 1719), 29; Thomas Wilson, *An Essay Towards An Instruction For The Indians, Explaining the most Essential Doctrines of Christianity. . . .* (London: J. Osborn, 1740), xxi.

32. Alexander Garden, *Six Letters to The Rev. Mr. George Whitefield . . .*, 2nd ed. (Boston: T. Fleet, 1740), 51–52.

33. See the Abstract of Proceedings printed with Thomas Secker, *A Sermon Preached before the Incorporated Society for the Propagation of the Gospel in Foreign Parts . . . On Friday, February 20, 1740–1* (London: J. and H. Pemberton, 1741), 82–83.

34. Alexander Garden to Secretary, May 6, 1740, quoted in Frank J. Klingberg, *An Appraisal of the Negro in Colonial South Carolina: A Study in Americanization* (Washington, DC: Associated Publishers, 1941), 104–5.

35. SPG–L, Alexander Garden to Secretary, May 20, 1741, B9/124; Apr. 9, 1742, B10/138; July 3, 1742, B11/204; Sept. 24, 1742, B10/139; and "Bill of Sale for Andrew and Harry," July 3, 1742, B10/140.

36. Abstract of Proceedings printed with Secker, *A Sermon Preached before the Incorporated Society*, 82; Abstract of Proceedings printed with John Gilbert, *A Sermon Preached before the Incorporated Society for the Propagation of the Gospel in Foreign Parts . . . On Friday, February 17, 1743–4* (London: J. and H. Pemberton, 1744), 54; SPG–L, Alexander Garden to Secretary, Oct.(?) 10, 1743, B11/204–06.

37. Philip Bearcroft, *A Sermon Preached before the Incorporated Society for the Propagation of the Gospel in Foreign Parts . . . On Friday, February 15, 1744* (London: Edward Owen, 1744/5), 18.

38. On the Bryans, see Allan Gallay, *The Formation of a Planter Elite: Jonathan Bryan and the Southern Colonial Frontier* (Athens: University of Georgia Press, 2007), 30–54; Gallay, "The Origins of Slaveholders' Paternalism: George Whitefield, the Bryan Family, and the Great Awakening in the South," *Journal of Southern History* 53, no. 3 (Aug. 1987): 169–94; Harvey H. Jackson, "Hugh Bryan and the Evangelical Movement in Colonial South Carolina," *WMQ*, 3rd ser., 43, no. 4 (Oct. 1986): 594–614; and Leigh Eric Schmidt, "'The Grand Prophet,' Hugh Bryan: Early Evangelicalism's Challenge to the Establishment and Slavery in the Colonial South," *South Carolina Historical Magazine* 87, no. 4 (Oct. 1986): 238–50.

39. SPG–L, Lewis Jones to Secretary, June 3, 1736, A26/360.

40. Jackson, "Hugh Bryan," 605.

41. Quoted in Gallay, *Formation of a Planter Elite*, 45.

42. Gallay, "The Origins of Slaveholders' Paternalism," 386–88.

43. Ibid., 387–88.

44. Milton C. Sernett, "Bryan, Andrew," *ANBO*.

45. *South-Carolina Gazette*, Apr. 10–17 and Apr. 17–24, 1742. See also Frank Lambert, "I Saw the Book Talk: Slave Readings of the First Great Awakening," *Journal of African American History* 87 (Winter 2002): 15–16.

46. Klingberg, *Appraisal of the Negro*, 114.

47. Darold D. Wax, "The Great Risque We Run": The Aftermath of Slave Rebellion at Stono, South Carolina, 1739–1745," *Journal of Negro History* 67, no. 2 (Summer, 1982): 143. On the school's role in combating evangelical religion among enslaved people see also Bolton, *Southern Anglicanism*, 116–19.

48. Klingberg, *Appraisal of the Negro*, 115; SPG–L, Alexander Garden to Secretary, Oct. 18, 1744, B12/119; Sept. 9, 1750, B18/182; Secretary to Alexander Garden, Apr. 27, 1745, B13/349; July 2, 1746, B15/206; Apr. 5, 1751, B20/14–15; and SPG to Alexander Garden, Power of Attorney, Oct. 16, 1746, South Carolina Archives, Miscellaneous Records (Main Series), S213003, vol. HH (1746–50), 250.

49. Abstract of Proceedings printed with Secker, *A Sermon Preached before the Incorporated Society*, 82–3.

50. SPG–L, Minutes of a Meeting of the SPG's Codrington Attorneys, June 29, 1741, B8/62–63; J. Harry Bennett, *Bondsmen and Bishops: Slavery and Apprenticeship on the Codrington*

Plantations of Barbados, 1710–1838 (Berkeley: University of California Press, 1958), 83–84; and SPG–L, Sampson Smirk to Society, Apr. 6, 1741, B8/53.

51. Abstract of Proceedings printed with John Thomas, *A Sermon Preached before the Incorporated Society for the Propagation of the Gospel in Foreign Parts . . . On Friday, February 20, 1746* (London: Edward Owen, 1747), 55–56.

52. SPG–L, Secretary to Thomas Thompson, Apr. 11, 1753, B20, outgoing letters, 26–27.

53. See, for example, Thomas Hayter, *A Sermon Preached before the Incorporated Society for the Propagation of the Gospel in Foreign Parts . . . On Friday, February 21, 1755* (London: Edward Owen, 1755).

54. Abstract of Proceedings printed with Thomas Hayter, *A Sermon Preached before the Incorporated Society*, 57.

55. St. Philip's Parish, Transcript of Vestry Minutes, Mar. 17, 1768, South Carolina Archives, L630002; Bolton, *Southern Anglicanism*, 118–19; Olwell, *Masters, Slaves, and Subjects*, 120–21.

56. Klingberg, *Appraisal of the Negro*, 111.

57. For Wilson's long connection to the SPG, see Keble, *Life of . . . Thomas Wilson*, 1:148–49; 1:247–50; 2:912; 2:941–47. For his biography, see Carole Watterson Troxler, "Wilson, Thomas (1663–1755)," *ODNB*. On Wilson and Moravianism, see Colin Podmore, *The Moravian Church in England, 1728–1760* (Oxford: Clarendon Press, 1998), 192–95.

58. Thomas Wilson, *An Essay Towards An Instruction For The Indians, Explaining the most Essential Doctrines of Christianity. . . .* (London: J. Osborn, 1740).

59. Early editions were also "dedicated" to Oglethorpe and the George Trustees, but this was dropped by 1751, as Trustee rule in the colony was ending. Compare T. Wilson, *Essay Towards An Instruction For The Indians* (1740); T. Wilson, *The Knowledge and Practice of Christianity Made Easy To the Meanest Capacities . . .*, 2nd ed. (London: J. Osborn, 1741); and T. Wilson, *The Knowlege* [sic] *and Practice of Christianity Made Easy To the Meanest Capacities . . .*, 7th ed. (London: J. Osborn, 1751).

60. See, for example, T. Wilson, *Essay Towards An Instruction For The Indians*, xxxviii–xl, which includes excerpts from Martin Benson's 1740 SPG annual sermon and Wilson, *Knowledge and Practice of Christianity*, 5th ed. (1743), xx–xxxi, which adds excerpts from Thomas Secker's 1741 SPG annual sermon.

61. Thomas Wilson, *The knowledge and practice of Christianity made easy to the meanest capacities: or, An essay towards an instruction for children, and young persons; More especially those brought up in the Protestant charter-schools of Ireland* (Dublin: John Exshaw, 1750); T. Wilson, *Les Vérités et les devoirs du christianisme expliqués d'une manière accommodée à la capacité des plus foibles . . .*, trans. Jacob Bourdillon (Geneva: Heirs of Cramer and Philibert Brothers, 1744); and T. Wilson, *Gwybodaeth ac ymarfer o'r grefydd Grist'nogol . . .*, trans. Ddafydd Elis (London: J. a W. Olfir, 1774). The work was also reportedly translated into Italian by 1757. See Keble, *Life of . . . Thomas Wilson*, 2:921.

62. S. Austin Allibone, *A Critical Dictionary of English Literature and British and American Authors Living and Deceased from the Earliest Accounts to the Latter Half of the Nineteenth Century*, 3 vols. (London: Trubner, 1871) 3:2784.

63. Society for Promoting Christian Knowledge, *An Account of the Society for Promoting Christian Knowledge* (London: M. Downing, 1741), 33.

64. T. Wilson, *Knowledge and Practice of Christianity*, 5th ed. (1743), 270. See also, for example, the advertisements published in the 10th ed. (London: B. Dod, 1764) and 17th ed. (London: F. and C. Rivington, 1802).

65. For the younger Wilson's SPG membership, see Abstract of Proceedings printed with Isaac Maddox, *A Sermon Preached before the Incorporated Society for the Propagation of the Gospel in Foreign Parts . . . On Friday, February 15, 1733* (London: J. Downing, 1734), 40.

66. Abstract of Proceedings printed with Matthias Mawson, *A Sermon Preached before the Incorporated Society for the Propagation of the Gospel in Foreign Parts . . . On Friday, February 18,*

1742–3 (London: Somerset Draper, 1743), 34–35. Keble, *Life of ... Thomas Wilson,* 2:925, 931–32.

67. Allibone, *Critical Dictionary of English,* 3:2784.

68. Josiah Quincy, *The History of Harvard University,* 2 vols. (Cambridge: John Owen, 1840), 2:528.

69. SPG–L, Secretary to Sampson Smirk, Dec. 31, 1741, B8/75; Secretary to Abel Alleyne, Dec. 31, 1741, B8/74, SPG–X *Series,* Minutes of Barbados Committee Meeting, Oct. 14, 1742, X24; and Minutes of SPG Meeting, Nov. 16, 1744, X24.

70. Olwell, *Masters, Slaves, and Subjects,* 129, note 101; Klingberg, *Appraisal of the Negro,* 65–66; SPG–L, Alexander Garden to Secretary, Sept. 24, 1742, B10/139; Philip Bearcroft to William Vesey, June 14, 1743, B11/193a–194; Philip Bearcroft to Henry Barclay, June 14, 1743, B11/196–96a; and William B. Hart, "'For the Good of Our Souls': Mohawk Authority, Accommodation, and Resistance to Protestant Evangelism, 1700–1780" (PhD diss., Brown University, 1998), 237–38.

71. SPG–L, Samuel Frink to Secretary, July 3, 1767, C8/42; Christian Frederick Post to Secretary, July 31, 1767, B21/313.

72. SPG–L, Samuel Auchmuty to Secretary, Jan. 30, 1770, B2/35.

73. SPG–L, Philip Bearcroft to Roger Price, Nov. 6, 1742, B10/186a; Philip Bearcroft to William Shirley, Oct. 25, 1742, B10/186; Philip Bearcroft to Benning Wentworth, Apr. 25, 1743, B11/191a; Abstract of Proceedings with John Gilbert, *A Sermon Preached before the Incorporated Society for the Propagation of the Gospel in Foreign Parts ... On Friday, February 17, 1743–4* (London: J. and H. Pemberton, 1744), 45.

74. SPG–L, Philip Bearcroft to Francis Byam, Oct. 25, 1743(1742?), B11/203–03a; Philip Bearcroft to James Blair, Oct. 25, 1742, B11/202–03; Philip Bearcroft to William Gooch, Oct. 25, 1742, B11/203–04.

75. William Dawson, *A Letter from the Rev. Mr. Dawson, Commissary to the Lord Bishop of London. And President of William and Mary College, to the Clergy of Virginia in America* (London, 1745), 4.

76. Keble, *Life of ... Thomas Wilson,* 2:919.

77. SPG–L, Henry Addison to Secretary, Oct. 20, 1760, C8/4.

78. Olaudah Equiano, *The Interesting Narrative and Other Writings,* ed. Vincent Carretta (New York: Penguin Books, 1995), 78, 185. On the significance of Wilson's book to Equiano, see William C. Mottolese, "'Almost an Englishman': Equiano and the Colonial Gift of Language," *Bucknell Review* 41, no. 2 (1998): 160–71.

79. Hugh Pearson, *Memoirs of the Life and Correspondence of the Reverend Christian Frederick Swartz ...* 2 vols. (London: J. Hatchard and Son, 1834), 1:301.

80. "Extracts from The Barbados Mercury," *Journal of the Barbados Museum and Historical Society* 17, nos. 2 and 3 (Feb. and May 1950): 173.

81. Beilby Porteus, *A Letter to the Governors, Legislatures, and Proprietors of Plantation, in the British West-India Islands* (London: T. Cadell and W. Davies, 1808), 15.

82. Thomas Boyles Murray, *Pitcairn: The Island, The People, And The Pastor.* 8th ed. (London: SPCK, 1857) 113–15.

83. Wilson, *An Essay Towards an Instruction For the Indians* (1740), xviii–ix.

84. Ibid., 16.

85. Ibid., xix.

86. Ibid., xix–xx. On Wilson's text as a proslavery document, see also Mottolese, "Almost an Englishman," 161–63.

87. Society for the Propagation of the Gospel in Foreign Parts, *A Collection of Papers Printed by Order of the Society for the Propagation of the Gospel in Foreign Parts ...* (London: E. Owen, 1741), 44.

88. Wilson, *An Essay Towards An Instruction For the Indians* (1740), v.

89. Keble, *Life of ... Thomas Wilson,* 2:755–56, 2:764–68.
90. Ibid., 2:912–21. Keble's biography was connected to the Oxford Movement's embrace of Wilson as an intellectual and spiritual forebear. It is a rather uncertain guide to precisely how Wilson's texts were revised because Keble focused on criticizing the effect that the younger Wilson's Low Church tendencies had on his editing of his father's works.
91. Compare Wilson, *An Essay Towards An Instruction For the Indians* (1740), xix; and Wilson, *Knowledge and Practice of Christianity* (1741); viii.
92. Wilson, *An Essay Towards An Instruction For the Indians* (1740), xxi.
93. Ibid., xxii.
94. Richard R. Johnson, "Growth and Mastery: British North America, 1690–1748" in P. J. Marshall, ed. *The Oxford History of the British Empire,* vol. 2, *The Eighteenth Century,* ed. P. J. Marshall,(Oxford: Oxford University Press, 1998), 288–89. For an argument about the existence of a pan-Atlantic rebellion in the years around 1741, see Peter Linebaugh and Marcus Rediker, *The Many-Headed Hydra: Sailors, Slaves, Commoners, and the Hidden History of the Revolutionary Atlantic* (Boston: Beacon Press, 2000), 174–210. On slave rebellions in this period, see also David Barry Gaspar, *Bondmen and Rebels: A Study of Master-Slave Relations in Antigua* (Durham, NC: Duke University Press, 1993); Graham Russell Hodges, *Root and Branch: African Americans in New York and East Jersey, 1613–1863* (Chapel Hill: University of North Carolina Press, 1999), 91–98; and Jill Lepore, *New York Burning: Liberty, Slavery, and Conspiracy in Eighteenth-Century Manhattan* (New York: Knopf, 2005).
95. For omissions, compare T. Wilson, *An Essay Towards An Instruction For the Indians* (1740), xix–xxiv; and T. Wilson, *Knowledge and Practice of Christianity Made Easy* (1741), viii–xii.
96. T. Wilson, *An Essay Towards An Instruction For the Indians* (1740), xii; T. Wilson, *Knowledge and Practice of Christianity Made Easy* (1741), xi–xii.
97. Frey and Wood, *Come Shouting to Zion,* 118. Christine Leigh Heyrman estimated that 28 percent of all adult black people in the southern United States in 1835 were adherents of one of the three main evangelical denominations: Baptists, Methodists, and Presbyterians. See Heyrman, *Southern Cross: The Beginnings of the Bible Belt* (Chapel Hill: University of North Carolina Press, 1997), 265. See also Raboteau, *Slave Religion,* 149.
98. Frederick Cornwallis, *A Sermon Preached before the Incorporated Society for the Propagation of the Gospel in Foreign Parts ... On Friday, February 20, 1756* (London: Edward Owen, 1756), 7.

Chapter 5

1. Frank J. Klingberg, ed., *Codrington Chronicle: An Experiment in Anglican Altruism on a Barbados Plantation, 1710–1834* (Berkeley: University of California Press, 1949).
2. The most important study of Codrington is J. Harry Bennett, *Bondsmen and Bishops: Slavery and Apprenticeship on the Codrington Plantations of Barbados 1710–1838* (Berkeley: University of California Press, 1958). Because of its ownership by a record-keeping institution, Codrington is a particularly well-documented example of how an eighteenth-century sugar estate operated; Bennett considered his work, in part, as "a case study of plantation slavery." He also explored the Society's catechetical efforts, ultimately noting their failure in the face of hostility from other Barbadian planters. While less certain of the Society's altruism than his mentor, Klingberg, Bennett too saw nearly a century of Codrington's history as the precursor to reforms, which the SPG undertook in the nineteenth century.

Bennett opted to "treat the eighteenth century as one period through a series of topical chapters" while "the great changes of policy and practice" were "reserved to the chronological chapters with which this book ends." Framing Codrington's history in this way minimizes the significance and dynamism of eighteenth-century events and implies the ultimate redemption of enslaved people and the Society itself through a process culminating in emancipation. See Bennett, *Bondsmen and Bishops*, viii, 10, 75–87, 100–112. More critically, Richard Dunn took Codrington to exemplify "the full-blown West Indian slave system, in which several hundred blacks, kept docile and dumb through systematic semistarvation and a stupefying round of brute chores, functioned as dehumanized cogs in a very inefficient machine." See Richard S. Dunn, *Sugar and Slaves: The Rise of the Planter Class in the English West Indies, 1624–1713* (Chapel Hill: University of North Carolina Press, 1972), 324. An insightful examination of the plantation is Andrew Beahrs, "'Ours Alone Must Needs Be Christians': The Production of Enslaved Souls on the Codrington Estates," *Plantation Society in the Americas* 4, no. 2 and 3 (Fall 1997): 279–310.

3. J. Harry Bennett, "Of the Negroes thereon . . .," in Klingberg, ed., *Codrington Chronicle*, 96.

4. Vincent T. Harlow, *Christopher Codrington, 1668–1710* (London: Hurst and Co., 1990; repr. Oxford: Clarendon Press, 1928), 123; C. S. S. Higham, "The Negro Policy of Christopher Codrington," *Journal of Negro History* 10, no. 2 (Apr. 1925): 150–53.

5. SPG–J, Appendix B, Doc. #67.

6. Harlow, *Christopher Codrington*, 45. George Smalridge and another Tory clergyman with SPG connections, Francis Gastrell, received bequests from Codrington. Codrington also left £10,000 to his Oxford college, All Souls, for the founding of its still surviving Codrington Library: Harlow, *Christopher Codrington*, 217–19.

7. SPG–L, Archbishop of Canterbury to Secretary, Nov. 16, 1710, A6/24.

8. William Fleetwood, *A sermon preached before the Society for the Propagation of the Gospel in Foreign Parts . . . on Friday the 16th of February, 1710/11* (London: Joseph Downing, 1711), 32.

9. Printed in Harlow, *Christopher Codrington*, 218.

10. SPG–L, William Gordon to Secretary, July 25, 1710, C/Win/Bar1. See also William Gordon, *A Sermon Preach'd at the Funeral Of the Honourable Colonel Christopher Codrington . . .* (London: G. Strahan, 1710), 3–4.

11. Everild Young and Kjeld Helweg-Larsen, *The Pirates' Priest: The Life of Père Labat in the West Indies 1693–1705* (London: Jarrolds, 1965), 143–50. Labat was a Dominican, not a Jesuit; Codrington could well have known other Catholic priests.

12. Noel Titus, "Concurrence without Compliance: SPG and the Barbadian Plantations, 1710–1834," in Daniel O'Connor et al., *Three Centuries of Mission: The United Society for the Propagation of the Gospel, 1701–2000* (London: Continuum, 2000), 249. Codrington's biographer has suggested that the words relating to the establishment of a monastic clergy were "quietly deleted by Archbishop Tenison and nothing said." Harlow, *Christopher Codrington*, 213. See also Samuel Clyde McCulloch and John A. Schutz, "Of the Noble and Generous Benefaction . . .," in Klingberg, *Codrington Chronicle*, 24.

13. Dauril Alden, *The Making of an Enterprise: The Society of Jesus in Portugal, Its Empire, and Beyond 1540–1750* (Stanford, CA: Stanford University Press, 1996), 505, 513, 524–25; Frederick P. Bowser, "Africans in Spanish American Colonial Society," in *The Cambridge History of Latin America*, 11 vols., ed. Leslie Bethell (Cambridge: Cambridge University Press, 1984), 1:371. Nicholas P. Cushner has explored Jesuit slaveholding in several works. See, for example, Cushner, *Lords of the Land: Sugar, Wine, and Jesuit Estates of Coastal Peru, 1600–1767* (Albany: State University of New York Press, 1980).

14. Thomas Murphy, *Jesuit Slaveholding in Maryland, 1717–1838* (New York: Routledge, 2001), 45–47.

15. Sue Peabody, "'A Dangerous Zeal': Catholic Missions to Slaves in the French Antilles, 1635–1800," *French Historical Studies* 25, no. 1 (Winter 2002): 60, 70.

16. *Mission of the Church of the United Brethren, in the Danish West India Islands, St. Thomas, St. Croix, and St. Jan* . . . (London: [United Brethren], 1832), 14–16; Neville A. T. Hall, *Slave Society in the Danish West Indies: St. Thomas, St. John, and St. Croix*, ed. B. W. Hingman (Baltimore: Johns Hopkins University Press, 1992), 45–47; J. C. S. Mason, *The Moravian Church and the Missionary Awakening in England, 1760–1800* (Woodbridge, Suffolk, UK: Royal Historical Society, 2001), 90–113; Richard S. Dunn, *Moravian Missionaries at Work in a Jamaican Slave Community, 1754–1835*, The James Ford Bell Lectures, 32 ([Minneapolis]: The Associates of the James Ford Bell Library, University of Minnesota, 1994), 8. Moravian baptismal records from Barbados list, among several other items of information, who owned the slaves that were baptized by Moravian missionaries. Three slaves baptized in the 1770s and 1780s are listed as owned by the "Mission of the Brethren." Barbados Archives, RL1/73 A, 1, 53. On Moravians in the British Atlantic world, see also Katherine Carté Engel, *Religion and Profit: Moravians in Early America* (Philadelphia: University of Pennsylvania Press, 2008); Colin Podmore, *The Moravian Church in England, 1728–1760* (Oxford: Clarendon Press, 1998); and Jon Sensbach, *A Separate Canaan: The Making of an Afro-Moravian World in North Carolina* (Chapel Hill: University of North Carolina Press, 1998).

17. For descriptions of the estate see John A. Schutz and Maud E. O'Neil, "Of the Plantations Intire . . .," in Klingberg, *Codrington Chronicle*, 43; and Bennett, *Bondsmen and Bishops*, 2–3. See also SPG–L, Dudley Woodbridge to Henry Newman, Mar. 22, 1710, A6/66. An overview is provided in Fulham Papers, "Memorandum taken May 16, 1733 at Codrington College in Barbados of the Society's Plantation," vol. 16, 43.

18. SPG–L, Dudley Woodbridge and Gilbert Ramsay to Secretary, Mar. 17, 1711/12, C/WIN/Bar1/10.

19. For the varying fortunes of Codrington College, see Jean Bullen and Helen E. Livingston, "Of the State and Advancement of the College . . .," in Klingberg, *Codrington Chronicle*, 105–22.

20. SPG–J, July 15, 1720, vol. 4, 115–16. Rowland Tryon willed money for Codrington College at his death.

21. For examples of this movement of funds, see Abstract of Proceedings printed with Thomas Secker, *A Sermon Preached before the Incorporated Society for the Propagation of the Gospel in Foreign Parts . . . On Friday, February 20, 1740–1* (London: J. and H. Pemberton, 1741), 83–85; and Abstract of Proceedings printed with Thomas Greene, *A Sermon Preached before the Incorporated Society for the Propagation of the Gospel in Foreign Parts . . . On Friday, February 21, 1723* (London: J. Downing, 1724), 53–56.

22. SPG–J, Oct. 19, 1711, vol. 2, 96–106; Nov. 2, 1711, vol. 2, 109–12; Nov. 16, 1711, vol. 2, 113–17.

23. SPG–X, Minutes of SPG Meetings, July 15, 1743 and Nov. 16, 1744, X24.

24. Bennett, *Bondsmen and Bishops*, 69, 89. Granville Sharp later believed Drummond had become an abolitionist. See chap. 7.

25. On tenant farming families, see Hilary McD. Beckles, *White Servitude and Black Slavery in Barbados, 1627–1715* (Knoxville: University of Tennessee Press, 1989), 174.

26. SPG–X, Accounts, X40a. See also the reference to the conspicuously named person "Christian Clergy," who may have been another free person of color, SPG–X, Accounts, X40.

27. Sidney W. Mintz, *Sweetness and Power: The Place of Sugar in Modern History* (New York: Penguin Books, 1986), 47.

28. Bennett, *Bondsmen and Bishops*, 11–13.

29. Dunn, *Sugar and Slaves*, 107–18.

30. Philip D. Morgan, "The Black Experience in the British Empire, 1680–1810," in *Oxford History of the British Empire*, vol. 2, *The Eighteenth Century*, ed. P. J. Marshall (Oxford: Oxford University Press, 1998), 470.

31. SPG–X, X34, 75–85.

32. For the demographic history of British West Indian slave populations, see Morgan, "The Black Experience," 465–71.

33. On the prevalence of disease on the estate, see SPG–L, William Cattell to Secretary, Aug. 10, 1746, C/Win/Bar6/82; William Cattell to Secretary, July 20, 1747, C/Win/Bar6/82. See also B. W. Higman, *Slave Populations of the British Caribbean, 1807–1834* (Kingston: University of the West Indies Press, 1995), 341; Kenneth V. Kiple and Virginia H. Kiple, "Deficiency Diseases in the Caribbean," *Journal of Interdisciplinary History* 11, no. 2 (Autumn 1980): 206–13.

34. Bennett, *Bondsmen and Bishops*, 52.

35. See SPG–L, Barbados Attorneys to Secretary, Aug. 30, 1768, B6/79 and chap. 7.

36. Bennett, *Bondsmen and Bishops*, 138, 33, 54. It seems likely that Smalridge and other SPG managers chose to buy male slaves rather than being forced to do so by the nature of the slave trade. See David Eltis and Stanley L. Engerman, "Was the Slave Trade Dominated by Men?" *Journal of Interdisciplinary History* 23, no. 2 (Autumn 1992): 240–46; and David Eltis and Stanley L. Engerman, "Fluctuations in Sex and Age Ratios in the Transatlantic Slave Trade, 1663–1864," *Economic History Review*, n.s., 46, no. 2 (May 1993): 311–13.

37. SPG–L, Sampson Smirk to Secretary, Nov. 25, 1741, B8/56.

38. Bennett, *Bondsmen and Bishops*, 52. Many of the people the Society bought after 1761 were probably also African-born, but they had lived long enough on Barbados to have been considered "seasoned."

39. See, for example, John Thornton, *Africa and Africans in the Making of the Atlantic World, 1400–1800*, 2nd ed. (Cambridge: Cambridge University Press, 1992); and Mechal Sobel, *The World They Made Together: Black and White Values in Eighteenth-Century Virginia* (Princeton: Princeton University Press, 1987).

40. David Eltis, "The Volume and Structure of the Transatlantic Slave Trade: A Reassessment," *WMQ*, 3rd ser., 58, no. 1 (Jan. 2001): 36. This is in contrast to the view stressing the heterogeneous origins of colonial slave populations. See Sidney W. Mintz and Richard Price, *An Anthropological Approach to the Afro-American Past: A Caribbean Perspective* (Philadelphia: Institute for the Study of Human Issues, 1976), 4–11.

41. Compare, for example, Thornton, *Africa and Africans* and Philip D. Morgan, "The Cultural Implications of the Atlantic Slave Trade: African Regional Origins, American Destinations and New World Developments," *Slavery and Abolition* 18 (1997): 122–45. For the effect of this debate on the history of religion, see Sylvia R. Frey, "The Visible Church: Historiography of African American Religion since Raboteau," *Slavery and Abolition* 29, no. 1 (Jan. 2008): 83–110.

42. David Eltis, Stephen D. Behrendt, David Richardson, and Herbert S. Klein, eds., *The Trans-Atlantic Slave Trade: A Database on CD-ROM* (Cambridge: Cambridge University Press, 1999). In this period 223,706 slaves were embarked in Africa on ships destined for Barbados; 183,894 of these people survived the Middle Passage and were disembarked for sale in Barbados. The region of origin in Africa has been identified for 45.7 percent of the 223,706 slaves embarked. The estimate of 79 percent of imported Barbadian slaves being imported from the Bight of Biafra, the Bight of Benin, and the Gold Coast is a projection based on information about the 102,200 slaves for whom information on region of origin is known. Eltis et al. define the three regions under primary discussion here as follows: the Gold Coast–east of Assini River up to and including the Volta River; the Bight of Benin–east of the Volta River to the Nun River (at the city of Akassa); and the Bight of Biafra–east of the Nun River up to and including Cape Lopez.

43. Ibid. Because of the nature of shipping records available for the period, a particularly large number of slaves embarked for Barbados in the period between 1701 and 1750 came from unspecified parts of Africa. For this period, 68 percent of slaves shipped for Barbados came from unspecified regions; therefore estimates for the regional origins of slaves in this period should be treated with some caution. See also Eltis, "The Volume and Structure of the Transatlantic Slave Trade: A Reassessment," 39.

44. See the favorable comments made on Akans in Cecil Headlam, ed., *Calendar of State Papers, Colonial Series, America and West Indies, 1701, Preserved in the Public Record Office* (London: His Majesty's Stationery Office, 1910), 721; and Harlow, *Christopher Codrington*, 122.

45. SPG–L, John Smalridge to Secretary, June 4, 1725, C/Win/Bar2/27. "Calamantee" was a variant term for Gold Coast people: see Headlam, ed., *Calendar of State Papers*, 721.

46. Griffith Hughes, *The Natural History of Barbados. In Ten Books* (London: Printed for the author, 1750), 14. On Hughes's career, see also Mary Clement, ed., *Correspondence and Records of the S.P.G. Relating to Wales, 1701–1750* (Cardiff: University of Wales Press, 1973), 89–93. For Barbados and other planters' preferences for Akans see also Jerome S. Handler and Frederic W. Lange, *Plantation Slavery in Barbados: An Archaeological and Historical Investigation* (Cambridge, MA: Harvard University Press, 1978), 25.

47. Daniel C. Littlefield, *Rice and Slaves: Ethnicity and the Slave Trade in Colonial South Carolina* (Baton Rouge: Louisiana State University Press, 1981), 13; and John K. Thornton, "War, the State, and Religious Norms in 'Coromantee' Thought: The Ideology of an African American Nation," in *Possible Pasts: Becoming Colonial in Early America*, ed. Robert Blair St. George (Ithaca, NY: Cornell University Press), 181–200.

48. Harlow, *Christopher Codrington*, 122. See also Edward Long, *The History of Jamaica . . .*, 3 vols. (London: T. Lowndes, 1774), 2:403, 2:445–75.

49. SPG–L, Abel Alleyne to SPG Secretary, July 18, 1741, B8/48.

50. Handler and Lange, *Plantation Slavery in Barbados*, 25–28.

51. Robin Law, *The Slave Coast of West Africa, 1550–1750: The Impact of the Atlantic Slave Trade on African Society*, Oxford Studies in African Affairs (New York: Oxford University Press, 1991), 21–26. Planter ethnonyms for Africans cannot be relied on as completely accurate. People shipped from the Slave Coast, for example, may have been drawn from up to two hundred miles into the interior. See Handler and Lange, *Plantation Slavery in Barbados*, 27; and Law, *Slave Coast of West Africa*, 185–91.

52. Littlefield, *Rice and Slaves*, 13.

53. SPG–L, John Payne to Secretary, Aug. 20, 1746, C/Win/Bar3/37. Payne made this point to the Society repeatedly in the late 1740s, but did not specify these wild countries: see also SPG–L, John Payne to Secretary, Aug. 5, 1747, C/Win/Bar3/37; and John Payne to Secretary, June 21, 1748, C/Win/Bar3/37.

54. SPG–X, X33, Inventory of the Estate at the Death of John Smalridge, 1731.

55. SPG–X, X34, 74–75; SPG–L, "A List of All the Negroes that are Baptized and not Baptized . . . on Society's Estate in Barbados," Nov. 25, 1741, B8/58.

56. SPG–L, "List of the Negroes, Cattle, Horses and Asses Living the 31st of Dec., 1745," C/Win/Bar8/126.

57. SPG–L, "A List of All the Negroes that are Baptized and not Baptized . . . on Society's Estate in Barbados," Nov. 25, 1741, B8/58; "List of the Negroes, Cattle, Horses and Asses Living the 31st of Dec., 1745," C/Win/Bar8/126.

58. SPG–X, X33, "Inventory of the Estate at the Death of John Smalridge."

59. SPG–X, X33, Attorneys' Minutes, Aug. 21, 1750.

60. SPG–X, X32, 149, Inventory of Codrington Plantation, May 2, 1783.

61. Bennett, *Bondsmen and Bishops*, 105, 111–12.

62. SPG–X, X34, 191–92.

63. Ibid., 191–92, 205–7.

64. Bennett, *Bondsmen and Bishops*, 54.
65. SPG–X, X34, 34.
66. Ibid., 39.
67. Ibid., 33–38, 222–24.
68. Fulham Papers, Joseph Holt's Reply to "Queries from Bishop of London to be Answered by Ministers, Barbados, 1723/24," vol. 15, 207.
69. On Arthur Holt's interest in slave conversion, see Fulham Papers, Arthur Holt to bishop of London, May 28, 1730, vol. 15, 280–81; and Arthur Holt to bishop of London, Dec. 2, 1730, vol. 15, 292. See also John A. Schutz and Maud O'Neil, eds., "Arthur Holt, Anglican Clergyman, Reports on Barbados, 1725–1733," *Journal of Negro History* 31, no. 4 (Oct. 1946): 444–69.
70. SPG–L, Secretary to Attorneys in Barbados, July 26, 1726, C/Win/Bar2/28; and Secretary to John Smalridge, July 26, 1726, C/Win/Bar2/28.
71. Hazel Morse Hartley, "Of the Produce of the Plantations . . .," in Klingberg, ed. *Codrington Chronicle*, 70–71; Bennett, *Bondsmen and Bishops*, 50, 54.
72. SPG–L, Secretary to Attorneys in Barbados, Jan. 25, 1726/27, C/Win/Bar2/28.
73. Bennett, *Bondsmen and Bishops*, 54.
74. SPG–X, X37a. For Holt's complaints, see SPG–L, Arthur Holt to Secretary, Apr. 3, 1732, A24/267–70; Fulham Papers, Arthur Holt to Edmund Gibson, Aug. 16, 1732, vol. 16, 31–32.
75. SPG–X, X36, 3–7.
76. SPG–L, John Smalridge to Secretary, July 25, 1722, C/Win/Bar2/27.
77. SPG–L, Elias Neau to Secretary, Aug. 24, 1708, A4/68.
78. SPG–X, Accounts, X36, 23–25; and Secretary to SPG Attorneys in Barbados, Jan. 31, 1721, X37.
79. SPG–X, Accounts, X37a, 103–11.
80. Fulham Papers, Thomas Wilkie to Bishop of London, Mar. 7, 1726/27, vol. 15, 250.
81. SPG–L, Secretary to John Smalridge, Jan. 17, 1728/29, C/Win/Bar2/28.
82. Fulham Papers, Thomas Wilkie to Bishop of London, Mar. 7, 1726/27, vol. 15, 250.
83. SPG–L, Thomas Wharton to Secretary, Aug. 30, 1768, B6/80.
84. SPG–L, Elias Neau to Mr. Hodges, July 10, 1703, A1/106.
85. SPG–L, "Instructions of the Clergy of South Carolina given to Mr. Johnston . . .," Mar. 4, 1712, A8/423–38. On Sabbath keeping in plantation societies, see also Nicholas Beasley, *Christian Ritual and the Creation of British Slave Societies, 1650–1780* (Athens: University of Georgia Press, 2009), 40–45.
86. Leo Francis Stock, ed. *Proceedings and Debates of the British Parliaments respecting North America.* 5 vols. (Washington: The Carnegie Institution of Washington, 1924–1941), 3:237 and 3:295–96.
87. SPG–X, Secretary to Messrs. Woodbridge and Ramsay, Mar. 7, 1712, X34, 205–7; Secretary to John Smalridge, Mar. 7, 1712, X34, 208–9.
88. See SPG–L, "Minutes of a Meeting of the Attorneys," Sept. 12, 1728, C/Win/Bar3/33; Secretary to John Smalridge, Jan. 17, 1728/29, C/Win/Bar2/28; Joseph Bewsher to Secretary, Oct. 5, 1745, C/Win/Bar6/79; Thomas Rotheram to Secretary, Oct. 7, 1745, C/Win/Bar6/78; Thomas Wharton to Secretary, Aug. 30, 1768, B6/80; John Pinder to Secretary, Jan. 22, 1819, C/Win/Bar5/67; John Packer to Secretary, July 31, 1828, C/Win/Bar5/68; and "Minutes of a Meeting on the Estate," Sept. 1, 1829, C/Win/Bar7/107. For the evolution of the issue of Sunday work in colonial Georgia, see Betty Wood, "'Never on a Sunday?' Slavery and the Sabbath in Lowcountry Georgia 1750–1830," in *From Chattel Slaves to Wage Slaves: The Dynamics of Labour Bargaining in the Americas,* ed. Mary Turner, (Kingston: Ian Randle, 1995), 79–96.
89. In 1746 the Society considered leasing the plantation and entered into ultimately unsuccessful discussions with potential tenants. Based on the Society's stipulation that slaves be

given half of Saturday off—one-twelfth of the six-day workweek—to work for themselves, the prospective lessors argued that one-twelfth should be taken off their annual rent. SPG–L, Henry Lascelles and David Maxwell to Society, Oct. 22, 1746, C/Win/Bar3/36. See also Bennett, *Bondsmen and Bishops*, 22–23; and Beahrs, "'Ours Alone Must Needs Be Christians,'" 291. Beahrs argues that the Sunday work dispute on Barbados "was not informed by rational, economic calculation, but by an immediate anxiety that the day might be imbued with a new, sacred meaning, which the slaves might access and appropriate." I believe the issue had cultural and economic significance on Codrington.

90. SPG–L, William Duke to Secretary, Dec. 30, 1740, B8/39.
91. SPG–L, Joseph Bewsher to Secretary, Oct. 5, 1745, C/Win/Bar6/79.
92. SPG–L, Barbados attorneys to Secretary, Aug. 30, 1768, B6/79.
93. SPG–L, "John Codrington English" to Secretary, July 20, 1778, C/Win/Bar3/42.
94. SPG–L, "Invoice of Goods to be sent from England to Barbados," Jan. 12, 1756, B6/63.
95. Abstract of letter from William Thomas to Secretary, May 14, 1796, quoted in Bennett, *Bondsmen and Bishops*, 14.
96. Bennett, *Bondsmen and Bondsmen*, 49.
97. Ibid., 24–25.
98. Ibid., 26–27. The Society's representatives tried but failed in both cases to have the death sentences commuted. In accordance with Barbados law, the estate received monetary compensation for both of the people executed.
99. SPG–L, John Vaughton to Secretary, July 15, 1738, C/Win/Bar3/34; John Vaughton to Secretary, July 26, 1738, C/Win/Bar3/34.
100. SPG–L, Philip Bearcroft to Barbados attorneys, Dec. 31, 1741, B8/74.
101. SPG–L, Abel Alleyne to Secretary, Sept. 11, 1741, B8/49.
102. SPG–J, vol. 3, 388–91.
103. SPG–X, SPG Meeting Nov. 16, 1744, X24; Bennett, *Bondsmen and Bishops*, 83.
104. SPG–L, Joseph Bewsher to Secretary, Oct. 5, 1745, C/Win/Bar6/79.
105. SPG–X, Attorneys' Meeting, July 6 and 7, 1744; and Attorneys' Meeting, Mar. 21 and 22, 1744/45, X33.
106. See, for example, Vincent Brown's observations about colonial Jamaica, where "supernatural beliefs and the machinery of the colonial state were inextricably enmeshed" and "in practice, neither masters nor slaves recognized a distinction between material and supernatural power." Vincent Brown, *The Reaper's Garden: Death and Power in the World of Atlantic Slavery* (Cambridge, MA: Harvard University Press, 2008), 151.
107. Fulham Papers, Thomas Wilkie to Bishop of London, Mar. 7, 1726/27, vol. 15, 250.
108. SPG–L, Thomas Rotheram to Secretary[?], Oct. 7, 1745, C/Win/Bar6/78.
109. Bennett, *Bondsmen and Bishops*, 14.
110. SPG–L, Sampson Smirk to Secretary, Apr. 16, 1741, B8/53–55.
111. Bennett, *Bondsmen and Bishops*, 85; SPG–X, Barbados Committee Meeting, Nov. 18, 1760, X26.
112. Whether masters or slaves played a primary role in naming slaves has been debated. Several historians have seen naming patterns as important indicators of the tenacity of enslaved peoples' commitment to their African heritage, as indicators of the gradual transformation of African cultures into an African American culture, and as one of the myriad ways that slaves challenged masters' domination. See Cheryll Ann Cody, "There was No 'Absalom' on the Ball Plantations: Slave Naming Practices in the South Carolina Low Country, 1720–1865," *American Historical Review* 92, no. 3 (June 1987): 563–96; John Thornton, "Central African Names and African-American Naming Patterns," *WMQ*, 3rd ser., 50 (1993): 727–42; and John C. Inscoe, "Carolina Slave Names: An Index to Acculturation," *Journal of Southern History* 49, no. 4 (Nov. 1983): 527–54. For an argument that Jamaican "evidence suggests that slave owners, rather than slaves, were the originators of

slave names," see Trevor Burnard, "Slave Naming Patterns: Onomastics and the Taxonomy of Race in Eighteenth-Century Jamaica," *Journal of Interdisciplinary History* 31, no. 3 (Winter, 2001): 326, 328. Because they were owned by a record-keeping institution, the names of hundreds of Codrington's enslaved people were preserved. Since names seemingly derived from West African roots were prevalent on Codrington, its records have been used to support the argument "that Barbadian slaves played a larger role in naming themselves and their children than has been supposed by scholars of Caribbean slavery." See Jerome Handler and JoAnn Jacoby, "Slave Names and Naming in Barbados, 1650–1830," *WMQ,* 3rd ser., 52 (1996): 724. There is limited but direct evidence from the early 1740s that, at least in that period, the Society's white employees played an important part in selecting the names preserved in the Society's records. See SPG–L, Sampson Smirk to Secretary, Nov. 25, 1741, B8/56. Regardless of who named people on Codrington, what the continuing prevalence of African-derived "plantation" names there suggests most strongly is the continuing weight of African culture on the estate, which was apparent to both white and black residents.

113. On West African religion in Barbados, see Handler and Lange, *Plantation Slavery in Barbados,* 208–9. Particularly because the SPG owned Codrington, it might be seen as a site where the weight of slavery's coercive power prevented the whole-cloth reproduction of African religious *systems,* but it is clear that important elements of African religious *practice* long continued to exist on the estate. For the distinction, see Jon Butler, *Awash in a Sea of Faith: Christianizing the American People* (Cambridge, MA: Harvard University Press, 1990), 129–63. On the centrality of practice to understanding colonial religion, see David D. Hall, "From 'Religion and Society' to Practices," in St. George, *Possible Pasts,* 159.

114. John Thornton, *Africa and Africans,* 254, 322; Thornton, *Kingdom of Kongo: Civil War and Transition, 1641–1718* (Madison: University of Wisconsin Press, 1983), xiv–xv, 62–68. For a similar pattern in Senegambia, see George E. Brooks, *Eurafricans in Western Africa: Commerce, Social Status, Gender, and Religious Observance from the Sixteenth to the Eighteenth Century* (Athens: Ohio University Press, 2003), 68–101. Annette Laing has considered this dynamic with regard SPG activity in South Carolina in "'Heathens and Infidels?' African Christianization and Anglicanism in the South Carolina Low Country, 1700–1750." *Religion and American Culture* 12 (2002): 197–228.

115. Anne Hilton, *The Kingdom of Kongo* (Oxford: Clarendon Press, 1985), 101–2; John Thornton, *The Kongolese Saint Anthony: Dona Beatriz Kimpa Vita and the Antonian Movement, 1684–1706* (Cambridge: Cambridge University Press, 1998), 149–50.

116. SPG–X, "Mr. Smalridges Acct of the Negroes," (1712), X34, 74–75; Accounts, X40; Slave Inventory, July 13, 1762, X41a.

117. Michael Gomez, *Exchanging Our Country Marks: The Transformation of African Identities in the Colonial and Antebellum South* (Chapel Hill: University of North Carolina Press, 1998), 59–87; Gomez, "Muslims in Early America," *Journal of Southern History* 60, no. 4 (Nov. 1994): 671–710. See also Gomez, *Black Crescent: The Experience and Legacy of African Muslims in the Americas* (Cambridge: Cambridge University Press, 2005); Gomez, *Reversing Sail: A History of the African Diaspora* (Cambridge: Cambridge University Press, 2005); Sylviane A. Diouf, *Servants of Allah: African Muslims Enslaved in the Americas* (New York: New York University Press, 1998); Sultana Afroz, "The Unsung Slaves: Islam in Plantation Jamaica," *Caribbean Quarterly* 41, no. 3/4 (1995): 30–44; and Alan D. Austin, *African Muslims in Antebellum America: A Sourcebook* (New York: Garland, 1984).

118. On the long-term presence of Islam in West Africa see, for example, Ivor Wilks, *Wa and the Wala: Islam and polity in Northwestern Ghana* (Cambridge: Cambridge University Press, 1989); Diouf, *Servants of Allah,* 4–10; and Paul E. Lovejoy, ed. *Slavery on the Frontiers of Islam* (Princeton, NJ: Markus Wiener Publications, 2004).

119. SPG–L, Sampson Smirk to Secretary, Apr. 16, 1741, B8/53–55; "A List of All the Negroes that are Baptized and not Baptized . . . on Society's Estate in Barbados," Nov. 25, 1741, B8/58; Gomez, "Muslims in Early America," 686–88.

120. Morgan Godwyn, *The Negro's & Indians Advocate, Suing for their Admission into the Church*. . . . (London: Printed for the author, by J. D., 1680), 33.

121. Jerome S. Handler and Kenneth M. Bilby, "On the Early Use and Origin of the Term 'Obeah' in Barbados and the Anglophone Caribbean" *Slavery and Abolition* 22, no. 2 (Aug. 2001): 87–100; Brown, *Reaper's Garden*, 144–52.

122. On the practice of obeah and resistance to slavery, see Walter Rucker, "Conjure, Magic, and Power: The Influence of Afro-Atlantic Religious Practices on Slave Resistance and Rebellion," *Journal of Black Studies* 32, no. 1 (Sept. 2001): 84–103; Brown, *Reaper's Garden*, 148–56.

123. SPG–L, Extract of a Letter from Arthur Holt to Henry Newman, Feb. 18, 1728/9, B6/62.

124. Fulham Papers, Arthur Holt to Bishop of London, Mar. 7, 1729, vol. 15, 266–67.

125. Hughes, *Natural History of Barbados*, 15.

126. Vincent Brown, "Spiritual Terror and Sacred Authority in Jamaican Slave Society" *Slavery and Abolition* 24, no. 1 (Apr. 2003): 35–37; Jerome S. Handler, "Slave Medicine and Obeah in Barbados, circa 1650 to 1834" *New West Indian Guide* 74, no. 1/2 (2000): 57–90. For archaeological evidence on the high status of obeah practitioners within their communities, see Jerome Handler, "An African-Type Healer/Diviner and His Grave Goods: A Burial from a Plantation Slave Cemetery in Barbados, West Indies," *International Journal of Historical Archaeology* 1, no. 2 (1997): 103–4; and Douglas V. Armstrong and Mark L. Fleischman, "House Yard Burials of Enslaved Laborers in Eighteenth-Century Jamaica," *International Journal of Historical Archaeology* 7, no. 1 (Mar. 2003): 46–47, 55–56.

127. Handler, *Plantation Slavery in Barbados*, 181–82.

128. Harlow, *Christopher Codrington*, 218.

129. Bennett, *Bondsmen and Bishops*, 40; SPG–X, X40, Accounts for 1745.

130. SPG–L, "List of the Negroes, Cattle, Horses and Asses Living the 31st of Dec., 1745," C/Win/Bar8/126; Sampson Smirk to Secretary, Apr. 16, 1741, B8/53–55; "A List of All the Negroes that are Baptized and not Baptized . . . on Society's Estate in Barbados," Nov. 25, 1741, B8/58.

131. Fulham Papers, Arthur Holt to Bishop of London, Apr. 30, 1725, vol. 15, 216.

132. Fulham Papers, Thomas Wilkie to Bishop of London, Mar. 7, 1726/7, vol. 15, 250.

133. SPG–L, William Duke to Secretary, Dec. 30, 1740, B8/39.

134. Bennett, *Bondsmen and Bishops*, 85.

135. SPG–L, Abel Alleyne to Secretary, July 18, 1741, B8/48.

136. Ibid.

137. SPG–L, Sampson Smirk to Secretary, Apr. 6, 1741, B8/53.

138. SPG–L, Abel Alleyne to Secretary, Dec. 9, 1741, B8/51.

139. SPG–X, Barbados Committee Meeting, Oct. 3, 1745, X25.

140. SPG–L, "Minutes of a Meeting of the SPG's Attorneys in Barbados," May 26, 1748, C/Win/Bar3/35; see also Bennett, *Bondsmen and Bishops*, 6.

141. Bullen and Livingston, "Of the State and Advancement of the College," in Klingberg, *Codrington Chronicle*, 109.

142. Bennett, *Bondsmen and Bishops*, 84.

143. W. P. Courtney, "Rotheram, John (1725–1789)," DNB Archive (1897) in *ODNB*. See also Nigel Aston, "Rotheram, John (1725–1789)," *ODNB*.

144. SPG–L, "Report of the Special Committee," Feb. 18, 1761, C/Win/Bar20/f2.

145. John Hodgson to Secretary, July 17, 1760, quoted in Bennett, *Bondsmen and Bishops*, 85; SPG–J, vol. 15, 17–40.

146. SPG–L, James Butcher to Secretary, May 4, 1769, B6/86.

147. Bennett, *Bondsmen and Bishops*, 70–74 and chap. 7.

148. SPG–L, James Butcher to Secretary, July 15, 1770, C/Win/Bar6/87.

Chapter 6

1. Important studies of this missionary work include: F. L. Bartels, "Philip Quaque, 1741–1816," *Transactions of the Gold Coast and Togoland Historical Society* 1 (1952–1955): 153–77; Frank J. Klingberg, "Philip Quaque: Pioneer Native Missionary on the Gold Coast, 1765–1816," *Journal of Negro Education* 8, no. 4 (Oct. 1939): 666–72; Margaret Priestley, "Philip Quaque of Cape Coast," in *Africa Remembered: Narratives by West Africans from the Era of the Slave Trade,* ed. Philip D. Curtin (1967; Prospect Heights, IL: Waveland Press, 1997), 99–139; Ty M. Reese, "'Sheep in the Jaws of So Many Ravenous Wolves': The Slave Trade and Anglican Missionary Activity at Cape Coast Castle, 1752–1816," *Journal of Religion in Africa* 34, no. 3 (2004): 348–72; and Vincent Carretta and Ty M. Reese, eds., *The Life and Letters of Philip Quaque, The First African Anglican Clergyman* (Athens: University of Georgia Press, 2010).

2. Thomas Thompson, *An Account of Two Missionary Voyages. By the Appointment of the Society for the Propagation of the Gospel in Foreign Parts. The one to New Jersey in North America, the other from America to the Coast of Guiney.* (London: Benjamin Dod, 1758), 11.

3. Ibid., 23.

4. A. W. Lawrence, *Fortified Trade-Posts: The English in West Africa 1645–1822* (London: Jonathan Cape, 1969), 164–79.

5. George Metcalf, "A Microcosm of why Africans Sold Slaves: Akan Consumption Patterns in the 1770s," *Journal of African History* 28, no. 3 (1987): 377–94; David Northrup, "West Africans and the Atlantic, 1550–1800," in *Black Experience and the Empire*, Oxford History of the British Empire Companion Series, ed. Philip D. Morgan and Sean Hawkins (Oxford: Oxford University Press, 2004), 35–40.

6. Ralph M. Wiltgen, *Gold Coast Missionary History, 1471–1880* (Techny, IL: Divine Word Publications, 1956).

7. Lawrence, *Fortified Trade Posts*, 165–68.

8. David Eltis, Stephen D. Behrendt, David Richardson, and Herbert S. Klein, eds., *The Trans-Atlantic Slave Trade: A Database on CD-ROM* (Cambridge: Cambridge University Press, 1999).

9. A. D. C. Hyland, "The Architectural History of Cape Coast," *Transactions of the Historical Society of Ghana* 16, no. 2, n.o., 1 (Jan. 1995): 163–67.

10. Henry Merideth, *An Account of the Gold Coast of Africa: With a Brief History of the African Company* (London: Longman, Hurst, Rees, Orme, and Brown, 1812), 95.

11. Eveline C. Martin, *The British West African Settlements, 1750–1821: A Study in Local Administration* (1927; repr., New York: Negro University Press, 1970), 7–14; K. G. Davies, *The Royal African Company* (London: Longmans, 1957), 344–45.

12. Martin, *British West African Settlements*, 29–42.

13. Thomas Thompson, *A Letter From New Jersey, in America, Giving Some Account and Description of that Province* . . . (London: M. Cooper, 1756); and Thompson, *Account of Two Missionary Voyages.*

14. For a report on Thompson's mission see, Thompson, *Account of Two Missionary Voyages,* 33–77. For his belief in the possibility of large-scale conversions, see Ibid., 77–87.

15. Eric Hinderaker, "The 'Four Indian Kings' and the Imaginative Construction of the First British Empire," *WMQ*, 3rd ser., 53, no. 3 (July 1996): 487–526; SPG–J, vol. 2, 296–97, 300, 338–39, 395; vol. 3, 32–33; SPG–L, Gideon Johnston to Secretary, Aug. 20, 1714, A9/22–23; Sept. 30, 1715, A11/99–100; Dec. 19, 1715, A11/101–5; Apr. 4, 1716, A11/117–21; and Prince George to Secretary, Dec. 8, 1715, A11/77.

16. Douglas Grant, *The Fortunate Slave: An Illustration of African Slavery in the Early Eighteenth Century* (London: Oxford University Press, 1968), 97–98.

17. Ira Berlin, "From Creole to African: Atlantic Creoles and the Origins of African-American Society in Mainland North America," *WMQ*, 3rd ser., 53, no. 1 (Apr. 1996): 254–65.

18. Jacobus Elisa Johannes Capitein, *The Agony of Asar: A Thesis on Slavery by the Former Slave,* trans. Grant Parker (1742; repr. Princeton, NJ: Markus Wiener, 2001); F. L. Bartels, "Jacobus Eliza Johannes Capitein, 1717–1747," *Transactions of the Historical Society of Ghana* 4 (1959): 3–13; and Jon F. Sensbach, *Rebecca's Revival: Creating Black Christianity in the Atlantic World* (Cambridge, MA: Harvard University Press, 2005), 162–71.

19. Thompson, *Account of Two Missionary Voyages,* 66–67; SPG–L, Thomas Thompson to John Moore, Feb. 10, 1762, C/AFR/W/1/1b; Philip Quaque to Secretary, Mar. 7, 1767, C/AFR/W/1/11; and Margaret Priestley, *West African Trade and Coast Society: A Family Study* (London: Oxford University Press, 1969), 10–24.

20. Grant, *Fortunate Slave,* 145–47; Priestley, *West African Trade and Coast Society,* 20–21, 36–37; and Reese, "'Sheep in the Jaws of So Many Ravenous Wolves,'" 352–54.

21. RAC, Charles Bell to the Committee of the Company of Merchants Trading to Africa, Mar. 20, 1756, T70/30, fols. 76–77.

22. Thompson, *Account of Two Missionary Voyages,* 66–67; SPG–L, Thomas Thompson to John Moore, Feb. 10, 1762, C/AFR/W/1/1b; and Priestley, *West African Trade and Coast Society,* 10–24.

23. SPG–L, Philip Quaque to Secretary, Sept. 28, 1766, C/AFR/W/1/10.

24. See *Gentleman's Magazine* 23 (Dec. 1753): 588, 25 (Apr. 1755): 184; RAC, Minutes of Company of Merchants Trading to Africa, 1750–55, T70/143J, fols. 167, 173; J. Crooks, *Records Relating to the Gold Coast Settlements from 1750 to 1874* (London: Taylor and Francis, 1973), 28–30.

25. SPG–L, John Moore to Secretary, Jan. 15, 1766, C/AFR/W/1/7; Philip Quaque to Secretary, Mar. 14, 1766, C/AFR/W/1/9; Sept. 28, 1766, C/AFR/W/1/10; and Records of Guy's Hospital London, London Metropolitan Archives, HO9/GY/B1/8/1, HO9/GY/B1/9/1.

26. Travis Glasson, "Missionaries, Methodists, and a Ghost: Philip Quaque in London and Cape Coast, 1756–1816," *Journal of British Studies* 48 (Jan. 2009): 29–50.

27. On Methodism and the Black Atlantic, see Vincent Carretta and Philip Gould, "Introduction," in *Genius in Bondage: Literature of the Early Black Atlantic,* (Lexington: University of Kentucky Press, 2001), 3; Vincent Carretta, ed., *Unchained Voices: An Anthology of Black Authors in the English-Speaking World of the Eighteenth Century* (Lexington: University of Kentucky Press, 1996), 7–10. For ties between Africans and early Methodist leaders, see Randy J. Sparks, *The Two Princes of Calabar: An Eighteenth-Century Atlantic Odyssey* (Cambridge, MA: Harvard University Press, 2004), 106–26; and James Albert Ukawsaw Gronniosaw, *A Narrative of the most remarkable particulars in the life of James Albert Ukawsaw Gronniosaw, an African prince, written by himself* (Newport, RI: Bath, 1774), 2, 33–35.

28. Ignatius Sancho, *The Letters of Ignatius Sancho,* ed. Paul Edwards and Polly Rewt (Edinburgh: Edinburgh University Press, 1994), 44, nn. 8 and 9, 51, 59, 60 n. 3; Olaudah Equiano, *The Interesting Narrative and Other Writings,* ed. Vincent Carretta (New York: Penguin Books, 1995), 183–93, 220–21, 304–5, n. 674.

29. SPG–L, John Moore to Secretary, Jan. 15, 1766, C/AFR/W/1/7; Philip Quaque to Secretary, Mar. 7, 1767, C/AFR/W/1/11.

30. *Gentleman's Magazine* 35 (Mar. 1765): 145.

31. SPG–L, Philip Quaque to Secretary, Feb. 29, 1766, C/AFR/W/1/8.

32. Christopher R. DeCorse, "Culture Contact, Continuity, and Change on the Gold Coast, AD 1400–1900," *African Archaeological Review* 10 (1992): 168.

33. David Birmingham, "A Note on the Kingdom of Fetu," *Ghana Notes and Queries* 9 (Nov. 1966): 30–33; Martin, *British West African Settlements,* 48–52.

34. For the political and social history of Cape Coast, Fetu, and Fante, see A. Adu Boahen, "Asante and Fante A.D. 1000–1800," in *A Thousand Years of West African History,* ed. J. F. Ade Ajayi and Ian Espie (Ibadan, Nigeria: Ibadan University Press, 1970), 165–90; Kwame

Yeboa Daaku, *Trade and Politics on the Gold Coast, 1600–1720. A Study of the African Reaction to European Trade* (Oxford: Clarendon Press, 1970); K. G. Davies, *The Royal African Company* (New York: Octagon Books, 1975), 282–83; J. K. Fynn, *Asante and Its Neighbours, 1700–1807* (London: Longman, 1971), 86–87; David P. Henige, "Abrem Stool: A Contribution to the History and Historiography of Southern Ghana," *International Journal of African Historical Studies* 6, no. 1 (1973): 1–18; Wilhelm Johann Muller, "Description of the Fetu Country, 1662–1669," in *German Sources for West African History, 1599–1669,* ed. Adam Jones (Weisbaden: Franz Steiner Verlag GMBH, 1983), 134–259; R. A. Kea, "Firearms and Warfare on the Gold and Slave Coasts from the Sixteenth to the Nineteenth Centuries," *Journal of African History* 12, no. 2 (1971): 185–213; Priestley, *West African Trade and Coast Society,* 12–17; James Sanders, "The Expansion of the Fante and the Emergence of Asante in the Eighteenth Century," *Journal of African History* 20, no. 3 (1979): 352–57; and Ivor Wilks, *Asante in the Nineteenth Century: The Structure and Evolution of a Political Order* (Cambridge: Cambridge University Press, 1975), 24–29.

35. George Metcalfe, "Gold, Assortments, and the Trade Ounce: Fante Merchants and the Problem of Supply and Demand in the 1770s," *Journal of African History* 28, no. 1 (1987): 31; Roger S. Gocking, *Facing Two Ways: Ghana's Coastal Communities Under Colonial Rule* (Lanham, MD: University Press of America, 1999), 29–30; and Ty M. Reese, "The Drudgery of the Slave Trade. Labor at Cape Coast Castle, 1750–1790," in *The Atlantic Economy during the Seventeenth and Eighteenth Centuries,* ed. Peter A. Coclanis (Columbia: University of South Carolina Press, 2005), 278–79.

36. Gocking, *Facing Two Ways,* 29–33; Priestley, *West African Trade and Coast Society,* 15–17; and Priestley, "Philip Quaque of Cape Coast," 99–139, 105, n. 11. On Cudjoe's kinship ties, see also Crooks, *Records Relating to the Gold Coast Settlements,* 36.

37. Thompson, *Account of Two Missionary Voyages,* 34–35.

38. Gocking, *Facing Two Ways,* 29–33.

39. For how similar elites functioned across coastal West Africa, see Northrup, "West Africans and the Atlantic, 1550–1800," 35–57.

40. Thompson, *Account of Two Missionary Voyages,* 70.

41. Philip Quaque to Samuel Johnson, Nov. 26, 1767, in *Samuel Johnson President of King's College: His Career and Writings,* ed. Herbert Schneider and Carol Schneider, 4 vols. (New York: Columbia University Press, 1929), 1:427.

42. DeCorse, "Culture contact, continuity, and change on the Gold Coast," 172; Reese, "The Drudgery of the Slave Trade," 278–93. See also Ty M. Reese, "Toiling in the Empire: Labor in Three Anglo-Atlantic Ports, London, Philadelphia, and Cape Coast Castle, 1750–1783" (PhD diss., University of Toledo, 1999), 113–56.

43. SPG–L, Philip Quaque to Secretary, Feb. 8, 1786, C/AFR/W/1/45.

44. Martin, *British West African Settlements,* 53–54; Crooks, *Records Relating to the Gold Coast Settlements,* 38; and Ty M. Reese, "An Economic Middle Ground?: Anglo/African Interaction, Cooperation and Competition at Cape Coast Castle in the Late Eighteenth Century Atlantic World," Interactions: Regional Studies, Global Processes, and Historical Analysis. Mar. 28–Feb. 3, 2001. Library of Congress, Washington, D.C. Accessed June 28, 2005. <http://www.historycooperative.org/proceedings/interactions/reese.html>.

45. SPG–L, Philip Quaque to Secretary, Sept. 28, 1766, C/AFR/W/1/10; Philip Quaque to Secretary, Sept. 5, 1768, C/AFR/W/1/14. On the similarly multi-ethnic nature of other Gold Coast and West African slave trading ports, see H. M. Feinberg, "Africans and Europeans in West Africa: Elminans and Dutchmen on the Gold Coast during the Eighteenth Century," *Transactions of the American Philosophical Society* 79, no. 7 (1989): 85–86; Larry W. Yarak, "Elmina and Greater Asante in the Nineteenth Century," *Africa: Journal of the International African Institute* 56, no. 1 (1986): 33–52; Christopher R. DeCorse, *An Archaeology of Elmina: Africans and Europeans on the Gold Coast, 1400–1900* (Washington: Smith-

sonian Institution Press, 2001); George E. Brooks, *Eurafricans in Western Africa: Commerce, Social Status, Gender, and Religious Observance from the Sixteenth to the Eighteenth Century* (Athens: Ohio University Press, 2003), 283–316.

46. Thompson, *Account of Two Missionary Voyages*, 54.

47. Ibid., 53–55.

48. SPG–L, Philip Quaque to Secretary, Sept. 5, 1768, C/AFR/W/1/14.

49. Ibid., Sept. 28, 1766, C/AFR/W/1/10.

50. Ibid., June 12, 1780, C/AFR/W/1/35.

51. Ibid., Jan. 17, 1778, C/AFR/W/1/30.

52. Ibid., Sept. 5, 1768, C/AFR/W/1/14. See also Thompson's account of his encounters with a "Fetish man" and "Fetish Woman," *Account of Two Missionary Voyages*, 63–65.

53. For the characteristics of Fante religion and European understandings of it, see De Corse, *An Archaeology of Elmina*, 179–91; and T. C. McCaskie, "Nananom Mpow of Mankessim: An Essay in Fante History," in *West African Economic and Social History: Studies in Memory of Marion Johnson*, ed. David Henige and T. C. McCaskie (Madison: Board of Regents of the University of Wisconsin System, 1990), 133–50.

54. Thompson, *Account of Two Missionary Voyages*, 35–41; and SPG–L, Philip Quaque to Secretary, [no day or month] 1767, C/AFR/W/1/12.

55. Ruth A. Fisher, "Extracts from the Records of the African Companies," *Journal of Negro History* 13, no. 3 (July 1928): 366–67.

56. Ibid., 384–85, 388.

57. Thompson, *Account of Two Missionary Voyages*, 36.

58. Fisher, "Extracts from the Records of the African Companies," 354, 371, 375, 381, 383.

59. SPG–L, Philip Quaque to Secretary, [no day or month] 1767, C/AFR/W/1/12.

60. Ibid., Sept. 28, 1766, C/AFR/W/1/10.

61. Ibid., Mar. 7, 1767, C/AFR/W/1/11; Sept. 5, 1769, C/AFR/W/1/16; Apr. 12, 1770, C/AFR/W/1/17; RAC, Gilbert Petrie to the Committee, Jan. 31, 1767, T70/31, fols. 119–25.

62. SPG–L, Philip Quaque to Secretary, Apr. 12, 1770, C/AFR/W/1/17; Mar. 8, 1772, C/AFR/W/1/21.

63. Ibid., Oct. 13, 1811, C/AFR/W/1/53. Priestley noted that Quaque's disputes with his extended family involved competing notions of private and familial property and paternal and maternal inheritance patterns. See Priestley, "Philip Quaque of Cape Coast," 138–39, n. 82.

64. SPG–L, Philip Quaque to Secretary, [no day or month] 1767, C/AFR/W/1/12; Apr. 15, 1769, C/AFR/W/1/15.

65. C. F. Pascoe, *Two Hundred Years of the SPG . . ., 1701–1900* (London: SPG, 1901), 257.

66. SPG–L, Philip Quaque to Secretary, Oct. 20, 1781, C/AFR/W/1/37. See also SPG–L, Philip Quaque to Secretary, Aug. 6, 1782, C/AFR/W/1/38.

67. Ibid., Philip Quaque to Secretary, Oct. 13, 1811, C/AFR/W/1/53.

68. Ibid.

69. Ibid., [no day or month] 1767, C/AFR/W/1/12.

70. Ibid., Apr. 12, 1770, C/AFR/W/1/17.

71. Ibid., Sept. 28, 1766, C/AFR/W/1/10.

72. Ibid., May 12, 1773, C/AFR/W/1/25; Mar. 19, 1774, C/AFR/W/1/26.

73. Ibid., Apr. 12, 1770, C/AFR/W/1/17; Feb. 6, 1771, C/AFR/W/1/19; Oct. 20, 1781, C/AFR/W/1/37; Writing Exercises Signed by Willoughby Senior, C/AFR/W/1/54d, C/AFR/W/1/54e. Nassau Senior is noted in Priestley, *West African Trade and Coast Society*, 47.

74. SPG–L, Philip Quaque to Secretary, Jan. 28, 1789, C/AFR/W/1/49; C/AFR/W/1/50; C/AFR/W/1/51; Bartels, "Philip Quaque," 168–74; and Crooks, *Records Relating to the Gold Coast Settlements*, 75, 77, 80.

75. Philip Quaque to Samuel Johnson, Nov. 26, 1767, in Schneider and Schneider, *Samuel Johnson*, 1:424–27; SPG–L, Philip Quaque to Secretary, Sept. 5, 1769, C/AFR/W/1/16.

76. SPG–L, Philip Quaque to Secretary, Apr. 15, 1769, C/AFR/W/1/15; and Philip Quaque to Samuel Johnson, Apr. 5, 1769, in Schneider and Schneider, *Samuel Johnson*, 1:427–30.

77. Ibid.

78. The National Archives (Kew, England), Records of the Board of Trade, Miscellanea, List of Company Slaves at Cape Coast Castle, Apr. 1771, BT 6/1.

79. Gocking, *Facing Two Ways*, 29–35; and Reese, "The Drudgery of the Slave Trade," 278–79.

80. Crooks, *Records Relating to the Gold Coast Settlements*, 78.

81. SPG–L, Request from the Privy Council for Trade for Information on SPG missionaries to West Indies and Africa and Copy of Secretary's Response, Feb. 1788, C/AFR/W/1/47 and 48.

82. Reese, "'Sheep in the Jaws of So Many Ravenous Wolves,'" 358–59; 371, n. 76.

83. RAC, John Grossle to Committee, Oct. 26, 1769, T70/31, fols. 189–91.

84. SPG–L, Anthony Benezet to the SPG, Apr. 26, 1767, C/AM/4/55; Daniel Burton to Anthony Benezet, Feb. 3, 1768, printed in George S. Brookes, *Friend Anthony Benezet* (Philadelphia, 1937), 417–18.

85. Thomas Thompson, *The African Trade for Negro Slaves, Shewn to be Consistent with Principles of Humanity, and with the Laws of Revealed Religion* (Canterbury: Simmons and Kirkby, 1772).

86. Philip Quaque to Samuel Johnson, Nov. 26, 1767 and Apr. 5, 1769, in Schneider and Schneider, *Samuel Johnson*, 1:424–30.

87. SPG–L, Philip Quaque to Secretary, May 12, 1773, C/AFR/W/1/25; Mar. 19, 1774, C/AFR/W/1/26; David S. Lovejoy, "Samuel Hopkins: Religion, Slavery, and the Revolution," *New England Quarterly* 40 (June 1967): 227–43; and Phillis Wheatley to Samuel Hopkins, May 6, 1774, printed in William H. Robinson, *Phillis Wheatley and Her Writings* (New York, 1984), 337.

88. SPG–L, Philip Quaque to Secretary, Feb. 6, 1771, C/AFR/W/1/19; Aug. 19, 1771, C/AFR/W/1/20.

89. SPG–L, Philip Quaque to Edward Bass, July 31, 1775, C/AFR/W/1/28.

90. SPG–L, Philip Quaque to Secretary, Sept. 1, 1782, C/AFR/W/1/39.

91. Ibid., Apr. 6, 1781, C/AFR/W/1/36.

92. Ibid., Feb. 14, 1785, C/AFR/W/1/42; Apr. 6, 1785, C/AFR/W/1/43.

93. Beilby Porteus, *A Sermon Preached before the Incorporated Society for the Propagation of the Gospel in Foreign Parts . . . On Friday, February 21, 1783* (London: T. Harrison and S. Brooke, 1783).

94. Christopher Leslie Brown, *Moral Capital: Foundations of British Abolitionism* (Chapel Hill, NC: University of North Carolina Press for the Omohundro Institute of Early American History and Culture, 2006), 352–77.

95. William St. Clair, *The Door of No Return: The History of Cape Coast Castle and the Atlantic Slave Trade* (New York: Bluebridge, 2007), 219.

96. Johannes Menne Postma, *The Dutch in the Atlantic Slave Trade, 1600–1815* (Cambridge: University of Cambridge, 1990), 167; Selena Axelrod Winsnes, trans. and ed., *Letters on West Africa and the Slave Trade: Paul Erdmann Isert's Journey to Guinea and the Caribbean Islands in Columbia* (Oxford: Oxford University Press, 1992), 176; David Eltis, Stephen D. Behrendt, David Richardson, and Herbert S. Klein, eds., *The Trans-Atlantic Slave Trade: A Database on CD-ROM* (Cambridge: Cambridge University Press, 1999), Voyage Identification Number 10890; and SPG–L, Philip Quaque to Secretary, Feb. 8, 1786, C/AFR/W/1/45.

97. Great Britain. Parliament. House of Commons, *Abridgement of the minutes of the evidence taken before a committee of the whole House, to whom it was referred to consider of the slave-trade, 1790* ([London, 1790]), 228.

98. Alexander Falconbridge, *An Account of the Slave Trade on the Coast of Africa* (London: J. Phillips, 1788).

99. Great Britain. Parliament. House of Commons, *Abridgement of the minutes of the evidence taken before a committee of the whole House, to whom it was referred to consider of the slave-trade, 1791* ([London, 1791]), 22; *An Abstract of the Evidence Delivered before a Select Committee of the House of Commons in the Years 1790 and 1791; on the Part of the Petitioners for the Abolition of the Slave Trade* (Edinburgh, 1791), 22.

100. SPG–L, Philip Quaque to Secretary, July 21, 1792, C/AFR/W/1/51. Prior to his suspension, Quaque also had been serving as an "Assistant Writer" to the Company. See Carretta and Reese, *Life and Letters of Philip Quaque*, 180.

101. SPG–L, Philip Quaque to Secretary, Apr. 15, 1769, C/AFR/W/1/15; Apr. 11, 1777, C/AFR/W/1/29; June 19, 1795, C/AFR/W/1/52; Oct. 13, 1811, C/AFR/W/1/53.

102. SPG–L, Request from the Privy Council for Trade for Information on SPG missionaries to West Indies and Africa and Copy of Secretary's Response, Feb. 1788, C/AFR/W/1/47 and 48.

103. Morice's letter was printed in: Great Britain. Parliament. House of Commons, *Report of the Lords of the Committee of Council Appointed for the Consideration of all Matters Relating to Trade and Foreign Plantations; . . . concerning the present state of the trade to Africa, and particularly the trade in slaves; . . .* ([London]: n.p., 1789), Part I, "Detached Pieces of Evidence Relating to the Trade to Africa Generally," no. 3.

104. SPG–L, Philip Quaque to Secretary, Oct. 13, 1811, C/AFR/W/1/53.

105. Carretta and Reese, *Life and Letters of Philip Quaque*, 14.

106. SPG–L, Opinion of Lancelot Shadwell, Feb. 2, 1821, C/AFR/W/1/54.

107. SPG–L, William Phillip to Archbishop of Canterbury, Mar. 8, 1817, C/AFR/W/1/55. See also Crooks, *Records Relating to the Gold Coast Settlements*, 113–14.

108. SPG–L, Philip Quaque to Secretary, June 12, 1780, C/AFR/W/1/35.

109. Equiano, *Interesting Narrative*, 221–23.

110. SPG–L, Philip Quaque to Secretary, June 30, 1783, C/AFR/W/40; Aug. 23, 1783, C/AFR/W/41; July 1, 1785, C/AFR/W/44.

111. Mrs. R. [Sarah] Lee. *Stories of Strange Lands; and Fragments from the Notes of A Traveller* (London: Edward Moxon, 1835), 133–34. Over the course of a long literary career, Lee became best known for her works popularizing natural history.

112. Priestley, "Philip Quaque of Cape Coast," 112. Quaque was buried within Cape Coast Castle's courtyard, where a marker can still be seen.

113. John Beecham, *Ashantee and the Gold Coast. Being a sketch of the History, Social State and Superstitions of the inhabitants of those countries with a notice of the state and prospects of Christianity among them.* Introduction and notes by G. E. Metcalfe (1841; repr. London: Dawsons, 1968), 258–59.

114. Brodie Cruickshank, *Eighteen Years on the Gold Coast of Africa including an account of the native tribes, and their intercourse with Europeans.* 2nd ed. with an Introduction by K. A. Busia (1853; London: Frank Cass, 1966), 183. It is interesting to note that similar charges of apostasy were leveled against Quaque's near contemporary Jacobus Capitein. See S. R. B. Attoh Ahuma, *Memoirs of West African Celebrities: Europe, &c. (1700–1850). With Special Reference to the Gold Coast* (Liverpool: D. Marples, 1905), xi–xii.

115. John S. Pobee, "The Anglican Church in Ghana and the SPG," in *Three Centuries of Mission: The United Society for the Propagation of the Gospel, 1701–2000*, ed. Daniel O'Connor et al., (London: Continuum, 2000), 411.

116. Bartels, "Philip Quaque," 174; Adrian Hastings, *The Church in Africa 1450–1950* (Oxford: Clarendon Press, 1994), 178–79; Priestley, "Philip Quaque of Cape Coast," 111.

117. J. F. Ade Ajayi, "Samuel Ajayi Crowther of Oyo," in Curtin, *Africa Remembered*, 289–98.

Chapter 7

1. See, for example, the various treatments of Quaker, Dissenting, and evangelical networks in Roger Anstey, *The Atlantic Slave Trade and British Abolition, 1760–1810* (Atlantic Highlands, NJ: Humanities Press, 1975); Christopher Leslie Brown, *Moral Capital: Foundations of British Abolitionism* (Chapel Hill, NC: University of North Carolina Press for the Omohundro Institute of Early American History and Culture, 2006); David Brion Davis, *The Problem of Slavery in the Age of Revolution, 1770–1823* (New York: Oxford University Press, 1999); Seymour Drescher, *Abolition: A History of Slavery and Antislavery* (Cambridge: Cambridge University Press, 2009); and Drescher, *Capitalism and Antislavery: British Mobilization in Comparative Perspective* (New York: Oxford University Press, 1987).

2. An important exception is Larry Tise, *Proslavery: A History of the Defense of Slavery in America, 1701–1840* (Athens: University of Georgia Press, 1987), 25. While Tise did not analyze all of the authors discussed here, and he focused on the American debate over slavery, he observed that "The circle of associates who promoted the program of the Anglican SPG were also active proponents of proslavery ideology."

3. The key text in this regard is Frank Klingberg, *Anglican Humanitarianism in Colonial New York* (Philadelphia: Church Historical Society, 1940), which reprinted three SPG sermons critical of slavery and the slave trade in their entirety. Jon Butler, considering the history of the SPG and slavery from the perspective of religious history rather than the history of abolitionism, viewed the SPG as propping up colonial masters. See Butler, *Awash in a Sea of Faith: Christianizing the American People* (Cambridge, MA: Harvard University Press, 1990), 149–63.

4. Anthony Benezet to the SPG, Apr. 26, 1767, printed in George S. Brookes, *Friend Anthony Benezet* (Philadelphia: University of Pennsylvania Press, 1937), 272–73.

5. Daniel Burton to Anthony Benezet, Feb. 3, 1768, printed in Brookes, *Friend Anthony Benezet*, 417–18.

6. William Warburton, *A Sermon Preached before the Incorporated Society for the Propagation of the Gospel in Foreign Parts . . . On Friday, February 21, 1766* (London: E. Owen and T. Harrison, 1767).

7. Anthony Benezet, *A Caution and Warning to Great Britain and Her Colonies, in A Short Representation of the Calamitous State of the Enslaved Negroes in the British Dominions. . . .* (Philadelphia: Henry Miller, 1766).

8. Warburton, *A Sermon Preached before the Incorporated Society*, 29.

9. Ibid., 26.

10. B. W. Young stressed the uniqueness of Warburton's thought in a range of areas: see Young, *Religion and Enlightenment in Eighteenth-Century England: Theological Debate from Locke to Burke* (Oxford: Clarendon Press, 1998), 167–212.

11. [William Knox]. *Three Tracts Respecting the Conversion and Instruction of the Free Indians, and Negroe Slaves in the Colonies. Addressed to the Venerable Society for Propagation of the Gospel in Foreign Parts* ([London]: n.p. [1768]). This work's author and original publication date are clarified in its second edition, published in 1789.

12. Leland J. Bellot, "Evangelicals and the Defense of Slavery in Britain's Old Colonial Empire," *Journal of Southern History* 37, no. 1 (Feb. 1971): 27; Tise, *Proslavery*, 21–22. Knox again inserted himself into the debate about slavery in 1790: see W[illiam] K[nox], *A Letter from W. K. Esq. to W. Wilberforce, Esq.* (London: J. Debrett, 1790). In this work Knox notes that he wrote his *Three Tracts* in 1768 at the desire of Archbishop Secker, and he attributed the lack of progress the SPG had made in converting slaves in the years between 1760 and 1790 to the death of Secker. In his biography of Secker, Beilby Porteus wrote "Whenever any Publications came to his [Secker's] Knowledge that were manifestly calculated to corrupt

good Morals, or subvert the Foundations of Christianity, he did his utmost to stop the Circulation of them," and when such writings could not be suppressed "he engaged Men of Abilities to answer them, and rewarded them for their Trouble. His Attention was every where." Beilby Porteus, *A Review of the Life and Character of The Right Rev. Dr. Thomas Secker, Late Lord Archbishop of Canterbury,* 5th ed. (London: F. and C. Rivington, 1797), 70–71.

13. Leland J. Bellot, "Knox, William (1732–1810)," *ODNB.*

14. Bellot, "Evangelicals and the Defense of Slavery," 19–40; J. Harry Bennett, *Bondsmen and Bishops: Slavery and Apprenticeship on the Codrington Plantations of Barbados, 1710–1838* (Berkeley: University of California Press, 1958), 88; and Bellot, "Knox, William (1732–1810)," *ODNB.* For Knox's part in supervising Codrington, see SPG–X, Barbados Committee Minutes, 1771–79, X27.

15. On Knox, see Jack P. Greene, "William Knox's Explanation for the American Revolution," *WMQ,* 3rd. ser., 30, no. 2 (Apr. 1973): 293–306; Leland J. Bellot, *William Knox: The Life and Thought of an Eighteenth-Century Imperialist* (Austin: University of Texas Press, 1977); Brown, *Moral Capital,* 226–28; and David Waldstreicher, *Runaway America: Benjamin Franklin, Slavery, and the American Revolution* (New York: Hill and Wang, 2004), 186–92.

16. Rena Vassar, "William Knox's Defense of Slavery (1768)" *Proceedings of the American Philosophical Society,* 114 (Aug. 1970), 310–26.

17. Footnotes in the *Three Tracts* 1789 edition show Knox also took issue with Warburton's 1766 sermon.

18. [Knox], *Three Tracts* [1768]), 18–19.

19. Ibid., 26.

20. Ibid., 31–41.

21. See Vassar, "William Knox's Defense of Slavery," 310; and Brown, *Moral Capital,* 197. SPG annual sermons in the late 1760s also suggest more support for Knox's position on slavery than Warburton's. See John Green, *A Sermon Preached before the Incorporated Society for the Propagation of the Gospel in Foreign Parts . . . On Friday, February 19, 1768* (London: E. Owen and T. Harrison, 1768), 19; Thomas Newton, *On the imperfect Reception of the Gospel. A Sermon Preached before the Incorporated Society for the Propagation of the Gospel in Foreign Parts . . . On Friday, February 19, 1769* (London: E. Owen and T. Harrison, 1769), 27.

22. Abstract of Proceedings printed with Frederic Keppel, *A Sermon Preached before the Incorporated Society for the Propagation of the Gospel in Foreign Parts . . . On Friday, February 16, 1770* (London: T. Harrison and S. Brooke, 1770), 55.

23. Thomas Thompson, *The African Trade for Negro Slaves, Shewn to be Consistent with Principles of Humanity, and with the Laws of Revealed Religion* (Canterbury: Simmons and Kirkby, 1772), 12.

24. James Oldham, "New Light on Mansfield and Slavery," *Journal of British Studies* 27, no. 1 (Jan. 1988), 53–54.

25. *Monthly Review,* 46 (May 1772), 541–42.

26. Granville Sharp to Anthony Benezet, Aug. 21, 1772, in Wilson Armistead, *Anthony Benezet. From the Original Memoir* (London: A. W. Bennett, 1859), 32–33.

27. Granville Sharp, *An essay on slavery, proving from Scripture its inconsistency with humanity and religion; in answer to a late publication, entitled, "The African trade for Negro slaves shewn to be consistent with principles of humanity, and with the laws of revealed religion."* (Burlington, NJ: Isaac Collins, 1773).

28. Granville Sharp, *The just limitation of slavery in the laws of God, compared with the unbounded claims of the African traders and British American slaveholders* (London: B. White, 1776).

29. Granville Sharp, *A Tract on the Law of Nature, and Principles of Action in Man* (London: B. White and E. and C. Dilly, 1777), 2–3.

30. Thomas Clarkson, *An essay on the slavery and commerce of the human species, particularly the African, translated from a Latin dissertation* . . . (London: J. Phillips, 1786), xx–xxi.

31. Granville Sharp to Anthony Benezet, Aug. 21, 1772, in Armistead, *Anthony Benezet*, 32–33.

32. Shute Barrington, *A Sermon Preached before the Incorporated Society for the Propagation of the Gospel in Foreign Parts* . . . *On Friday, February 17, 1775* (London: T. Harrison and S. Brooke, 1775), xxii; E. A. Varley, "Barrington, Shute (1734–1826)," *ODNB*.

33. Brown, *Moral Capital*, 456.

34. Of the 296 Anglican clergymen serving in the thirteen colonies in 1775, only 130 remained at their posts in 1783. James B. Bell, *The Imperial Origins of the King's Church in Early America, 1607–1783* (New York: Palgrave Macmillan, 2004), 201.

35. See for example Douglas R. Egerton, *Death or Liberty: African Americans and Revolutionary America* (New York: Oxford University Press, 2009); Simon Schama, *Rough Crossings: Britain, the Slaves, and the American Revolution* (New York: Ecco, 2006); Sylvia R. Frey, *Water from the Rock: Black Resistance in a Revolutionary Age* (Princeton: Princeton University Press, 1991).

36. James W. St. G. Walker, *The Black Loyalists: The Search for a Promised Land in Nova Scotia and Sierra Leone 1783–1870* (London: Longman, 1976), 2, 66–67; Alexander X. Byrd, *Captives and Voyagers: Black Migrants Across the Eighteenth-Century British Atlantic World* (Baton Rouge: Louisiana State University Press, 2008), 154–76.

37. Walker, *Black Loyalists*, 40–41.

38. Egerton, *Death or Liberty*, 207.

39. Robin M. Winks, *The Blacks in Canada: A History*, 2nd ed. (Montreal: McGill-Queen's University Press, 1997), 57–59.

40. SPG–L, Jacob Bailey to Secretary, Oct. 28, 1784, C/Am/6/16. On denominational diversity in these communities, see Walker, *Black Loyalists*, 64–79.

41. Bennett, *Bondsmen and Bishops*, 71–73. Clarke's bankruptcy, which was felt widely in Atlantic mercantile circles, is analyzed in S. D. Smith, "Gedney Clarke of Salem and Barbados: Transatlantic Super-Merchant," *New England Quarterly* 67, no. 4 (Dec. 2003): 499–549.

42. John A. Schutz and Maud E. O'Neil, "Of the Plantations Intire . . .," in *Codrington Chronicle: An Experiment in Anglican Altruism on a Barbados Plantation, 1710–1834*, ed. Frank J. Klingberg (Berkeley: University of California Press, 1949), 57.

43. Beilby Porteus, *A Sermon Preached before the Incorporated Society for the Propagation of the Gospel in Foreign Parts* . . . *On Friday, February 21, 1783* (London: T. Harrison and S. Brooke, 1783), 7, 16, 18–20. Porteus based many of his factual claims on the research of the West Indian clergyman James Ramsay. See Brown, *Moral Capital*, 354; and James Ramsay, *Essay on the Treatment and Conversion of African Slaves in the British Sugar Colonies* (London: James Philips, 1784). See also Bob Tennant, "Sentiment, Politics, and Empire: A Study of Beilby Porteus's Anti-Slavery Sermon," in Brycchan Carey, Markman Ellis, and Sara Salih, *Discourses of Slavery and Abolition: Britain and its Colonies, 1760–1838* (Houndmills: Palgrave Macmillan, 2004), 158–74.

44. Robert Hodgson, *The Life of the Right Reverend Beilby Porteus, D.D. Late Bishop of London* (New York: Ezra Sargeant, 1811), 67–70.

45. Brown, *Moral Capital*, 352–64.

46. Porteus, *A Sermon Preached before the Incorporated Society*, 24–25.

47. Lillian M. Penson, *The Colonial Agents of the British West Indies: A Study in Colonial Administration Mainly in the Eighteenth Century* (London: F. Cass, 1971), 251.

48. Schutz and O'Neil, "Of the Plantations Intire," in Klingberg, *Codrington Chronicle*, 57–58.

49. Frederick V. Mills, *Bishops by Ballot: An Eighteenth-Century Ecclesiastical Revolution* (New York: Oxford University Press, 1978), 300–301; G. M. Ditchfield, "Sharp, Granville

(1735–1813)," *ODNB*; and Pascoe, *Two Hundred Years of the SPG . . ., 1701–1900* (London: SPG, 1901), 749–50.

50. Prince Hoare, *Memoirs of Granville Sharp, Esq.* (London: Henry Colburn, 1820), 435; Walker, *Black Loyalists*, 67–87, 99–100; Pascoe, *Two Hundred Years of the SPG*, 259.

51. Granville Sharp to John Moore, Aug. 1, 1786, printed in Hoare, *Memoirs of Granville Sharp*, 261–64. In this letter Sharp also asked Moore to support sending Patrick Fraser to Sierra Leone. Sharp first complained to Bishop Barrington about Burton's reply to Benezet in 1774. See Davis, *Problem of Slavery in the Age of Revolution*, 374–75.

52. Thomas Thurlow, *A Sermon Preached Before the Incorporated Society for the Propagation of the Gospel in Foreign Parts . . . On Friday February 17, 1786* (London: T. Harrison, 1786), 19–20.

53. John Warren, *A Sermon Preached Before the Incorporated Society for the Propagation of the Gospel in Foreign Parts . . . On Friday February 16, 1787* (London: T. Harrison and S. Brooke, 1787), xx.

54. Warren, *A Sermon Preached before the Incorporated Society*, xx.

55. Anstey, *Atlantic Slave Trade and British Abolition*, 289.

56. Ramsay, *Essay*, 101.

57. Ibid., 233.

58. [Anonymous], *An Answer to the Reverend James Ramsay's Essay, on the Treatment and Conversion of Slaves, in the British Sugar Colonies. By some Gentlemen of St. Christopher* (Basseterre, St. Christopher: Edward Low, 1784).

59. [Anonymous], *An Answer to the Reverend James Ramsay's Essay*, 57–58, 99.

60. Simon David Smith, *Slavery, Family and Gentry Capitalism in the British Atlantic: The World of the Lascelles, 1648–1834* (Cambridge: Cambridge University Press, 2006), 273–77. Gibbes, Brathwaite, and the Barbados planter/clergyman Henry Evans Holder joined six other Barbadian planters in putting their names on a 1786 work, *Instructions for the Management of a Plantation*, that pursued a similar agenda.

61. Philip Gibbes, *Instructions for the Treatment of Negroes* (London, 1797), 96–97, 100.

62. Olaudah Equiano singled out Gibbes, who subscribed to his autobiography's first edition, as a benevolent master. See Equiano, *The Interesting Narrative and Other Writings*, ed. Vincent Carretta (New York: Penguin, 1995), 105–6.

63. [James Tobin], *Cursory Remarks upon the Reverend Mr. Ramsay's Essay on the Treatment and Conversion of African Slaves in the Sugar Colonies* (London: G. and T. Wilkie, 1785), 102–5.

64. *Morning Chronicle* (London), Feb. 21, 1788.

65. James Ramsay, *Objections to the abolition of the slave trade, with answers. To which are prefixed, strictures on a late publication, intitled, "Considerations on the emancipation of negroes, and the abolition of the slave trade, by a West India planter."* (London: James Philips, 1788).

66. Ibid., 24.

67. Ibid., 2nd ed., 33–35.

68. John Walsh, "Peckard, Peter (bap. 1717, d. 1797)," *ODNB*.

69. [Peter Peckard], *Am I Not a Man? And a brother? With all humility addressed to the British Legislature* (Cambridge: J. Archdeacon, 1788), 20.

70. SPG secretary William Morice's harsh criticism of Philip Quaque, which seems also to have been informed by new, harder attitudes toward human difference within the Society's ranks, was also published in 1789.

71. Knox, *Three Tracts*, 2nd ed. (London: J. Debrett, 1789).

72. [Anonymous], *No Abolition . . .* (London: J. Debrett, 1789), 48.

73. Samuel Hallifax, *A Sermon Preached before the Incorporated Society for the Propagation of the Gospel in Foreign Parts . . . On Friday, February 20, 1789* (London: T. Harrison and S. Brooke, 1789), xxvi–xxix.

74. Ibid., xxix–xxxiv.
75. On Francklyn as a spokesman for the West Indian interest, see Davis, *Problem of Slavery in the Age of Revolution*, 382.
76. Gilbert Francklyn, *Observations, Occasioned by the Attempts Made in England to Effect the Abolition of the Slave Trade* ... (London: Logographic Press, 1789), 62–63.
77. Gilbert Francklyn, *An answer to the Rev. Mr. Clarkson's essay on the slavery and commerce of the human species* ... (London: Logographic Press, 1789), xiv–xv, 88–89.
78. Ibid., 88–89.
79. Robert Norris, *Memoirs of the reign of Bossa Ahádee, King of Dahomy, an Inland country of Guiney.* ... 2nd ed. (London: W. Lowndes, 1789), 165–66. Norris first made similar claims about the SPG in *A short account of the African slave trade.* ... (Liverpool: Ann Smith, 1788), 11–12.
80. James Makittrick Adair, *Unanswerable arguments against the abolition of the slave trade.* ... (London: J. P. Bateman, [1790?]), 176.
81. John Holroyd, *Observations on the Project for Abolishing the Slave Trade* ... (London: J. Debrett, 1790), 65–66.
82. Great Britain. Parliament. House of Commons, *The debate on a motion for the abolition of the slave-trade, in the House of Commons on Monday and Tuesday, Apr. 18 and 19, 1791, reported in detail.* 2nd ed. (London: James Philips, 1792), 74.
83. John Douglas, *A Sermon Preached before the Incorporated Society for the Propagation of the Gospel in Foreign Parts* ... *On Friday, February 15, 1793* (London: S. Brooke, 1793), 19–21.
84. F. C. Mather, *High Church Prophet: Bishop Samuel Horsley (1733–1806) and the Caroline Tradition in the Later Georgian Church* (Oxford: Oxford University Press, 1992), 237 (quote), 233–44.
85. *Substance of the Bishop of Rochester's Speech in the House of Peers, Friday, July 5, 1799* ... (London: J. Robson, 1799), 35–43.
86. Charles Manners-Sutton, *A Sermon Preached before the Incorporated Society for the Propagation of the Gospel in Foreign Parts* ... *On Friday, February 17, 1797* (London: S. Brooke, 1797), 16–17; W. M. Jacob, "Sutton, Charles Manners-(1755–1828)," *ODNB*.
87. Edward Venables-Vernon, *A Sermon Preached before the Incorporated Society for the Propagation of the Gospel in Foreign Parts* ... *On Friday, February 16, 1798* (London: S. Brooke, 1798), 19–20; Nigel Aston, "Harcourt, Edward (1757–1847)," *ODNB*. Venables-Vernon changed his name to Harcourt in 1830.
88. On Edwards as the "pre-eminent statesman-intellectual" of the British West Indies, see Davis, *Problem of Slavery in the Age of Revolution*, 188.
89. Richard B. Sheridan, "Edwards, Bryan (1743–1800)," *ODNB*; Davis, *Problem of Slavery in the Age of Revolution*, 184–95.
90. Bryan Edwards, *The History, Civil and Commercial, of the British Colonies in the West Indies.* 2 vols. (Dublin: Luke White, 1793), 2:34–35.
91. *Times* (London), Feb. 10, 1807, 3. This list records only those who voted in person for the bill, not those who voted for it by proxy, voted against it, abstained, or were absent. Twenty-six English and Welsh bishops and four Irish bishops sat in the House of Lords in 1807.
92. On these maneuverings, see Anstey, *Atlantic Slave Trade and British Abolition*, 364–402; Stephen Farrell, "'Contrary to the Principles of Justice, Humanity and Sound Policy': The Slave Trade, Parliamentary Politics and the Abolition Act, 1807," *Parliamentary History* 26 (June 2007): 141–202; M. W. McCahill, *The House of Lords in the Age of George III (1760–1811)* (Chichester: Wiley-Blackwell, 2009), 70–95, 264–73, 355–59; and Drescher, *Abolition*, 226–28.
93. J. Harry Bennett, "The Problem of Slave Labor Supply at the Codrington Plantations," *Journal of Negro History* 37, no. 2 (Apr. 1952): 141.

94. Robin Blackburn, *The Overthrow of Colonial Slavery, 1776–1848* (London: Verso, 1988), 316–26.

95. Ibid., 421–23.

96. John Riland, *Memoirs of a West Indian Planter . . .* (London: Hamilton, Adams, and Co., 1827), vii, 115–16, 197–99.

97. The *Christian Observer* article is printed verbatim in *Christian Remembrancer, or, The churchman's biblical, ecclesiastical & literary miscellany* 10:1 (Jan. 1828), 32.

98. Ibid., 32–42.

99. Riland printed his replies to S.H.P. as a separate pamphlet. John Riland, *Two Letters, Severally Addressed to the Editor of the Christian Observer and the Editor of the Christian Remembrancer Relative to the Slave-Cultured Estates of the Society for the Propagation of the Gospel* (London: John Hatchard and Son, 1828), 2.

100. *Anti-Slavery Reporter* 2, no. 45 (Feb. 1829), 413–27.

101. Letter by "Philalethes," *Christian Remembrancer* 11, no. 4 (Apr. 1829), 243–47; and "Progress of Religious Instruction in the West Indies," *British Critic* 5, no. 10 (Apr. 1829): 407–54.

102. John Riland, *On the Codrington Estates. A Letter to the Most Reverend William, Lord Archbishop of Canterbury, President of the Society for the Propagation of the Gospel in Foreign Parts on the Connection of that Institution with Codrington College, in the Island of Barbadoes* (London: J. Hatchard and Son, 1830).

103. [Society for the Propagation of the Gospel in Foreign Parts], *A Statement Relative to Codrington College; Extracted from the Reports of the Society for the Propagation of the Gospel in Foreign Parts* (London: G. Woodfall, 1829), 4. This *Statement* was inserted in its entirety in the sympathetic *Christian Remembrancer* 11, no. 12 (Dec. 1829). See also Drescher, *Capitalism and Antislavery*, 233, n. 6.

104. The Society's *Statement* and defenses of Codrington in the *Christian Remembrancer* and *British Critic* were criticized in the *Anti-Slavery Reporter* 2, no. 47 (Apr. 1829): 457–62. See also the *Anti-Slavery Reporter* 4, no. 18 (Nov. 1831): 487–91.

105. [Society for the Propagation of the Gospel in Foreign Parts], *Report from the Committee of the Codrington Trust* (London: G. Woodfall, 1831), 2.

106. The practical ineffectiveness of these plans for reform and gradual emancipation on Codrington are discussed in Bennett, *Bondsmen and Bishops*, 125–35.

107. SPG, *Report from the Committee of the Codrington Trust*, 3.

108. *To the People of Great Britain and Ireland . . .* (London: Maurice and Co., 1831).

109. George Stephen, *Anti-Slavery Recollections: In a Series of Letters Addressed to Mrs. Beecher Stowe*, 2nd ed. with an introduction by Howard Temperley (London: Frank Cass, 1971 [1854]), 96–97, 114; Leslie Stephen, "Stephen, Sir George (1794–1879)," rev. Peter Balmford, *ODNB*.

110. Frank J. Klingberg, "The Evolution of the Humanitarian Spirit in Eighteenth-Century England," *Pennsylvania Magazine of History and Biography* 66, no. 3 (July 1942): 266; Klingberg, ed., *Codrington Chronicle*, 10. Klingberg did not provide information on the source or context for Stephen's remarks.

111. Stephen, *Anti-Slavery Recollections*, 117.

112. Bennett, *Bondsmen and Bishops*, 131–35.

Conclusion

1. For these institutional and political changes see, C. F. Pascoe, *Two Hundred Years of the SPG . . .*, 1701–1900 (London: SPG, 1901); H. P. Thompson, *Into All Lands: The History of the Society for the Propagation of the Gospel in Foreign Parts, 1701–1950* (London: SPCK, 1951); and Daniel

O'Connor et al., *Three Centuries of Mission: The United Society for the Propagation of the Gospel, 1701–2000* (London: Continuum, 2000).

2. Sylvia R. Frey and Betty Wood, *Come Shouting to Zion: African American Protestantism in the American South and British Caribbean to 1830* (Chapel Hill: University of North Carolina Press, 1998), 212.

3. Frederick Keppel, *A Sermon Preached before the Incorporated Society for the Propagation of the Gospel in Foreign Parts . . . On Friday, February 16, 1770* (London: E. Owen and T. Harrison, 1770), 17.

4. SPG–L, Philip Quaque to Secretary, Oct. 13, 1811, C/AFR/W/1/53.

SELECT BIBLIOGRAPHY

This list includes a selection of secondary works particularly relevant to the history of the SPG's transatlantic missionary work among enslaved people before 1838. Full references to the primary and secondary sources used in the book may be found in the notes.

Allen, W. O. B., and Edmund McClure. *Two Hundred Years: The History of the Society for Promoting Christian Knowledge, 1698–1898.* London: SPCK, 1898.

Anderson, James S. M. *The History of the Church of England in the Colonies and Foreign Dependencies of the British Empire,* 3 vols. London: Francis and John Rivington, 1845–56.

Anesko, Michael. "So Discreet a Zeal: Slavery and the Anglican Church in Virginia, 1680–1730." *Virginia Magazine of History and Biography* 93, no. 3 (July 1985): 247–78.

Anstey, Roger. *The Atlantic Slave Trade and British Abolition, 1760–1810.* Atlantic Highlands, NJ: Humanities Press, 1975.

Armitage, David. *The Ideological Origins of the British Empire.* Cambridge: Cambridge University Press, 2000.

Armitage, David, and Michael J. Braddick, eds. *The British Atlantic World, 1500–1800.* 2nd ed. New York: Palgrave Macmillan, 2009.

Bailyn, Bernard. *Atlantic History: Concept and Contours.* Cambridge, MA: Harvard University Press, 2005.

Bartels, F. L. "Philip Quaque, 1741–1816." *Transactions of the Gold Coast and Togoland Historical Society* 1 (1952–1955): 153–77.

Beahrs, Andrew. "'Ours Alone Must Needs Be Christians': The Production of Enslaved Souls on the Codrington Estates." *Plantation Society in the Americas* 4, no. 2 and 3 (Fall 1997): 279–310.

Beasley, Nicholas M. *Christian Ritual and the Creation of British Slave Societies, 1650–1780.* Athens: University of Georgia Press, 2009.

Bell, James B. *The Imperial Origins of the King's Church in Early America, 1607–1783.* New York: Palgrave Macmillan, 2004.

Bellot, Leland J. "Evangelicals and the Defense of Slavery in Britain's Old Colonial Empire." *Journal of Southern History* 37, no. 1 (Feb. 1971): 19–40.

———. *William Knox: The Life & Thought of an Eighteenth-Century Imperialist.* Austin: University of Texas Press, 1977.

Bennett, G. V. *White Kennett, 1660–1728, Bishop of Peterborough: A Study in the Political and Ecclesiastical History of the Early Eighteenth Century.* London: SPCK, 1957.

Bennett, J. Harry. *Bondsmen and Bishops: Slavery and Apprenticeship on the Codrington Plantations of Barbados, 1710–1838.* Berkeley: University of California Press, 1958.

Bennett, Robert A. "Black Episcopalians: A History from the Colonial Period to the Present." *HMPEC* 43, no. 3 (Sept. 1974): 231–45.

Blackburn, Robin. *The Overthrow of Colonial Slavery, 1776–1848.* London: Verso, 1988.

Bolton, S. Charles. "South Carolina and the Reverend Doctor Francis Le Jau: Southern Society and the Conscience of an Anglican Missionary." *HMPEC* 40, no. 1 (Mar. 1971): 63–79.

———. *Southern Anglicanism: The Church of England in South Carolina.* Westport, CT: Greenwood Press, 1982.

Bonomi, Patricia U. *Under the Cope of Heaven: Religion, Society, and Politics in Colonial America.* Rev. ed. New York: Oxford University Press, 2003.

Bonomi, Patricia U., and Peter R. Eisenstadt. "Church Adherence in the Eighteenth-Century British American Colonies." *WMQ,* 3rd ser., 39, no. 2 (Apr. 1982): 245–86.

Braude, Benjamin. "The Sons of Noah and the Construction of Ethnic and Geographical Identities in the Medieval and Early Modern Periods." *WMQ,* 3rd ser., 54, no. 1, (Jan. 1997): 103–42.

Bridenbaugh, Carl. *Mitre and Sceptre: Transatlantic Faiths, Ideas, Personalities, and Politics 1689–1775.* New York: Oxford University Press, 1962.

Brown, Christopher Leslie. *Moral Capital: Foundations of British Abolitionism.* Chapel Hill: University of North Carolina Press for the Omohundro Institute of Early American History and Culture, 2006.

Brown, Vincent. *The Reaper's Garden: Death and Power in the World of Atlantic Slavery.* Cambridge, MA: Harvard University Press, 2008.

Butler, Jon. *Awash in a Sea of Faith: Christianizing the American People.* Cambridge, MA: Harvard University Press, 1990.

———. "'Gospel Order Improved': The Keithian Schism and the Exercise of Quaker Ministerial Authority in Pennsylvania." *WMQ,* 3rd ser., 31, no. 3 (July 1974): 431–52.

———. "Les 'Hymnes ou cantiques sacrez' d'Elie Neau: Un nouveau manuscrit du 'grand mystique des galères.'" *Bulletin de la société de l'histoire du protestantisme français* 124 (1978): 416–23.

Byrd, Alexander X. *Captives and Voyagers: Black Migrants Across the Eighteenth-Century British Atlantic World.* Baton Rouge: Louisiana State University Press, 2008.

Calam, John. *Parsons and Pedagogues: The SPG Adventure in American Education.* New York: Columbia University Press, 1971.

Carpenter, Edward. *Thomas Tenison, Archbishop of Canterbury: His Life and Times.* London: SPCK, 1948.

Carretta, Vincent, and Ty M. Reese, eds. *The Life and Letters of Philip Quaque, The First African Anglican Clergyman.* Athens: University of Georgia Press, 2010.

Clark, J. C. D. *English Society 1660–1832: Religion, Ideology and Politics during the Ancien Regime,* 2nd ed. Cambridge: Cambridge University Press, 2000.

———. *The Language of Liberty, 1660–1832: Political Discourse and Social Dynamics in the Anglo-American World.* Cambridge: Cambridge University Press, 1994.

Clarke, W. K. Lowther. *Eighteenth Century Piety.* London: SPCK, 1944.

———. *A History of the SPCK.* London: SPCK, 1959.

Claydon, Tony, and Ian McBride, eds. *Protestantism and National Identity: Britain and Ireland, c. 1650–c. 1850.* Cambridge: Cambridge University Press, 1998.

Clifton, Denzil T. "Anglicanism and Negro Slavery in Colonial America." *HMPEC* 39, no. 1 (Mar. 1970): 29–70.

Colley, Linda. *Britons: Forging the Nation, 1707–1837.* New Haven, CT: Yale University Press, 1992.

Cox, Jeffrey. *British Missionary Enterprise Since 1700.* New York: Routledge, 2008.

Cross, Arthur Lyon. *The Anglican Episcopate and the American Colonies.* New York: Longmans, Green, and Co., 1902.

Daaku, Kwame Yeboah. *Trade and Politics on the Gold Coast, 1600–1720. A Study of the African Reaction to European Trade.* Oxford: Clarendon Press, 1970.

Davis, David Brion. *The Problem of Slavery in the Age of Revolution, 1770–1823.* New York: Oxford University Press, 1999.

———. *The Problem of Slavery in Western Culture.* New York: Oxford University Press, 1966.

DeCorse, Christopher R. "Culture Contact, Continuity, and Change on the Gold Coast, AD 1400–1900." *African Archaeological Review* 10 (1992): 163–96.

Doll, Peter M. *Revolution, Religion, and National Identity: Imperial Anglicanism in British North America, 1745–1795.* Madison, NJ: Fairleigh Dickinson University Press, 2000.

Drescher, Seymour. *Abolition: A History of Slavery and Antislavery.* Cambridge: Cambridge University Press, 2009.

———. *Capitalism and Antislavery: British Mobilization in Comparative Perspective.* New York: Oxford University Press, 1987.

Dunn, Richard S. *Sugar and Slaves: The Rise of the Planter Class in the English West Indies, 1624–1713.* Chapel Hill: University of North Carolina Press for the Institute of Early American History and Culture, 1972.

Egerton, Douglas R. *Death or Liberty: African Americans and Revolutionary America.* New York: Oxford University Press, 2009.

Eltis, David, Stephen D. Behrendt, David Richardson, and Herbert S. Klein, eds. *The Trans-Atlantic Slave Trade: A Database on CD-ROM.* Cambridge: Cambridge University Press, 1999.

Etherington, Norman, ed. *Missions and Empire.* Oxford History of the British Empire Companion Series. Oxford: Oxford University Press, 2005.

Foote, Thelma Wills. *Black and White Manhattan: The History of Racial Formation in Colonial New York City.* New York: Oxford University Press, 2004.

Frey, Sylvia R. "The Visible Church: Historiography of African American Religion since Raboteau." *Slavery & Abolition* 29, no. 1 (Jan. 2008): 83–110.

———. *Water from the Rock: Black Resistance in a Revolutionary Age.* Princeton: Princeton University Press, 1991.

Frey, Sylvia R., and Betty Wood. *Come Shouting to Zion: African American Protestantism in the American South and British Caribbean to 1830.* Chapel Hill: University of North Carolina Press, 1998.

Gaustad, Edwin. *George Berkeley in America.* New Haven, CT: Yale University Press, 1979.

Gibson, William. *The Church of England, 1688–1832: Unity and Accord.* London: Routledge, 2001.

Glasson, Travis. "'Baptism doth not bestow Freedom': Missionary Anglicanism, Slavery, and the Yorke-Talbot Opinion, 1701–30." *WMQ,* 3rd ser., 68, no. 2 (Apr. 2010): 279–318.

———. "Missionaries, Methodists, and a Ghost: Philip Quaque in London and Cape Coast, 1756–1816." *Journal of British Studies* 48, no. 4 (Oct. 2009): 29–50.

Gocking, Roger S. *Facing Two Ways: Ghana's Coastal Communities Under Colonial Rule.* Lanham, MD: University Press of America, 1999.

Goetz, Rebecca Anne. "Rethinking the 'Unthinking Decision': Old Questions and New Problems in the History of Slavery and Race in the Colonial South." *Journal of Southern History* 75, no. 3 (Aug. 2009): 599–612.

Gomez, Michael. *Exchanging our Country Marks: The Transformation of African Identities in the Colonial and Antebellum South.* Chapel Hill: University of North Carolina Press, 1998.

Gould, Eliga H. "Prelude: The Christianizing of British America." In Etherington, *Missions and Empire,* 19–39.

Greene, Jack P., and Philip D. Morgan, eds. *Atlantic History: A Critical Appraisal.* New York: Oxford University Press, 2009.

Hall, David D. "From 'Religion and Society' to Practices." In St. George, *Possible Pasts: Becoming Colonial in Early America,* 148–59.

Handler, Jerome S., and Frederic W. Lange. *Plantation Slavery in Barbados: An Archaeological and Historical Investigation.* Cambridge, MA: Harvard University Press, 1978.

Hannaford, Ivan. *Race: The History of an Idea in the West.* Washington, DC: Woodrow Wilson Center Press, 1996.

Harlow, Vincent T. *Christopher Codrington, 1668–1710.* London: Hurst and Co., 1990. First published 1928.

Harris, Leslie M. *In the Shadow of Slavery: African Americans in New York City, 1626–1863.* Chicago: University of Chicago Press, 2003.

Hastings, Adrian. *The Church in Africa 1450–1950.* Oxford: Clarendon Press, 1994.

Haynes, Stephen R. *Noah's Curse: The Biblical Justification of American Slavery.* New York: Oxford University Press, 2002.

Hempton, David. *Religion and Political Culture in Britain and Ireland: From the Glorious Revolution to the Decline of Empire.* Cambridge: Cambridge University Press, 1996.

Heyrman, Christine Leigh. *Southern Cross: The Beginnings of the Bible Belt.* Chapel Hill: University of North Carolina Press, 1997.

Hodges, Graham Russell. *Root and Branch: African Americans in New York and East Jersey, 1613–1863.* Chapel Hill: University of North Carolina Press, 1999.

Hudson, Nicholas. "From 'Nation' to 'Race': The Origin of Racial Classification in Eighteenth-Century Thought." *Eighteenth-Century Studies* 29, no. 3, (1996): 247–64.

Irons, Charles F. *The Origins of Proslavery Christianity: White and Black Evangelicals in Colonial and Antebellum Virginia.* Chapel Hill: University of North Carolina Press, 2008.

Jacob, W. M. *Lay People and Religion in the Early Eighteenth Century.* Cambridge: Cambridge University Press, 1996.

Jernegan, Marcus W. "Slavery and Conversion in the American Colonies." *American Historical Review* 21, no. 3 (Apr. 1916): 504–27.

Jordan, Winthrop D. *White Over Black: American Attitudes Toward the Negro, 1550–1812.* Chapel Hill: University of North Carolina Press for the Institute of Early American History and Culture, 1968.

Kidd, Colin. *British Identities before Nationalism: Ethnicity and Nationhood in the Atlantic World, 1600–1800.* Cambridge: Cambridge University Press, 1999.

———. "Ethnicity in the British Atlantic World, 1688–1830." In Wilson, *A New Imperial History: Culture, Identity, and Modernity in Britain and the Empire, 1660–1840,* 260–77.

———. *The Forging of Races: Race and Scripture in the Protestant Atlantic World 1600–2000.* Cambridge: Cambridge University Press, 2006.

Kidd, Thomas S. *The Great Awakening: The Roots of Evangelical Christianity in Colonial America.* New Haven, CT: Yale University Press, 2007.

Klingberg, Frank J. *Anglican Humanitarianism in Colonial New York.* Philadelphia: Church Historical Society, 1940.

———. *The Anti-Slavery Movement in England, a Study in English Humanitarianism.* Hamden, CT: Archon Books, 1968. First published 1926.

———. *An Appraisal of the Negro in Colonial South Carolina: A Study in Americanization.* Washington, DC: Associated Publishers, 1941.

———, ed. *The Carolina Chronicle of Dr. Francis Le Jau, 1706–1717.* Berkeley: University of California Press, 1956.

———, ed. *Carolina Chronicle: The Papers of Commissary Gideon Johnston, 1707–1716.* Berkeley: University of California Press, 1946.

———, ed. *Codrington Chronicle: An Experiment in Anglican Altruism on a Barbados Plantation, 1710–1834.* Berkeley: University of California Press, 1949.

———. "The Efforts of the SPG to Christianize the Mosquito Indians, 1742–1785." *HMPEC* 9 (1940): 305–32.

———. "The Indian Frontier in South Carolina as Seen by the S.P.G. Missionary." *Journal of Southern History* 5, no. 4 (Nov. 1939): 479–500.

———. "Philip Quaque: Pioneer Native Missionary on the Gold Coast, 1765–1816." *Journal of Negro Education* 8, no. 4 (Oct. 1939): 666–72.

Laing, Annette. "'Heathens and Infidels'? African Christianization and Anglicanism in the South Carolina Low Country, 1700–1750." *Religion and American Culture* 12 (2002): 197–228.

Law, Robin. *The Slave Coast of West Africa, 1550–1750: The Impact of the Atlantic Slave Trade on African Society*. Oxford Studies in African Affairs. New York: Oxford University Press, 1991.

Marshall, P. J., ed. *The Oxford History of the British Empire*, vol. 2. *The Eighteenth Century*. Oxford: Oxford University Press, 1998.

Monaghan, E. Jennifer. *Learning to Read and Write in Colonial America*. Amherst: University of Massachusetts Press, 2005.

Morgan, Philip D. "The Black Experience in the British Empire, 1680–1810." In Marshall, *Oxford History of the British Empire*, vol. 2, *The Eighteenth Century*, 465–86.

———. "The Cultural Implications of the Atlantic Slave Trade: African Regional Origins, American Destinations and New World Developments." *Slavery & Abolition* 18, no. 1 (1997): 122–45.

Morgan, Philip D., and Sean Hawkins, eds. *Black Experience and the Empire*. Oxford History of the British Empire Companion Series. Oxford: Oxford University Press, 2004.

Nelson, John K. *A Blessed Company: Parishes, Parsons, and Parishioners in Anglican Virginia, 1690–1776*. Chapel Hill: University of North Carolina Press, 2001.

O'Connor, Daniel et al. *Three Centuries of Mission: The United Society for the Propagation of the Gospel, 1701–2000*. London: Continuum, 2000.

Olson, Alison Gilbert. *Making the Empire Work: London and American Interest Groups, 1690–1790*. Cambridge, MA: Harvard University Press, 1992.

Olwell, Robert. *Masters, Slaves, and Subjects. The Culture of Power in the South Carolina Low Country, 1740–1790*. Ithaca, NY: Cornell University Press, 1998.

Paley, Ruth, Cristina Malcolmson, and Michael Hunter. "Parliament and Slavery, 1660–c. 1710." *Slavery & Abolition* 31, no. 2 (June 2010): 257–81.

Pascoe, C. F. *Two Hundred Years of the SPG . . ., 1701–1900*. London: SPG, 1901.

Pestana, Carla Gardina. *Protestant Empire: Religion and the Making of the British Atlantic World*. Philadelphia: University of Pennsylvania Press, 2009.

———. "Religion." In Armitage and Braddick, *The British Atlantic World, 1500–1800*, 71–91.

Porter, Andrew. *Religion versus Empire? British Protestant Missionaries and Overseas Expansion, 1700–1914*. Manchester: Manchester University Press, 2004.

Priestley, Margaret. "Philip Quaque of Cape Coast." In *Africa Remembered: Narratives by West Africans from the Era of the Slave Trade*, edited by Philip D. Curtin. Prospect Heights, IL: Waveland Press, 1997, 99–139. First published 1967.

———. *West African Trade and Coast Society*. London: Oxford University Press, 1969.

Reese, Ty M. "The Drudgery of the Slave Trade. Labor at Cape Coast Castle, 1750–1790." In *The Atlantic Economy during the Seventeenth and Eighteenth Centuries*, edited by Peter A. Coclanis. Columbia: University of South Carolina Press, 2005, 277–93.

———. "'Sheep in the Jaws of So Many Ravenous Wolves': The Slave Trade and Anglican Missionary Activity at Cape Coast Castle, 1752–1816." *Journal of Religion in Africa* 34, no. 3 (2004): 348–72.

Raboteau, Albert J. *Slave Religion: The "Invisible Institution" in the Antebellum South*. Rev. ed. Oxford: Oxford University Press, 2004.

Rhoden, Nancy L. *Revolutionary Anglicanism: The Colonial Church of England Clergy during the American Revolution*. New York: New York University Press, 1999.

Rupp, Gordon. *Religion in England 1688–1791*. Oxford: Clarendon Press, 1986.

St. Clair, William. *The Door of No Return: The History of Cape Coast Castle and the Atlantic Slave Trade.* New York: Bluebridge, 2007.

St. George, Robert Blair, ed. *Possible Pasts: Becoming Colonial in Early America.* Ithaca, NY: Cornell University Press, 2000.

Schama, Simon. *Rough Crossings: Britain, the Slaves, and the American Revolution.* New York: Ecco, 2006.

Sensbach, Jon F. *Rebecca's Revival: Creating Black Christianity in the Atlantic World.* Cambridge, MA: Harvard University Press, 2005.

Sparks, Randy J. *The Two Princes of Calabar: An Eighteenth-Century Atlantic Odyssey.* Cambridge, MA: Harvard University Press, 2004.

Stevens, Laura M. *The Poor Indians: British Missionaries, Native Americans, and Colonial Sensibility.* Philadelphia: University of Pennsylvania Press, 2004.

Strong, Rowan. *Anglicanism and the British Empire, c. 1700–1850.* Oxford: Oxford University Press, 2007.

———. "A Vision of an Anglican Imperialism: The Annual Sermons of the Society for the Propagation of the Gospel in Foreign Parts, 1701–1714." *Journal of Religious History* 30, no. 2 (June 2006): 175–98.

Sykes, Norman. *Edmund Gibson Bishop of London, 1669–1748: A Study in Politics and Religion in the Eighteenth Century.* Oxford: Oxford University Press, 1926.

———. *From Sheldon to Secker; Aspects of English Church History, 1660–1768.* Cambridge: Cambridge University Press, 1959.

Thompson, H. P. *Into All Lands: The History of the Society for the Propagation of the Gospel in Foreign Parts, 1701–1950.* London: SPCK, 1951.

Thornton, John. *Africa and Africans in the Making of the Atlantic World, 1400–1800.* 2nd ed. Cambridge: Cambridge University Press, 1998.

Tise, Larry. *Proslavery: A History of the Defense of Slavery in America, 1701–1840.* Athens: University of Georgia Press, 1987.

Updike, Wilkins. *A History of the Episcopal Church in Narragansett, Rhode Island . . .* 2nd ed., Edited by Daniel Goodwin. 3 vols. Boston: D. B. Updike, 1907.

Van Horne, John C. "Impediments to the Christianization and Education of Blacks in Colonial America: The Case of the Associates of Dr. Bray." *HMPEC* 50, no. 3 (Sept. 1981): 243–69.

———, ed. *Religious Philanthropy and Colonial Slavery: The American Correspondence of the Associates of Dr. Bray, 1717–1777.* Urbana: University of Illinois Press, 1985.

Vassar, Rena. "William Knox's Defense of Slavery (1768)." *Proceedings of the American Philosophical Society* 114 (Aug. 1970): 310–26.

Vaughan, Alden. *Roots of American Racism: Essays on the Colonial Experience.* New York: Oxford University Press, 1995.

Vibert, Faith. "The Society for the Propagation of the Gospel in Foreign Parts: Its Work for the Negroes in North America Before 1783." *Journal of Negro History* 18, no. 2 (Apr. 1933): 171–212.

Wahrman, Dror. *The Making of the Modern Self: Identity and Culture in Eighteenth-Century England.* New Haven, CT: Yale University Press, 2004.

Walker, James W. St. G. *The Black Loyalists: The Search for a Promised Land in Nova Scotia and Sierra Leone 1783–1870.* London: Longman, 1976.

Walsh, John, Colin Haydon, and Stephen Taylor, eds. *The Church of England c. 1689–c. 1833: From Toleration to Tractarianism.* Cambridge: Cambridge University Press, 1993.

Wheeler, Roxanne. *The Complexion of Race: Categories of Difference in Eighteenth-Century British Culture.* Philadelphia: University of Pennsylvania Press, 2000.

Wilson, Kathleen. *The Island Race: Englishness, Empire and Gender in the Eighteenth Century.* London: Routledge, 2003.

————, ed. *A New Imperial History: Culture, Identity, and Modernity in Britain and the Empire, 1660–1840*. Cambridge: Cambridge University Press, 2004.

Winks, Robin W. *The Blacks in Canada: A History*, 2nd ed. Montreal: McGill-Queen's University Press, 1997.

Winner, Lauren F. *A Cheerful and Comfortable Faith: Anglican Religious Practice in the Elite Households of Eighteenth-Century Virginia*. New Haven, CT: Yale University Press, 2010.

Wood, Betty. "'Never on a Sunday?' Slavery & the Sabbath in Lowcountry Georgia 1750–1830." In *From Chattel Slaves to Wage Slaves: The Dynamics of Labour Bargaining in the Americas*, edited by Mary Turner, 79–96. Kingston: Ian Randle, 1995.

Wood, Peter H. *Black Majority: Negroes in Colonial South Carolina from 1670 through the Stono Rebellion*. New York: Alfred A. Knopf, 1974.

Woolverton, John Frederick. *Colonial Anglicanism in North America*. Detroit: Wayne State University Press, 1984.

Young, B. W. *Religion and Enlightenment in Eighteenth-Century England: Theological Debate from Locke to Burke*. Oxford: Clarendon Press, 1998.

INDEX

abolitionism, 7, 11, 195, 199, 239. *See also*
    antislavery, emancipation
    colonial, 206
    emancipationism compared to, 224–25
    Parliament and, 224, 226, 295n91
    Porteus and, 210–12, 218–19, 223
    Ramsay and, 216–17
    SPG and, 199–225
Acosta, José de, 61
Addison, Henry, 133
Adoy, Frederick, 175
Africa. *See also* Africans, Company of
    Merchants Trading to Africa,
    Gold Coast
    Methodism in, 194
    Quaque SPG mission, 171–95
    Roman Catholic Church in, 106, 173
    Thompson initiating activity, 172–73
Africans, 9
    and Cape Coast mission, 174–84
    on Codrington Plantation, 150–53, 162–64
    in New York, 77
    Quaque attitude towards, 181–82
    in South Carolina, 92–93, 104, 106
African Americans, 9. *See also* enslaved
    people
    as Anglicans, 33–34
    Christianity, 137, 236
    colonial population, 20
    as "heathens," 4, 9
Afro-Caribbean people, 5, 9, 137, 151, 153–54,
    162, 234–35. *See also* Creoles
agriculture, 143
    practices on Codrington Plantation, 148–49
    settled, 70, 262n113
Akan people, 177–78
    on Codrington Plantation, 151–53
    religion, 180
Alleyne, Abel, 160–61
    catechizing, 132

on enslaved people's practices, 165–66
American Episcopalianism, 3, 7, 212
American Revolution, 22, 84
    aftermath, 32, 137, 233
    Codrington Plantation and, 169, 208–9
    role in antislavery, 199, 207–9, 224
    SPG and, 7, 207–9, 233, 254n77
Andrew (enslaved catechist), 124, 127–28
antislavery. *See also* abolitionism, emancipation,
    proslavery
    activism, 6, 189, 199
    American Revolution and, 207–9
    Benezet and, 200–2, 224
    bishops and, 206–7, 213, 216, 224–25, 231
    Clarkson dissertation, 206, 220
    countermovement to, 209
    movement history, 231
    Porteus and, 210
    Quaque and, 185–89
    religious networks and, 199–200
    Sharp and, 212–13
    SPG and, 199–232
Anti-Slavery Reporter, 228
Anti-Slavery Society, 231
Archbishop of Canterbury, 130, 212, 220, 229
    Cornwallis as, 137
    Manners-Sutton as, 222
    Moore as, 212
    Potter as, 148
    Secker as, 202
    as SPG president, 22
    Tenison as, 20
Asante, 178, 192
Associates of Dr. Bray, 9, 17, 32, 34, 111, 125,
    131, 208
Atlantic world, 3–8, 19, 22, 26, 30, 32, 34–37, 39,
    110, 125, 233, 236, 239
Atterbury, Francis, 23–24
Auchmuty, Samuel, 29, 35
Australia, 235

CPSIA information can be obtained
at www.ICGtesting.com
Printed in the USA
BVHW03s0324260818
525470BV00005B/104/P